Obama's Detractors In The Right Wing Nut House

Howard A. DeWitt

Horizon Books
P. O. Box 4342
Scottsdale, AZ. 85261-4342

E Mail: Howard217@aol.com

First Published 2012

Copyright Howard A. DeWitt,

All quotations fall within permitted use.

All rights reserved
Without limiting the rights under copyright reserved above, no part of this publication may be reproduced, stored in or introduced into a retrieval system, or transmitted in any form or by any means (electronic, mechanical, photocopying, recording or otherwise) without the prior written permission of both the copyright owner and the above publisher of this book

Every effort has been made to contact copyright holders. Any errors and omissions will be amended in subsequent editions.

ISBN: 0-938840-05-3

Library of Congress Catalogue Number: 2012911418
CreateSpace,
North Charleston,
South Carolina

Copyright © 2012 Howard A. DeWitt
All rights reserved.

ISBN: 1-4699-2562-1
ISBN-13: 9781469925622

Dedication

THIS BOOK IS DEDICATED TO THE MEMORY AND SCHOLARSHIP OF RICHARD HOFSTADTER AND MY PROFESSORS AUGUST RADKE, RICHARD F. W. WHITTEMORE, BERNARD BOYLAN, HARLEY HILLER, KEITH A. MURRAY, EARL S. POMEROY, JAMES H. SHIDELER, DONALD SWAIN, JAMES BEATSON AND HERMAN BATEMAN. ALSO TO MY HISTORY FRIENDS LOU ISAACS, DAVID L. PAGE, JOE GILLILAND, WARREN JOHANSON AND HARVEY SCHWARTZ WHO ARE MORE ACCOMPLISHED THAN ANYONE I KNOW. CONVERSATIONS WITH CLAUDE AMERSON HELPED THIS BOOK, HE IS THE MOST ASTUTE POLITICAL INDEPENDENT IN SCOTTSDALE.

"Here is to the political wisdom of my friends who share the most intelligent opinions on matters of politics and the selection of friends. None of their opinions, ideas and input embraces the following pages. That is my loss."

TABLE OF CONTENTS

Preface: Why Is This Book Needed?   xi
Prologue: The Lunatic Fringe And President Obama   xvii

PART ONE: THE PARANOID STYLE AND THE RIGHT WING   1
Chapter 1: Richard Hofstadter's Paranoid Style
In American Politics   7
Chapter 2: Will Bunch, What Is This Guy Doing In a Book About Right Wing Lunatics?—He Explains The Paranoids   17
Chapter 3. The Koch Brothers Invented The Tea Party   31

PART TWO: THE PROFESSORS, THE HIGH SCHOOL AUTHORS AND THE PUNDITS   49
Chapter 4: The Professor as Critic: The Corsi Book On The Cult of Personality   55
Chapter 5: Why Yale, Joe Lieberman And The College Professors Led Glenn Beck To Thomas Paine   69
Chapter 6: The Professor Is An Attack Dog: Jerome Corsi, Where Is The Birth Certificate?- The Case That Barack Obama Is Not Eligible To Be President   89

PART THREE: SELLING BOOKS THROUGH SENSATIONALISM AND BIG BROTHER   101
Chapter 7: Selling Books Via A Title: David Freddoso's, Gangster Government: Barack Obama and the New Washington Thugocracy   105
Chapter 8: If I Had Brains I Would Be In The Big Time: David Limbaugh, Crimes Against Liberty And The Indictment of President Barack Obama and Pamela Geller's Outrageous Claims   117
Chapter 9: Overstated Language: Michelle Malkin, Culture of Corruption: Obama And His Team of Tax Cheats, Crooks and Cronies   129

PART FOUR: I USED TO BE A DEMOCRAT OR A BEAUTY QUEEN: NOW I AM A PISSED OFF CRITIC   149
Chapter 10: I'm 5-4 But I Am Trying To Be 6-5: Dick Morris, The Political Consultant With A Seven Foot Ego   153
Chapter 11: The Six Barack Obama Books From The Fringe   165
Chapter 12: Barbie on Steroids: Ann Coulter, Demonic: How The Liberal Mob is Endangering America   179
Chapter 13: She Is Not Quite Barbie But I'm Trying: Laura Ingraham's Books   195
Chapter 14: Right Wing Lunatics And Obama's Dijongate Scandal That Includes Catsup   203

PART FIVE: THE RIGHT WING AND OTHER CRITICS WHO MAKE SENSE BUT ARE STILL OVER THE TOP   213
Chapter 15: Bill O'Reilly: You May Not Like His Pomposity, But He Has Some Intelligent Criticism   217
Chapter 16: The Nincompoop Nominee: Newt Gingrich   235
Chapter 17: Dinesh D'Souza and The Anti-Business Obama   261
Chapter 18: Anti-Obama Books Sell: A Conclusion   278
Chapter 19: From The Coffee Shop   283

ROCK N ROLL BOOKS
BY HOWARD A. DEWITT

Van Morrison: Them and the Bang Era, 1945-1968 (2005)

Stranger In Town: The Musical Life of Del Shannon (with D. DeWitt (2001)

Sun Elvis: Presley In The 1950s (1993)

Paul McCartney: From Liverpool To Let It Be (1992)

Beatle Poems (1987)

The Beatles: Untold Tales (1985, 2nd edition 2001)

Chuck Berry: Rock 'N' Roll Music (1981, 2nd edition 1985)

Van Morrison: The Mystic's Music (1983)

Jailhouse Rock: The Bootleg Records of Elvis Presley (with Lee Cotton) (1983)

HISTORY AND POLITICS

The Road to Baghdad (2003)

A Blow To America's Heart: September 11, 2001, The View From England (2002)

Jose Rizal: Philippine Nationalist As Political Scientist (1997)

The Fragmented Dream: Multicultural California (1996)

The California Dream (1996)

Readings In California Civilization (1981, 4th edition revised 2004)

Violence In The Fields: California Filipino Farm Labor Unionization (1980)

California Civilization: An Interpretation (1979)

Anti Filipino Movements in California: A History, Bibliography and Study Guide (1976)

Images of Ethnic and Radical Violence in California Politics, 1917-1930: A Survey (1975)

NOVELS

Stone Dead: A Rock 'N' Roll Mystery (2012)

PREFACE: WHY IS THIS BOOK NEEDED?

This book examines how and why President Barack Obama's critics operate. There is a great deal of money made from books, television shows and speaking appearances for conservatives. The essays are divided into five sections to demonstrate the various levels of conservative thought.

As Richard Hofstadter remarks: "American politics has often been an arena for angry minds. In recent years, we have seen angry minds at work mainly among extreme right wingers." When Hofstadter made these remarks in the November, 1964, issue of **Harper's** Magazine, his criticism centered upon an increasingly conservative trend; Barry Goldwater was taking the right into the political mainstream. Few people realized the danger of this growing reactionary political direction. It was Goldwater's resounding 1964 defeat, which led the right wing to carefully direct a comeback. It has taken half a century, as well as a major economic crisis, but the conservative juggernaut is back. The Tea Party advocates include Michele Bachmann, Sarah Palin and other right wing critics who threaten free speech. Sarah Palin became the Queen of the right wing nut house when she left the Alaska Governorship to line her pockets with lucrative speaking engagements and million dollar book contracts.

Consider the October 30, 2011, Bachmanns comment regarding the children of undocumented immigrants: "Their parents are the ones who brought them here…they did not have the legal right to come to the United States." She implies that if you have any support for immigration reform, then you are less than a good American. She fails to realize that there are two sides to the argument. There is only one solution, she argues, get rid of the undocumented workers. When Michele Bachmann spoke in Newton, Iowa in October 2011, she suggested that President Obama be impeached. Her comments make her eligible for immediate induction into the Right Wing Nut House Hall of Fame. Bachmann wants the President impeached because he is African American.

The stupidity continues for Bachmann in late November 2011, when she stated that the American embassy in Tehran would be closed if she were elected president. When the Iranian revolutionary leader the Ayatollah Khomeini endorsed militants, the U. S. government formally severed diplomatic relations with Iran in April 1980. There is no U. S. Embassy in Tehran. Unfortunately, Bachmann is not privy to this American policy. She also spoke of three countries that formed a new Axis of evil. Bachmann identified those countries as Iran, North Korea, China, Russia and Syria. Someone needs to tell her to learn to count, as it's five countries. Rick Perry is giving Bachmann logic and memory lessons. These examples are what prompted me to write this book. Bachmann and Perry not only embarrass the Republican Party, but they also embarrass America.

On December 12, 2011, Bachmann appeared on the TV show, Face The Nation, and she evoked the image of the Founding Fathers when she talked about Newt Gingrich's character. She implied that he didn't have Washington's character. What George Washington and Newt have in common is a mystery. Her inability to handle the media is obvious in her appearances on Face The Nation. While she hit hard at Gingrich's wealth, Bachmann had no facts and little analysis.

The money issue is an important one. In 2008, Bachmann's net worth was less than a million dollars. Then she became a media darling, and in October 2010, her net assets were at least $1.28 million. Her husband's counseling clinic in Lake Elmo, Minnesota, is worth in excess of a million dollars. By 2012, when Bachmann's name was all over the right wing nut house, her estimated total worth was approaching three million dollars. A sub-thesis of this book is that there is a great deal of money to be made from conservative books and speaking engagements. How does the right wing nut house help politicians become rich? The answer is in the following chapters.

The American voter is well educated, careful in his or her opinions and diligent about going to the polls. There is no lack of information to help voters make decisions.

Why is the literary lunatic fringe so successful? The answer is a mixed one. Some authors are respected politicians like Newt Gingrich; others are well known political consultants like Dick Morris, and the rest are media figures like Michael Savage. All of these critics believe in their vision. The problem is that they present a view of President Barack Obama obfuscated by race. The critics are not racist, but they are troubled by Obama's background. Is he a citizen? Is he a Communist? Is he a Socialist? These are ridiculous questions; ones that we asked in the 1950s when Senator Joe McCarthy terrorized America.

By 2010, there were forty-six best selling anti-Obama books. The popularity of these books was demonstrated by the fact that more than fifty million copies sold in the first year of publication. No president has been attacked with such vigor. When Franklin D. Roosevelt was elected in 1932, the right wing book industry was born. But FDR didn't experience the personal attacks, the vindictive language and the outright falsehoods that Barack Obama endures. Even Bill Clinton, who was increasingly the object of right wing conservative attacks, had less written about his personal life and more about his presidential problems. The vibrant economy helped Clinton escape much of the criticism.

The conservatives who attack Obama are, for want of a better term—-nuts. Take David Limbaugh's books. He accuses President Obama of war crimes. President Obama could be accused of leading a stagnant economy, he could be criticized for his foreign policy, and he could be charged with campaigning while in office. War crimes! I don't think so.

The anti-Obama books are turned out from the pens of radio and television personalities who have little in-depth knowledge of, or for that matter interest in, politics. They are into selling books.

There is one ringer in this study. The book by Will Self is critical of the right wing lunatics. He is in this book to see if you read it. Enjoy!

The truth is that the radical right is a danger to all Americans. They have little regard for the opinions of their opponents, and they have an ideology that promotes racism, sexism, classism, anti-immigrant feeling, homophobia and anti-intellectual behavior. They also distort the facts while invoking the blessing of Jesus. Kinky Friedman is not amused. Fox News is the worst. Somewhere George Orwell is turning over in his grave. The following analysis exposes and dissects the radical rights' attempt to subvert American democracy. When I finished my doctoral dissertation "Hiram W. Johnson And American Foreign Policy, 1917-1941," I mentioned in a question-answer session that I had with Senator Barry Goldwater at Cochise College in 1966 that I had studied responsible extremism. Goldwater commented: "Extremism is often hidden in excessive patriotism."

Obama's Detractors: In The Right Wing Nut House is an attempt to demonstrate the danger, as well as the demeaning criticism, of the radical right. In politics, good manners, fair criticism and a sense of honor no longer are a part of the political landscape.

When I watch the Fox News Channel, I love Bill O'Reilly. He is funny. He is entertaining. He is intelligent. He has charisma. He has integrity. He has a great wit. He is a wonderful writer. Now before I bronze him and put up an O'Reilly statue next to Mother Theresa let me state my reservations. O'Reilly and his ilk at Fox News appeal to a fanatical fringe of voters who seldom read. They are in the main college educated, and they are generally the polar bears. That is the crowd over sixty who are retired, and since they don't read and can only play three or four rounds of golf or shuffleboard a week, they sit around watching O'Reilly and his impersonator Glenn Beck rally the troops. The rally is to get rid of the Mexicans, the terrorists hiding all over America, and they also hope to make state's rights the new credo. If there is a father figure leading this revolt, it is Phoenix, Arizona, Sheriff Joe Arpaio. Maybe a statue of Sheriff Joe Arpaio next to Mother Theresa is more appropriate.

Malcolm Gladwell's **Outliers: The Story of Success**, published in 2008, the same year that President Barack Obama was elected gives a clue to the president's success. An outlier is defined as "something that is situated away from or classed differently from a main or related body." There is no better description of the president than that of the outlier. Because President Obama is so different from his predecessors, he has been subjected to outrage, innuendo, and conservative manipulation of the facts.

After graduating from Harvard Law School, Barack Obama was not content with a job on Wall Street in the high six figures column. So there must be something wrong with him. He strove for the American Dream and then he failed to cash in on it. The man must be a Socialist, Communist or Radical. This is the message of the right wing nut house.

There are four voices of reason within conservative circles. Bill O'Reilly on Fox TV News does his best to be fair in a moderate conservative manner. Former House Speaker Newt Gingrich understands government more than most politicians, but he is anything but fair. However Gingrich is so knowledgeable that he is able to raise questions that are important to the Republicans in general and the nation at large. Dinesh D'Souza provides excellent analysis of why and how he sees Obama as the most significant anti-business president since Theodore Roosevelt. The last sane critic, Michael Savage, is an over the top radio host who thinks and writes brilliantly. They all have one thing in common; they have written books critical of President Obama. Not surprisingly, their books sell well. There is a lot of money in the anti-Obama book field.

Much of what I have written is influenced by the work of Columbia University History Professor Richard Hofstadter. The late Richard F. W. Whittemore, Bernard Moylan, Keith Murray and August Radke of Western Washington State University stressed Hofstadter's analysis and its importance in analyzing the radical right. Earl S. Pomeroy and Herman Bateman, my MA and PhD advisers, are important to this book as they provided the intellectual stimulus. I can never equal their scholarship, but I thank them for the inspiration.

The level of vitriolic criticism in American democracy is at an all time high. There is little civility, and no one listens to both sides of the argument. This comes at a time when our nation is at a crossroads. The problem is the divisive nature of the differences between the Republican and Democratic parties.

Senator Mitch McConnell, the Republican from Kentucky, is the perfect example of a politician who sees a conspiracy of people of color attempting to take over American democracy. His demeaning comments, mean spirited politics and pompous declarations are a greater danger to our country than anything. Richard Hofstadter defined Senator McConnell in 1964 when he observed that extreme conservatives see "a vast or gigantic conspiracy as the motive force in historical events. History is a conspiracy, set in motion by demonic forces of almost transcendent power…." (Hofstadter, **The Paranoid Style In American Politics**, p. 29)

One day Senator McConnell looked at his wife and screamed: "My goodness, there is a Negro in the White House." His second wife, Elaine Chao, the former Secretary of Labor under President George W. Bush and the first Asian American woman to serve in the Cabinet, asked McConnell. "Would you support an Asian president?" He responded: "Would you pass the mashed potatoes and gravy?" Although Senator McConnell is not the brightest bulb in the U. S. Senate, he knew enough to placate his wife. Now if he could only do that for the voters.

There is another reason for writing this book. A survey by Zombie International in 2008 rated Bill O'Reilly as the second most trusted newsman in America. Rush Limbaugh was the most trusted.

The Fox TV News channel is a conservative outlet, and that is within the tradition of broadcast journalism. What has happened is that the right wing nut house has taken over Fox News. Roger Ailes, who was a Richard M. Nixon apologist, has orchestrated the radical right message for Fox News. The problem is that there is an undue influence from Fox News and Richard Hofstadter's notion of the influence of the "paranoid style" in American politics is once again relevant.

What is the role of media? Another question: What happens to those in the right wing nut house who make such profits from their books? Is this what American democracy intended? Somewhere George Washington or Thomas Jefferson are rolling over in their graves. Glenn Beck is probably having someone ghost write a book on the subject.

PROLOGUE: THE LUNATIC FRINGE AND OBAMA

"THERE IS NO SECRET, BRILLIANT STRATEGY. THE WHITE HOUSE IS IN A BUBBLE. THEY THINK THEY'RE WINNING WHEN THE ROOF IS ABOUT TO CAVE IN." CENQ UNGER

The hatred generated toward President Barack Obama is unprecedented. Hate is not a new theme in the political arena. By early 2011, there were forty-six well-written, carefully researched and highly articulate books about President Obama. The motivation was to defeat him in his quest for reelection in 2012.

The anti-Obama books have turned into a profitable industry for conservative authors. Ann Coulter, who shows up dressed like a fashion model, is the poster Barbie for the right wing nut house. Her good looks are mitigated by a truck driver's mouth and a vocabulary straight out of the political sewer. With three million books sold, Coulter is the darling of the American right wing. She is also a brilliant speaker and a consummate businessperson. But she is essentially a victim of the demand to make money in the marketplace. Her research is sketchy, but her writing is clear and well crafted. This helps to cover her lack of research and analysis.

The Fox News Network is the drug of choice for the elderly and infirmed who see Barack Obama as the coming of Satan. They sit in front of their flat screen TVs wondering what in the hell happened to America. It sure has gone to hell, they muse. Hank Williams, Jr., is a regular watching the Fox News channel. So he is the fountain of knowledge for inane anti-Barack Obama remarks. When Williams appeared on Fox TV News, he compared President Obama to Hitler. He was eased from the show. Like most of these conservatives, Williams is incensed that an African American is in the White House. But as Hank would tell you, it is not about racism. Hank just doesn't like the fact that Obama doesn't use ketchup on his hamburger.

Former President Jimmy Carter remarked in September 2009 that much of the criticism directed toward President Barack Obama is due to inherent racism. "When a radical fringe element of demonstrators and others begin to attack the president of the United States as an animal or as a reincarnation of Adolf Hitler, or when they wave signs in the street that said we should have buried Obama with Kennedy, those kinds of things are beyond the bounds," Carter told students at Emery University.

Former John F. Kennedy adviser and Harvard trained historian, Arthur M Schlesinger, Jr., stated the problem with the lunatic right wing succinctly in a quote for a 1996 reissue of Richard Hofstadter's book **The Paranoid Style In American Politics**: "Recent months have witnessed an attack of unprecedented passion and ferocity against the national government. Unbridled rhetoric is having consequences far beyond anything that antigovernment politicians intended. The flow of angry words seems to have activated and in a sense legitimized what the historian Richard Hofstadter called: "the paranoid strain in American politics."

The attempts to smear President Barack Obama are numerous, but there is none more alarming than the debate over whether or not he is an elitist. The paranoia of the radial right and the Fox TV News channel is endless. It is obvious that the news media is influencing the American voter. The struggling economy and foreign policy issues also contribute to Obama's declining popularity. The conservative media has brought American politics closer to the right wing nut house. Paranoia runs rampant on the right, and, as Richard Hofstadter observed, the radical right will take away our privileges to protect democracy. They suggest this without realizing how fragile American democracy is in the Age of Terrorism.

In 2001, Theodore Dalrymple's **Life At The Bottom: The Worldview That Makes The Underclass** argued that a lack of personal responsibility and the inability of the lower class to work made them the so-called "underclass." Dalrymple, a British writer, doctor and psychiatrist, became the darling of conservative, right wing pundits because he defined poverty and the reasons for it. To Dalrymple, government assistance is the culprit.

What makes Dalrymple significant to American audiences is his notion that the underclass lacks the drive and motivation for success. He also argues that immigrants have trouble adjusting to a new society. He based this odious conclusion on the problems between Indian Sikhs and

Pakistani Muslims in the United Kingdom. The truth is that Dalrymple is an angry English white man who can't adjust to cultural change.

Thomas Sowell, the conservative academic apologist, called the book "brilliant and insightful." Sowell pointed out that Dalrymple analyzed the social destructiveness of the left's welfare state mentality. The right embraced Dalrymple, a respected British psychiatrist, who defined the reason for poor people. The poor emerged due to liberal programs, Dalrymple argued, and his theory supported the idea of eliminating the welfare state.

By concentrating on forces in the media right wing nut house, it is obvious that the profits, fame, speaking engagements and book contracts provide a lucrative flow of income. This encourages conservatives to accentuate their political drift to the right.

The Koch brothers are an example of wealthy political donors who have had and will continue to have a strong influence upon American conservatism. Although they are conservative billionaire industrialists, they are serious and thoughtful people with a fear that America is heading in the wrong direction. As a result, they have funded and supported the Tea Party. Neither of the Koch brothers is a fanatic. They are simply thoughtful conservatives and should be taken that way.

In American politics, the use of pressure groups, lobbying organizations and media watchdogs are important, but with the advent of Rupert Murdoch's Fox TV News there are new pressures on liberals. America is experiencing a financial crisis that is unparalleled since the Great Depression. This has heightened the conservative message and created a host of previously unknown government critics. Most of these people are regulars on Fox TV News, and they have a disproportionate influence on national attitudes.

The conservative messages of Glenn Beck, Michelle Malkin, David Freddoso, David Limbaugh, Pamela Geller, Ann Coulter, Laura Ingraham and Dick Morris, among others, suggest that there is a wide divergence of right wing opinion. These writers and television personalities are well-educated, accomplished people who write and present themselves with skill. They are angry. Morris is a perfect example of a writer-commentator thrown out by President Bill Clinton who has struck back with a vengeance. Focus, political honesty and fairness are what Morris lacks. Others like Ann Coulter and Laura Ingraham are not only angry with liberals but with feminists, abortion advocates and anyone else with a liberal agenda. Pamela Geller is Jewish and some of her comments have New York Rabbis rolling their eyes.

The following books are examples of extreme writing, with excellent sales and wonderful royalties. The content of Aaron Klein's, **The Manchurian President: Barack Obama's Ties to Communists, Socialists And Other Anti-American Extremists**; R. Lee Prescott's, **Barack Obama's Plan to Socialize America and Destroy Capitalism**; John Graham's, **Obama's Change: Communism in America**; Michael Savage's, **Trickle Up Poverty: Stopping Obama's Attack on Our Borders, Economy and Security**; Pamela Geller and Robert Spencer's, **The Post-American Presidency The Obama Administration's War on America** and Mike Cullen's, **Whiny Little Bitch: The Excuse Filled Presidency of Barack Obama** are perfect foils for this books thesis. That is that over the top journalism sells. The inclusion of Newt Gingrich, Dinesh D'Souza and Bill O'Reilly is designed to suggest that some right wing critics are fair and balanced. For all of O'Reilly's pomposity, he is an excellent newsperson, and he attempts to be fair. Dinesh D'Souza is not only a brilliant writer, but he is a calm and rational voice on radio and television. His books address some controversial subjects, and he often has excellent points. Why include Newt Gingrich? He is after all a politician. The reason is a simple one. Gingrich, after receiving a doctorate in European history, rose from a small college to Speaker of the House of Representatives, and along the way, for a brief time, he positioned himself for the 2012 presidential nomination. By May, 2012, Gingrich dropped out of the presidential race, but he continued to cash his large checks from his books. With almost thirty books to his credit, he is an unusually prolific political author. He has also made a fortune on his book deals. The use of Richard Hofstadter's "paranoid style" is important. It is the feeling of excessive paranoia that drives the conservative right wing. Hofstadter's writing defended the liberal values of tolerance, civil liberties and academic freedom. There was an open mind in Hofstadter's writing and this trait is missing in much of recent conservative writing. The use of language inciting the viewer or voter to exaggerate statements is another problem. At Fox TV News, there is often a shouting match. Then the pompous host, be it Bill O'Reilly, Glenn Beck or Sean Hannity smiles and tells the audience that they are "fair and balanced." Many educated people repeat this statement without analyzing what they have watched. As Blanche from Iowa stated: "I just love Fox because all those broadcast people know their history." That is the danger of the right wing nut house. Richard Hofstadter demonstrated that there is a long standing right wing mentality. It is nothing new, and the notion of conspiracy, dishonest government and politicians as crooks continues to proliferate. There is a frightening aspect to recent conservatism. If one can imagine a political movement created in a moment of national anxiety, dominated by fundamental Christians, its origins depending on grass roots organization by the Tea Party, its funding provided by industrialists who view government as socialistic and its goals is to replace an African American president. The conclusion would be that this is the Ku Klux Klan. Perhaps it is the modern version of the KKK. This makes what follows even more frightening. The insipid smell of white racism wafts through modern day conservatism. But the right wing nut house for a time could trot out presidential hopeful Herman Cain, former Congressman J. C. Watts or Supreme Court Justice Clarence Thomas to disprove any sense of racism. It doesn't disprove a thing. The racial nature of the new conservatism is obvious.

To understand how the right wing nut house operates, it is necessary to rethink Richard Hofstadter's "paranoid style" in American politics. One of the sub-themes of this book is the manner in which the media directs American politics. There is a decidedly conservative bias to the media. The general belief is that the media is liberal. This is, of course, not true as a study by Harvard University in 2003 concluded that conservatives own, hire and run the major news outlets. So the idea that the media is a liberal bastion is an erroneous one. The Shorenstein Center at Harvard concluded that liberal newspapers, the **New York Times** and **Washington Post** were more critical of Bill Clinton than George W. Bush. The reason is that these newspapers went out of their way to be fair, and the result was harsh attitudes toward liberalism.

Another problem with American politics resulted from the reports emanating from the right wing think tanks. A good example of the influence of the right is the Americans For Prosperity propaganda on the Obama administration and the environment. The Koch brothers funded the AFP's attempts to defeat state laws granting rebates for solar energy. Conservative lobbying groups have been active since the early twentieth century, but during the 1970s they grew with alarming regulatory. During the 1990s, more than one billion dollars funded right wing think tanks. By 2003, the Heritage Foundation had a budget of $30 million and 180 employees. They also had their own television studio in an eight story Washington building. Why is President Barack Obama attacked? Those who reside in the right wing nut house see indisputable facts. They argue that there is no way to explain Obama's friendship with and support of Chicago's Reverend Jeremiah Wright. The radical African American minister is hostile to whites, and he is a strong supporter of welfare programs. The right argues that President Obama's friendship with and support of Wright is evidence that he dislikes white people. The right concludes that he is a reverse racist intent upon supporting federal funds for African American organizations that misuse government money. Another contention is that 1960s Weather Underground radical, Bill Ayers, influenced Obama's politics. There is also the assertion that the radical political organizing skills of Saul Alinsky dominate Obama's approach to political organization. Since Alinsky was a poor people's advocate, this philosophy appealed to Obama. But it was Alinsky's organizational genius that attracted the future president. There are also questions from the right about his father's Communist leanings. There is concern that his birth certificate is fraudulent. This has led many to argue that he is not eligible to run for the presidency. The birther controversy is no longer an issue. For a time, Barack Obama lived in Indonesia. There are questions about his education in that country. The attacks continue and most of the issues are straw ones. The so-called indisputable facts about his birth, his education, his family, his politics and his philosophical direction as president are motivated by one fact. The fact is that his critics can't stand the thought of an African American president. Pure and simple, it is latent racism that drives the arguments against President Barack Obama

When House Speaker John Boehner addressed the nation on July 25, 2011, he was answering a speech that President Obama delivered on the debt-ceiling crisis. In only 930 words Boehner was inarticulate and showed great anxiety over the debt issue. His speech demonstrated a lack of leadership and little insight into America's fiscal problems. In sharp contrast, President Obama delivered a 2300 word speech that showed a clear understanding of the debt crisis. The reaction to their speeches created a storm of criticism directed toward President Obama from the right wing nut house.

PART I
THE PARANOID STYLE AND THE RIGHT WING

"PRESIDENT OBAMA WILL REMIND US THAT HE'S PUT OFF CALLS FROM HIS PARTY TO RENEW THE OLD CLINTON ASSAULT WEAPONS GUN BAN....THE PRESIDENT WILL OFFER THE SECOND AMENDMENT LIP SERVICE AND HIT THE CAMPAIGN TRAIL, SAYS HE'S ACTUALLY BEEN GOOD FOR THE SECOND AMENDMENT." WAYNE LAPIERE, EXECUTIVE VICE PRESIDENT OF THE NATIONAL RIFLE ASSOCIATION

The rise of Fox TV News changed the direction of American politics. The various news and talk shows made media stars of Bill O'Reilly, Sean Hannity, Dick Morris, Glenn Beck, Ann Coulter, Laura Ingraham and a host of right wing pundits. Initially, it seemed a nice balance to the liberal media. Then the ratings arrived and the money began rolling into Fox TV News. The book companies, the agents, the major television talk shows, satellite radio and even Broadway came calling. These news people were now media stars. The celebrity status of the radical right brought recognition to a host of news people who influenced politics in an extraordinary manner.

The end result is that public opinion polls, the news, op-ed pieces and the traditional, if boring, CBS NBC, ABC and CNN hard news programs are competing with the entertainment news. This is the news that attacks, pillars and demeans politicos on a daily basis. Barack Obama is the main target of the criticism.

The real danger to this type of television is to incite and agitate the electorate. The other danger is the misuse of information, data and statistics. The Fox News Network is a brilliant, moneymaking institution that divides this nation.

By demonizing President Barack Obama and Vice President Joe Biden, the Fox talking heads have created a news system that perverts and distorts. Voters are angry. Voters are sophisticated. Voters are frustrated. These forces add up to make Fox TV News one of the most significant sources for political information. The opinions of Sean Hannity, Glenn Beck and Bill O'Reilly have a disproportionate influence on political issues. Voters are increasingly turning to Fox TV News and acting on its recommendations. It is not, as some liberal critics have suggested, due to the uneducated voter. On the contrary, the average Fox TV News viewer is proportionally better educated than the average American. Why is Fox News so successful? The simple answer is that Fox TV News dissects issues that are important to the majority of American voters. Like it or not, they are highly influential and do present one viewpoint with authority and clarity; if it is not always accomplished with accuracy. Clearly, voters respond to the conservative message.

How did fringe conservatism go mainstream? The notion of conspiratorial fantasies is at a record high. Many Americans see the coming apocalypse. Fox TV News feeds that fear. The notion of President Barack Obama as a "Commie Liberal Puppet," to quote Chip Berlet, has led to a reemergence of the witch-hunt atmosphere that pervaded America during the time of Senator Joseph McCarthy. The difference is that the radical right is more sophisticated, and its more persistent members have learned to use the media to trumpet conservative ideology. They also suggest that they are "fair, balanced and impartial." The conservatives who have lost their way, not to say their minds, imagine that there will be a liberal roundup of patriotic conservative Americans. Then their guns will be taken away, and they will be hustled to reeducation camps. Maybe reading George Orwell was a bad idea. The specter of Hollywood manipulation runs through the anti-Obama literature.

No one states the argument better than Floyd Brown and Lee Troxler's, **Obama Unmasked: Did Slick Hollywood Handlers Create The Perfect President?** All we need is for Frank Sinatra to walk out of the grave and re-make the Manchurian Candidate II. Perhaps Karl Rove could direct it.

President Obama's campaign has launched a website, "Attack Watch," to counter smears and innuendo as well as unfair and unsavory Republican criticism. Seth Mandel, at **Commentary**, suggests that conservative criticism is getting to the administration. He fears that Obama, like Nixon, will keep an enemies list. Perhaps the president is tired to reading that he was educated in a Madrassa, or he is weary of reading that he or someone in his administration committed federal crimes.

The truth is that paranoid politics are out of hand. In 2009, Ken Eisold, writing in **Psychology Today**, stated the problem clearly: "Those

Obama's Detractors

who see a fascist (or communist) take-over of the Federal Reserve Bank, or attempts to indoctrinate school children...are nuts." People forget when Richard Hofstadter used the term "the paranoid style," he wasn't making a medical diagnosis, rather he was referring to an analogy. Politics, with the right pressures, can revert to a "paranoid syndrome."

The Paranoid Style in American Politics appeals to white voters who are threatened by change. Ironically, these voters have watched their portfolios, their formerly expanding 401Ks, their home values and their jobs slide into oblivion. They blame liberals, immigrants and big government for their plight. Richard Hofstadter has defined this group as those whose "loss of status" has driven them to the far right.

The controversy over President Obama's birth certificate is the best example of the paranoid mentality. Hawaii has released the president's birth record, the Obama administration has released a long version of the birth certificate. Yet, there are still concerns. This comes from the belief that the president is so powerful that he can alter the course of history.

The paranoid style in American politics is nothing new. It harkens back to the late nineteenth century when farmers and others threatened by immigrants, industrialization, technology, urbanization and a changing world order envisioned the end of American life as they knew it. The same notion drives conservatives today, and they hope to put the radicals, the liberals and the free thinkers into a powerless position. It is a frightening time as whackos like Sarah Palin and Glenn Beck teach us about American history. It is a history that exists in their minds, and they present a distorted view of the American experience.

The Internet is filled with intellectual crackpots. One common tale is that after Barack Obama left Occidental College, he traveled around the world. The right wing nuts ask: Who paid for his trip? They also point out that his two roommates were Mohammad Hasan Chandoo and Wahid Hamid, who were from Pakistan. If the blogger had paid attention Wahid Hamid is a Senior Vice President at Pepsi Cola and Mohammad Hasan Chandoo is a respected businessman working in New York for Oppenheimer and Company. Neither is a terrorist. Obviously, these blogs suggest they were terrorists. Tony Rezko, a Syrian, is another friend who is portrayed as brainwashing Obama with radical socialist ideas. The irony is that Rezko is a super capitalist. None of these people are Obama's close friends. President Barack Obama is what he says he is. He is a middle of the road Democrat, who was born in Hawaii, and who was educated in the United States. He is a man who has devoted his life to politics. He could have made millions as a lawyer or a corporate pirate. Instead he has served his country.

To understand the depth of conservative depravity in the right wing nut house, it is important to examine their characteristics. There are fifteen characteristics of the paranoid style.

FIFTEEN CHARACTERISTICS OF THE PARANOID STYLE

1. A FEAR OF EXCESSIVE TAXES
2. A FEAR OF GOVERNMENT CONTROLS
3. A FEAR OF DECLINING CIVIL RIGHTS
4. A FEAR OF THE LOSS OF STATES' RIGHTS
5. A FEAR OF MUSLIM INFLUENCES UPON GOVERNMENT
6. A FEAR OF IMMIGRANTS
7. A FEAR OF COMMUNISM INUNDATING AMERICAN GOVERNMENT
8. A FEAR OF SOCIALISM CREEPING INTO GOVERNMENT POLICIES
9. A FEAR OF COMMUNITY ORGANIZERS
10. A FEAR OF EXCESSIVE POLITICAL PROTESTS
11. A FEAR OF A WEAK FOREIGN POLICY
12. A FEAR OF THE END OF RELIGIOUS INFLUENCES IN GOVERNMENT
13. A FEAR OF EXCESSIVE GUN CONTROL
14. A FEAR OF GAY MARRIAGE
15. A FEAR OF LAWS AGAINST ABORTION

How does the present criticism of President Barack Obama differ from the past? The concept of the "loyal opposition" is as old as American politics. There has never been a time when Americans believed that their president was a Muslim, not a citizen, a Socialist or a Communist. These popular feelings combined, with his African-American heritage, made Obama a prime candidate for attack from the right wing.

On January 9, 2009, eleven days before Barack Obama was sworn in as president, in the midst of national euphoria over the possible recovery of American prosperity, Senate Republican Leader Mitch McConnell and then House Minority Leader John Boehner announced that they had a different agenda from the president. This is not surprising as they are Republicans. Yet, their rhetoric and body language suggested that they were outraged. An African American was in the White House, and they made it clear that they would do everything they could to make him a one-term president.

This is not typical of American politics. Soon the personal attacks upon Barack Obama's heritage and family reached epic proportions. When Obama's father wrote an article suggesting how Kenya might escape from British colonial rule and achieve independence, right wing critics charged that the President was intent upon changing the Constitution. The critics somehow equated President Obama with his father's ideas. They did this without evidence.

The media has been a witting and unwitting partner in publicizing Obama's detractors. They have reported that President Obama is influenced by former Weather Underground radical William Ayers. He hardly knows Ayers, and there is no evidence that the president has had more than a cursory relationship with Ayers.

Sean Hannity accused President Obama of initiating a foreign policy that blamed America for the world's problems. This was a conclusion Hannity reached after President Obama spoke at Cairo University in June 2009. The President was concluding a campaign promise he made to have a major speech in a Muslim nation. He vowed to bring us closer to all people in the world.

There are other scurrilous attacks on Barack Obama. The most disgusting is that he spent four years in an Indonesian Madrassa. As early as 2008, a report surfaced that Obama was engaged in the Wahhabi doctrine. This is a doctrine that denies the rights of non-Muslims. In January 2007, the Fox TV program, Fox And Friends, aired a report by co-host, Steve Doocy reporting that Obama was a Muslim with Wahhabi leanings. The Wahhabi's are a conservative reform movement dedicated to purifying Islam. The Wahhabi's are extremists who have a strong feeling against any reinterpretation of the Quran.

Michael Savage on his radio show remarked: "Now we have....a candidate who went to a Madrassa in Indonesia and, in fact, was a Muslim." The notion is that he is a Muslim like his father. Again, with no evidence, this argument flooded the media. Congress was no better in its hostility to President Obama.

It was when the Republican Party took control of the 112th Congress on January 3, 2011 that House Majority Leader John Boehner and Senate Minority Leader Mitch McConnell flexed their political muscles.

Obamacare, the president's health plan, was attacked as the radical right accused the Democrats of attempting to enforce "medical socialism."

The **Los Angeles Times** headlined: "Not Quite A Do Nothing Congress, But It's Close." The reason for a do nothing House of Representatives is traced to the leadership of John Boehner. In his role as House Speaker, Boehner is a constant foe of Democratic legislation. The reasons for Boehner's intransigent political leadership have less to do with the Democrats and more to do with President Obama. He cringes at the thought of Obama's policies. Consequently, he opposes any and all of his programs.

Not one Republican voted for the final health care reform bill. They also failed to introduce a counter proposal. It is all about defeating President Obama's legislative programs. Most people viewed this as politics as usual. The truth is that racial overtones controlled the opposition. The hostility of Fox TV News, the rise of anti-Obama books, the popularity of radio commentators like Rush Limbaugh and the TV Barbie's, Ann Coulter and Laura Ingraham, brought unprecedented criticism.

From 2008 to 2012, the right wing nut house blossomed in American politics. One of the byproducts of this conservative surge was the money made from books, television and radio shows, blogs, newspaper columns and speeches.There was also paranoia about America's future. Richard Hofstadter's notion of the "Paranoid Style in American Politics" flourished.

Chapter 1
RICHARD HOFSTADTER'S PARANOID STYLE IN AMERICAN POLITICS

"AMERICAN POLITICS HAS OFTEN BEEN AN ARENA FOR ANGRY MINDS...WHICH HAVE NOW DEMONSTRATED IN THE GOLDWATER MOVEMENT, HOW MUCH POLITICAL LEVERAGE CAN BE GOT OUT OF THE ANIMOSITIES AND PASSIONS OF A SMALL MINORITY...THERE IS A STYLE OF MIND...I CALL IT THE PARANOID STYLE, SIMPLY BECAUSE NO OTHER WORD ADEQUATELY EVOKES THE SENSE OF HEATED EXAGGERATION, SUSPICIOUSNESS, AND CONSPIRATORIAL FANTASY THAT I HAVE IN MIND." RICHARD HOFSTADTER

When Richard Hofstadter's essay: "The Paranoid Style in American Politics" appeared in **Harper's**, he traced the conspiracy theory influences upon American history. This essay provided liberals with an argument to attack conservatives for ignoring national concerns. When Hofstadter delivered his ideas at the Herbert Spencer Lecture in the U. K. at Oxford University in November 1963, America had just experienced the assassination of President John F. Kennedy. There were conspiracy fears everywhere. Was Oswald the killer or was he a Communist dupe? That question had the conspiracy nuts suggesting many alternatives to the Kennedy assassination. This accentuated the drift into the right wing nut house. Barry Goldwater's supporters envisioned government conspiracies everywhere. The voters on the right were concerned about the decline of traditional American values. When Hofstadter's essay appeared in Harper's magazine in November 1964, there was a public debate over the paranoid style. Hofstadter's book, **The Paranoid Style in American Politics** appeared as Arizona conservative Senator Barry Goldwater made an ill-fated run for the presidency, and the Republican Party suffered an ignoble defeat.

The mistake that critics make is to label right wing conservatives as conspiratorial and suspicious. Hofstadter made the case that right wing critics were paranoid about the changes in American politics. Nothing describes the state of Obama criticism better than the word paranoid. The paranoid style, as Hofstadter reminds us, harkens back to the late nineteenth century. The newly emerged paranoid direction is one that continues to protest American policy into the Cold War years. It is America's involvement in world affairs that created the earliest signs of right wing activism. Combine the fear of foreign influences with a sagging economy, and the right wing nut house is open for business.

QUOTES FROM THE CONSPIRACY MINDED

"PROOFS OF A CONSPIRACY AGAINST ALL THE RELIGIONS AND GOVERNMENTS OF EUROPE CARRIED ON IN THE SECRET MEETINGS OF FREE MASONS, ILLUMINATI AND READING SOCIETIES" THIS IS A BOOK TITLE FROM 1797

"IT IS A NOTORIOUS FACT THAT THE MONARCHS OF EUROPE AND THE POPE OF ROME ARE AT THIS VERY MOMENT PLOTTING OUR DESRUCTION." TEXAS NEWSPAPER 1855

"AS EARLY AS 1865-1866 A CONSPIRACY WAS ENTERED INTO BETWEEN THE GOLD GAMBLERS OF EUROPE AND AMERICA...FOR NEARLY THIRTY YEARS THESE CONSPIRATORS HAVE KEPT THE PEOPLE QUARRELING...." THE POPULIST PARTY

SOURCE: HOFSTADTER, THE PARANOID STYLE IN AMERICAN POLTICS

In June 1951, at the height of the Cold War, Wisconsin Senator Joseph McCarthy commented: "How can we account for our present situation unless we believe that men high in this movement are conniving to deliver us to disaster." McCarthy was a true demagogue who abused his

Obama's Detractors

power. Bill O'Reilly, Glenn Beck, Rush Limbaugh and a host of hostile white bread critics echo McCarthy. They have the advantage of an electronic media to influence those who sit in front of the Fox News Network watching people scream about President Barack Obama. It is enough to make anyone paranoid.

What makes the paranoid style so popular is that Fox TV News sees itself, through its commentators, as "manning the barricades of civilization," to quote Hofstadter. It also leads to an increasing frustration over the direction of American politics. Rather than political debate or a dialogue over issues, the paranoid style creates a mindset that the enemy has to be defeated. The enemy is Barack Obama. One right wing critic after another castigates liberals and the Obama administration for their malfeasance, dereliction of duty and nefarious socialist programs.

But President Obama is not the only one who is tarred by the political paranoia. When Texas Governor Rick Perry was introduced at a rally in 2011, his minister suggested that Republican frontrunner Mitt Romney practiced a cultish religion. Some critics suggested that Perry's alleged bigotry and intolerance forced him to drop out of the race.

Rick Perry is the classic politician in the right wing nut house. The Texas Governor, by December 2011, faded in his quest for the Republican presidential nomination. So he took matters in his own hands. He ran an ad that stated he's "not afraid to admit he's a Christian." In the ad, he verbally abused gays, he complained that children couldn't openly celebrate Christmas, and he concluded the ad by promising to end President Obama's war on religion. This advertisement qualifies Governor Perry for admission into the right wing hut house Hall of Fame. He sees a conspiracy to poison the military with gays, a plan to Islamize all children in school, and he views the president as abolishing organized religion. To their credit, most Republicans shied away from Governor Perry. Yet, there are those who love Perry's message. It is an extremist viewpoint that some people embrace. Why? The answer is a simple one. The right feels it has lost power and has little political influence.

Glenn Beck employs "conspiratorial fantasy" to couch his arguments. He is a garrulous, photogenic television personality with looks like someone between Porky Pig and Bob at the buffet table. Beck sees the old order of the small village collapsing from liberals, Socialists, Communists, labor unions, radicals and feminists. **Time's** David Greenburg asks the leading question: "What moved people or subcultures to embrace the paranoid style?" The main reason for the paranoid style is government intrusion upon the individual.

Arizona's Senate Bill 1070 occupies much of the focus in 2012 over the rights of the state visa via immigration and those of the government. Hofstadter argued that this has less to do with immigration and more to do with "status politics." This is the notion that the movement of social class is too fluid and leadership roles are changing. Immigrant economic success threatens status. Status politics is best understood as "the effort of Americans of diverse cultural and moral persuasions to win reassurance that their values are respected by the community at large…." (Richard Hofstadter, **The Paranoid Style In American Politics**, p. 87) As Hofstadter observed, the media has created a window into the personal life of political figures. Conservative Republicans have too much information about Barack Obama, and they have used his personal life and accomplishments to denigrate the president. Obama is the classic American success story, and this has driven the right wing nut house into apoplexy. As a result, they attack him as a radical figure. Richard Hofstadter summed up the hatred for Barack Obama when he wrote that status values rather than economic ideas motive pseudo-conservatives.

In 1948, Hofstadter's **The American Political Tradition And The Men Who Made It** contained a warning about the coming of the right wing nut house. Hofstadter wrote: "The fierceness of the political struggles has often been misleading; for the range of vision embraced by the primary contestants in the major parties has always been bounded by the horizons of property and enterprise." Some sixty years later, the Tea Party formed out of a fear of a loss of property and enterprise.

On the other side of the right wing nut house there is a morality, which argues that the Tea Party is restoring traditional American values. This is simply a euphemism for white power.

President Barack Obama not only is an African American, he has a Muslim father, he had a free spirited mother with a PhD and after he was granted a Harvard law degree, he went to work in Chicago to help the poor and underprivileged. To Glenn Beck, President Obama has to be a Communist. Why wouldn't he take a six-figure salary to begin to career on Wall Street? What Beck suggests is that by not accepting a plush legal position, Obama demonstrated his political radicalism.

It is the fear of big government that drives right wing conservatives. They believe that Americans who see a one-world socialism are everywhere. The notion that the old values are eroding is a popular one. A more plausible conclusion is that, as Bob Dylan said, "the times they are a changing." That is the force that agitates the paranoid right. It is this fluctuating social-economic scene that drives politicians on the right to impose their policies.

David Greenberg, writing in **Time**, postured that Hofstadter wouldn't "understand the birthers and town hall screamers and Glenn Beck acolytes of today." There is one hidden thesis that few deal with in American politics. That is the race issue. Almost every critical and demeaning book written about Barack Obama has a preface where the author tells you that he or she has an African American friend. One wonders if there are enough people of color to befriend the right wing. The paranoia over an African American president runs rampant.

Historians have demonstrated the slow, but steady, growth of the right wing. A number of Hofstadter's ideas still apply to American politics. The status politics argument in **The Age of Reform** introduced the theory that people act less from pure economic self-interest than from a strong desire to preserve their social standing. Hofstadter's dignified and elegant prose stands in sharp contrast to his critics.

Lloyd Gardner, one of the foremost New Left critics, answered Hofstadter's argument on the paranoid style in a November 1964 article in **Harper's**. As a former Hofstadter graduate student, Gardner discussed his reaction to his mentor's brilliant book, **The Age of Reform**. What Gardner does is to show how the Populist Movement, which was an agrarian political uprising in the late nineteenth century, helped Senator Joe McCarthy create a coalition of voters who envisioned bankers, businessmen and foreign interests leading America to bankruptcy.

What President Obama can learn from Hofstadter's ideas is clear. Politics is not a battle for the middle. It is a battle to define the policies and direction of American democracy. The economic well being of the common man is the role of the Democratic Party. This is another lesson that Obama must recognize.

In 2007, the year before anyone had heard of Barack Obama, Scott Horton writing in **Harper's** reminded us that the paranoid style was well and alive in American politics. As Obama quietly organized his campaign for the presidency, he realized that the forces of conservatism would bash and attack his candidacy and later his presidency. He neutralized the right wing nut house, and he was elected president.

The primacy of the right wing nut house is demonstrated in the constant, never ending, remarks by former Alaska Governor and hockey mom, Sarah Palin. She is the voice of the right wing nut house, and her explanations are ready made for a media looking for sensationalism.

THE WIT AND WISDOM OF SARAH PALIN

"ALL I EVER NEEDED TO KNOW I LEARNED ON THE BASKETBALL COURT, ANCHORAGE DAILY NEWS

"I'M CONFIDENT THAT A PREGNANT WOMAN SHOULD NOT AND DOESN'T HAVE TO BE PROHIBITED FROM DOING ANYTHING INCLUDING RUNNING FOR VICE PRESIDENT," ANCHORAGE DAILY NEWS

"POLLS ARE FOR STRIPPERS AND CROSS COUNTRY SKIERS," QUOTE FROM A TEA PARTY RALLY, SEPTEMBER 3, 2011

"IF WE WERE REALLY TERRORISTS, PRESIDENT OBAMA WOULD WANT TO BE PALLING AROUND WITH US." AUGUST 2, 2011

"I HAVEN'T HEARD THE PRESIDENT STATE THAT WE'RE AT WAR. THAT'S WHY I TOO DO NOT KNOW—DO WE USE THE TERM 'INTERVENTION' DO WE USE WAR? DO WE USE SQUIRMISH?" A QUOTE ON THE US AND NATO BOMBINGS OF LIBYA, JANUARY 12, 2011

One of Hofstadter's primary points is that the right wing has a defined pedantry. To support their conclusions, conservatives employ questionable and highly biased data. Recently, Bill O'Reilly was on the David Letterman Late Night Show, and O'Reilly wanted to bet Letterman a weeks salary that nine plus per cent of America was on some sort of medication or needed help for drug or alcohol problems. Not only is the statistic incorrect, but also the capricious manner in which O'Reilly attacked Letterman, albeit in a pseudo friendly manner, indicated the level of his deception. Hofstadter predicted this type of behavior when there is little knowledge and even less thought forming a political opinion.

Obama's Detractors

Those who practice the paranoid style of politics envision conspiracies, Communists, Socialists, free loaders and liberals. If Professor Richard Hofstadter is the foremost critic of the radical right, a new right wing professorial darling is Jerome Corsi, PhD. No one in or out of academic life puts PhD behind their name, unless they want to impress you with their credentials. So Jerome Corsi emerged in 2008 with a book that questioned not only Barack Obama's credentials but also his alleged ties to Communists, Socialists, New Left Radicals and liberals. The inane arguments in Corsi's books should have been dismissed. However, the efforts of a major publisher and thirty-five pages of footnotes prompted Mary Matalan to label the book one of sound scholarship. She often failed to mention that she was the editor and the force behind a book with the obnoxious subtitle: "Leftist Politics and The Cult of Personality."

The problem with political forums today is that they are stratified, either left or right. There is little consensus as well as a lack of manners, fairness and honesty. Politics has always been a contentious business. However, the level of vitriolic criticism toward President Barack Obama is more intense and personal than at anytime in presidential history.

There are some definitional points to the paranoid style. First, the enemy has to be identified. The Fox TV News crew does that daily. But to make the paranoid style effective the enemy has to be shown as malicious and forceful enough to alter the traditional freedoms of American Democracy. Hence, the large number of books on Obama taking over America and making it a "socialist utopia." Second, the paranoid style uses the process of "psychological projection," that is the crafting of dangerous politics that must be defeated. The rhetoric used by Fox TV News commentators on the 2012 presidential election validates this point. Third, the paranoid style sees the danger of Barack Obama's presidency as a key component of a national conspiracy to rob the nation of its independence.

The paranoid style is not a strictly American phenomenon. There is a nationalistic megalomaniac view of the world. The French have proven that insular nationalism is rampant. They see conspiracies abounding. The problem is when a mass movement actively seeks out a chauvinistic nationalism; the result is a paranoid group of critics bastardizing history.

Everyone has a specialized view of history. This is what makes the profession useful. The problem is outright distortion and a bending of historical facts to meet the demands of a copious ideology. This results in the misuse of our past.

Despite the general gloom over the conservative, right wing political conspiracy that threatens our use of free speech, there are four conservatives who make some interesting points. Michael Savage on the radio, Dinesh D'Souza in print, Newt Gingrich on the political stump and Bill O'Reilly on television are conservatives with a message. They provide intelligent, well-informed and interesting conservative commentary. They are alone in this realm.

WHY THE RIGHT FEELS DISPOSSESSED

The 21st Century right wing conservatives are vastly different than their predecessors. They feel dispossessed by a country taken over by immigrants, left-wing intellectuals, subversives and those with anti-American values. The modern day conservatives see themselves taking back America.

They believe that the traditional American virtues of piety, hard work, competitive capitalism and individualism have been taken over by intellectuals and big government. Right wing conservatives see a treasonous side to America

The conspiracy advocates argue that President Franklin Delano Roosevelt introduced a liberalism that fostered the government take over of business initiative, and the Democrats created a bureaucracy that threatens our existence.

What Richard Hofstadter never envisioned was that television would bring McCarthyism and its attack on free speech back into the vortex of American political thought. The mentality of those in the right wing nut house is to use the term, as Bill O'Reilly does, "fair and balanced," and then proceed to destroy any other viewpoint. To disagree, to demonstrate, to protest and to challenge are now badges of political dishonor.

Political dialogue between Republicans and Democrats has all but vanished. The nasty and partisan political tone is the most vitriolic in American history. This does not bode well for the country.

Richard Hofstadter envisioned political change but not to the extent of the influence of modern day conservatism. "Important changes may also be traced to the effects of the mass media," Hofstadter continued. "The villains of the modern right are much more vivid than those of their paranoid predecessors, much better known to the public...." The following pages suggest how correct Hofstadter is in predicting the non-palpable influence of the radical right. It is all due to television radio and anti-Obama books with help from key publishers.

The Paranoid Style in American Politics, as Hofstadter defines it, is a fear that the world is catching up with American technology, military strength and innovative capitalism. As Hofstadter pointed out, the affinity for sensationalism and the negativity of the conservative news reports created an angry and pro-active electorate. By examining Hofstadter's arguments it is obvious that the paranoid style in American politics is running rampant.

MITT ROMNEY USES THE PARANOID STYLE

No one uses the paranoid style in American politics better than Republican presidential candidate Mitt Romney. In March 2012, he appeared on Fox News claiming that gas prices were too high thanks to President Obama. This inane comment ignores the facts. The gasoline conspiracy theory is one that has helped the Republican right wing to castigate the Obama administration. The notion that President Obama wants higher gas prices is absurd. The right wing nut house argues that the Obama presidency has an impact upon world oil prices. This is simply insane. The U.S. uses only about a tenth of the world oil production, and they are in no position to influence oil prices.

In order to understand the growth, the success and the continual drive for power, it is necessary to look at a book critical of conservative politics. Will Bunch, a Philadelphia journalist, has the clearest explanation of the present condition of the right wing nut house.

Chapter 2
WILL BUNCH: WHAT IS THIS GUY DOING IN A BOOK WITH RIGHT WING LUNATICS? -HE EXPLAINS THE PARANOIDS

"THERE ARE A FEW RONALD REAGAN QUALITIES THAT OBAMA WOULD BE WISE TO STUDY...THE 40TH PRESIDENT'S ABILITY TO COMMUNICATE DIRECTLY WITH AMERICANS AND CONVEY A SENSE OF OPTIMISM...." WILL BUNCH

Ronald Reagan was one of the key presidential persuaders. Will Bunch suggests that President Barack Obama needs to develop some of Reagan's style. Bunch's **Tear Down The Myth: The Right-Wing Distortion of the Reagan Legacy** is a detailed account of why the right wing commentators on the Fox TV Network, those in the Tea Party, and the talking heads in the general media have legitimacy.

Will Bunch, a progressive journalist, has spent an enormous amount of time analyzing the structure and direction of the Tea Party. His prize winning writing in the **Philadelphia Daily News** led to the Reagan book. As Bunch analyzes the Reagan Presidency, he points out the positive and negative aspects of Reagan's policies to lower taxes, to deregulate the market and to stand tough against foreign enemies. In sharp contrast, President George W. Bush employs many of the same strategies. He finds himself mired in controversy, economic decline and international hostility. President Reagan was more popular, because he created an easily understood political climate that brought compromise and bipartisan legislation. This is lost in the current political climate.

It is this clear political direction that makes President Reagan the poster child for reorienting American history. When American historians ranked President Reagan low in their studies of his presidency, the Ronald Reagan Legacy Project was created to name schools, roads and landmarks for Reagan.

Not all historians rate Reagan as an average president. Some historians see him as an innovator and a leader. Not only did three of America's most respected historians write in-depth, well researched and carefully written studies of the Reagan presidency, but they also agree that he was a seminal figure in the rise of responsible conservatism. John Lewis Gaddis, a Professor of History at Yale University, argues that President Reagan's strategy of containment led to the fall of Communism. Douglas Brinkley, a distinguished historian at Rice University and a noted television personality, edited **The Notes: Ronald Reagan's Private Collection of Stories and Wisdom**, and he provides notes, anecdotes and analysis for the great conciliator. The best single volume on Reagan is by liberal, left wing historian, John P. Diggins, **Ronald Reagan: Fate, Freedom and the Making of History**, published in 2007. Diggins points out that Reagan was marginalized after leaving office. He believes that Reagan is one of America's three greatest presidents. The Diggins book is a surprise, because the author is a staunch left wing critic. The reason for Diggins' analysis is the president's diplomatic dealings with Russian leader Mikhail Gorbachov. This led to the realignment of American foreign policy, making the U. S. stronger in world affairs through diplomacy rather than armaments. Reagan also reigned in big government, while expanding states' rights. As Diggins suggests, the Reagan model is one that every conservative Republican adopts without understanding the need for persuasion and conciliation. The right wing political nut house was born after President Reagan. They need to embrace Reagan's conciliatory voice.

Bunch's argument is that the rehabilitation of President Reagan helps the right wing, but they must avoid "the myth of Ronald Reagan." The right neither understands nor is able to implement his policies.

Had the conservative critics paid more attention to Professor John Gaddis, they would have discovered a brilliant academician who has spent decades interviewing those close to Ronald Reagan. The result

Obama's Detractors

is that Gaddis concluded that former presidents Ronald Reagan and George W. Bush presented a "grand strategy" that has provided American foreign policy with a context that creates world stability.

Gaddis is one historian who understands not only the Cold War, but also the way in which it fits into the current American political scene. The President's exercise of power, Professor Gaddis argues, made the world safer for democracy. Gaddis approves of this concept. While Gaddis is critical of Bush's overblown rhetoric and hard line comments, he believes in the principle of America's military strategy in Iraq. The Bush Doctrine of preemptive war, unilateralism and American hegemony is the right course for the nation. What is obvious is that President Obama is attempting to work his way out of the Bush Doctrine. It is a difficult task.

What Gaddis' work demonstrates is that the right wing doesn't understand the Cold War and its aftermath. What is tragic is that during the marathon Republican presidential debates in the early months of 2012, the candidates were not well informed on the future of American foreign policy. Newt Gingrich was the only candidate with a sense of America's world future. Yet, Gingrich often overstates his opinions, as when he labels Palestinians "an invented people." Herman Cain insulted the people of Uzbekistan, and he had little or no sense of foreign policy. Then Mr. Winkey took him out of the race. Mitt Romney's foreign policy is a hawkish hard line approach. None of the Republican candidates have a viable foreign policy, as they concentrate on the domestic economy. Republican indecision in foreign policy is largely the result of the stranglehold that the Tea Party has on candidates and issues.

THE TEA PARTY IS THE NEW GOP

The Tea Party has altered the traditional direction of the Republican Party. Increasingly, Republicans take their orders from Fox TV News. The Republican Party is no longer the vehicle of fiscal responsibility and personal freedom. It is now the party that panders to racism, incites old people to worry about losing their social security, warns of imminent Muslim attacks and paints a picture of criminals and thugs inhabiting the Obama administration The corporate crazies are directing the Republican Party, via Tea Party influences, down the road to ruin.

The Tea Party is virtually all white, socially conservative, disgruntled with traditional Republicans and fearful of immigrants. The new America is multicultural and less bigoted. This enrages the Tea Party.

Not only does the Tea Party fail to point out that President George W. Bush turned a $236 billion surplus into a $1.2 trillion deficit. They fail to point out that the Republican president led us into two wars that helped to bankrupt the nation.

What causes critics to reflect on the Tea Party? The answer is a simple one. Some of its most important participants belong to suspect organizations. Peter Gemma in Florida is a leader in the white supremacist organization, the Council For Conservative Citizens. Gemma is a long time conservative activist with ties to religious fundamentalist leader Pat Buchanan. Billy Joe Roper in Arkansas is a Tea Party advocate, who is the founder of the White Revolution. Roan Garcia Quintana in South Carolina is a director of the Council For Conservative Citizens, and he was a leader in the 2010 tax day Tea Party in Greenville, South Carolina. They all have a narrow view of American democracy that does not include immigrants, women or people of color.

The image of the Tea Party is one of apple pie and patriotism. The workings are quite different, as right wing extremists attempt to destroy Medicare, social security and any form of government entitlements. While it looks like an uprising of concerned American citizens, the reality is that the Tea Party is a sophisticated version of white supremacy.

WHEN DID THE TEA PARTY START TO FUNCTION?

The Tea Party is a recent phenomenon. It began to function in January 2009, in the aftermath of President Obama's election. Fox TV News had to find a new story. It came in their extensive and highly favorable Tea Party coverage. They likened the movement to that of a new burst of patriotism. The truth is that it was an angry white reaction to an African American president.

When Glenn Beck headlined a Tea party event held at the Alamo, the media was transfixed with the movement. The Tea Party would have vanished into the land of fanatics had it not been for the media's fascination with the right. The level of paranoia reflected in the Tea Party soon became part and parcel of the media. The press treated them like they were a part of the Founding Fathers rather than a racially insensitive group. The size and authenticity of the Tea Party is in question. They are a fringe group with little clout. The beauty of Will Bunch's writing is that he has succinctly and honestly placed the Tea Party in perspective. His analysis suggests that they are dangerous.

BUNCH: ANALYZING THE TEA PARTY

In order to appreciate the brilliance of Bunch's analysis, it is important to understand the Tea Party. He is also the author who has documented the rise of the right wing in the well researched and beautifully written **The Backlash: Right Wing Radicals, High-Def Hucksters and Paranoid Politics In the Age of Obama,** which Harper Collins published in 2010.

Bunch presents a fresh interpretation of political subjects. You may wonder what a liberal and intelligent journalist is doing in a book analyzing right wing fanatics. The answer is that Bunch is one of the more astute minds looking into the right wing phenomena. Bunch defines the three reasons for the rise of the Tea Party: 1.) This movement reflects the genuine anger and the frustration of rank and file conservatives; 2.) The rise of the radio and television talk gurus, notably Glenn Beck, Rush Limbaugh and Bill O'Reilly, have fueled voter hostility and given credible voices to the right; 3.) The business or capitalistic right sees this as a time to return to the George W. Bush era of little government involvement. Big business is attempting to cash in on voter anger by demanding reduced taxes and less governmental regulation. As Bunch suggests, "the pure profit hucksters" are eager to cash in on voter anger. It is through the Tea Party that the increasingly hostile and often repugnant attacks on President Obama are planned and carried out.

The Tea Party has received an inordinate amount of publicity. Its goals and direction are attuned to extreme conservatism. Its primary concern is in defeating the alleged socialism that President Obama advocates.

The Tea Party is a coalition determined to change the direction of American government. Some critics, notably the **New York Times**, describe it as "an antigovernment, grass roots political movement that began in 2009...."

As a coalition of disgruntled citizens the Tea Party promotes candidates and targets elections. They were successful in the 2010-midterm Congressional elections, as the Republican Party took control of the House of Representatives. Not all Tea Party candidates were successful in the public eye. One candidate, Christine O'Donnell, is a rank amateur.

O'Donnell was a perpetual embarrassment to the Republican Party. She has few qualifications for public office, other than the Koch Brothers' money and Tea Party support. Her comments on President

Obama suggest her lack of credibility. "He's anti-American. He did not vote for English as the official language." As the Delaware Senate candidate, O'Donnell was a constant reminder that the power of the Tea Party is real. Where did O'Donnell come from and what are her qualifications?

After O'Donnell helped to found and work for two advocacy organizations for twenty years, she became a conservative electoral favorite. With money from the Koch brothers and Tea Party activists, she won the Delaware Republican primary for the U. S. Senate in 2010. She defeated nine-term U. S. Congressman Michael Castle from Delaware's Tenth District.

It is Castle's defeat that provides a microcosmic look at the Tea Party's power. He had a lengthy career in Delaware politics as a state legislator, then as governor and then he ascended to Congress in 1992 in a bipartisan deal with Democrat Tom Carper that the press labeled "the swap." Each took the other's job, and they called it "The Delaware Consensus." Or "The Delaware Way." In other words, Delaware was an old boys' political state. Castle was not used to criticism or opposition. He was a tall, be speckled, shy man who had trouble campaigning. It didn't seem to matter, the Delaware Way guaranteed his reelection. This consensus ended when the Tea Party backed O'Donnell.

It was when Castle toured Delaware speaking in favor of health care reform that throngs of Tea Party advocates sabotaged his town hall meetings. Although Castle was the great-great-great-great-great grandson of Benjamin Franklin, a Tea Party member hollered at a Town Hall meeting that "he could go fly a kite." The Tea Party was responsible for altering Delaware's political culture.

In the general election, O'Donnell ran against Democrat Chris Coons, who won by a 57% to 40% margin. She displayed little knowledge of the intricacies of politics, and she was less savvy on campaigning, and as a Monica Lewinsky look alike she was a campaign joke. She made Sarah Palin look like a rocket scientist. O'Donnell was invented by the Tea Party. She was a total failure until the Tea Party latched onto her. She also ran in 2008, losing 65% to 35% to the incumbent Joe Biden. Her understanding of politics, her grasp of the issues, and her inability to answer tough media questions exposed her lack of qualification for public office. What was frightening is that the Tea Party could successfully place a person with little intelligence, and even less charisma, in a position to enter high public office. For that reason alone, politicians were scared of the Tea Party.

Christine O'Donnell's inability to answer questions was highlighted when she appeared on CNN's Piers Morgan show to publicize **Troublemaker: Let's Do What It Takes To Make America Great Again**. She walked out on the interview when she couldn't answer questions on fiscal policy and gay marriage. She demanded that she be allowed to tell Morgan what questions to ask. He smiled. She accused Morgan of being rude. He described her behavior as "weird." O'Donnell is typical of Tea Party candidates.

Mario Rubio, of Florida, and Rand Paul, of Kentucky, are examples of Tea Party success in the U. S. Senate. Paul, the son of Ron Paul, is a major figure in the Tea Party youth movement. While voters elected Paul and Rubio in Kentucky and Florida, the Tea Party lost a Delaware seat when the voters rejected Christine O'Donnell. This is one indication that the confrontational Tea Party didn't appeal to all voters. In the House of Representatives, one hundred thirty Tea Party backed candidates ran but only forty were elected. The U. S. Senate had more dramatic results as five of ten Tea Party backed candidates won their elections.

THE TEA PARTY DEFINES THE TEA PARTY

In 2012, Mark Meckler and Jenny Beth Martin's **Tea Party Patriots: The Second American Revolution** outlined the movement's role and success. There are more than 3,500 Tea Party chapters in America. On April 15, 2009 more than 1.2 million people attended Tea Party meetings. Where did the movement come from and why did it grow so rapidly? The authors argue that they have the same "source code" for America as its citizens. That is fiscally responsible government with limited federal power and free markets.

Using references from Thomas Jefferson and other Founding Fathers, the Tea Party argues that the economic path is to "get the government off our backs and free the people to do what Americans do best: create wealth, jobs and prosperity." (p. 46) Fiscal and entitlement reform are key arguments. That government spending should be discretionary, not mandatory, is a key Tea Party argument. (p. 60) Meckler and Martin applaud the attempt to curtail social security, Medicare and Medicaid.

The Tea Party leaders have a messianic quality. They see themselves as "the path to liberty." (pp. 81-110) Meckler and Martin have some strange arguments. They see Harlem as the Tea Party's next bastion. They argue that once Harlem parents recognize that they can't send their children to charter schools, they will rise up and organize a Harlem Tea Party chapter. "So these kids wound up as illiterate casualties of Harlem's failing public schools." (p. 113) These comments angered Harlem's parents, and they were contrary to the facts. There are some excellent Harlem public schools. Since 1974, Harlem Week is a college expo that places African American students in a wide variety of universities. The Tea Party suggests that a government controlled, union run, school system has stunted Harlem's academic growth. In fact, just the opposite is true.

Much of the argument in favor of Tea Party politics centers on American exceptionalism. The core belief system for exceptionalists is that egalitarianism, individualism, populism and laissez-faire economics dominate American values. Ironically, it was Soviet dictator Joseph Stalin who first used the term "American exceptionalism" in 1929. He did so to point out that America's natural resources, its geographical isolation and its absence of rigid social class distinctions made it a special nation. With that in mind, Stalin and others have posited exceptionalism's influence.

THE TEA PARTY INFLUENCE IS REAL

The Tea Party has enormous influence on House Speaker John A. Boehner. They persuaded him to support deep cuts in the 2011 budget, and they have pressured him to oppose President Obama at every turn. When he is not playing golf, smoking cigarettes or drinking bourbon, Boehner screams the Tea Party credo. Boehner has talked tough on spending while attending private meetings with Tea Party members. They have helped craft his politics. If only the Tea Party could teach him to speak without looking like he was constipated. Boehner also sees conspiracies everywhere but on the golf course.

When politicians appear on national news shows there is an overwhelming notion of conspiracy. When Bill O'Reilly had Kris W. Kobach, the Kansas Secretary of State, as a guest it was a high rated show. Kobach labeled Obamacare as an invasion of privacy and individual rights. The Republican Kobach is typical of politicians who envision a massive government conspiracy to collect information on all citizens.

Kobach, a Harvard law graduate, played a significant role in the drafting of Arizona SB 1070, a state law to control illegal immigration. He was also the key author of Alabama HB 56, which is even tougher than Arizona's anti-immigrant legislation.

Obama's Detractors

Despite politicians like Kris W. Kobach, the Tea Party movement faltered. It is not surprising, as they launched candidates that had little to offer.

WHY THE TEA PARTY FAILED

The Tea Party is comprised of the major nut cases in American politics. They are so disgusting that some Republicans are running for cover. They failed for many reasons. In the Republican successes of 2010, the Tea Party was influential but that hegemony has faded. The Tea Party fails for many reasons. Here are the Top Eleven Reasons for the Tea Party failure: 1.) Americans are tired of hearing "I want my country back." 2.) Americans are not listening to the notion that government is not responsive. 3.) The Tea Party is in bed with corporate America. 4.) The Tea Party acts like they are the victims. 5.) The Tea Party is anti-government with no platform or program that makes sense. 6.) The Tea Party is obsessed with sex. Same sex marriage is a no-no. 7.) Glenn Beck's paranoid ranting is in line with the rhetoric of the Tea Party. 8.) The Tea Party defends legal decisions that restrict personal rights while the average Tea Party member seeks excessive wealth. 9.) The Tea Party fears and opposes liberal protest. The Wall Street demonstrations are a perfect example of this strain of paranoia. 10.) The Tea Party envisions health reform as a government conspiracy.11.) The Tea Party wants limits on free speech. David Letterman won't be reading a Tea Party Top Eleven.

The problem is the Tea Party leadership. They have leaders who are out of touch with urban problems, immigration, ethnic sensitivity or mainstream political issues. The head wacko, Sarah Palin, makes millions from her books and her speeches. She is equally out of touch with the key issues.

THE HEAD WACKOS IN THE TEA PARTY: SARAH PALIN AND OTHER WACKOS

Sarah Palin is the poster child for the Tea Party. Her book, **Going Rouge**, published in 2009, has a chapter on the media. She begins chapter 5 "The Thumpin" by relating that she didn't run for the U. S. Senate because "who would be the hockey manager...." (p. 341)

Joe McGinniss' **The Rogue: Searching For The Real Sarah Palin** is an excellent study of the shallow nature and prejudicial direction of her life. McGinniss reported that temper tantrums, shopping sprees, ignorance of issues, emotional instability and personal excesses clouded her ability to govern. He bought a house next door to Palin, and the result is more trivia about her life than one can endure.

There is a mean spirited direction to McGinnis' book. It is fun to read. As the **New York Times** critics suggested, it is filled with too much trivia. McGinnis went so far as to include a map on how to find Palin's secluded Alaska home. The cartoon strip Doonesbury included references to Palin and the McGinnis tome. The McGinnis volume did provide some hilarious observations. She has a toilet that didn't work well. She allegedly had an affair with former NBA player Glen Rice. His friends commented that Rice had better judgment. Palin, according to McGinnis, told friends that God asked her to enter politics. She also purged all books about homosexuality from her local library. McGinnis attempts some serious issues. He charges that Palin wants religious controls of government, and she also represents the more significant Alaska business interests. There is nothing surprising about these conclusions.

Geoffrey Dunn's, **The Lies of Sarah Palin: The Untold Story Behind Her Relentless Quest For Power** is an in-depth look at her ambition. It is a frightening insight into a politician who is ill equipped for national office. The people who support her talk of God, country, family and fiscal independence are homophobic, conspiratorial right-wingers. The truth is that she has virtually no knowledge of foreign affairs, panders to racism, targets people to attack and labels President Obama a Muslim, a socialist and a criminal.

When Palin remarked that she believed Africa was a country, not a continent, she charged her remarks were taken out of context. In her public statements, speeches and press conferences, Palin is a master of the arcane and implausible. She is condescending, evasive, ill informed and steeped in platitudes.

Here is another irony. Palin accused the Fox TV Network of character assassination. She wrote that Senator John McCain's campaign staff leaked materials to Fox newsperson Carl Cameron, and she was humiliated and insulted. One wonders did she have something to do with the humorous tales of her life.

WHERE DOES SARAH PALIN FIT IN THE RIGHT WING NUT HOUSE?

As the self appointed Queen of the Tea Party, Sarah Palin is the voice of the white middle class. She became the conservative favorite in August 2009, when she wrote on Facebook: "The America I know and live in is not one in which my parents or my baby with Down Syndrome will have to stand in front of Obama's death panel...." Palin's comment was directed at President Obama's health care reforms. She alleged that Down Syndrome children would not get the same care as other babies. This is, of course, untrue. The right wing rallied behind her statement. Palin's "death panel" comment drew a strong reaction from the **St. Petersburg Times** who labeled her comment "the biggest political lie of the year." Fox TV News failed to analyze Palin's remark.

The "death panel" quote was spectacular, and continued to have a media life. The comment does have some merit. It was aimed at a provision in a bill introduced by Democratic House member Earl Blumenauer from Oregon who co-authored the bill, which included the "end of life counseling." This provision was an amendment to America's Affordable Health Choices Act of 2009, and it was Blumenauer's amendment that led to the "death panels" quote. Sarah Palin told anyone who would listen that his amendment would be a cover for U. S. government death panels. Republican Senator Johnny Isakson of Georgia called Palin's "death panel" notion "nuts."

The point is a simple one. The media reported every weird, crazy and politically laughable Sarah Palin quote. It made for good news. It also created profits for the media.

WILL BUNCH'S ARGUMENTS

The key arguments in Bunch's book are interesting ones. He suggests that Rush Limbaugh and his radio talk show imitators have established a critical, political forum without actual journalism. In other words, they fabricate, distort and use history in a clearly dishonest manner. An example of this direction is the controversy over President Obama's birth certificate.

The big business agenda is another argument. The unregulated economy, the real estate bubble and the easy credit of the George W. Bush years prevented reform. However, the right wing seldom criticized Bush's lack of financial scrutiny. Bunch's view of Glenn Beck's audience is often cruel. He describes those who listen to Beck: "Not only did it turn out that the revolution was televised after all, but it also needed assistance out to its car." This nasty comment is close to the truth as retirees, the grey headed political conservatives and those who detest big government come together to sing the praises of Glenn Beck's use of history. That is after happy hour in the country club or over the shuffleboard court at the over 55 gated community.

It is the entertainment value, or lack of it, of political television that is subverting the political arguments and issues that Americans should consider. In 1985, Neil Postman's **Amusing Ourselves To Death: Public Discourse In The Age of Show Business** suggested that George Orwell's **1984** and Aldous Huxley's **Brave New World** predicted the future of American politics. The result is the news becomes a packaged entertainment commodity. This was Postman's argument prior to the rise of Fox TV News. During his lifetime, Postman died in 2003, he was an educator and held the Paulette Goddard Chair of Media Ecology at New York University. His seventeen books studied the connection between media, education and politics. Postman predicted the decline of serious political dialogue, and the rise of the talking heads on the Fox TV Network. He did this before Rupert Murdoch invented the genre. What he didn't envision or predict is that the conservative media wouldn't just report the news, it would employ it to destroy Barack Obama's presidency.

One of Bunch's concerns is the amount of money that Glenn Beck makes from his program. When Fox TV News blares "fair and balanced," the viewers throw this in your face. Bunch not only is concerned that the bilious Beck has created a merchandise empire, but he argues that the conservative media exists to sell books. Of course, those books contain opinions. Those opinions generally bare little resemblance to the truth.

Once again we are back to Richard Hofstadter's "The Paranoid Style in American Politics." Hofstadter explains the notion that President Obama's critics see themselves as "populists" or the voice of the people. The so-called populists have a weapon that Hofstadter couldn't imagine. That is they have a television outlet, Fox TV News, and a book company, Regnery Publishing that provides the political propaganda.

The two best recent examples of the right wing electing politicians are Republican Scott Brown taking Edward M. (Teddy) Kennedy's normally liberal Massachusetts Senate Democratic seat, and Tea Party favorite Marco Rubio capturing the Republican nomination for the Florida Senate seat. Both politicians owe their victories to support from the right wing, the Tea Party and the Koch brothers.

Bunch argues that the Tea Party appeals to the older, white middle-class conservatives who have trouble accepting change. They are attached to the conservative media like Fox TV News. The confluence of conservatives educated by the media leads to strong grassroots opposition to continued government social programs.

Obama's Detractors

The feeling of lost status sent the Tea Party out into politics. As Richard Hofstadter observed, the loss of status, the rise of immigrants, the continually developing social programs and the fear of foreign enemies galvanized the Tea Party. The changes brought by the Tea Party created a conservative group of political activists, who are an army for immediate social-economic-political change. The downside is that it brings politically inexperienced amateurs like Michele Bachmann and Christine O'Donnell into the mainstream of American politics.

The irony is that the Tea Party is described as a grass roots political movement. The Koch brothers and other free market billionaires, who oppose President Obama, are pulling the strings of the Tea Party movement. They hate President Barack Obama. This is not a recipe for future American political success.

WHAT BUNCH'S BOOKS TELL US

Bunch's message in his Reagan book is that the right wing has hijacked the former president's legacy. He maintains that the Tea Party and the Koch brothers have no idea about the depth of sophistication of President Reagan's policies. Unlike some historians, who see in Reagan's policies a bold direction, Bunch concludes that Reagan presided over an ineffective military, his tax cuts weighed heavily toward the rich and his support of Wall Street deregulation contributed to current economic problems.

Bunch writes: "By picking Reagan's Air Force One and the artifacts of his life as proper for a Republican presidential debate, that would be watched by an estimated 4 million Americans, CNN showed what would have been a more obvious motif: the news of 2008." (p.2) This quote speaks to the heart of Bunch's thesis. He sees Reagan's image used by the Republican Party, the major news networks, select candidates and the media to explain current political directions. Bunch demonstrates that this is a mistake. In the process, he illustrates how the Reagan myth is at the center of a segment of American politics.

It is Bunch's **The Backlash: Right Wing Radicals, High-Def Hucksters, and Paranoid Politics In the Age of Obama** that highlights the paranoid, conspiracy oriented right wing nut house. What Bunch demonstrates is that Barack Obama's election brought out a hard core and highly organized right wing to attempt to make him a one-term president. In the process, the media abandoned its middle of the road reporting and there was a media war on the left, right and center. The book publishers jumped in with contracts for those in the right wing nut house, and this irrevocably altered American politics.

Chapter 3
THE KOCH BROTHERS INVENTED THE TEA PARTY

"I THINK THE RE-ELECTION OF BARACK OBAMA WOULD BE THE END OF FREEDOM." RICK SANTORUM, MARCH 25, 2012

A sophisticated political machine that is led by two billionaire brothers, whose family lineage has a history of opposing liberal Democratic presidents since Franklin Delano Roosevelt, directs the hostility to President Barack Obama. When Jane Meyer in the **New Yorker** published an in-depth critique of the Koch Brothers: "The Billionaire Brothers Who Are Waging A War Against Obama," they hired investigators and attempted to find evidence to discredit her. They didn't succeed. Who are the Koch brothers?

WHO ARE THE KOCH BROTHERS?

Fred Koch, the family patriarch, was born in 1900 and died in 1967. A chemical engineer, as well as a skilled entrepreneur, he founded the oil refinery that became Koch Industries. It grew into the second largest privately held company in America.

The son of a Dutch immigrant, Koch was born in Quanah, Texas. He was a brilliant student. He graduated from the Massachusetts Institute of Technology with a degree in chemical engineering. He also studied for two years at Rice. When Fred founded his Texas Company in Port Arthur, he was on his way to making a massive fortune. In 1927, he developed a method of turning crude oil into gasoline. It was this technology that made him a multi-millionaire, and he quickly headed his family into billionaire territory.

But it was not easy for Fred Koch. After he discovered a method to reform crude oil into gasoline, the major oil companies sued him. After forty-four different lawsuits, Koch won all but one. That one decision against his financial interests was later overturned. When the lawsuit ended Koch held a personal grudge against the federal government, the courts and his competitors. He also suspected that politicians were bribed to slander Koch Industries. He wasn't amused. These lawsuits turned Koch into a writer who warned America of impending Socialist and Communist influences. He quickly became a political activist. He saw dire consequences for a liberal democracy.

THE KOCH BUSINESS EMPIRE AS THE FOUNDING OF ACTION POLITICS

Fred Koch's business empire was the foundation of his politics. Had it not been for the huge sums of money that the businesses generated, there would not have been funds for conservative political activism.

He developed a disdain for government that bordered on the obsessive. The federal government was a bane to his existence. He instilled in his family a skeptical notion of the government's ability to represent the people. Fred argued that big government eroded individual enterprise. He predicated his business career on challenging government's intrusion upon private enterprise. As he looked at the world economy, Fred Koch concluded that other nations, particularly Russia, threatened individual business rights. An examination of Koch's world business interests confirms this conclusion.

Not only was Koch a brilliant engineer, he was an equally adept businessmen who realized that there were foreign business opportunities. He built 15 crackings in the Soviet Union to make gasoline from oil. While in the USSR, he developed a latent fear of Communism. He saw it as a violent, anti-capitalistic system with a police state mentality. By 1940, Koch's fortune was enormous, and he thought of ways to challenge big government.

He founded the Wood River Oil and Refining Company, and it is this entity that today is known as Koch Industries. In 1966 his son, Charles Koch, began the day-to-day management. Another son, David, quickly came into the mix a few years later. They took their dad's political philosophy into the national arena. They subscribed to and improved their father's political philosophy.

Political conservatism dominated Fred. He viewed Joseph Stalin as a tyrant and Communism as a threat to capitalism. His 1960 book, **A Business Man Looks At Communism,** didn't find a receptive audience. It is a reasonable book that highlighted Fred's time in the USSR. He described the people's hunger, the terror of the KGB and the day-to-day living conditions that made Russian life virtually unbearable. Fred Koch was not a fanatic. He was a reasoned man with a view of Russia that was historically accurate. The advent of John F. Kennedy's presidency, and the rise of persistent liberalism made Koch a critical political voice. His sons, Charles and David, reflect their father's political convictions.

Fred Koch had four sons. The two sons who operate Koch Industries, Charles and David, are brilliant businessmen, technical innovators, and they are among the most influential American political lobbyists. They not only inherited their conservatism from their father, but doing business in the USSR influenced them.

While he was in the Soviet Union, Fred socialized with a number of local engineers. He watched as the people changed from bullish on Russia into fearful citizens, as a result of central government power. Many of the engineers who befriended Fred were later purged from the Communist Party, and some of Fred's friends were sent to labor camps. The lack of political-economic progress and the decline of civil liberties frightened Koch. He feared these influences would take root in America. It is one of the reasons that he was a founding member of the John Birch Society. From his business in Texas, and later Missouri, he envisioned a multitude of dangers to American democracy.

THE KOCH BROTHERS IN POLITICS

"The Koch Brothers are the financial engine of the Tea Party." This is a quote in an internal memo from the Mitt Romney campaign, and it suggests the Koch's fiscal importance. This November, 2011, memo is an indication that without the Koch Brothers, and the Tea Party, the Romney candidacy would not have had an easy road to the Republican nomination. Rather than head to Iowa to campaign two months before the Iowa Caucuses, Romney delivered the 2011 keynote address to the Koch brothers funded pressure group Americans For Prosperity. Since 2004, this organization has trained and supported conservative candidates and causes. It is the training ground for the Tea Party.

In addition to supporting conservative candidates, right wing lobbying groups and reactionary research institutions, the Koch brothers make their case effectively in the media. A case in point is the money spent on television advertising to inform the nation that President Obama and his Democratic administration pumped millions of dollars into the Solyndra energy company without doing the necessary research on company solvency.

Solyndra's ties to the Obama administration were well known, but there is no evidence of criminal malfeasance. David and Charles Koch disagreed. They funded the Americans For Prosperity, who spent $2.4 million to run anti-Solyndra ads blaming the Obama administration for giving money to a company that was going bankrupt. The ads ran almost 4,000 times, and this illustrates the depth to which the Koch brothers will go to end the Obama administration's power.

This prompted the Democrats to strike back. The founding of Priorities USA Action, a pro-Obama group, created with the help of Bill Burton, a former White House spokesman, who was given a million dollars to counter the Solyndra ads. Burton attempted to explain the Solyndra situation. The Solyndra solar panel company went bankrupt after the government granted a $535 million loan. Koch Industries pointed out the obvious fact that Solyndra talked about helping the environment, when in fact it was their pocketbook that prospered. The Koch brothers also emphasized that the clean energy loan program was introduced and started by President George W. Bush. They believed the Bush policies were superior on the environment. The Koch's characterized President Obama as an empty suit who had little understanding of the environment. He was, the television ads argued, helping his donors to survive in a difficult business climate.

AMERICANS FOR PROSPERITY AND REFORM

David Koch and his wife, Julia, fund conservative candidates seeking election and support key conservative issues. They intensified their conservative political efforts when they founded the Americans For Prosperity; the organization is based in Washington D. C. and is a tax-exempt political advocacy group. This AFP hosts an annual convention to promote American values. In 2007, the annual meeting concentrated upon government spending and taxation policies. Some of those who attended included Senator John McCain, Congressman Ron Paul, conservative author Dinesh D'Souza, future presidential candidate Herman Cain and media stars Mike Huckabee and John Stossel. As Barack Obama conducted a successful campaign and was elected president, the Koch brothers increased their donations to oppose his policies.

By 2008, the Koch brothers donated more than $7 million to fund Americans For Prosperity. Surprisingly, this was less than a third of the groups $22 million budget. There are many other conservatives who follow the Koch brothers, and they do so because of clearly defined goals. Americans For Prosperity has an agenda. They oppose a climate tax, and they believe that a government backed health care system is contrary to American law.

The Democratic Party and the Obama administration are critical of Americans For Prosperity. They argue that the organization should lose its tax-exempt status for being overtly political. The Democratic Congressional Campaign Committee filed a formal Federal complaint against the organization. The Americans For Prosperity fired back that the Democratic Party and President Obama are filing "a nuisance complaint to intimidate." The fact remains that the organization and its supporters, primarily the Koch brothers, are important to presidential candidates. Without the Koch brothers funding, most of the major candidates would not have had a chance to oppose President Obama in the 2012 election.

CHARLES KOCH ON HOW TO SOLVE THE ECONOMIC CRISIS

In March 2011, Charles G. Koch wrote an op-ed editorial piece for the **Wall Street Journal**. It is a perfect statement of his fears. The cause of the present economic crisis, Koch maintains, is government overspending. It is not just federal spending but state and local government economic policies that concern Koch. He casts equal blame on Republicans and Democrats.

He does make some excellent points. He demonstrates that politicians have made few serious proposals for cuts in military spending and entitlements. He points out that Social Security, Medicare and Medicaid have exceeded $106 trillion. This is over $300,000 for every person in America.

Koch maintains that the solution to these problems is to reduce federal spending. He points to Canada cutting federal spending to 25% of the GDP and the prosperity that ensued. The worst thing about government spending, according to Koch, is when government dispenses special funds to business. When businesses lobby for special favors they decline in profit, Koch maintains, and he sees "crony capitalism" as one of the worst political problems in the Obama administration.

On federal regulation, Koch points out that his ethanol business suffers because of government regulations. Koch remarked: "We believe that ethanol-and every other product in the marketplace-should be required to compete on its own merits, without mandates, subsidies or protective tariffs." He argues that government regulation drives prices up.

The **Wall Street Journal** op-ed piece was a rare insight into Koch's thinking. "I am confident that businesses like ours will hire more people and invest in more equipment when our country's financial future looks more promising," Koch concluded. Most business people echo this statement.

THE DEMONIZATION OF THE KOCH BROTHERS

The Koch brothers are among the most demonized political activists in America. Yet, surprisingly, they have stayed under the radar. That is until the last couple of years. They crave anonymity. They are nervous public figures. It was when they funded the Tea Party that the press became interested.

The anonymity was shed when Charles Koch's op-ed piece for the **Wall Street Journal** appeared. He wrote: "Society as a whole benefits from great economic freedom." Not exactly revolutionary, but it is a simple and accurate description of their ideological direction. There are also millions of Americans who agree with Charles Koch as the 2010 elections demonstrated.

It was in 2009 that news about the Koch brothers surfaced on MSNBC and in the **Huffington Post**. Then President Obama spoke out against the Koch brothers. "You don't know if it's a foreign controlled corporation," Obama remarked of Koch Industries. "You don't know if it's a big oil company, or a bank." David Axelrod stated in September 2010 that the Koch brothers are "billionaire oilmen secretly underwriting what the public has been told is a grass-roots movement for change in Washington."

The media comments on the Koch brothers suggest that they are no longer under the radar. The press is intrigued by the secret meetings undertaken by lobbyists and pressure groups funded by the Koch brothers.

Robert Greenwald, the Hollywood director who brought Olivia Newton-John to the screen in Xanadu, produced a documentary on the Koch brothers. At the Lincoln Center, he screened it and among the scenes in Greenwald's documentary are his filmmakers knocking on the doors of the five homes the brothers own in the U. S. They attempted to elicit a comment, but they were not successful. So far there is no word from the Koch brothers. In the documentary, Greenwald compares the Koch homes, which he dubs "luxury porn," along side the houses of average Americans. These pictures suggest the degree of wealth at a time when working class Americans are struggling to pay their bills.

MEDIA COMMENTS ABOUT THE KOCH BROTHERS

1. THEY HAVE AN INTEREST THAT IS HARD CORE IDEOLOGICAL CONSERVATIVE AND DAD'S MONEY TO PURSUE THAT AGENDA...." RACHEL MADDOW MSNBC
2. "THEY ARE INHERITANCE BABIES WHO DON'T WANT TO PAY THEIR TAXES." MIKE PAPANTONIO
3. "WHAT THE KOCH BROTHERS HAVE BOUGHT WITH THEIR HUGE POLITICAL OUTLAYS IS...THE FREEDOM TO POLLUTE." PAUL KRUGMAN
4. "THEY ARE FAT CATS." FRANK RICH
5. "WE DON'T WANT THE RIGHT WING BUYING ELECTIONS," HOWARD DEAN

WHIAT WOULD RICHARD HOFSTADTER SAY?

According to the Obama administration, the Koch brothers provide the financing, the misinformation and disinformation, as well as the conspiracies that produce paranoid right wing thinking. This may have been true in the past, but the Koch brothers are reasoned and intelligent men, who simply view themselves as changing the political landscape.

Each brother is worth roughly twenty-two billion dollars. While they have been private, there have been some previous political campaigns. In 1980, David Koch was the Libertarian Party Vice Presidential nominee. During this campaign, the Libertarian Party platform called for the abolition of social security, most federal regulatory agencies as well as the FBI and CIA. Since this time David Koch has been an elusive political figure

Long before they were the financial benefactors of the Tea Party, the Koch brothers supported efforts to educate American voters. In 1977, they established the Cato Institute to promote economic and political reform. The Cato Institute is a think tank that turns out exceptionally well-documented articles and reports on the dangers of big government. The website for the Cato Institute claims it supports "Individual Liberty, Free Markets And Peace." The Koch brothers continue to fund this organization as a means of influencing government policy. Downsizing Government.org is an offshoot of the Cato Institute and it contains a department-by-department guide to cutting the government's budget.

The Cato Institute is a major source of conservative news. It is a sophisticated organization analyzing why conservative policy is needed.

Some examples of Cato Institute articles and reports are Gene Healy's "Newt Gingrich Is No Conservative," John Samples' "Laws Shouldn't Supersede Free Speech" and the Cato Pocket Constitution, "Can The Government Do That, Check The Constitution?" There are also hundreds of reports from mainstream magazines like the **US News and World Report** and more conservative publications such as **The National Interest**. Whether or not one agrees with the Cato Institute, the reports are clearly written, supported with excellent research, and they point toward the future direction of American politics. In many respects, the Tea Party has taken the best of the Cato Institute reports and presented this information to the American public. This would have been impossible without the Koch brother's financial support. They are information gurus who attempt to educate Americans to the conservative point of view. The notion in the media that they are right wing crackpots is an incorrect one. They are conservatives, who believe in putting their thoughts out to the electorate.

COMMENTS FROM CATO INSTITUTE SUPPORTERS

"THE CATO INSTITUTE IS THE FOREMOST UPHOLDER OF THE IDEA OF LIBERTY IN THE NATION…." GEORGE WILL

"IF YOU'RE LOOKING FOR A CONSISTENT COMMITMENT TO PRESERVING ALL FORMS OF INDIVIDUAL LIBERTY, JOIN THE CATO INSTITUTE," WENDY KAMINER, THE AMERICAN PROSPECT

"CATO IS NOW THE HOT POLICY SHOP, REPSECTED FOR NOT COMPROMISING ITS CORE BELIEFS EVEN WHEN THEY GET IN THE WAY OF PRACTICAL POLITICS," WASHINGTON POST

THE KOCH BROTHERS AND LABOR UNIONS

Labor Unions are the bane of the Koch brothers. They believe that the unionization process is anathema to American democracy. As a result, they support an anti-union group, the Associated Builders And Contractors of Ohio, who introduced a right to work constitutional amendment on the Ohio state ballot. They also supported similar efforts in Wisconsin, Illinois and Pennsylvania.

Obama's Detractors

The Koch brothers realized that President Obama has a good chance of carrying Ohio in the 2012 presidential election. As a result, they poured money into Ohio to support a right to work law. They believe that the depressed economy creates anti-labor union sentiment. What the Koch supporters desire is to end collective bargaining. The hope of defeating Obama and labor unions drives them.

In Wisconsin, the Koch brothers were behind the effort to end public unions. In their subtle, yet understated manner, they funded Governor Scott Walker, who argues that tough economic times are responsible for ending the public employees right to collective bargaining.

In June 2012, Wisconsin voters failed to recall Governor Scott Walker. The 900,000 recall signatures resulted from cuts in the public employees unions, their loss of bargaining status and the cuts in state government. Walker's victory over Democratic challenger Tom Barrett was by eight points, which was close to his victory margin when he was elected governor in 2010.

The media reported the main issue as labor unions and the Democratic Party attempting to recall Governor Walker. In reality, there were two issues. The right wanted to severely reduce public employee unions and there was also the specter of Walker's anti-abortion stance versus Barrett's pro-abortion position. The Republican Party spent forty-five point six million dollars to beat back the recall, whereas the Democrats spent seventeen point nine million dollars to make Milwaukee Mayor Barrett the new governor. Lurking in the shadows the specter of the Koch brothers dominated the electoral process.

The investigative magazine, **Mother Jones,** discovered that long before the issues of public collective bargaining came to the table, the Koch brothers were prime movers in electing Governor Walker. The Koch brothers were the second largest contributor to Walker's campaign. The housing and building industry donated most of the funds for Walker's gubernatorial bid. Then the Americans For Prosperity arrived in the dairy state to run ads supporting the end of collective bargaining for public employees. The Cato Institute brought in its scientific studies to demonstrate that public labor unions were not needed. The Reason Foundation and the Competitive Enterprise Institute were other organizations that supported an end to collective bargaining. The public sector is under attack and the Koch brothers are in the forefront of the assault.

Governor Walker also opposed the Wisconsin Clean Energy Job Act. The Koch brothers were flushed with success as their minions from the Americans For Prosperity flooded the state with self-righteous arguments on the right to work.

Mary Ellen Burke, the spokesperson for Americans For Prosperity, stated that the organization was bussing in supporters to end the collective bargaining process for public employees. The issue was not about collective bargaining in Wisconsin, the Koch brothers were going after President Obama.

THE CHARITABLE SIDE OF THE KOCH BROTHERS

From Wichita, the Koch brothers funded conservative and libertarian groups. Since 1980, they have donated more than $100 million to conservative politics. Their crowning achievement is the Tea Party. But there is more to the Koch brothers than politics. They are also patrons of the arts.

On May 17, 2011, a black tie audience at New York's Metropolitan Opera House applauded a tall, good-looking billionaire, David H. Koch, as he celebrated his donation of two and a half million dollars to support the New York Opera Company. At seventy, Koch is one of New York's more prominent philanthropists. His hundred million dollar donation to modernize Lincoln Center's New York State Theater building is a generous gift. He was also applauded for adding twenty million to the American Museum of Natural History. Koch is by all accounts a respected philanthropist.

As the crowd cheered for Koch, there was one person missing the festivities. The event's third honorary co-chair, Michelle Obama, was absent. Her office cited a scheduling conflict. The real reason is that the Koch brothers are not only financing the Tea Party, but also they are contributing more than money to the Mitt Romney presidential campaign. The Koch brothers are not only critical of the policies and programs of the federal government, they are intent upon blaming the present fiscal crisis solely upon Barack Obama.

The Koch's believe that incipient Socialism, a form of viral Communism and the federal entitlement programs are subverting traditional democratic values. David Koch is a man who clearly fears for the future of his country. His seventy-four year old brother, Charles, is a courtly gentleman who has control of most of Koch Industries. With oil refineries in Alaska, Texas and Minnesota, they are at odds with President Obama's energy policies. They have made fortunes in the energy industry, timber speculation, and the chemical business. So naturally they are the focal point of attack from environmentalists.

Forbes ranks Koch Industries as the number two private corporation in America. The Koch brothers are the seventh richest men in America, according to a 2011 **Forbes** article. They were once ranked third and another time fifth. The Koch brothers have specific political interests. They are libertarians who advocate lower personal and corporate taxes, minimal social services and less governmental regulation.

There are some business negatives to Koch Industries. The environmentalists paint an ominous picture of Koch Industries. The University of Massachusetts Amherst Political Economy Research Institute ranked Koch Industries as a major air polluter. Greenpeace labeled the company the "kingpin of climate science denial." Both organizations claim that the Koch business model out distanced Exxon Mobil in giving money to organizations fighting legislation on climate control. Greenpeace reported that fifty-five million dollars from the Koch brothers was spent on opposing climate change regulation.

Koch Industries vigorously defends its business practices. They claim that Greenpeace "distorts the environmental record of our companies." They also believe that the press attacks them unfairly. There is no evidence of law breaking at Koch Industries. Not everyone sees it this way. Charles Lewis, the founder of the Center For Public Integrity, disagrees as he compares the Koch brothers to the late nineteenth century robber barons.

The Center For Public Integrity, in August 2011, published an article by John Aloysius Farrell on how Koch Industries was able to lobby against increased regulation on financial markets. This think tank pointed out that in 2004 Koch Industries spent $857,000 lobbying. The company disputes this figure. It is difficult to pinpoint the amount of money that the Koch brothers donate to oppose environmental laws, cut social security and oppose Medicare.

KOCH INDUSTRIES ANSWERS BACK

The Americans For Prosperity is a Koch supported group that hosts summits on defending the American dream. In 2004, the initial meeting, held in Austin Texas, was a training ground for the emergence of the Tea Party. It was here that Tea Party activists met to train and discuss strategy.

The Koch brothers are establishing a nationwide database to bring voters together who share their anti big-government, libertarian views. The alleged voter file is two years old, and it was started with almost three million dollars. It is called Themis, after the Greek goddess who imposed divine order on human affairs. The purpose of Themis is to gather information that will be useful in future political campaigns. In reality, it is a voter list that allows the conservative views that the Tea Party advocates to be shared with millions of likeminded Americans. This database is one that conservatives developed after watching Democrats use this tactic in local elections. Themis is taking the database nationally to influence presidential elections. The use of sophisticated technology suggests that the Koch brothers are not political amateurs. They are smart, driven and ideologically directed.

THE KOCH BROTHERS' CONSERVATIVE SEMINARS

In January, 2011, while two hundred conservatives met in California's desert east of Los Angeles, for a Koch sponsored seminar, the environmental group, Greenpeace, was in action. They launched a blimp with liberal political slogans over the luxury spa housing the meeting. Protesters held signs outside demanding that corporations be kept out of politics. As more than a thousand liberal activists marched around Rancho Mirage, adjacent to Palm Springs, the Koch brothers' security was taken up a notch. Trade unionists, a citizen's lobby group, Common Cause, and a cast of California liberals joined Greenpeace. The Koch's booked the entire Rancho Mirage resort for the weekend. So the formidable private security staff quickly ejected intruders.

What the annual retreat indicates is that any attempt to label the Koch brothers as part of the right wing nut house is a mistake. They are serious, smart, moneyed, and they are determined to bring political change. That was demonstrated in 2011 when Virginia Republican Representative Eric Cantor was a strong presence at their meetings.

Ken Langone was another significant voice in these meetings. Langone, the founder of Home Depot, is a venture capitalist, banker and former director of the New York Stock Exchange. He helped Karl Rove organize the **American Action Network** and the **American Action Forum** to support conservative causes.

WHERE IS AMERICA HEADED BECAUSE OF THE RIGHT WING?

The Koch brothers aren't responsible for the rise of right wing pressures on government, they are simply the financial benefactors. Where is America headed due to nascent conservatism? **Rolling Stone** called the Republican Party "the Party of the one-percent-the Party of the Rich." The fiscal conservatism that is required to bring America out of its economic doldrums is nowhere to be found. Neither the Republican nor the Democratic Party can figure out how to solve the economic riddle that is driving the U.S. to the brink of bankruptcy.

What is obvious is that there is enormous income, social, cultural and educational inequality. Since 1997, the Republican political machine has pressured for less taxation, less regulation and less government meddling in the economy. The result is that the income of the four hundred highest taxpayers has tripled in the last fifteen years. The average billionaire pays a seventeen per cent tax, while the middle class American kicks in a thirty-two to forty per cent tax. Yet, tax receipts are at their lowest level since the early 1950s.

There are fourteen million Americans out of work and one in seven families collect food stamps. The Republicans response is to extend tax credits to millionaires and billionaires. There are also arguments for tax credits to large corporations. The rich can do no better than investing in Washington politics, as it gives them enormous tax credits.

"Starve the Beast" is the latest Republican strategy. That is to force cuts in federal spending by bankrupting the country. In 1980, Irving Kristol suggested that the strategy of cutting taxes and imposing a financial strain on the federal government would end federal interference in the business sector. Since that time right wing Republicans have embraced that strategy.

When Newt Gingrich was House Speaker in 1994, he led a Republican revolt that hoped to eliminate taxes on investment income and abolish the inheritance tax. The result was a bitter fight between President Bill Clinton and Gingrich. In the midst of this brouhaha, capital gains taxes were cut to twenty per cent. There were other tax incentives for the rich, and these laws doubled the amount of money that the rich passed on to their heirs. This was the beginning of the program designed to eliminate the middle class, and it has been a Republican mandate since the mid-1990s.

In 2002, the Koch brothers funded the Mercatus Center, and they based it at George Mason University. This was a brilliant strategy to bring in academic specialists, but they also needed a media person. They found one when they hired Lawrence Kudlow, a CNBC co-host who later went on to host his own show, The Kudlow Report. Public documents report that Mercatus spent almost $300,000 for more than forty trips to influence lawmakers and their aides.

When Barack Obama became president in January 2009, the policies of George W. Bush had bankrupted the country. The Bush presidency not only exposed the hypocrisy behind the notion that tax cuts for the rich would help the economy grow, but the rise of special interests hindered the Democrats from passing reform legislation. The tax cuts for the wealthy produced lower growth and a decrease of the middle class.

Virginia Republican Eric Cantor is in the forefront of the program to shield the rich from increased taxes. During the stimulus debate, Cantor issued the sound bite: "No Tax Increase To Pay For Spending." When the Bush presidency ended, Republicans remarked that deficits didn't matter. When Barack Obama assumed the presidency, they blamed him for the economy continuing to decline.

Republicans opposed Obamacare, and vilified it as a socialist program that took away the fundamental right to select health insurance. Or for that matter the decision not to have health insurance. In one of the more rancorous debates in American politics, the Republican Party neglected to inform the voters why they opposed Obamacare. The usual lame argument was that it took away an individuals right to select his or her insurance. They also charge that it downgraded medical care. The real reason that right wing conservatives lobbied Republicans to end Obamacare is that the money came from increasing Medicare taxes on the wealthy. The top 400 American taxpayers would contribute eleven million dollars yearly to Medicare. Not surprisingly, these four hundred Americans spend more than a million dollars each year to lobby against Obamacare.

The 2012 presidential campaign, according to the liberal magazine **Mother Jones**, is one that Charles Koch viewed as a battle "for the life or death of this country." He allegedly made this comment at a political summit in June 2011. **Mother Jones**, despite heavy security, obtained tapes of the Koch brothers at the political summit in Vail Colorado. This meeting at the Ritz Carleton Bachelor Gulch was important as three hundred of the most prominent conservatives met to plan a strategy to defeat President Obama.

The Koch brothers hold twice-yearly seminars and they are extremely well funded. At the Vail meeting, Texas Governor Rick Perry was a prominent attendee. Another important figure, retired Superior Court Judge Andrew P. Napolitano, remarked that the Second Amendment was created to ensure "the right to shoot at the government if it is taken over by tyrants."

When Ronald Reagan was president, he advocated a trickle down economy. Since the Presidency of George W. Bush it has been trickle up to the wealthy. Eric Cantor, advocates ending consumer protection, he supports less environmental regulation, the subsidizing of agribusiness, the stifling of health care and a decline in taxes for the wealthy.

In August 2011, the Congressional Super Committee began work on reducing the debt ceiling. It remained on the job with very few concrete accomplishments. Representative Cantor reminded voters and those in the Republican Party to resist tax increases. He continued to lobby for governmental budget cuts.

THE KOCH BROTHERS AS REFORMERS AND CHRISTIANS

The Koch brothers are not only skilled businessmen but they are reformers with integrity. A Koch Industries subsidiary in southern France was paying bribes for contracts. Suspecting wrong dong, the Wichita Company sent Ludmila Egorova-Farines, its compliance officer and ethics manager, to France where she uncovered the illegal practices. She notified management in Wichita, and Koch Industries sent an investigative team. The unauthorized payments were uncovered and the French Koch-Glitsch affiliate reported their findings to local authorities.

What is impressive is that Koch Industries could have ignored these violations of law. They didn't. Koch Industries found impropriety and took action. What bothered the media was that court documents were not available to the press. The wrongdoing was documented and corrected in private.

David and Charles Koch are Christian conservatives that are concerned about the moral, ethical and political direction of American democracy. They see the Republican Party as the vehicle of salvation. They are also an important influence upon decision-making. The House Energy and Commerce Committee had nine of its twelve Republican members sign a pledge to oppose any and all of the Obama administration's attempts to control greenhouse gases. Koch Industries argue that federal controls hurt their profits.

AMERICANS FOR PROSPERITY: SOME CONCLUSIONS

The Tea Party is not as dangerous as Americans For Prosperity. What AFP has done is to hamper public sector unionization in Ohio, Indiana, Pennsylvania and Wisconsin as well as combat health care reform, oppose environmental regulation while arguing that Barack Obama's defeat is essential to American prosperity.

In an economy that is faltering, the AFP argues that taxes and regulation are destroying America. They use the term "people's grassroots democracy" to push for less government. By supporting Tea Party candidates, the Koch brothers are the puppet masters and the legislatures who accept their money are the puppets. Since 2004, when they split from the Citizens For A Sound Economy, the AFP has been a prime mover in educating voters about government economic policy and mobilizing the vote for lower taxes and limited government.

SUMMING UP THE KOCH BROTHERS

It was the January 2011 meeting in Palm Springs that brought the Koch brothers into the public eye. They had met many times previously with a minimum of press coverage. What the Koch's didn't realize was that Think Progress, the investigative arm of the Center For Public Progress, publicized the Koch meeting. The result was a group of protesters showing up to demonstrate at the conservative gathering.

When Common Cause protested outside the hotel, the press recorded the event. Suddenly the Koch brothers' were front-page news. The Koch brothers were an important force in attacking the Obama administration. They effectively publicized the increase in unemployment from 7.7% to 10% at its peak. They failed to mention that when Barack Obama was inaugurated, the Dow Jones increased over fifty per cent. It is corporate money and grass roots support that has made the Koch brothers so effective. Koch money attacked former President Bill Clinton when he proposed an energy tax or carbon tax.

It is through their organizations, Freedom Works and Citizens For A Sound Economy, that the Koch influence has permeated every segment of the American political and economic sector. These organizations had little impact until President Obama took office, and then they exploded with a frenetic zeal. On April 15, 2009 six hundred different tax day rallies took place throughout America, and this led to countless protests at town hall meetings led by the Tea Party.

To attack President Obama, Americans For Prosperity organized "Porkulus," which was a rally against Obama's $787 billion stimulus program. The Koch political organization funded 57 separate anti-Obama groups. With protests like the "Defending The American Dream" meeting in Crystal City, Virginia, held in October 2009, the Koch brothers funded an organization that drew Newt Gingrich as its featured speaker.

The Koch brothers are no longer conservative voices in the wilderness. They are front-runners for political change.

On January 5 2012, the Koch brothers were vindicated in their drive for political influence. John Boehner was introduced as the House Speaker for the 112th Congress. The Koch brothers had a private meeting with Boehner and other members of the House showed up for wine and cheese with the billionaire benefactors of the conservative arm of the Republican party.

There are a number of media figures that share the Koch brothers' politics and trumpet their message on national television. Charles Krauthammer, a columnist for the **Washington Post** and a regular commentator on Fox TV News, is a strong Koch supporter. Ramesh Ponnuru, a senior editor at the **National Review**, who wrote a 2006 book, **The Party Of Death**, which pilloried the Democratic Party, is a major Koch supporter. Tim Carney, a political columnist for the **Washington Examiner**, is another voice of the Koch brothers. He is a former editor of the Evans-Novak Political Report. The Koch influence is all over the conservative media.

The Koch brothers are a strong influence on American society. They have what Bob Dylan calls: "With God On Our Side," as the major justification for their actions. They are a force to be reckoned with in American politics.

PART TWO
THE PROFESSORS, THE HIGH SCHOOL AUTHORS, THE COLORING BOOKS AND THE PUNDITS

> "SO HERE YOU HAVE BARACK OBAMA GOING IN AND SPENDING THE MONEY ON EMBRYONIC STEM CELL RESEARCH.... IN CASE YOU DON'T KNOW WHAT EUGENICS LED US TO; A MASTER RACE, A PERFECT PERSON...." THE GLENN BECK PROGRAM, MARCH 9, 2009

The right wing pundits, like Jerome Corsi, argue that President Barack Obama represents a cult. Corsi claims that Obama is a revered figure, who believes that he is above criticism. In the right wing nut house the facts, the course of history and the flow of world events are seldom considered. Other writers, like Glenn Beck, use a high school brand of history to criticize. Beck will tell you what George Washington thought, but, as he told Don Imus, he is too busy to write his books. A ghostwriter takes Beck's ideas and translates them for the millions who purchase books from the right wing nut house.

The authors who attack President Obama have little regard for the facts or the truth. The more absurd the argument the better the book sells. But it is the pundits who are most interesting. The first wave of anti-Obama books was directed toward defeating his re-election. To that end, the critics attack his character, his integrity and his persona.

This tactic divides America and prevents bipartisan political compromise necessary to govern our nation.

This section is one that demonstrates that the well-educated, the professors, the media darlings, like Glenn Beck, and the so-called cute critics, take your pick, all have little to offer in the way of serious political criticism.

But the general public likes their nonsense. Jerome Corsi, who has written two books charging President Obama with a personality disorder, is the most dangerous critic. He is literate as well as a good writer. He has carefully researched his subject. The problem is that the presentation is so skewed, if in a literate way, that it is hard to tell truth from fiction. But as one of Corsi's friends remarked, he allegedly never let the truth get in the way of a good story.

Glenn Beck is equally dangerous. He uses history to make his points. Or to be more accurate, he is the most prominent critic who abuses and misuses historical material. His outrageous claims that President Obama is racist, his open promotion of the John Birch Society, and his criticism of the "New World Order," suggests that he is a writer on the lunatic fringe. Yet, he has a wide following.

If Richard Hofstadter were alive, he would nominate Glenn Beck as the role model of the media host who promotes poisonous and hateful conspiracy theories. Beck predicts the future is one nationally where paramilitary right wing militias will protect America. He also has said that concentration camps run by FEMA were well and alive. He has had several portions of his program supporting the secession of Texas from the Union. Beck sees the forces of Socialism, Communism and Middle Eastern dictators (are there any left) creating a One World Government.

Beck is suspicious of central banking, and he regularly complains about declining states rights. He is subtle, but clear, in a controlled anti-Semitic manner. Hitler he finds interesting, and his admiration for Henry Ford avoids the manufacturers blatant anti-Semitism.

Al Gore is a frequent Beck target. Gore may be guilty of bad hair and too many hot fudge sundaes, but he is not an extremist. By promoting environmental awareness among young people, Beck suggests, Gore is creating a new type of socialism. It is eco-socialism.

It is in his use of history that Beck is most dangerous. He spent two weeks listening to some Yale University professors and he figured that he could do it better. So he started reading about history, Jesus, Bob Dylan and Kinky Friedman.

Some of his harshest criticism is for the victims of 9/11/. He hates them for asking questions, he chides them for seeking compensation. He made comments on September 9, 2005 that are egregious. Beck remarked: "You know it took me about a year to start hating the 9/11 victims' families. I don't hate all of them. I hate probably about ten of them. But when I see a 9/11 victim family on television…I'm so sick of them because they're always complaining." The irony is that two days later Beck didn't seem to know that it was the fourth anniversary of 9/11.

In this section, two pundits, Jerome Corsi and Glenn Beck, challenge the direction of American politics. Corsi is a career conspiracy writer with thoughtful, intelligent books that are easily digested. The danger of the Corsi books comes from the notion that President Obama is disingenuous.

The Glenn Beck books are more dangerous. They are poorly grounded in fact, they misrepresent history and they are written in a style that suggests he is not involved in all aspects of the books. Another strange statistic is that Beck has written in different categories that include children's picture books. He is most qualified to write the children's tomes. Both Corsi and Beck use inflamed rhetoric. Corsi does it intelligently. Beck does it with a sledgehammer.

The Beck and Corsi attacks on President Obama have yielded a reaction. When Democratic Representative Anthony Weiner got caught in a scandal in New York's 9th Congressional District, Beck was an instant and moralistic critic. Weiner's revenge came when he demonstrated that one of Beck's sponsors, Goldline, allegedly ripped off investors. Beck and Weiner argued as federal prosecutors looked toward prosecuting Goldline. Weiner was implicated in an Internet sex message scandal. The controversy resulted in Weiner's resignation, and, in a special election, in a dominant Democratic Congressional district, a Republican, Bob Turner, won handedly. What is strange is that this is a New York, highly Democratic district that sent Geraldine A. Ferraro to Congress. Weiner had represented New York's Ninth Congressional district for twelve years, and he was disparaged for good reason by Beck.

After graduating from the Elliott Spitzer marriage school of ethics and integrity, Weiner did the right thing by resigning from Congress. What did the Weiner scandal demonstrate? Plenty! It showed that writers like Jerome Corsi and TV personalities like Glenn Beck have a ready-made audience for Democratic scandal. But, on a more serious note, the election of a conservative Republican to the House in a dominant, liberal Democratic district sent a clear message to the Obama administration. There is a need to reform the economy, clean up the budget mess and bring the troops home.

Does this mean that the voting public is unaware? No! It is just the opposite, American voters are angry. They are also well-educated and the voting public is ready for a change.

WHAT RICHARD HOFSTADTER DIDN'T ENVISION

One summer Richard Hofstadter and Southern historian C. Vann Woodward rented a vacation home. Hofstadter quietly got out of bed early in the morning, took his notes cards to the kitchen and he prepared to write a chapter on the paranoid style in American politics. He was surprised to see C. Vann Woodward working at the table. They refilled their coffee cups and talked. The topic was about extremists in American politics. Hofstadter was off to England to deliver a speech at Oxford. It was published in **Harper's** magazine, and the following year in the seminal book **The Paranoid Style In American Politics**, he defined the right wing nut house. What Hofstadter never envisioned was the power of Jerome Corsi or TV personalities like Glenn Beck. Yet, Hofstadter did describe traits common to both critics.

Hofstadter pointed out that the paranoid searched for evil doers (Barack Obama) and flaws in the system (health care, foreign policy) and rather than working within the political system to change it, they advocate a complete overhaul.

The animosity and passions of hate surprisingly spur a large segment of the voting public. As Hofstadter suggests, the right wing America has been around almost two centuries. What Hofstadter never envisioned is that the right wing would develop into a multi-million dollar book, radio and television industry.

When the Republican Party produced a minute long web-video, they used President Obama's comment: "We haven't made enough progress on the economy," as well as "We've lost our ambition, our imagination," the President continued. "We've gotten a little soft." This angered Americans.

The authors in this section are virulent Obama critics. They have a hatred for the president and the Democratic Party. This not only clouds their analysis but the level of writing. Jerome Corsi and Glenn Beck not only despise Barack Obama, but they do everything in their power to criticize and embarrass the president. The problem is that this attitude influences their objectivity and credibility. It makes for a nasty combination of misplaced facts, highly judgmental writing, without factual verification, as well as plain and simple vindictive conclusions. They are like those kids in high school that want to get even with the star football player or the head cheerleader. In other words, they are small-minded individuals. Unfortunately they have a mainstream audience.

Chapter 4
THE PROFESSOR AS CRITIC THE CORSI BOOK ON THE CULT OF PERSONALITY

THE GOAL IS TO DEFEAT OBAMA. I DON'T WANT OBAMA TO BE IN OFFICE." JEROME CORSI

Jerome Corsi is the classic writer employing the paranoid style in American politics. His convoluted conclusions are based on what he claims to be irrefutable factuality. To this end, Corsi's book on President Obama and the cult of personality is loaded with footnotes. The majority of the footnotes have little resemblance to his arguments. This is intellectual posturing. He concludes that radicals, Communists, Socialists and terrorists support and influence President Barack Obama. Corsi's **The Obama Nation: Leftist Politics And The Cult of Personality**, released in 2008, inaugurated the proliferation of anti-Obama books.

He is also a popular writer and a persistent blogger. He believes that a conspiracy exists to create a plan for a North American government. This notion is one that argues that Mexico, Canada and the United States will organize a European Union type organization to dominate the North American economy. Corsi argues that this would require an element of conspiracy. He disguises his criticism in the words of a serious academic. The critics, however, site many inaccuracies in his books.

He is the worst type of academic writer. He introduces his concept that President Obama does not have a proper birth certificate by announcing that: "This is a story President Obama and his team do not want told. They would prefer that American voters forget about the attack they launched against McCain...." In convoluted logic and sparkling prose, Corsi claims that the Democrats questioned John McCain's eligibility to be president. McCain was born in the Panama Canal Zone. Corsi accuses the Democratic Party of raising the issue of his eligibility to run for President for political, not legal, reasons. This attack was designed to deflect criticism from Obama's birth certificate. This twisted logic and imprecise thinking is only part of the problem. Few people had heard of Jerome Corsi, and he has a circuitous background. His first book on Obama dealt with the years prior to Obama's presidency. This ill-conceived tome employed pop psychology and right wing hatred.

WHO IS JEROME CORSI?

Jerome Corsi is an American intellectual with five well-regarded books. He hit the spotlight in 2004 co-authoring, **Unfit For Command: Swift Boat Veterans Speak Out Against John Kerry**, which challenged the Democratic presidential nominee, John Kerry, on his Vietnam record. From that point on, Corsi was a favorite with conspiracy theorists. His columns appear on conservative websites **WorldNet Daily** and **Human Events**. He is a Roman Catholic and a favorite with the Tea Party.

His professor credentials are strange ones. He received a PhD in political science from Harvard University in 1972. He was never able to secure an academic appointment. This seems strange. A Harvard doctorate is a lifetime credential to a cushy professor position. By 1981, Corsi was in banking, and, more than a decade later, he launched a mutual fund to invest in the formerly Communist Poland. After the fall of Russian control, Corsi reasoned that there was money to be made in Poland, but he lost 1.2 million dollars. The twenty some Minnesota investors who provided the money sued. When two of those who sued won a judgment, they were unable to collect. All of Corsi's money was in his second wife's name. In his defense, the FBI found no criminal activity. It was simply a poor business investment. This is not against the law.

In January 2005, the **Boston Herald** quoted Corsi as planning to challenge Democratic Senator John Kerry for his U. S. Senate seat in Massachusetts. Corsi stated that he would run as a Republican or perhaps an independent. The Constitution Party nominated him for the U. S. Senate, but he dropped out. His rage and rancor in not being able to face Kerry in the general election was reflected in his writing. He hated Kerry, and Corsi vowed to expose his weaknesses.

THE DANGERS TO CORSI'S ARGUMENTS

The danger is that Corsi is a brilliant writer, a diligent researcher, but his conclusions are often at variance with the facts. He has no sense of fairness or independent judgment. The criticism of Democratic politicians and the inflated conspiracy theories are the twin engines driving Corsi's work.

In 2008, the **London Guardian** labeled Corsi anti-Semitic, anti-Muslim, anti-Catholic and homophobic. The London newspaper described Corsi as a writer attempting to scare white America into submission. In 2005, Corsi's **Atomic Iran: How The Terrorist Regime Bought the Bomb And American Politicians** advanced the thesis that Democratic politicians influenced by Iranian money helped develop the path to nuclear weapons in Tehran. He also co-authored, **Black Gold Stranglehold: The Myth of Scarcity And the Politics of Oil**, with Craig R. Smith. This book argues that the U. S. is being blackmailed by oil wealthy nations. These books cemented his credentials with the right wing.

Corsi is equally critical of Republicans and Democrats. He charges that President George W. Bush was trying to create a North American Union. This is a group that promoted economic and social integration between Mexico, Canada and the United States. It is led by business, political and academic minds supported by the Council on Foreign Relations and funded by the Independent Task Force On the Future of North American along with help from the Mexican and Canadian governments. The idea of a common North American government in Corsi's mind is a conspiracy about to become fact.

He also promoted the preposterous charge, posted on **WorldNet Daily**, that Senator John McCain had strong support from criminal drug networks and al-Qaeda. Despite these inane and highly suspicious arguments, Corsi's books have found a receptive audience. He has criticized the Republican Party because the "Rockefeller Wing" once controlled it. This is, of course, the liberal, money oriented faction in the Republican Party. What does Corsi dislike about the Rockefeller Wing? They are simply too liberal. In 2008, he endorsed his good friend, Chuck Baldwin, the candidate of the Constitution Party for president. Baldwin is a politician who is determined to challenge the September 11, 2001 inquiries. He is often the voice of the 9/11 Truth Movement. Not surprisingly, Baldwin is a co-writer or contributor to Corsi's books.

An even stranger allegation suggests that Obama had "extensive connections to Islam." Rather than laughing at this premise, book sales rocketed due to Corsi's mean spirited diatribe.

Corsi's book is subtitled: "Leftist Politics And The Cult of Personality," and it is a road map for his didactic attack. The right wing media, notably Sean Hannity, Glenn Beck and Bill O'Reilly, bronzed Corsi's elegant prose and Three Stooges conclusions.

There is a great deal that is suspect in Corsi's book. He experienced bulk sales to Christian bookshops and large Christian wholesalers. This smells of right wing political money shipping books for a position on the **New York Times** best-seller list.

The main problem with the Corsi book is the publisher Simon and Schuster. They placed Mary Matalan in charge of the project. As a former Republican strategist and long time right wing defender, Matalan smelled dollar signs. She spent months refining the writing and his arguments.

One wonders what Matalan's husband, liberal Democratic strategist, James Carville, thought when she discussed Professor Corsi at the dinner table. I would have loved to be at that dinner table. Then again the book was hidden under an inauspicious imprint. You have to look long and hard to find the Simon and Schuster imprint.

The books imprint under Threshold Publications saw Simon and Schuster distancing itself from the product. They feared a backlash. There wasn't a need for this tactic as the right celebrated Corsi's dubious conclusions and self-righteous explanations.

Matalan also had Karl Rove's memoirs to finish. The level of bakery goods and Bibles piled up in her office, as she guided Corsi's book to the marketplace, was astonishing. She is literally a one-person publishing machine getting the message of the radical right to the American public.

The outline of Corsi's book is a strange one. In part one, which Corsi labels "Roots," he does his best to destroy the memory and the image of Obama's father. He is also tangentially hostile to the President's mother, Stanley Ann Dunham, and her hapless second husband Lolo. He is kind to the grandparents, the Dunham's, who raised Obama in Hawaii. They sent him to private school. It was in a private school that young Barack Obama experienced his earliest lessons in class differences. This is surprising as the Dunham's were white, well educated, conservative, moneyed and well intentioned. Barack Obama experienced the degradation of color. To his credit, he ignored it, but he never forgot neither the slights nor the judgments. He vowed to educate himself in a manner to overcome these negative attitudes.

This part of the book stretches the analysis by suggesting some dubious conclusions. Corsi writes that Hawaii is the most ethnic or integrated place in live for Americans. But he doesn't understand Hawaiian history. Corsi writes: "Hawaii in 1971 was in many ways the most racially diverse state in the nation." (p. 71) He fails to mention the power of the sugar plantations, white politicians and New England patricians controlled the state's history. He finds Obama's early rage a puzzle, when in fact, it was little more than an honest reaction to white repression. It wasn't until the 1980s that ethnic politics took hold in Hawaii.

In a chapter, "Black Rage, Drugs, And A Communist Mentor," Corsi attempts to tie Obama to the ideas of Frantz Fanon. He also points out that Obama read James Baldwin, Ralph Ellison and W. E. B. DuBois. Rather than praising the future President for his curiosity and wide spread literary-political interests, Corsi takes this as a badge of radicalism. Millions of college students in the 1970s shared the same books.

The notion that Fanon influenced Obama is not factually based. In Corsi's own words, he is stretching the truth. He writes: "The connection with Fanon may still seem slim, until we get to chapter 5, 'The Facts of Blackness." Corsi alleges that Obama accepted Fanon's notion of "denegrification." This is singularly the most absurd part of the book, as he quotes Obama as recalling an African American who harmed himself with chemicals to alter his skin. What is the evidence for this startling conclusion? Corsi's footnotes cites Fanon's book, **Black Skin, White Mask**, published in 1967 and Barack Obama's **Dreams From My Father**. The connection is not only dubious but also downright dishonest. This is not the end of his disastrous scholarship. Corsi cites a well respected book Alistair Horne's **A Savage War Of Peace: Algeria, 1954 To 1962**, published in 1977, to tie Obama to Fanon's radical thought. There is no tie.

The worse part of this book is the notion that President Obama "struggles to find his own racial identity." (p. 83) This is of course utter nonsense but it sounds good. When Corsi spends two pages (pp. 90-91) on the influence of Malcolm X, he is stretching the truth. Most students in high school or college read **The Autobiography of Malcolm X**. It is part and parcel of the education process among the more liberal and progressive schools. This doesn't turn someone into a Communist or unrequited radical. In fact, it more likely allows for understanding. Even more ridiculous is Corsi's assertion that one paragraph in the Malcolm X autobiography stuck in Obama's mind. The passage is: "If I could drain away his blood that pollutes my complexion, I'd do it! Because I hate every drop of the rapist's blood that's in me." This makes for exciting reading but as scholarship it is a joke. President Obama has never stated that he is angry over the white blood flowing through his veins. To suggest this is insulting. It gets worse. Corsi goes on to conclude that Obama doesn't want to be white but Corsi writes: "Obama wants to will all the white blood out of himself so he can become pure black." (p. 91) His proof for this conclusion is Obama's book **Dreams From My Father**. He should read the book. If he did, he would alter his conclusions. But Corsi never lets the truth get in the way of a good story.

CORSI'S THE MAKING OF A RADICAL POLITICIAN

In part two, Corsi entitles it: "The Making of A Radical Politician." Much of this section centers on a Chicago political manipulator Tony Rezko and Pastor Jeremiah Wright. Both are less than savory characters, and they share a penchant for grandiose braggadocio while hogging the media spotlight. Whether or not they were an important influence on President Obama is debatable.

Tony Rezko, a Chicago based real estate tycoon, owns a great deal of low-income property. He is a successful businessman. He owns a number of restaurants, and he is a well-known political fundraiser. He is also a strong Obama supporter who began contributing money in 1996 to Obama's political efforts. He continues to the present day to support President Obama. There is no evidence of wrongdoing between Rezko and Obama, but those in the right wing nut house continue to charge collusion. There have been some embarrassing incidents in Rezko's life, and he is the target of those in the right wing nut house for some of his business dealings, as well as his support for President Obama. The charges of public corruption against Rezko are factually based. This did happen. However, it had nothing to do with Barack Obama. They were acquaintances and not friends.

What Corsi does is to suggest that when a federal grand jury convicted Rezko of sixteen of twenty-four counts of political influence peddling in 2008, that this was related to Obama's political career. When Rezko was indicted on federal charges in October 2006, it was for using political connections to Illinois state boards to demand kickbacks from businesses that hoped to secure state contracts. What Corsi fails to mention is that Rezko pleaded not guilty. Eventually, he was found guilty on sixteen of twenty-four indictments. On November 23, 2011, Rezko was sentenced to ten and a half years in prison. By linking Rezko's legal problems with Obama's political career, Corsi has unfairly manipulated the facts. What Corsi suggests is that Obama's relationship with Rezko was "politics as usual." (p. 153).

Here is where Corsi is intellectually flawed. He writes: "The story is so complicated that tracking the key players virtually requires a flow chart so complex that most prosecutors would balk at explaining the connections to a jury." (pp. 153-54) This is a convenient way of allowing Corsi to state his opinions, but he never offers proofs as everything is "so complicated."

Now comes the innuendo. Corsi points out that Antoin "Tony" Rezko sounds like an Italian name, but he is Syrian. The implication is clear. Warning! He may be a terrorist. Things get more absurd when Corsi includes a section: "Rezko Recruits Obama At Harvard." (pp. 156-157) Corsi alleges that Rezko went to Harvard and attempted to hire Obama to work for his recently opened real estate firm. Wherever and whenever the Obama-Rezko meeting took place is disputed. The clear fact is that the future president did not go to work for Rezko. The real estate developer was so taken with Obama's vision, he became a staunch political supporter.

As a well-known Chicago real estate developer, Rezko helped the Obama's purchase their dream home. The doctor who owned the house wanted to sell the home and a vacant lot next door to the same person. To make sure that the Obama's could purchase the house, Tony Rezko's wife bought the vacant lot and the Obama's negotiated the purchase of their home for $1.65 million. As Corsi points out, this was $300,000 less than the asking price. It is common in real estate transactions to make an offer. The doctor accepted the offer. The **Wall Street Journal's**, John Fund, wrote a series of articles on the Obama-Rezko connection, and he editorialized in reference to the two real estate deals: "both actions would be clear violations of Senate ethics rules barring the granting or asking of favors." That conclusion is debatable.

There is no evidence that Barack Obama broke the law. There is also no evidence of ethics violations. If there is a misdeed, it is that Barack Obama supported a friend in time of need. Obama said it best to David Jackson of the **Chicago Sun Times**: "I had known him for a long time and he had acted in an above-board manner with me and I considered him a friend."

The housing scandal proved little or nothing. As Obama stated: "I am not perfect." In his manic writing, Corsi found a tenuous Rezko connection with Saddam Hussein. This is singularly the most preposterous point in the book. But give Corsi credit, he makes the Rezko connection with Saddam Hussein brilliantly. What Corsi does is to investigate Rezko's tangled finances and he concludes that a cousin of Saddam Hussein, Nadhmi Shakir Auchi, helped Rezko secure financing. Then in March 2008 Rezko held a dinner at Chicago's Four Seasons for Hussein's cousin, Nadhmi Shakir Auchi, and Barack Obama was asked to drop by and say hello. The future president helped his friend out with a quick handshake, and a minute later he was gone to another engagement. It is from this thirty-second introduction that Corsi concludes that Barack Obama and Saddam Hussein were co-conspirators

There is one other problem with the story. Auchi disavows any connection to Saddam Hussein. There is also no love lost between Auchi and Rezko. They had a tumultuous business fallout. Rezko also asked Auchi to contribute money to Obama's future political campaigns.

Right wing blogs continue to argue that an Obama-Rezko-Auchi partnership existed to elect Obama. Andrew Walden alleges that a "secret $3.5 million loan from an Auchi company to key early-money Barack Obama fundraiser Antoin Rezko was exposed..." This is a sensational charge that is factually unsupported.

The chapter on the Reverend Jeremiah Wright focuses upon the 'black liberation" theology that Wright preaches. It became a controversial part of the 2008 campaign. What is black liberation theology? It is an intellectual notion from the Rev. James Cone. It arose from the 1960s civil rights conflicts, and it is a theology that views God as concerned with the poor and weak. In the hands of Rev. Wright it became a concept demeaning to everyone. Wright charged in 2003, that God did not bless America because the nation killed innocent people. Cone's message was quite different from Wright's interpretation. Cone believes that African Americans need to embrace their black roots and Christian values at the same time. Wright erroneously interpreted "black liberation" theology. It is a half-baked and intellectually indefensible notion. What the author alleges is that President Obama needs to "renounce black liberation theology itself." (p. 177) This is an interesting notion as Obama has neither accepted nor embraced this doctrine. The notion that Wright and Obama have the same "black liberation" view is nonsense. But put in an academic manner with footnotes, it sounds plausible.

When Obama stated that he read Martin Luther King and Malcolm X, he found some interesting material. Corsi takes this statement as the battle cry of a radical. A more acceptable conclusion is that like every other bright college student, Obama read about and reacted to the lives of these extraordinary men. The academic trick that Corsi uses to fool his readers is to quote books like Frantz Fanon's **The Wretched of the Earth**. This book espoused a revolutionary socialist dogma that has nothing to do with Barack Obama's political thought.

Perhaps the most egregious problem with the chapter on Reverend Wright is the section: "Obama Decides To Become A Christian." (pp.184-186) When Obama suggested in his memoir **The Audacity of Hope** that he "was not raised in a religious household," (p. 202) he did not mean that he wasn't a Christian.

It is Corsi's simplistic view that Obama joined Wright's church because he saw a "Free Africa" sign in the church window. The truth is that Barack Obama was a rising political figure and joining a well-established African American church was to his political advantage. The president has always been, and will always be, a political animal. Hence, the decision to become a member of Wright's church. The sin for Barack Obama was not to investigate Wright's political, social and media megalomania.

By the time that Obama left the Trinity Church, Reverend Wright was famous. He used his friendship with President Obama to promote his own agenda. The reverend charged that the U. S. created the AIDS virus to kill African Americans. He allowed another pastor, a Catholic, to mock Hillary Clinton and Wright was unrepentant in his arrogance. The sin that Obama committed was remaining loyal to a church, a neighborhood and a concept of Christian compassion that Reverend Wright forgot in his lust for power, prestige and wealth. The reverend is mean spirited, and he is now a joke.

BARACK OBAMA EXPLAINS HIS RELATIONSHIP WITH REV. WRIGHT

"The pastor of my church, Rev. Jeremiah Wright, who recently preached his last sermon and is in the process of retiring, has touched off a firestorm over the last few days. He's drawn attention as the result of some inflammatory and appalling remarks he made about our country, our politics, and my political opponents. Let me say at the outset that I vehemently disagree and strongly condemn the statements that have been the subject of this controversy. I categorically denounce any statement that disparages our great country or serves to divide us from our allies. I also believe that words that degrade individuals have no place in our public dialogue, whether it's on the campaign stump or in the pulpit. In sum, I reject outright the statements by Rev. Wright that are at issue.

Because these particular statements by Rev. Wright are so contrary to my own life and beliefs, a number of people have legitimately raised questions about the nature of my relationship with Rev, Wright and my membership in the church. Let me therefore provide some context. As I have written about in my books, I first joined Trinity United Church of Christ nearly twenty years ago. I knew Rev. Wright as someone who served this nation with honor as a United States Marine, as a respected biblical scholar, and as someone who taught or lectured at seminaries across the country, from Union Theological Seminary to the University of Chicago. He also led a diverse congregation that was and still is a pillar of the South Side and the entire city of Chicago. It's a congregation that does not merely preach social justice but acts it out each day, through ministries ranging from housing the homeless to reaching out to those with HIV/AIDS."

THE REV. WRIGHT AND THE JEWS

Reverend Wright ended the controversy with Barack Obama when he charged: "Them Jews aren't going to let him talk to me." This was the pastor's reaction to Obama leaving the Trinity United Church of Christ in Chicago. There was no way to defend Wright's actions and rhetoric. Once he began appearing on national television, Wright went over the top. He did more to discredit himself and his church than he did to harm Obama's presidential bid and eventually his presidency.

In an example of highly offensive rhetoric, Reverend Wright accused Obama of "not wanting to offend the Jews." He continued his tirade, Wright charged: "Ethnic cleansing is going on in Gaza. Ethnic cleansing of the Zionist is a sin and a crime against humanity, and they don't want Barack talking like that because that's anti-Israel." Is there is need to comment on this statement?

The Reverend Wright tried to back off from his anti-Semitic references. He put on a smart brown shirt and a yellow-brown tie and said that he "misspoke." He said he didn't mean to use the term "Jews," what he meant was "Zionists." The damage had been done. The Reverend Wright had his day on national television. He humiliated himself, cast aspersions on the president and ruined his church. Not a bad effort for fifteen minutes of fame.

The Anti Defamation League released a statement condemning Wright's remarks as "inflammatory and false." Reform Jewish leaders issued a press release placing the controversy in its proper perspective.

REFORM JEWISH LEADERS CONDEMN REVEREND WRIGHT
"Reverend Wright's recent press comments that were derogatory toward Jews, contending that members of the Jewish community dictate President Obama actions, are unacceptable and worthy of repudiation. Yesterday's events at the U.S. Holocaust Memorial Museum demonstrate that hateful speech can spiral into tragedy and thus cannot go unanswered. Words have consequences, and Reverend Wright has contributed to a dangerous culture of anti-Semitism. Legitimate disagreements about policy differences can never be allowed to spill into ugly religious or ethnic characterizations. As the Reverend John H. Thomas, General Minister and President of the United Church of Christ, wisely noted in his response to Reverend Wright's comments, we must remember the importance of respectful disagreement and maintain vigilance against that which diminishes or caricatures others. Reverend Wright would justly not tolerate racist statements about his community and his propagation of anti-Semitism should be condemned from all quarters.

Source: Religion Action Center For Reform Judaism

From the vantage point of 2012, conservative right wing critics argue that the 78% Jewish vote that President Obama received in the 2008 election is slipping. This is of course pure nonsense. The Jewish vote is continually Democratic. This is primarily due to the malevolent attitudes and dirty politics of the radical right. For conservatives, the only thing worse than an African American President, one Jewish leader argued, is the presence of pro-Israeli politicians in the White House. The truth is that Obama's strong support for Israel has increased his vote.

IS THE CANDIDATE THE MESSAGE?
In part three, Corsi employs the subtitle: "The Candidate Is the Message." This is a convenient way of stating that there is little, if any, substance to Barack Obama. Whether you are a supporter or critic of the president, the universal conclusion is that he is a brilliant man. One who can talk on any subject or deliver a polished speech. He is also an in-depth thinker. So what is it that bothers Corsi? The answer is a simple one. How could a black man get so far? Corsi seldom uses the term Af-

rican American. He prefers Black or Negro. There is a dangerous path for a person with this mind set. Yet, there is absolutely no evidence that Corsi is a racist. To the contrary, he appears racially enlightened, despite his research, writing and conclusions.

The question of race analysis is what bothers most readers. In campaigning for the presidency, Obama did his best to appear to be an average, middle-class American. He isn't. But after all this is politics. So Corsi criticizes him on a campaign junket for not being able to bowl. What Corsi may not realize is that he has fallen into the upper class white thought mode. His subconscious states that Obama should be a football or basketball player. But it gets worse. Corsi uses the outdated thoughts of Marshall McLuhan, as he describes Obama's campaign as a visual one with little substance to the message. The medium is not the message. It is Barack Obama's substance as a politician that Corsi questions.

Corsi's "The Cult of Personality" predicted that chief strategist David Axelrod will manipulate the election "by promoting the personality of the candidate, not issues." (p. 215) This suggests a low opinion of the American voter. The reviewers were critical of Corsi's research as well as his lack of accuracy, his misuse of facts, the irregular footnotes, the manipulation of the data, the use of suspicious innuendo and the tendency to make outrageous statements. There were those reviewers who not only challenged his credentials, but they argued that Corsi was a public relations flax for the right wing. He continually displayed insensitivity to race. The facts were often at variance. Corsi has Obama attending a fiery and radical sermon by the Reverend Jeremiah Wright in Chicago, when in fact, he was delivering a speech in Florida. He also misstated Obama's drug use. The term "extensive connections to Islam" is another Corsi means of implanting radical ideas. When Barack Obama lived in Indonesia, he was not a practicing Muslim. This fact has been substantiated by more than a hundred interviews with the president's friends.

The main problem is the mean spirited criticism and the lack of balance. If the Hawaiian newspapers were manipulated, as the critics of the birth certificate controversy suggest, this would be one of the strangest events in history. On the cult of personality, there have been many presidents with this trait.

WHAT THE CRITICS SAY ABOUT THE CORSI BOOK

"SEVERAL OF THE BOOK'S ACCUSATIONS, IN FACT, ARE UNSUBSTANTIATED OR INACCURATE." JULIE BOSMAN, THE NEW YORK TIMES, AUGUST 12, 2008

CONSERVATIVES SHOULD NOT HITCH THEIR HOPES TO CORSI'S BOOK BECAUSE IT SEEMS TO BE RIDDLED WITH FACTUAL ERRORS," PETER WEHNER, COMMENTARY, AUGUST 15, 2008

'INNUENDO FILLED, MISTAKE RIDDLED BIOGRAPHY," ANNE E. KORNBLUT, AUGUST 15, 2008

"CORSI'S BOOK LEFT A TRAIL OF WILD THEORIES, VITRIOL AND DOGMA THAT HAVE CALLED INTO QUESTION HIS CREDIBILITY." KENNETH P. VOGEL, THE POLITICO, AUGUST 15, 2008

"THE BOOK CONTAINS POTENTIALLY OFFENSIVE PASSAGES ABOUT BARACK OBAMA'S PERSONAL AND FAMILY LIFE," ELI SASLOW, THE WAHSINGTON POST, AUGUST 15, 2008

"AN ABOMINATION," THE CHICAGO SUN TIMES, AUGUST 15, 2008

The Corsi book did little to sully President Obama's reputation or to defeat his political agenda. In fact, just the opposite took place, as he was defined as a visionary and a leader.

Chapter 5
WHY YALE, JOE LIEBERMAN AND THE COLLEGE PROFESSORS LED GLENN BECK TO THOMAS PAINE

> "WHEN HE'S 18 YEARS OLD, AS HE'S GETTING READY TO... SEEK OUT THE MARXIST PROFESSORS, HE CHANGES HIS NAME FROM BARRY...TO BARACK. NOW WHAT DOES THAT TELL YOU? YOU KNOW IMMIGRANTS USED TO CHANGE THEIR NAME TO FIT IN...." GLENN BECK ON PRESIDENT BARACK OBAMA, FEBRUARY 4, 2010

Glenn Beck is a bilious, vile and insensitive television host. On the radio, he is even more overbearing. The good news is that you don't have to look at him. Despite his demeanor, or maybe because of it, he is one of the more popular talk show gurus. He is also a giant on XM Satellite radio. He is number three behind Rush Limbaugh and Sean Hannity in ratings. For a guy who could barely read and write through high school, this is a marvelous reincarnation. He has hit a nerve in the right wing nut house. That nerve makes him millions of dollars and sells his books and half-baked political theories.

Time magazine put Beck on its cover with the title "Mad Man." But there is a serious side to his writing. He has found that using history is the key to his popularity. He employs the technique of a blackboard and a pointer to highlight his political contentions. He masquerades as a professor.

The salary that Glenn Beck commands in the right wing nut house is an astronomical one. In 2009, sources close to Fox TV News reported an income of twenty-five million dollars. In 2010, his earnings rose to thirty-two million. There is no doubt that the misapplication of history, sensational posturing about the president, and his hefty books make for a millionaire lifestyle. The tragedy is that the use of history in the right wing nut house is in sending America into an era of entrenched conservatism.

It is in Beck's early writings that the focus of his later, more sophisticated, criticism is revealed. Cleon Skousen's books, **The 5000 Year Leap** and **The Naked Communists** were major influences upon Beck's thinking and writing. Skousen, a Mormon, argues that the U. S. Constitution limits the federal government's oppressive powers. A sub-theme is that history is being taught incorrectly. Rather than rely on trained historians, Skousen's view is that the average person should interpret history. Like many in the right wing nut house, Skousen believes that the Christian faith is ignored in the classroom and on the written page. He argues that the conservative and high-minded individual is the best person to interpret history. To that end, Skousen concludes that welfare and civil rights reforms are unconstitutional. Edwin Brown Firmage, a professor of law at the University of Utah, complained that Skousen is "a right wing buzzard." Glenn Beck used Skousen's ideas as the main source for his writing and political rants.

GLENN BECK'S EARLY WRITINGS

Glenn Beck was not an overnight sensation. At least not as a writer; it took Fox TV News to build his reputation before his books sold. When he charted on the **New York Times** bestseller list, it was due to conservatives. His 2003 book, **The Real America: Early Writings From The Heart And the Heartland**, had a strong impact. It was an egomaniacal book that featured pictures of Beck with such famous people as Matt Drudge and George H. W. Bush. There isn't much to recommend here.

The Real America is filled with clichés. Some examples of his clichés are: 1.) "In the Real America our current plastic politicians will be replaced by the more genuine…." (p. 5) 2.) "In the Leave It To Beaver years, the background noises were things like Goodness, Common Decency and Courtesy." (p. 8); 3.) "I've included jingoistic on my word calendar….My word calendar has only one word a month…I'm not smart like the **New York Times**." (p. 29). These comments suggest Beck's anti-intellectual attitudes.

Obama's Detractors

Richard Hofstadter's 1964 book **Anti-Intellectualism In American Life** argues that the strong conservative foundation of American society featured intellectual writers like Leo Strauss, Irving Kristol and William F. Buckley. They had marvelous writing skills, used factual material well and spun a believable story about the dangers of liberalism. This is no longer the case as those in the right wing nut house are like Glenn Beck, who shouts out obscenities. There is also Rush Limbaugh who employs facts that allegedly have little to do with reality, and Sarah Palin whose comments indicate that she doesn't have even a minimal understanding of American history. It is a sad commentary on present day conservatism. The terminal condition of the right wing nut house was demonstrated when South Carolina Republican Senator Jim DeMint proposed that unmarried pregnant women be banned from teaching in the public schools. The Tea Party is a strong DeMint supporter, and he is a Glenn Beck clone.

The worst excess in the right wing nut house resulted from Allen West's comment that there were "about 78 to 81 House Democrats" who are members of the Communist Party. While addressing a town hall meeting in Jensen Beach, Florida, Representative West uttered this fact. He also claimed that the Congressional Progressive Caucus housed the Communist Democrats. This comment has no basis in fact and calls into question Representative West's qualifications. He sees conspiracies where none exist. West is not alone. Glenn Beck goes on using a blackboard to point out the decline of American values.

Beck's message is a clear one. He wails on about the decline in personal responsibility, the nasty nature of partisan politics, and he suggests Hitler and Jesus had one thing in common; that is the ability to mesmerize an audience. You do get a list of 1963 Communist goals; for what reason no one knows.

Why are Becks books so successful? The answer is a simple one. His history of America comes with apple pie, picket fences, blueberry cobbler, flags, neighbors who care and religious values. Nasty politicians and minorities are something we must bear, Beck informs us, and this is a message that appeals to a lot of frustrated Americans.

Beck might as well be writing: "There is a Negro in the White House! Help!" He doesn't say this but it is implicit in his writing. There are numerous examples of Beck's racial insensitivity. He called the civil rights movement "an abomination." He has labeled President Obama "a racist," and he defends slavery as necessary to American history.

He sees other dangers. One of them is Barbra Streisand. Beck writes of Streisand's singing and her politics: "Shut up you big-nosed, cross-eyed freak!" (p. 65) But Beck claims not to be anti-Semitic, he says that he does have some Jewish friends. At least one. He is simply an arrogant jerk who is using stereotypes and hatred to sell his books. He did learn something from reading about Adolph Hitler.

In chapter four, on partisan politics, he doesn't analyze the phenomena, Beck simply lists people and then writes hundreds of times "blah, blah, blah." (p. 87) The number of blah, blah words was in the thousands in this chapter. **The Real America** is a ranting piece of imperceptive journalism that is difficult to understand. But if you hate Barbra Streisand, it is the book for you.

There is a formula to Beck's writing. The federal government and the president are the bad guys. The Tea Party and the zealots, who want to cut government spending, are the good guys.

THE USE OF HISTORY IN THE RIGHT WING NUT HOUSE

Glenn Beck's bragging point is his use of history. He fashions himself a historian. Many of his fans embrace his knowledge. Beck has no professional historical training, and he even failed to finish a college course. His explanation is that after a few weeks at Yale, he had a better grasp on the subject than the professors. Maybe he is right! He has written a number of best selling historical treatises. What does this tell us? It is an indication of how history is used in the right wing nut house to promote a conservative viewpoint.

On Becks' television show, he frequently has David Barton as a guest. His guest looks like a history professor. He talks like a history professor. He dresses like a history professor. He is nerdy looking like a history professor. His lack of formal training shouldn't be a problem. That said, he should still get a chance to prove his meddle. Barton does possess a B.A. in religious education from Oral Roberts University. Some of Barton's opinions are: 1.) Homosexuals die decades earlier than heterosexuals. 2.) Suicide is higher among non-Christians. 3.) African Americans have a higher rate of disease than white people. The good news here is that Barton is not analyzing American Foreign Policy or for that matter the economy. He is also closely connected to Beck's publications.

David Barton, like Beck, believes in the unsung, the unknown or the obscure historical anecdote. He operates a website out of Texas, "Wall Builders," dedicated to what he labels the forgotten heroes in American history. One page highlights Frederick Douglass, a prominent

African American, and then the website goes on to suggest the legislators would promote Biblical instruction, and then the website spends an inordinate amount of time on African American history. The website means well but distorts African American history. No one has told Barton that Douglass is a major African American historical figure.

Beck's use of history has led to enormous best sellers on Thomas Paine and George Washington. This prompted the Reverend Jerry Falwell's Liberty University to confer an honorary doctorate upon Beck. This is not surprising, as Beck is the Fox TV News resident historian. Newt Gingrich is virtually tied with Beck for this honor. While earning a million dollars a month, Beck is one of the world's highest paid writers. His message is that Franklin D. Roosevelt, Woodrow Wilson, Theodore Roosevelt and anyone else who embraced Progressivism began the long road to taking away American freedoms. He views Franklin D. Roosevelt as a "closet racist." He argues that Teddy Roosevelt's New Nationalism and Woodrow Wilson's New Freedom were policies that brought an end to states' rights. These programs promoted federal aid to Americans who were not yet middle class. What Beck fails to recognize is that the dream of prosperity for all Americans came to fruition due to the Roosevelt and Wilson leadership. These programs curtailed exploitation of the worker, including women and children, provided for minimum wage, allocated restraint on working hours, modified horrific factory conditions, prevented food contamination, policed medical practices and began the road to the middle class. In modern hindsight, many people believe that unions, medical supervision by federal authorities, wage and hour restrictions and other devices guarantee the health and safety of citizens. These governmental devices were necessary due to predatory big business schemes that violated personal rights and endangered the growth and health of the newly emerging middle class.

It was President Theodore Roosevelt who stated the basic belief of the New Nationalism and executive power in general: "The New Nationalism regards the executive power as the steward of the public welfare." This pronouncement had an impact upon President Obama who took this dictum as his role.

The present day audience is an educated one. But they are not ready for simple answers to complex questions. Americans are well educated and intelligent, but they are frustrated with the economy, partisan politics and changes threatening the American dream. Many citizens believe that government imposes too many limits on private business, and that there is a constant threat to individual rights. There is a renewed concern for individual liberty, and this is often reflected in rebellion against laws that limit individual initiative. This is the sane conservative viewpoint. Religion is the driving force behind conservative politics and it challenges rational political decision making.

Gordon S. Wood, a Brown University Professor, writing in the **New York Review of Books**, stated: "We can't solve our current disputes over religion by looking back to the actual historical circumstances of the Founding; those circumstances are too complex, too confusing, and too biased toward Protestant Christianity to be used in courts today...." Yet, this is exactly what Beck does in his history books. He is a demagogue who continually misuses the historical process.

Anthony Grafton, the President of the American Historical Association, wrote: "We need to mobilize the formal collective intellect of our discipline…to defend and explain our enterprises." While Grafton has a point, it is not historians who are under attack but history itself. The misuse of history for nationalistic purposes is a dangerous phenomenon. It is usually in the hands of people like Adolph Hitler that history is the excuse for atrocities. But lately the Glenn Beck's of the world have entered the marketplace. It is a frightening prospect to believe that readers will take Beck's half-baked theories seriously.

He is also a barometer for anti-Semitic thought. He has talked negatively at length about the Holocaust and Nazis. This in itself is not surprising. This is a topic that is important. What Beck fails to understand is that his insensitive opinions cause pain and emotional scars. When Beck accused a fourteen-year-old Jewish boy, hiding with a Christian family in Hungary, of sending them to death camps, he went beyond the bounds of good taste. He has also called media executives Nazis. Ignorance and insensitive are the keys to Beck's opinions.

BECK'S SUCCESSES ARE REAL: HOW HIS EARLY BACKGROUND INFLUENCED HIS CAREER

As a success story, there are few people who have achieved more than Glenn Beck. His parents died at an early age. Beck's mother was divorced, then she drowned while boating with a male friend. His stepbrother also committed suicide. Beck and his elder sister went to live with their father in Bellingham, Washington. This is a small town in northern Washington with the state's best liberal arts college, Western

Washington University. The town is a calm one with less than one hundred thousand people when Beck went to school.

When Beck looked up at WWU or walked up the hill to the campus, he felt alienated. He wasn't smart enough for college. This fact frustrated him and he disparaged college students when he snuck into Cap Hanson's for a beer with the college crowd. He had a sense of his inferiority and he would take it out on the educated people.

He graduated from Sehome High School in 1982, and he began his radio career. He had a well-publicized battle with drugs and alcohol. He was diagnosed with Attention Deficit Hyperactivity Disorder. His main asset was a larger than life personality, and this helped Beck overcome some early career obstacles.

Beck took a job at Washington D.C.'s WPGC in February 1983, and this began his rise to prominence in talk radio. For the next decade, he was erratic and at times suicidal. His pain was dulled by alcohol and marijuana. When his wife, Claire, divorced him in 1994, he began attending Alcoholics Anonymous. But the failure of his marriage haunted him.

After he hit rock bottom in 1994, Beck imagined that he would commit suicide by shooting himself. It was while listening to Kurt Cobain's "It Smells Like Teen Spirit" that Beck started attending A. A. meetings. When he stopped drinking in November 1994, he began a spiritual quest. He moved to New England. It was amidst the Ivy League's intellectual atmosphere that Beck reconsidered his minimal education. He was bright but not well read.

While working in radio in the New Haven area at WELI, the same station that broadcast Yale football games, Beck took a theology class at Yale University. Senator Joe Lieberman recommended him for admission to Yale into a program for non-traditional students. The "Early Christology" course sparked his intellectual curiosity. He soon dropped out of this academic endeavor. He had an agenda. It was to begin a self-educating process necessary to a life of political criticism.

Here is the crux of Beck's intellectual fury. While attending Yale for a very brief time, he was incensed over the professor's role. He found the college professors arrogant, short tempered, biased and ill thought out in their political conclusions. So he began a furtive reading program aimed at self-education.

Beck's program of self-education took a strange direction. He called his reading list: "The Library Of A Serial Killer." He read books on law by Alan Dershowitz, the writings of Pope Paul II, the writings, the speechmaking and the biographies of Adolph Hitler, the works of evangelist Billy Graham, the theories of scientist Carl Sagan and the wandering intellect of philosopher Friedrich Nietzsche. It was from this strange combination of books that Beck's formidable intellect emerged.

When Beck blogged about the books he read, there were some interesting insights into his intellectual development. Slavery was one of his earliest interests. Rather than reading Kenneth Stampp's **The Peculiar Institution** or another serious book, he derived his thoughts on the 3/5ths person rule in the U. S. Constitution by reading Judge Andrew Napolitano's comments. Not surprisingly Napolitano hosts Fox TV News shows. The Judge is neither a brilliant journalist nor a respectable historian. His judicial career suffered from mediocrity. He also supported the peculiar institution. Like Beck, he believed that slavery was essential to American history.

There are a number of key books that continue to shape other parts of Beck's persona. Peter Schweizer's **Throw Them All Out: How Politicians And Their Friends Get Rich Off Insider Stock Tips, Land Deals, And Cronyism That Would Send The Rest of Us To Prison**, published in 2011, feeds the various conspiratorial fears of the right wing nut house. Schweizer is a fellow at Stanford's Hoover Institution, and his focus is on the Cold War and the struggle against Communism. He was hired as an adviser on foreign policy to Sarah Palin. He is a brilliant writer and thinker, and he titillated Beck's curiosity over the decline of traditional American values and rights.

As Beck grew increasingly conservative, he adopted the Mormon faith, and he emerged as a crusader against big government. After he met his second wife, Tania, he described himself as a conservative with libertarian leanings. At this stage of his career, he supported the right to life, freedom of religion, limited government, and he proclaimed that the family was societies cornerstone. He is also an opponent of gun control. Beck is a frequent critic of government debt.

It is his reading of history that causes him to scream out against government. He spent some time devouring books on the Progressive Era. This is a period in American history from 1900 to 1917, that led to the income tax, social programs, a strong foreign policy, recognition of immigrant rights, the initiative, referendum and recall, the Pure Food And Drug Act, increasing federal laws regulating the state economy and some restrictions, through federal law, were placed on states rights.

Beck's misunderstanding of the Progressive Era framed his politics. He didn't realize that Theodore Roosevelt's New Nationalism protected the common man or that economic progress was the forte of Woodrow Wilson's New Freedom. Beck argued that big government and restrictions on business were the hallmark of Progressivism; when it fact the opposite is true. Government simply reigned in the tentacles of big business. Big Business no longer dominated the common man. Beck failed to recognize this simple fact.

He voiced his opposition to Progressivism in a 2010 keynote speech to the Conservative Political Action Conference, (CPAC). He turned to his audience and wrote "progressivism" on a blackboard. Then he labeled it a disease or cancer that was eating away at our Constitution. This established Beck as a constitutional authority with a great many people.

One of the ironies of Beck's criticism is that President Obama in 2011 echoed a portion of President Theodore Roosevelt's New Nationalism. In a speech during a cold December night in Kansas, Obama defended government aid to help the middle class retain its status. Much like Teddy Roosevelt, President Obama asked for the nation to come together for the greater good.

The tragedy is that Beck has little in-depth understanding of historical forces. Yet, he is natively bright. The problem is that his ideas are so peculiar that a large number in the Mormon faith, particularly its scholars, disavow Beck's quotes and theories. So why does he have multi-million dollar books? The answer is a simple one. He is on television. He is a key figure on Fox News, satellite radio and traditional media outlets. He can sell books. He makes his publisher a great deal of money.

In Beck's **Common Sense: The Case Against Out Of Control Government Inspired By Thomas Paine**, he charges that individual politicians attempt to restructure and redefine American politics. This is not a surprising conclusion. But Beck alleges these changes come without the will or consent of the people. They are there to "rebuild America into a country where individual liberties and personal property mean nothing, if they conflict with the plans and goals of the State."

Not all of Beck's ideas are irritating ones. In the introduction and chapter 1, he makes an intelligent case for changes in our political culture. He points out rightly that partisan politics is destroying the ability of elected politicians to govern. He quotes Thomas Paine's dictum that it is important to place principles over party affiliation, personal character over campaign promises, and it is common sense to make sure that the nation moves forward. This is a fine description of what needs to be done. Unfortunately, Beck's rhetoric and his egomaniacal identification with Thomas Paine leave a great deal to be desired.

Common Sense is Beck's attempt to make his bones as a political philosopher. He has difficulty making the grade. He demonstrates key prejudices against Ivy League educated politicians, the poor and liberals. He is concerned about elites, and he skewers environmentalists. He also attacks those supporting global warming, the tax structure, the public schools, and he views direct popular elections as an indication of liberal mob rule.

When Beck goes on the offensive, he is an attack dog. He has charged that there is a "Crime Inc." series of individuals conspiring to lead the clandestine conspiracy to take over America. Then they will transform the U. S. into a socialist nation. Normally, this type of political nonsense would be ignored. But if you have a show on Fox TV, a satellite radio program and a legion of followers your viewpoint is a respected one.

The politicians that Beck dislikes draw his ire. Beck charges that former Vice President Al Gore and President Barack Obama are working with Goldman Sachs, Fannie Mae, ACORN, Chicago Climate Exchange and the Center for American Progress to create a new America. The sheer nonsense of Beck's ideas prompted Princeton Historian Sean Wilentz to comment that not only does the radio talk show host employ "gross historical inaccuracies," but also he is doing nothing more than restating the discredited, right wing extremism of the John Birch Society.

The comments by Professor Wilentz get to the heart of the matter. That is the notion that not only does Beck distort history, but also he charges those who spend decades writing books with hiding that very history. In the **New Yorker**, Wilentz criticized Beck's "Restoring History" segment that had the host clenching a pipe in his mouth to make fun of professors. Then Beck went on the explain that Progressives "separate us from your Constitution and God." This is, of course, nonsense but it is a favorite theme in the right wing nut house. Beck accuses Progressives of conspiracies to alter American democracy. The truth is the reverse. American freedoms multiplied under the Progressives.

SEAN WILENTZ'S COMMENTS ON GLENN BECK

"Glenn Beck is trying to give viewers a version of American history that is supposedly hidden. Supposedly, all we historians—left, right and center—have been doing for the past 100 years is to keep true American history from you. And that true American history is what Glenn Beck is teaching. It's a version of history that is beyond skewed. But of course, that's what Beck expects us to say. He lives in a kind of *Alice in Wonderland* world, where if people who actually know the history say what he's teaching is junk, he says: 'That's because you're trying to hide the truth.'"

Glenn Beck's rise to prominence began in January 2006 when CNN's Headline News brought him in to host a nightly commentary show. This prime time program simply called Glenn Beck was an unconventional look at the news. Beck was an instant ratings success. Only Nancy Grace had higher numbers.

Fox News signed Beck in October 2008 and in January 2009, he began hosting the Glenn Beck Show. He was one of the earliest talk show hosts to bring Alaska Governor Sarah Palin on national television. By September 2009, Beck's ratings were higher than those at CNN, MSNBC and HLN for the same time slot. It was at this point that the inaccuracies caught up with him.

Howard Kurtz, writing in the **Washington Post**, called Beck's style one of "distorted or inflammatory rhetoric." Others have demonstrated that Beck not only plays loose with the facts, but his writing is turgid. He fails to look at both sides of an issue. The problem is that his books sell. He has convinced people that he knows the real history.

Government has an obligation to protect the people. This is one of the arguments of Thomas Paine's **Of Common Sense**, published in 1776. While Paine called government a "necessary evil," Beck has taken Paine's phrase and turned it into an aphorism for the Tea Party. Many of Paine's ideas are ignored in Beck's book. He doesn't discuss Paine's view of Christianity. Paine was also a radical liberal. This is not discussed.

Paine also believes in a form of social security. "To allow for each of these children ten shillings a year for the expense of schooling for six years each," Paine wrote. This convoluted prose demonstrates that Paine had concerns that are liberal and part of the welfare state. He also advocated a pension system for those over sixty. He understood the needs of the common person, Beck needs to read Paine who actually supports a welfare state. Paine also argued that the burden of taxation fell on the poor. "Government," Paine wrote, "even in the best state is but a necessary evil; in its worst state, an intolerable one." Beck should read Paine and understand him.

The critics point out the inconsistencies in Beck's thought. There is also the outright manipulation and distortion of Paine's ideas. Beck wants to abolish the Department of Education, where Paine spoke of "the expense of schooling." (**Common Sense**, p. 338) Unlike Beck, Paine argued that the burden of taxation fell upon the poor. (**Rights of Man**, p. 360) Beck doesn't understand Paine and when he talks of hunting down progressives, he fails to realize that Paine was a progressive thinker. Paine cared about economic and social differences, Beck wrote "Social justice and economic justice, they are code words." Sad!

Thomas Paine, in a 1796 tract **Agrarian Justice.** pointed out that "the common property of the human race…every man would have been born to property." He went on to argue that a national fund should be created to pay every person at age twenty one, "the sum of fifteen pounds sterling as a compensation in part, for the loss of his or her natural inheritance by the introduction of the system of lanced property." Had Beck paid attention to Paine's writing, he would have had a different view of this patriot.

GLENN BECK AND TAKING BACK LIBERTIES

The notion of taking back liberties is the message in a number of Beck's writings. There is no doubt that his books sell well due to the simple notion that the federal government is consistently taking away key rights. His supporters call Beck "a constitutional stalwart who supports traditional American values." This is a nice phrase but is it true? That is the question. A look at his books is necessary to answer the question.

The problem is that he links events to preposterous and indefensible ideas. The notion that health care reform came about due to 9/11 is one of Beck's more inane analogies. The use of "hidden history" is the ploy that Beck uses to convince his listeners, most of whom have never read a book on politics, that he has unique insights into history. Beck's ploy is to suggest that liberals and progressive have lied to the American people about the Founding Fathers. He describes the 3/5ths clause of the Constitution as anti-racist, but he missed the point. How could counting five African Americans as three voters not be racist? This clause was placed into the Constitution to guarantee Southern acceptance of the new nation. The three-fifths clause celebrated white supremacy, and Beck embraces it.

GLENN BECK'S BOOKS AND HIS COMMENTS: WRITING AND SPEAKING WITH CRAYONS

When Simon and Schuster, as a parody of Al Gore's 2006 documentary An Inconvenient Truth, published Beck's **An Inconvenient Truth: Real Solutions to The World's Biggest Problems**, it gave Beck a chance to make fun of the former Vice President, ecologists and liberals. The publicity was enormous and Beck's work rose to number one on the **New York Times** bestseller list. The book remained on the list for seventeen weeks.

What caused the flurry of publicity? Beck argued that former Vice President Al Gore was a Nazi. He suggested that Gore's campaign to raise concerns about global warming was to quote Beck "it's like Hitler. Hitler said a little bit of truth, and then he mixed in 'and it's the Jews' fault."

The arguments in Beck's book include his notion that the best way to fight global warming is the free market, he also weighs in on divorce rates (something he knows about personally), and he pillars liberals for their bias on college campuses. But there is more as Beck analyzes the income gap, illegal immigration and growing anti-Americanism.

Beck's popularity is a mystery. By examining his top nine quotes it is possible to gain a window into his mind. Dick Kurtzman compiled Beck's quotes: 1.) "This president, I think, has exposed himself over and over again as a guy who has a deep-seated hatred for white people...." This quote on the July 28, 2009 Fox And Friends Morning Show is a strange one. 2.) "I'm thinking about killing Michael Moore...." This quote came from a May 17, 2005 program on Fox. Moore, the filmmaker and liberal activist, is hardly a danger to American democracy. Moore does from time to time expose and criticize Beck's stupidity. So maybe he does deserve to die at the hand of Glenn Beck. The instrument of death will be Beck's tongue. No, he will not lick Moore to death. Then again he might. 3.) "When I see a 9/11 victim family on television... I'm so sick of them...." This September 9, 2005 comment suggests that Beck lacks humanity. He also has problems with sensitivity. 4.) "The only (Katrina victims) we're seeing on television are the scumbags." Another September 9, 2005 quote. 5.) "Sir, prove to me that you are not working with our enemies...." This is an example of Beck questioning Minnesota Democratic Congressman Keith Ellison. The irony is that Ellison is the first Muslim member of the House of Representatives. 6.) "Al Gore's not going to be rounding up Jews and exterminating them. It is the same tactic...that's what Hitler did." This is a comment from a May 1, 2007 Glenn Beck program. I wonder if Ian Kershaw footnotes him. (Editor: Kershaw is Hitler's most astute biographer) 7.) Beck remarked: "So here you have Barack Obama going in and spending the money on embryonic stem cell research....In case you don't know what Eugenics lead us to....A master race." This is a March 2009 quote on the Glenn Beck Show, and once again the idea of linking Obama and Hitler is ludicrous. 8.) "You have the artwork of Mussolini...here in New York at Rockefeller Plaza...." This September 2, 2009 quote from the Fox News Channel is an attempt to link the Obama Administration to the fascist Italian dictator. If you can't link Obama to Hitler, Mussolini is your next choice. 9.) "Oligarchy." This is a word that Beck placed on his black board and he misspelled it, Oligarchy is what President Obama is creating, Beck told his listeners. If there is a poster boy for American the politics of paranoia, it is Glenn Beck. He fears nothing.

GLENN BECK AND RICHARD HOFSTADTER

When Richard Hofstadter wrote: "The Modern right wing...feels dispossessed, America has been largely taken away from them and their kind, though they are determined to try to repossess it and to prevent the final destructive act of subversion," he predicted the political activism of the radical right.

Hofstadter is correct about the right wing feeling dispossessed, but he didn't fully recognize the authoritarian, anti-Democratic thrust in the right wing. The Republican Party is firmly controlled by the conservative right. Mitt Romney, in the spring of 2012, continually readjusted his campaign to placate the radical right.

Glenn Beck fits into Hofstadter's paranoid theory in a number of ways. First, Beck believes that concentration or re-education camps are being prepared for conservatives. Second, he predicts that America is headed toward a totalitarian state. Third, Obama is going to eliminate elections and disband the U. S. Supreme Court. He sees FEMA as the advanced agent of totalitarian control. The re-education camps in Louisiana, Beck suggests, are the first step toward a totalitarian state. This is a dangerous trend as Beck is pandering to Americans who believe that the Democratic Party is attempting to turn America into a socialist or communist state.

WHAT HOFSTADTER SUGGESTED AND HOW BECK FITS INTO IT

Hofstadter's essay in a 1964 issue of **Harper's** created a stir in the academic world. A sub-thesis to Hofstadter's the paranoid style is that right wing critics would silence the center and left. This certainly seems to be the case with Beck's program. He goes too far in criticizing and pillorying the left, but, in the process, he has created an army of anti-Democratic Party critics. Suddenly suburban housewives and their golfing husbands gather at their over 55 adult community to play shuffleboard and talk about the radical, socialist president. These suburbanites, who have retreated to their gated, private communities, fear for America's future. It is a sad commentary on the divisive nature of recent politics. As they hang on Glenn Beck's every word, they see the apocalypse. Then it's happy hour and they forget their fears.

When Beck is challenged for inaccurate reporting, poor taste or outright manipulation of the facts, he selects the Don Imus excuse. It is simply comedy. Beck argues, where is your sense of humor? Imus has insulted people for years in the guise of comedy. The real issue is censorship, and the attack upon freedom of expression. Beck is the icon of censorship in the right wing nut house. A central theme to Hofstadter's writing is that the academy would be prevented from legitimate criticism. He was particularly concerned that the professors who were unpopular critics of presidents, news figures and assorted politicians would be denied tenure and prevented from publishing their devastating critiques of the radical right.

One of Beck's conspiracy theories is that the government has taken charge of Google and the U. S. government controls the online information giant. While he is worshiped by millions of his followers, they seldom question his remarks. Google is a lot of things; it is not a propaganda agent for President Obama. Beck commented: "Don't do a Google search, it seems to me that Google is pretty deeply in bed with the government...are they just a shill for the United States Government?" It is Beck's outrageous comments that place him squarely in the right wing nut house.

The paranoid style in American politics works to perfection. Beck's sources make him suspect. He uses a video from one of Timothy McVeigh's militia group to analyze whether or not FEMA is setting up concentration camps. Yet, Beck insists that he is not political. He is simply retelling American history. He can't name any of the history books

that he has read or his favorite history authors. He does have one——
Glenn Beck.

It is Beck's behavior that has caused Fox TV News to limit his appearances. When Beck attacked Van Jones, an African American, who is a senior fellow at the Center For American Progress, the White House "green jobs" czar resigned his position and challenged Beck to a debate. When Jones' attorney, Joseph Sandler, sent a cease and desist order to Dianne Brandi, at Fox TV News, the battle lines were drawn. Beck's sensational and inflammatory statements were challenged as "unequivocally and absolutely false." The six page letter from Jones' attorney complained that Beck labeled his client as "an avowed Communist…a far left kook…." This didn't slow Beck down, and he continued his irresponsible attacks toward a Jewish-American financier, George Soros.

ATTACKING GEORGE SOROS

It is the Jewish-American community that is most critical of Beck. He has made continual comments about financier George Soros and how this Jewish businessman has abused his business relationships. He charges Soros with stealing from Jews. This seems a strange charge, as Soros is a Hungarian Jew. Abraham Foxman of the Anti-Defamation League remarks that Beck is "totally over the top." What really bothers Beck is that Soros was listed as the 46th richest man in the world in 2011. There is a populist anti-Semitism in much of Beck's rhetoric. This is one of his fundamental appeals to those who inhabit the right wing nut house.

Who is George Soros? He was born Gyorgy Schwartz on August 12, 1930 in Hungary. The Schwartz's were non-practicing Jews who changed the family name to Soros to assimilate into the Gentile population. Soros watched as the Nazis took control of Hungary in the 1930s. Soros had a protector who claimed that the young man was not Jewish.

After moving to England, Soros attended the London School of Economics. He was a brilliant student and he moved to New York City in 1956, where he quietly amassed a fortune on Wall Street. It was in hedge funds and currency speculation that Soros made his money. By 1992, he was a billionaire. Soros is not without his critics. The French government fined him 2.9 million dollars for felony insider trading.

The press labeled Soros as "The Man Who Broke The Bank of England" due to his one billion dollars in profit from the Black Wednesday U. K. currency crisis. This is a reference to the September 16, 1993 action by the British Conservative government when they were forced to withdraw the pound sterling from the European Exchange Rate mechanism. Soros was the most important currency market investor and he made his billion dollar profit by short selling sterling.

David Horowitz, a right wing darling, argues that Soros has taken over the Democratic Party. Horowitz' book, written with Richard Poe, **The Shadow Party: How George Soros, Hillary Clinton And Sixties Radicals Seized Control Of The Democratic Party** argues: "The architect and guiding genius of the Shadow Party…its Lenin…is billionaire activist George Soros." (Chapter 1) Then Horowitz traces a rise to power of the Hungarian billionaire and charges that Soros indirectly controls the American economy. Of Soros' power, he writes: "Few private individuals in the history of finance have possessed the power to break currencies with a single utterance." (Chapter 1)

It is as a writer and investor that Soros is brilliant. His book, **The New Paradigm For Financial Markets**, published in 2008, predicted a global super bubble. In retrospect, Soros' book is a reminder that he is a wise man.

Beck's attacks on Soros are unconscionable. He labels him the puppet master of the progressives. He also criticizes Soros for not giving enough money to Jewish charities. In a two-part Fox TV program, "the Puppet Master," there were veiled references to Soros that smacked of anti-Semitism.

Since the financial collapse of 2007, Soros has written a series of brilliant essays on banking and the financial system. He sees a need for globalism and international fiscal cooperation. This is antithetical to Glenn Beck. In October 2011, Soros brought out a seven-point plan to save the Eurozone. Beck and other conservatives trashed Soros' ideas. His book **Financial Turmoil In Europe And the United States**, published in 2011, is a reasoned and intelligent approach to the financial crisis.

THE REAL GEORGE SOROS

George Soros is not the devil. Glenn Beck and those in the right wing nut house will be surprised to discover the real George Soros. From 1979 through 2011, Soros awarded over eight million dollars to human rights, educational and public health organizations. He is also a prime mover in African education with money granted to the University of Cape Town. He is also a supporter of democracy in Russia and its satellite nations. For all the right wing hostility to his politics and economic endeavors, his philanthropy and support for democratic causes presents another George Soros.

It is Soros' large donations to defeat President George W. Bush that has prompted much of the right wing criticism. The real George Soros is a tough businessman with a political agenda. He watched as the Nazis, and later the Communists, compromised European civil liberties. He fears the same treatment is in store for America.

He remarked that removing Bush from office was "the central focus of my life...a matter of life and death." In an interview with Laura Blumenfeld in the **Washington Post**, Soros defined his opposition to President Bush. "When I hear Bush say, 'You're either with us or against us,' it reminds me of the Germans." The nightmare from living in Nazi Germany remains a persistent thought with Soros.

The press has unfairly vilified Soros. He is a tough businessman, but he has a strong humanitarian side that most journalists ignore. This is a tragedy as Soros is a shrewd observer of the political-economic scene. He has a lot to offer. He also has a strong reason for his political activism.

It is the resurgence of anti-Semitism that is at the heart of Soros' political activism. "There is a resurgence of anti-Semitism in Europe," Soros continued. "The policies of the Bush administration and the Sharon administration contribute to that....The new anti-Semitism holds that Jews rule the world." It is this fear that drives Soros' politics.

Those who criticize Soros argue that he is a secular Jew. They point that religion is not important in his life, he is a politically obsessive person. Since he doesn't practice his religion, he has thoughts and a defined philosophy on government. To promote his ideas, he has enlisted the American educational system. His more than 400 million dollar donations to major Universities has resulted in his ideas being popular in the university, in government and amongst liberals. Soros' critics argue that he is unduly influential on those who write about government theory. He wants government broken down, reformed and placed in a more socialistic mode. He believes that the present form of capitalism in the United States is not the best system, because it is corrupt and unsupportable. What does Soros mean by unsupportable? He believes that we attempt to impose our will on other countries. Soros supports a world order. The notion of world order suggests that everyone thinks the same in political and economic terms, and this is one of Soros' most significant theoretical ideas. He is a typical liberal Jewish activist. That does not go down well in the right wing nut house.

LIBERAL JEWISH ACTIVISTS AND GLENN BECK

For liberal Jewish activists, Beck has gone too far. In January 2011, he made what many consider inappropriate references to the Holocaust. Jewish leaders charged that Beck was practicing the worst form of historical revisionism.

When 400 Rabbis petitioned Fox TV News to sanction Beck, the Jewish Fund For Open Justice placed an open letter in **The Wall Street Journal** asking Rupert Murdoch to "sanction Glenn Beck" for his repeated use of Holocaust and Nazi imagery. This letter was the result of Beck's unsavory treatment of a Holocaust survivor. Insensitivity and ignorance is not a crime. However, it should not be tolerated on national television. A talk show host should not be allowed to pander to bigoted listeners. What is ironic is that Glenn Beck doesn't see justice, security, freedom and opportunity resulting from government. This is a sad commentary from an otherwise intelligent man.

QUOTATIONS FROM CHAIRMAN GLENN BECK

Glenn Beck": "If you have a priest that is pushing social justice, go find another parish. Go alert your Bishop."

Glenn Beck on President Obama's Civilian National Security Force- "This is what Hitler did with the SS."

Beck Compared Al Gore to Germany's Propaganda Minister Goebbels: "The Government and Its Friends Are Indoctrinating Our Children For the Control of Their Minds."

Glenn Beck: "Not a single time have we gotten a right from Congress or from the President? We get them from God."

Glenn Beck: "Darwin is the father of modern day racism."

GLENN BECK USES THE RACE CARD

One of the more frightening aspects of Glenn Beck's personality is his ability to use popular subjects to attack his foes. No charge is more dangerous to a person, a candidate or an organization than the blatant charge of racism. In December 2011, Beck interviewed Newt Gingrich on the Fox Business show, "Freedom Watch." In an incendiary and inflammatory interview, Beck charged that Gingrich's supporters were racist. They supported Newt not because of his politics, Beck alleges, but they are in his political camp due to a hatred for Obama.

Because Barack Obama is the child of a black man and a white woman some critics, like Glenn Beck, have been usually vicious. Beck went so far as to call Obama "colorless." As Beck remarked: "As a white guy, you don't notice that he is black. So he might as well be white." This gratuitous comment suggests a lack of civility in Beck's approach to political criticism.

The race card is one that Glenn Beck uses and the result is that it may incite violence.

DOES THE RIGHT INCITE VIOLENCE?

There is no doubt that Glenn Beck incites anger and at time violence toward the left. The use of violent metaphors is a fact of life often taken to extremes. The legion of followers who support Beck's books, his radio show, his television appearances and his speaking engagements are suburban, middle class white people frightened by the changes in American society. The white, frightened middle class are educated, they are affluent, they are the new Ku Klux Klan, and they continue to be the right wing's dominant force. Unlike the blatant ignorance of the KKK, they are persuasive, as well as bright, and this makes them a danger to our future civil liberties.

When Fox TV News parted company with Glenn Beck, it didn't bring an end to his popularity. What it reflected was the fall in ratings that doomed Beck's TV program. He moved over to Satellite radio and continues to rant and rave about America's bleak future. Fortunately, his day has passed and he remains an entertainer not a newsperson. As a comedian, he is as funny as Don Imus. Those in the right wing nut house still love him.

Chapter 6
THE PROFESSOR IS AN ATTACK DOG: JEROME CORSI, WHERE IS THE BIRTH CERTIFICATE: THE CASE THAT BARACK OBAMA IS NOT ELIGIBLE TO BE PRESIDENT

"MY WORK IS INVESTIGATIVE, NOT PROSECUTORIAL," JEROME CORSI

The specter of Barack Obama's presidential nomination gave Jerome Corsi gas. He has a sly smile, he is slightly overweight and he looks like the guy that people beat up in junior high school. He went to Harvard and received a PhD. He can now examine President Obama's birth certificate. The only problem is that he says that he can't find it.

The question that Jerome Corsi asks: "Is the 44th president of the United States of America, Barack Hussein Obama, illegally occupying the Oval Office?" That said Corsi goes on to conclude that no one has presented a verifiable birth certificate. How and why did Corsi come to occupy the "Professor Right Wing" mantle amongst conservatives? The answer lies in his background.

Jerome Corsi was born on August 31, 1946, and he came of age during the John F. Kennedy years. He was unable to explain Kennedy's assassination, and, as a young man, he was filled with conspiracy theories. It was while growing up in East Cleveland, Ohio that he watched his father, Louis E. Corsi, work as a union public relations director, and he came to detest the blue collar, working man. He vowed never to accept this life. While he studied for his B. A. his interest in economics was an integral part of his personality. He was interested in banking and finance, but he didn't study it in college. His political science degree clouded his view of economics as did the direction of American history.

While pursuing graduate work at Harvard University, Corsi researched the protesters who surrounded the 1972 Democratic and Republican National Conventions. He concluded that they were a danger to American democracy. At his undergraduate school, Case Western Reserve University, Corsi had a low opinion of his professors. This was due to their professorial liberalism. He found Harvard intellectually oppressive. He entered the world of banking and finance, where he was comfortable. The political protests of the 1960s and the early 1970s were ingrained in his psyche. He came to view America as a land beset by Communists, Socialists and radicals. He developed anti-Islamic, anti-Catholic, anti-Semitic and homophobic views, according to the **London Guardian**.

When Corsi wrote the birth certificate book, he not only questioned Barack Obama's citizenship, but he made it clear that there was a conspiracy to hide the documentation. Corsi writes: "All too often, documents relating to Obama's past turn out conveniently lost or reported destroyed...." (p. vi) But, according to Corsi, there are more missing documents. The marriage records for his parents. The President's travel-records, as well as his law school writings, are missing. But even worse, suggests Corsi, Obama is a Muslim. All of these things, according to Corsi, make Obama ineligible to be President of the United States.

To Corsi's credit, he is an excellent researcher, he knows his political history and he is a marvelous writer. But he is a fanatic. "Those of us who believe the Constitution of the United States is worth preserving, protecting and defending intend to continue pressing the Obama eligibility issue," Corsi observes. (p. ix)

In part one, he paints a picture of a young man who scarcely knew his family and parentage. He also suggests that there were myths about

Obama Sr. that his son obscured. This is difficult, if no impossible, in the media age. He labels President Obama's family "strangers in a strange land." The irony here is that Barry Obama, as he was then known in Hawaii, had a white bread upbringing, and he attended an exclusive private school that was the antithesis of radicalism.

The final chapter in part one entitled "Kenya, Odinga, Communism and Islam" is a personal and political hatchet job. Corsi's attempt to link Obama with African nationalism and the Muslim faith lacks conviction. With seventy-two references to Kenya and Obama's involvement in that nation, Corsi concludes that President Obama "doesn't meet the simple requirements" for office. There is also an attempt to link Barack Obama with Kenya's Prime Minister Raila Odinga. During his time leading Kenya, Odinga arrested homosexuals, and he persecuted professors who challenged his rule. He became a born again Christian who controlled elections while terrorizing his people. There is no connection to President Obama, but Corsi attempts to link the Democratic president to this regime. The reason, Obama's father lived there. This is all circumstantial. It has nothing to do with Barack Obama.

But the key question remains. Did Barack Obama forge his birth certificate? The president tried to point out that he had more serious issues, but this one did not go away. So the White House posted the long version of the birth certificate. This led the right wing conspiracy nuts to suggest that seven to nine revisions of the document had taken place. The notion of his middle name was Mohammed came out. The two birth certificates that were released did not end the controversy.

The copies of the Hawaii birth certificates appear authentic, but there is still some question in the minds of many about their legality. Those who believe that the birth certificate is false, point to the use of modern technology. They argue that watermarks from Photoshop prove it is a tampered document and hence a fake. The independent fact-checking organization, **FactCheck.org** concluded that the document "meets all the requirements from the State Department proving U. S. citizenship." There are claims that the document doesn't possess a raised seal or a valid signature, but, after an extensive investigation, **FactCheck.org** concluded that the charges are false.

The steady flow of anti-Obama books fueled the belief that he was a Muslim, not native born and a radical. The Pew Research Center found that nearly twenty percent of Americans believe that Barack Obama is a Muslim and the Democratic Corps Polling Center claims that fifty-five percent of Americans believe that President Obama is a socialist.

By November 2011, anti-Obama books topped the **New York Times** bestseller list. Jerome Corsi's **The Obama Nation** debuted at number one on the **NYT's** list. With this in mind, Corsi's book on Obama's birth certificate remains a best seller.

Politicians love to use President Obama's birth certificate as an issue. In late October 2011, Texas Governor Rick Perry spoke out against the Hawaiian birth document. While Governor Perry says that the birth certificate issue is "a dismissive one," he casts doubt on it. He continually flirts with the notion that President Obama was born in Kenya and schooled in Indonesia. Perry knows this is nonsense, but he also realizes that it is a popular issue with the voters. Even the major right wing brain, Karl Rove, condemned Perry for flirting with popular political notions that bear little resemblance to the truth.

HONOLULU ADVERTISER BIRTH ANNOUNCEMENTS AUGUST 1961

MR. AND MRS. BARACK OBAMA, 35 KALANIANAOLE HWY, SON, AUGUST 4

IS THIS THE REAL BARACK OBAMA BIRTH CERTIFICATE?

OR IS THIS BARACK OBAMA'S BIRTH CERTIFICATE?

THE ARGUMENT AGAINST BARACK OBAMA'S BIRTH CERTIFICATE

1. THE LACK OF AN EMBOSSED HAWAIIAN OFFICIAL STATE SEAL.
2. MINOR VARIATIONS IN THE HAWAII BIRTH CERTIFICATE.
3. THE LACK OF OFFICIAL STATE STAMPS ON THE DOCUMENT.
4. ALLEGATIONS OF 7 TO 9 CHANGES VIA COMPUTERS.
5. PHILADELPHIA ATTORNEY PHILIP BERG FILED A LAW SUIT ALLEGING A FORGED CERTIFICATE OF BIRTH AND FILED A SUIT IN THE U. S. DISTRICT COURT CHALLENGING BARACK OBAMA'S ELIGIBILITY FOR THE PRESIDENCY.
6. THE KAPI'OLANI MATERNITY AND GYNECOLOGICAL HOSPITAL WAS NOT KNOWN BY THAT NAME UNTIL 1978.

7. HE IS A MUSLIM WITH A MIDDLE NAME OF MOHAMMED AND HE WAS BORN IN AFRICA.

THE ARGUMENT FOR THE AUTHENTICITY OF BARACK OBAMA'S BIRTH CERTIFICATE
1. **THE BIRTH WAS ANNOUNCED IN TWO HONOLULU NEWSPAPERS, THE ADVERTISER AND THE STAR BULLETIN ON AUGUST 4, 1961.**
2. **IN OCTOBER 2008 A FEDERAL JUDGE DISMISSED THE COMPLAINT THAT BARACK OBAMA WAS NOT A CITIZEN.**
3. **THE HAWAII BIRTH CERTIFICATE IS CONSISTENT WITH OTHERS ISSUED AT THE TIME.**
4. **JUDGE SURRICK RULED THAT BERG'S CLAIMS "VENTURED INTO THE UNREASONABLE."**
5. **DR. CHIYOME FUKINO, HEAD OF THE HAWAII STATE DEPARTMENT OF HEALTH, VERIFIED THE BIRTH CERTIFICATE.**
6. **MEDICAL PEOPLE AND TEACHERS IN HAWAII REMEMBER THE EARLY YEARS.**

The birth certificate controversy continued in 2011, when entrepreneur Donald Trump suggested that President Obama needed to take a truth test. It was during a March 2011 interview on Good Morning America that Trump announced he was considering a presidential run. He talked of being a bit skeptical about President Obama's citizenship. "Growing up no one knew him," Trump announced. As Trump joined the ranks of the "birthers," he took credit for the release of the president's long form birth certificate.

Finally, in April 2011, a certified copy of Obama's original Certificate of Live Birth was released to the press. The controversy didn't go away but it was less important.

THE CONSPIRACY THEORIES ON PRESIDENT OBAMA'S BIRTH CERTIFICATE

It is Article Two of the U. S. Constitution that mandates a person be a natural-born citizen to run for the presidency. The birthers believe that since Obama's father is from Kenya, which means he has dual citizenship, that Barack Obama is not a natural-born citizen. This is, of courses, nonsense, but not to the truculent birthers.

At late as 2010, twenty-five per cent of adult Americans doubted that President Obama was American born. When the birther's controversy began it was alleged that anonymous e-mails from Hillary Clinton supporters ignited the controversy. Soon it was proven that Mrs. Clinton had nothing to do with the birth certificate fiasco.

Jim Heraghty, the **National Review Online** reporter, urged the candidate in June 2008 to release the birth certificate. Heraghty fueled the fire with the rumor that his middle name was Muhammad, rather than Hussein, and that his biological father was not a natural born citizen.

Then the Drudge Report got involved stating that the birth certificate was a forgery. They claimed that the document was made with image editing software. The conservative **National Review** concluded that the document was layered, and they announced that it was a forgery.

Republican Senator John McCain is one of the few people to have an ounce of integrity over the Obama birth question. In his 2008 campaign, his staff evaluated the citizenship question and declared that it was not a significant issue. What the McCain campaign failed to realize is that it was an important issue in the right wing nut house.

What the citizenship issue became was a means of raising funds for political candidates. The WorldNet Daily published more than two hundred articles, sold billboard ads, bumper stickers and postcards. The question they ask is "Where's The Birth Certificate?" At Tea Party meetings, there are birther signs. The irony is that the birther controversy has hurt rather than helped the Republican Party.

The bottom line is that America has an African American president and Southern conservatives are outraged that a black man is in the White House. It is pure and simple a racial issue. There is no other way to look at it.

Rachel Maddow, of MSNBC, has the best definition of the birther: "A specific new breed of American conspiracy theorists who believe that the real problem with Barack Obama being president is that he can't possibly have been born in the United States. The birth certificate is a fake. He's a foreigner."

President Barack Obama should have the last word. In a speech in February 2010, at the National Prayer Breakfast, the president remarked: "Surely you can question my policies without questioning my faith. Or for that matter my citizenship." Touché. In August 2010, during an interview with Brian Williams, the news anchor asked the president about his citizenship and his Christian values. Barack Obama remarked: "There is a mechanism, a network of misinformation that in a new media era can get churned out there constantly...I can't spend all my time with my birth certificate plastered on my forehead." Don't get Rick Perry started on this or he will want it plastered on the president's forehead.

EVEN RUSSIANS ARE IN THE RIGHT WING NUT HOUSE: THE CASE OF ORLY TAITZ

The birth certificate controversy has a life of its own. The website 2012 Barackobama.com reported in late November 2011 that elected officials were still questioning the president's birth records. In the New Hampshire House of Representatives, four Republicans supported a request by birthers, who wanted a hearing to have President Obama removed from the state primary ballot. The reason, he didn't have a valid birth certificate. In Arizona, a group organized demanding that Hawaii release the microfiche copy of President Obama's birth certificate.

A Russian woman, Dr. Orly Taitz, drove the late 2011 Obama birth certificate controversy in New Hampshire. Taitz, a leader in the birther movement, is one of the strongest voices alleging that Barack Obama is not a natural born citizen. Not surprisingly, she has filed frivolous lawsuits. Some courts have admonished her for abusing her law degree. She is an interesting character who has attracted national press attention.

Who is Orly Taitz? She was born on August 30, 1962 in Kishinev, Moldavian SSR in the USSR. Taitz is a well-educated individual. She is a dentist, lawyer, former real estate agent and businesswoman. So who is a better candidate to tell us that the president is not born in the U. S? Before she moved to America, Taitz was educated in Israel. Her dentistry degree is from Hebrew University. Since 1987, she has lived in the United States. Her law degree is from Taft Law School. This is a non-accredited online Internet law program. She was admitted to the California bar in December 2002. From her home in Laguna Nigel, California, a toney suburb south of Los Angeles, where she has a palatial home, Taitz directs her political criticism. She also has a dental practice in nearby Mission Viejo and Rancho Santa Margarita. She has three sons, and she is a black belt in Taekwondo. She also speaks five languages. How does she have time to go after President Obama?

Taitz is also a strong advocate for Israel. She told the **Orange County Register** in 2006 that she supported Israeli military actions again Hamas and Hezbollah. She claims to have lost relatives in the Holocaust. She is a strange figure to lead the birthers.

As the driving force behind the birthers in New Hampshire, Taitz led a movement to force President Obama's name off the primary ballot. The birthers website Birthreport.com reported that New Hampshire

State Representative Carol M. Vita was active in pursuing the president's false claims of an American birth certificate. But it is Taitz who is the motivator behind the New Hampshire birther controversy.

Taitz claims that President Obama is not a natural-born U. S. citizen. Her allegations are not only derogatory but down right insulting. She has suggested that a number of interviews that homosexuals (that's her use of the term) from Obama's church have died mysteriously. She also alleges that Obama has dozens of social security numbers. It gets worse. She points to an authentic Kenyan birth certificate for President Obama. She charges that Obama donated money to Hamas. There is a report that she has been threatened. Guess who? People close to the president are the ones looking for her. There were also reports that someone vandalized her car. That is the penalty for living in California.

Maybe Dr. Taitz is the wave of the future. While running for the U. S. Senate in 2012, She remarked: "Join me, uphold and defend the Constitution of the United States."President Obama is not Taitz' only concern. She is also convinced that Goldman Sachs runs the U. S. Treasury. In light of recent economic developments, I agree with this astute observation. She alleges that Ben Bernake is considering joining Goldman Sachs. She is also concerned about civil liberties. She points to Democratic Florida Congressman Alcee Hastings as one of the key proponents of building labor camps for non-patriotic Americans. Other inane charges include the notion that Hugo Chavez owns the software that runs American voting machines.

Not everyone finds Taitz amusing. She was ordered to pay $20,000 by the U. S. Supreme Court for filing a frivolous lawsuit in Georgia on belief of Army Captain Connie Rhodes, who refused to be sent to Iraq. In that case, Taitz argued that President Obama couldn't deploy Rhodes because Obama was not eligible to be President. The court was not amused. Bill O'Reilly summed up Taitz by saying she's "a nut." Thank you, Bill.

RACISM IS THE REAL ISSUE IN THE BIRTH CERTIFICATE CONTROVERSY

Racism is a delicate issue. When a person is labeled a racist, it is often a false statement. There needs to be proof. The vast majority of politicians, media types and professors who are unwilling to accept Obama's citizenship are betrayed by a small number of racially insensitive critics.

Tim Walker, writing in the **Minneapolis Star Tribune**, headlined: "Let's Call The Birthers What They Really Are: Racists." He went on to editorialize "these folks are not connected to reality." He continued: "The simple truth is that many birthers are simply racist." There is no doubt that racial attitudes influence the birth certificate controversy.

Any discussion of President Obama's birthplace or birth certificate is a code word for bigot or conspiracy minded lunatic. But it does sell books. The birthers have an extensive media following. Michael Savage remarked on his show: "We're getting ready for the Communist takeover of America with a noncitizen at the helm." There are credible people who mistakenly attacked Obama's birth certificate. Mike Huckabee stated in 2008 that Obama had been raised in Kenya. Then Huckabee went on the O'Reilly Factor and said that he had made a "verbal gaffe." Republican Representative Michele Bachmann told conservative radio host Jeff Katz: "If I was ever to run for president of the United States, I think the first thing I would do in the first debate is offer my birth certificate...."

The birthers have a long list of grievances, facts and assorted conspiracies. In their minds Barack Obama is not eligible for the Presidency. The list is bogus but it provides the right wing nut house with ammunition.

WHY THE BIRTHERS CONSIDER OBAMA INELIGIBLE FOR THE PRESIDENCY

1. **He obtained Indonesian citizenship when he lived there as a child.**
2. **Lieutenant Colonel Terry Larkin's attorney stated that any foreign born child could acquire a Hawaiian certificate of live birth.**
3. **Birthers argue that President Obama, although born in Hawaii, does not qualify as a natural-born citizen. This is because his father was not a citizen.**
4. **Birthers argue that a person cannot be a natural born citizen; he or she is a dual citizen at birth.**
5. **The Constitution Party campaigned for release of Obama's long form birth certificate. Jerome Corsi is a key figure in the Constitution Party.**

The birth certificate controversy is an example of how nasty American politics have become in the last decade. The right wing nut house tried to blame the controversy on Hillary Clinton by suggesting that her supporters ignited it in 2008 to help her in the presidential primaries. This is, of course, not true.

The media can't get enough of the Obama birth certificate story. The McClatchy newspaper chain alleged that President Obama hid much of his life from Americans. The notion that President Obama lost his U. S. citizenship when he lived in Indonesia is a staple of the right wing nut house. Fortunately, most people label the birth certification controversy a dead issue. Hallelujah!

There are many politicians who have suggested that President Obama is not qualified to occupy the Oval Office. In 2009, Senator Richard Shelby, a Republican from Alabama, questioned President Obama's citizenship. He later retracted his statement. A Missouri Congressman, Roy Blunt, complained that "the President couldn't produce a birth certificate." He later claimed his quote was taken out of context. Proving that women are smarter than men, Ohio Republican Congresswoman Jean Schmidt told a young lady who hollered that President Obama was not a citizen: "I agree with you. But the Courts don't." She didn't say that she was speaking out of context.

Ironically, Blunt mistake over the Obama birth certificate didn't hurt him politically. He ran for the U. S. Senate in 2010 and he was elected. He describes himself as a culture warrior. Blunt began his U. S. Senate career by introducing legislation allowing an employer to deny health services if they conflict with their religious beliefs or moral convictions. This proposed legislation firmly entrenched Blunt with those in the right wing nut house, and some say that he was elected to the U. S. Senate from Missouri due to his intransigent stand on health care. While Blunt tried to discredit President Obama on the birth certificate issue he failed, but he was elected to office in a small part due to the controversy.

What the birth certificate controversy suggests is a simple fact. President Obama's detractors have a long way to go before they can discredit him. The birth certificate fight is much adieu about nothing. A Pew Research Center Poll in 2009 found that 80% of Americans had heard of the controversy. The conclusion was that there was too much attention paid to it. The controversy went away shortly after President Obama's inauguration.

The final word on the birth certificate controversy came from Hawaii Governor Neil Abercrombie. When he took over as Hawaii's governor, he made it clear that he was a close friend with Stanley Ann Dunham and Barack Obama, Sr. He had spent time with young Barry. Abercrombie remarked of the President: "Obama's a big boy; he can take sticks and stones. But there's no reason on earth to have the memory of his parents insulted by people whose motivation is solely political."

The final word from Governor Abercrombie wasn't enough. Orly Taitz remarked: "To me this sounds like a very coordinated effort. As soon as a friend of the Obama family gets into the governor's office he has access to all documents." Taitz concluded that only herself and a detective could really decide if the president was really a citizen. Welcome to the right wing nut house.

SHERIFF JOE HEATS UP THE RIGHT WING NUT HOUSE

When it appeared that the birth certificate controversy was at an end, Phoenix Sheriff Joe Arpaio, at the behest of the Tea Party, investigated President Obama's birth certificate. As America's self-proclaimed toughest sheriff, Arpaio used his volunteer posse to look into the Obama birth certificate controversy.

Not surprisingly, Arpaio found that the long form birth document released by the White House in April 2011 was a computer-generated forgery. The investigation also stated that Obama's selective service card completed in 1980 in Hawaii was probably a forgery. "We don't know who the perpetrators are of those documents," Arpaio told the press. "I am not going after Obama," Arpaio remarked. "I'm just doing my job." Apparently, the Sheriff believes that his job is to monitor the president's daily activity. Somehow I feel safer. The real reason is that Sheriff Arpaio is under federal investigation for civil rights violations. A Federal Grand Jury is looking into criminal abuse of power allegations against Arpaio's office. He would do well to answer those potential charges.

The birth certificate controversy has a life of its own. At late as May 17, 2012, the birthers were once again questioning President Obama's birth certificate. In 1991, Obama's literary agency mistakenly handed out a publicity sheet stating that he was born in Kenya and raised in Indonesia. The conservative website Breitbart.com jumped on the story. The Drudge Report also weighed in questioning Obama's citizenship. Miriam Goodrich, the employee for the literary agency, Acton and Dystel, told the press that she simply didn't check her facts. Glenn Beck, David Limbaugh and virtually everyone else in the right wing literary establishment should take note. Something of importance did come from the controversy; it was revealed that Breitbart.com and the Drudge Report began their businesses on Mars. This explains a great deal about their claims regarding President Obama.

When Arizona Secretary of State, Ken Bennett, announced to the press, "I'm not a birther," the reporters at the press conference scratched their heads. Then he stated that his responsibility to the people of Arizona was to make sure that the state ballots were correct. So he needed to see a copy of President Obama's birth certificate. Arizona is the home of the right wing nut house and Bennett became the laughing stock of the nation with his lame request. What is Bennett doing? He is courting the Tea Party.

Secretary Bennett went on KFYI with Mike Broomhead and stated that he asked the state of Hawaii for verification of Barack Obama's birth. Then the truth came out. Bennett said that he was following the lead of Sheriff Joe Arpaio. He also respected the request of 250 members of the Tea Party who wanted the mystery solved. What mystery? Bennett said the mystery of the birth certificate. Then Bennett went over to Fed Ex and he purchased a five-dollar money order, which he promptly sent off to Hawaii. After two months there was still no word from the Aloha State. So maybe Barack Obama is not really a citizen. The mystery continues and Secretary Bennett has made every Arizonian the subject of national ridicule. It is better to be ridiculed than to be a Communist.

When Ken Bennett began his search for the birth certificate, he corresponded with Jerome Corsi. Not surprisingly, Bennett recently formed a committee to explore a potential run for governor. Then Corsi got in the act by posting on WorldNetDaily a blog that stated that Sheriff Arpaio's investigation "has not proven anything other than raised probable cause that the birth certificate posted on the White House website 'may be' a forgery." Corsi wants a Judge to hear the case.

Bennett had the last word. "If Hawaii can't or won't provide verification of the president's birth certificate, I will not put his name on the ballot." Where is Orly Taitz when you really need her?

Donald Trump continues to cry out that President Obama is not a citizen. Mitt Romney throughout the summer of 2012 was gracious and he believed that it was not an issue. This made Orly Taitz mad. Stay tuned; the right wing nut house is still after the birth certificate.

Jerome Corsi means well. He believes that Barack Obama is a danger to American society. He also believes that the president is leading the nation toward socialism. Joseph Farah, Corsi's editor remarked: "I believe with all my heart that Barack Obama is destroying this country, and I will continue to stand against his administration at every turn." After finishing this remark Farah stated that Corsi's book on President Obama's birth certificate "has become problematic and contains what I now believe to be factual inaccuracies…." That statement came after his publisher recalled the first 200,000 books and pulped them. This tells us all we need to know about Corsi's scholarship and writing.

PART THREE
SELLING BOOKS THROUGH SENSATIONALISM AND BIG BROTHER

"WITH SARAH PLAIN, DO YOU GET THE FEELING THAT IN HIGH SCHOOL SHE WAS VOTED LEAST LIKELY TO WRITE A BOOK AND MOST LIKELY TO BURN A BOOK," ROBIN WILLIAMS

The market for anti-Barack Obama books is a large one. Some of the less credible books published occupy small, but significant, sales in that they distort his record and malign the president. This section examines some of the best, if not the worst, of these odious tomes. The drive for fame and fortune is a persistent one. The authors in this section lust for fame and fortune, and they have received a degree of it. But their writing is atrocious, their public image is putrid and their personalities border on the obscene. Welcome to selling books through sensationalism and criticizing big brother. The right wing nut house is filled with authors who write for money and have neither integrity nor high-level analysis in their work.

The anti-Obama book industry by 2012 listed sixty-seven best selling tomes with little research and even less evidence. They all argued the same thing. That is the Obama is a socialist, anarchist, anti-democratic leader taking America down the path to permanent socialism. They also argue that he is a tool of big business and a politician determined to crush states rights. He is also accused of subverting the Constitution. In the right wing nut house, these arguments sound plausible.

Terry L. Cook's, **The Making Of An American Dictator Barack Hussein Obama** is a book that predicted the triumph of socialism by January 2012. It hasn't happened but Cook continues to warn Americans about impending socialist doom. Who is Terry L. Cook? He is a Christian fundamentalist researcher who has written sixteen books. He is a one trick pony, as his writing concentrates on one theme. The theme is that the government is intent upon controlling your life. Cook describes himself as "a fundamental Christian intelligence analyst." He is also a retired Los Angeles County Deputy Sheriff. As an ordained minister, he preaches about the coming of America's last days. He is a caricature of the right wing patriot. There are others in the right wing nut house that write better. A good example is David Freddoso.

The main ingredient for success in the right wing nut house book sales department is a good television appearance. No one is more adept at this than David Freddoso. His book, **The Case Against Barack Obama: The Unlikely Rise And Unexamined Agenda Of The Media's Favorite Candidate** is interesting. It also had a 300,000 initial print run. In person, Freddoso is articulate, well dressed, a strong interview, and he is a dedicated member of the anti-Obama hate machine. He labels the president and those around him as "gangsters." Somewhere Al Capone is rolling over in his grave.

Along the way, Freddoso has made a fortune through his books and media appearances. He is an excellent writer with a twisted view of the president. Ben Smith, writing in **The Politico**, labeled Freddoso's book "the first serious negative biography of Senator Barack Obama."

If David Freddoso is an impressive right wing critic, David Limbaugh and Pamela Geller are literally a second string set of critics. Limbaugh rides on the coattails of his big brother, Rush, and Pamela Geller wears bikinis on her blogs to suggest her hostility to Muslims. Neither is a responsible critic but they have a large following. Figure that out.

SENSATIONALISM IN THE MEDIA REGARDING PRESIDENT OBAMA

MICHAEL SAVAGE: "HE'S AN AFRO-LENINIST, AND I KNOW HE'S DANGEROUS."

GLENN BECK: "THIS GUY REALLY IS A MARXIST. HE BELIEVES IN THE REDISTRIBUTION OF WEALTH."

TOM DELAY, FORMER HOUSE SPEAKER: "HE'S A MARXIST BUT A VERY SMART ONE...HE DOESN'T LET ANYONE KNOW IT."

CHRISTINE O'DONNELL: "HE'S ANTI AMERICAN. HE DID NOT VOTE FOR ENGLISH AS THE OFFICIAL LANGUAGE."

Michelle Malkin is one of the few ethnic writers in the right wing nut house. Her Filipino heritage and liberal college education provide her with different way to view American politics. She is also something of a chameleon. After some liberal newspaper columns early in her career, she crossed over to the right wing nut house. Her income grew proportionally, and her books sold in large quantities. She is a brilliant writer, a devoted conservative and a shrewd businessperson. In addition to being a popular guest on Fox TV News, she has her own political website which provides a nice living.

Richard Hofstadter defined writers like Malkin when he observed that the paranoid style believed in "the existence of a vast, insidious, preternaturally effective international conspiratorial network designed to perpetrate acts of the most fiendish character." (Hofstadter, **The Paranoid Style in American Politics**, p. 14)

Malkin serves the right wing nut house through her daily video newscasts on Hot Air. This is the first conservative Internet news organization. It is kept alive through contributions and Hot Air is almost bankrupt. Hallelujah! Malkin refers to the president after he met with the Russian leader as "Comrade Obama." There is nothing like fairness in the media.

Chapter 7
SELLING BOOKS VIA A TITLE: DAVID FREDDOSO, GANGSTER GOVERNMENT: BARACK OBAMA AND THE NEW WASHINGTON THUGOCRACY: IS THIS A COMEDY ACT?

"OBAMA HAS THREE BANKERS INVOLVED IN HIS CAMPAIGN," DAVID FREDDOSO

The publishing dollar is a tough one. Only the top authors make money. The result is that publishers look for a title that will sell, maybe a gimmick, a far out argument or a fawning, complimentary book. These books are commissioned to recoup the author's advance. The amount of money publishers pay big time authors isn't always recouped. This has led to television and media personalities increasingly replacing serious political writers. The result is that in the realm of political criticism there has been a decline in quality.

The theory is that media types can promote their books better than the average writer. Enter the journalistic attack dog, David Freddoso. As a young, articulate, photogenic on-air personality with a nice suit, Freddoso is the master of conservative drivel. As a young man, he worked under and was trained by another right wing attack dog, Robert Novak. The result is some intelligent, if acerbic, writing. The specter of Novak hangs over Freddoso like a wet blanket.

Who is Robert Novak? He is a journalist, a columnist, a television personality and a leading conservative commentator. Novak's credibility comes from his work on television on CNN. He is one of the founding giants of CNN and his shows The Capital Gang, Crossfire, Evans, Novak, and Hunt and Shields established his reliable, conservative comments. Novak's abrasive personality is not well-suited to television. He is an intelligent analyst who talks down to his audience. Novak is often condescending to his guests and fellow commentators.

The difference between Novak and Freddoso is that the later has a personality. Freddoso increased his book sales due to media appearances on virtually every major news show. The interviews for his book, **The Case Against Barack Obama: The Unlikely Rise and Unexamined Agenda of the Media's Favorite Candidate**, published in 2008, established Freddoso's credible conservative credentials. His simple thesis is that the media was never critical of the candidate Barack Obama. What Freddoso does is to revive all the old horror stories of Tony Rezko's influence and the Bill Ayers-Sol Alinsky linchpin to socialism. He has no concrete evidence to back up his charges. There is little more than innuendo and circumstantial evidence to support Freddoso's allegations. But he writes beautifully, thinks clearly and exudes sincerity. He also is a brilliant title conceiver. His title tells you what you want to know, so there is no sense reading the book.

It is an example of a book sold by its title and not its content. It is also sold by the author's photogenic good looks. He spends so much time looking good; it is surprising that he has time to write. Freddoso is well dressed, handsome, articulate, but he is still a real journalist. He seems to possess a sincere message. That message has made him a lot of money.

Freddoso is described as "a card carrying member of the right wing smear machine." Surprisingly, this description is on Amazon's page for Freddoso hoping to sell his books. They have succeeded. His father, Notre Dame Professor of Philosophy, Alfred Freddoso, slinks into his office allegedly embarrassed by his son's conservative malfeasance. But the son doesn't have to live on a professor's salary.

When Freddoso's **The Case Against Barack Obama: The Unlikely Rise and Unexamined Agenda Of The Media's Favorite Candidate** had a first print run of 300,000, there was a buzz among reviewers. The book quickly hit the **New York Times Bookseller** list at number five. John K. Wilson, writing in the **Huffington Post** labeled the book "a hatchet job, " and he described it as "poorly written." Like most polemical tomes, it is filled with errors. Freddoso calls Obama "the least experienced politician in at least one hundred years to obtain a major party nomination for president...." (p. ix) This ignores the fact that George W. Bush had served only six years as Texas' governor, this gave him much less experience than Obama. Freddoso sees President Obama as the lead architect of a liberal plot to take over American government. In the final analysis, Freddoso suggests through innuendo that Socialist, Communist and conspiracy-oriented politicians are in control of the democracy.

The chapter titles are an ominous indication of Freddoso's critical direction. With titles like "The Accidental Candidate," "Obamessiah," "The Radical Influences" and "Abortion: Barack Obama's America," the direction of Freddoso's criticism is obvious. There is the story of a family friend, Frank, who young Obama visited and this whiskey breathed obscure poet was an influence. What Freddoso writes: "Obama doesn't give us the full identity of this man who influenced him as a kid. Such half-disclosure is in keeping with the tone of Obama's story-telling memoir..." (p. 133) The reality is that President Obama and others have fully described Frank, and they have suggested that he was no more than a subtle, but passing, influence.

Who was Frank? His full name was Frank Marshall Davis, and he is an African American who was not only a poet but also a political activist. He has published eleven books with such ubiquitous titles as **I Am An American Negro** and **Through Sepia Eyes**. He was an essayist and poet and the University of Wisconsin, the University of Illinois and the University Press of Mississippi are among his publishers. He was a highly literate essayist, a poet and an interpreter of American life. Freddoso mentions none of this.

In Freddoso's book, Frank appears as dangerous, poorly educated and a marginal person. The truth is that he was a radical civil rights advocate who lived in Hawaii, and he was incensed over the treatment of African Americans. Until he died in his early eighties, his essays reflected how one African American felt about the political system. He was a strong man with a message of radical political activism. Frank's preached that good relations between the races and faith, as well as dignity, would triumph over ignorance and prejudice. He told a young Barry Obama that social justice and human dignity were elements of American society that he should emphasize if he pursued a political career. While he may have been a rhetorical political radical, Frank Marshall Davis was a patriot. Something that David Freddoso fails to recognize. Instead sensationalism and a legal form of slander mark Freddoso's excellent writing and minimal thought.

WHY REGNERY LOVES FREDDOSO'S BOOK

Not surprisingly, the conservative press, Regnery, published the book in 2008, with the idea of defeating Barack Obama's bid for the presidency. It didn't work out, but in the process Freddoso established a career in the right wing nut house. In an over the top decision, the book has a sub-thesis that gangsters are in control of the White House. I guess that is better than rap or hip-hop artists!

Here is where it gets interesting. The best seller listing is bogus, not in an illegal way. Creative Response Concepts ordered thousands of Freddoso books for conservative bookstores, thereby driving up sales. Then The Christian bookstores jumped in with big orders. The book now sells for a penny on Amazon. Whether his books were sold or returned as remainders remains an unanswered question. So is David Freddoso a best selling author or not? I don't know. Where does Freddoso come from? After reading his book, I thought it was Mars. Turned out I wasn't too far off. It was New York City.

When his book appeared Freddoso told the press that he wanted to point out the media's uncritical stance. There are thirteen references to real estate developer and political contributor Tony Rezko. Like others in the right wing nut house, Freddoso tries to paint Rezko and Obama as best friends. In a chapter: "Pinstripe Patronage: Obama Takes Care Of His Friends," Freddoso claims "Obama could never have gotten where he is today without Rezko." (p. 211), and, then a few pages later, Freddoso writes: "By what criteria does a man choose his friends and end up with the likes of Tony Rezko, Jeremiah Wright and Bill Ayers?" (p. 234) This is an interesting quote. Freddoso might have explained that the President hardly knew Rezko, and Obama quickly got rid of

Wright and Ayers. Then to drive his point home, Freddoso alleges that Obama praised "Hugo Chavez as a champion of democracy." (p. 234) The theoretical radicalism of Barack Obama is Freddoso's message, and there are those who accept it as gospel.

It is Freddoso's handling of President Obama's foreign policy that gives his book a cutting edge. Freddoso writes: "How does he choose his advisors and end up with people who chat with terrorists, advocate reparations for slaves, and praise Hugo Chavez as a champion of democracy?" (p. 234) This is excellent writing but once again the facts get in the way of his elegant prose.

The Hugo Chavez interlude is an interesting tale of American foreign policy. The Venezuelan President was surprised when Obama walked across the room at the Summit of the Americas to shake Chavez's hand. The right wing nut house went ballistic. They failed to recognize that there was a need to repair Latin American relations. When Chavez handed President Obama a copy of **The Open Veins of Latin America: Five Centuries of the Pillage of A Continent** by radical Latin American author Eduardo Galeano, Obama upstaged Chavez by graciously accepting the book and vowing to increase trade and diplomatic relations with Latin America. Obama was praised for his diplomatic endeavors. When President Obama spoke to Chavez in Spanish it was an induction that the Bush policies toward Latin America were on the decline.

It is in the criticism of Obama's notion of and potential direction of other areas of foreign policy that Freddoso's book turns into a comedy act. He chides Obama for not visiting Iraq with regularity or for listening to General David Petraes. But, according to Freddoso, the Obama presidency does not go far enough toward stamping out our enemy. The strangest statement is when Freddoso writes that Obama "is especially disdainful of the so-called 'Star Wars' program, which was crucial to bankrupting the Soviets...." (p. 189) The truth is that Star Wars almost bankrupted the American military, and it didn't work. It is no longer in place. Even Ronald Reagan was critical of Star Wars.

Freddoso says that he doesn't want to smear Obama as a secret Muslim. There are only four references to Obama's Muslim influences and much to his credit; Freddoso does not dwell on this issue. He is too busy accusing the members of the president's inner circle of being gangsters. It sounds like John Gotti couldn't find work today.

Freddoso defends his analysis. "If you're a liberal, reading the following might make you support Obama even more....But if you're honest, I think you'll agree he's no centrist." This self-serving comment suggests the level of Freddoso's intellectual culpability.

BARACK OBAMA'S UNRECOGNIZED FAULTS

Freddoso's thesis is that the president has some unrecognized faults. He makes a number of unsubstantiated charges. He alleges that Obama was in bed with the old machine politicians and Chicago business interests. Freddoso claims that Obama manipulated Illinois politics to be elected to the United States Senate. He argues that Obama could hardly be considered a reformer. As a presidential candidate, Freddoso alleges Obama employed "dirty politics" to achieve his goals.

"He is the product of a marriage between two of the least attractive parts of Democratic politics-the hard-core radicalism of the 1960s era and Chicago's machine politics. Obama plays hardball and knows when to look the other way." (p. xi) This quote is typical of how Freddoso bends and shapes the material. His thesis is that the president lacks integrity and has no sense of leadership. Freddoso goes even further in linking President Obama to religious radicalism.

Freddoso attacks Obama's church affiliation with Reverend Jeremiah Wright. When he ended his relationship with Wright, Freddoso charges that Obama did so "without disowning the black community." (p. 168) Doesn't Freddoso realize that the Rev. Wright might not represent the entire black community? He went on to point out that the Obama-Wright tiff was due to the Wright's criticism of the presidential candidate, when in fact their differences had a deeper and more complicated past. The Rev. Wright not only used his friendship with Obama for personal gain, but he disrespected, lied about and attempted to manipulate the president. If anything President Obama should be applauded for his restraint and good manners in dealing with Wright.

Freddoso concludes that Obama is always a political animal and one without compassion. The use of statistics and facts is important to Freddoso, and he provides what he calls proofs of Obama's political duplicity. There are twenty-nine references to Reverend Wright, and they all point to the culpability of Barack Obama accepting Wright's radical message.

Freddoso views Obama as a man of minimal integrity, an empty suit who makes promises aimed for reelection, and he labels Obama a manipulator of the press and public opinion. Freddoso suggests that "the gangsters" surrounding him are proof of his lack of leadership.

DAVID FREDDOSO'S TOP NINE PROOFS OF BARACK OBAMA'S DECEPTION

1. BARACK OBAMA WON HIS FIRST ELECTION BY HAVING HIS LAWYERS MANIPULATE THE ELECTORAL PROCESS. (p. 1)
2. THE FRIENDSHIP WITH REVEREND JEREMIAH WRIGHT WAS A PERSONAL AND POLITICAL DECISION. (pp. 152, 163-164, 238, 244, 270)
3. THE PRESIDENT IS PRONE TO RADICALSIM BECAUSE HE KNOWS BILL AYERS, A 1960s ERA TERORIST BOMBER. (p. 121-122, 124, 126, 240)
4. TONY REZKO IS A FRIEND WHO HELPED OBAMA PURCHASE HIS HOUSE THROUGH SHADY DEALS AND HE SOLD HIM PART OF A LOT NEXT DOOR TO HIS HOUSE AT A BELOW MARKET PRICE.
5. OBAMA'S PROMISE TO PLANNED PARENTHOOD IN JULY 2007 TO SUPPORT ENDLESS ABORTIONS HAS NOT BEEN FULLY PUBLICIZED. (p. 197, 201, 203)
6. OBAMA SUPPORTS SCHOOL CHOICE THROUGH VOUCHERS OR TAX CREDITS WHILE SENDING HIS CHILDREN TO ELITE PRIVATE SCHOOLS. (p. 110)
7. BARACK OBAMA WAS NAMED THE MOST LIBERAL U. S. SENATOR IN 2007.
8. AS A U. S. SENATOR, HE VOTED REPEATEDLY FOR SPECIAL INTEREST LEGISLATION. (passim)
9. HE HAS CHALLENGED THE SIGNATURES OF ILLINOIS VOTERS ON ISSUES, PROPOSITIONS AND THE MEASURES HE HAS OPPOSED. (p. 2)

Reviewers point out many alleged errors. On the tax issue, Freddoso suggests that the Obama administration will vote to raise taxes on anyone with a sizeable income. This is, of course, blatant nonsense. Most of the Obama's tax plans were described incorrectly, as was much of the president's early life.

The key to Freddoso's writing is his analysis, which is often shallow, and he fails to support it statistically. An examination of Freddoso's questionable quotes demonstrate his intellectual malfeasance. He has a way with words, but there are generalizations that have little, if any, bearing in fact.

The problem is that Freddoso is glib, and he does have a solid command of the issues. Bernard Lewis, the eminent historian of the Muslim world, argued in his memoirs that there are many ways of interpreting the facts, but the use of innuendo is the worst sin of the serious analyst. Freddoso magnifies that sin.

THE 10 QUESTIONABLE FREDDOSO POINTS

1. He labels Barack Obama the least experienced elected public official to win the presidency. The truth is that Obama had 12 years of government experience eight as an Illinois State Senator and four as a U. S. Senator, whereas Jimmy Carter had 8, Ronald Reagan 8 and Dwight Eisenhower none. (Chapter 9)
2. He views Obama as part of a secret liberal plot to take over the economy and ruin the structure of American politics. (pp.75-76)
3. Freddoso envisions a new socialism with Obama in charge and he takes great pride in outlining the road to ruin. (pp. 130, 283)
4. Obama made money through connections with gangsters. (Passim)
5. The Stroger Families corruption in Cook County politics is given fourteen pages in the book, because Freddoso is able to link them to Obama. (There is no evidence of Obama's involvement in Cook County corruption) (pp. 6-21)
6. All of Obama's political successes are ignored. (passim)
7. The role of Mayor Richard Daley, Freddoso suggests, is to make sure all the gangsters support him. (p. 144)
8. Freddoso writes: "If Barack Obama is a reformer, he may be the first reformer to become president of the United States...." (p. 26) He flunks beginning American history as Theodore Roosevelt and Woodrow Wilson were respected progressive reformers who ascended to the office. Then again maybe Freddoso gets an A for irony or is that I for incomplete thought. (pp. 9, 12-13, 138, 210)
9. Freddoso argues that Obama never once did anything that cost him politically. This ignores the fact that he spoke out against the Iraq War in 2002. This is a fact Freddoso contests. (p. 177)
10. Freddoso argues that Obama won elections not because of his ability to campaign but "Obama has enjoyed success due to the failure of others." (p. 44)

The paranoid mentality is evident in Freddoso's writing. He predicts that Obama's dangerous agendas would become substantive upon his inauguration. This didn't happen in January 2009, as President Obama addressed the nation. This is Freddoso's clever way of suggesting that the Obama Presidency would abuse its power. It is his friends, Freddoso tells us, that "tarnishes" Obama's soul. The language in Freddoso's book is over the top and lacks credibility.

On President Obama's associates he writes: "What do these relationships tell us about his judgment and the type of people with whom he will entrust executive powers if elected." (p. 123) The best way to tarnish Obama is to use people like radical activist Bill Ayers as his so-called friend. The Reverend Wright and Tony Rezko complete the trilogy. All of these people are gone from President Obama's inner-circle. They were acquaintances rather than close friends.

To suggest that someone's reading list forms his or her character is another stretch. According to Freddoso, Obama's reading habits are dissected and with writers like Richard Wright and W. E. B. Dubois, Freddoso makes the point that Obama is "a fellow traveler." (p. 128) Wright and DuBois books are commonly assigned in college courses. There is no evidence that Wright's works did anything more than inspire Obama to academic excellence.

The question of race is a key one. Freddoso doesn't ignore it. He believes, like so many in the right wing nut house, that the president has secret anti-white thoughts. This is, of course, sheer nonsense.

FREDDOSO AND THE QUESTION OF RACE AND COMMUNISTS

It is on the question of race that Freddoso continually shows questionable judgment. He calls Condoleezza Rice a "race traitor." When is the last time Rice and Obama have been placed in a sentence let alone in politics. On the question of race in general, Freddoso is condescending.

Communists are everywhere. He points out that Frank Marshall Davis, the Communist poet, who was a close friend of Obama's grandfather, helped to form Barack Obama's character. "It would be foolish to fear Barack Obama just because he had a Communist father-figure when he was young," (p. 137) Freddoso concludes. It gets worse. Freddoso writes: "If Obama could understand and get along with radicals... Ayers and Bernadette Dohrn...it is because they share similar ideological influences." (p. 139) The red baiting is evident throughout the book. Princeton professor Cornell West is characterized as a progressive socialist who visited Venezuela and Harvard professor Charles Ogletree is condemned for supporting reparations for slavery. What they had to do with Obama and his presidency remains a mystery.

The use of factual material is woeful as Freddoso fills his inane book with examples of people close to Obama. He states that Obama was influenced by Dr. James Cone's book **Black Power And Black Theology**, which was published in 1969. The truth is Barack Obama had never heard of the book or of Cone. He probably has never heard of Freddoso.

THE GANGSTER GOVERNMENT BOOK

After the success of his first book, Freddoso's second critique **Gangster Government: Barack Obama And The New Washington Thugocracy**, published by Regnery, includes chapters with titles that are misleading: "Obamessiah" and "The Radical Influences." Once again the tired old arguments of a cult candidate and a president, who is controlled by radical thought, is restated. By writing for the **National Review** and **Regnery Publishing**, the content is a bit too emphatically anti-Barack Obama. That, in itself, is not a reason to dismiss this book, nor is the title, which suggests legal improprieties. Freddoso writes: "If you want to understand 'Gangster Government,' there's no better place to start than Chicago...." What Freddoso argues is that the union movement is the primary instrument that brought Obama to power. He is also in bed with big business, and Freddoso alleges President Obama protects the big automakers. He uses the Chrysler bankruptcy case, in which the federal government helped the automaker, as a prime example.

Congresswoman Michele Bachmann, a Republican from Minnesota, and the Texas governor, Rick Perry have picked up Freddoso's material, and they have used it in their failed campaigns for the presidency. In March 2011, Bachmann was challenged to define her use of "gangster Government" to describe the Obama administration. "I don't take back my statement on gangster government," Bachmann told one interviewer. This was a phrase she used in a speech at a Tea Party meeting. Shortly thereafter, Bachmann dropped out of the race. It was the same day she told the press that her husband had bought sunglasses for their dog.

What makes Freddoso's second book suspect is the analysis. He contends that Obama's political past is one littered with a lack of ethics and integrity. This is a sad conclusion, as there is no hard evidence that Barack Obama lacks an ethical approach to government. In fact, the opposite is apparent.

The theory that Obama won his election to the Illinois State Senate by forcing his main opponent off the primary ballot, due to election law technicalities, is simply not true. There is no credible evidence that he acted contrary to election law. The notion that a Chicago style thug government exists in the White House is a strange twist of the facts. Freddoso's thesis is that Obama, and his gang of political cohorts regularly abuse their power to create a socialist state. Subsequently, Freddoso argues, Barack Obama is a threat to our freedom. This is, of course, blatant nonsense. But with the economy in decline and foreign policy in transition, it makes sense in the right wing nut house. The only thing that gets in the way are the facts.

How does Freddoso prove his "gangster government" thesis? He cites the influence of organized labor. He has labor leaders wandering down the halls of the West Wing of the White House telling the president what to do. There is no documentation for his explosive charges and other inaccuracies. Freddoso's example of corrupt labor is Andy Stern, the president of the Service Employees International Union (SEIU), he claims that Stern was a guest in the White House nearly sixty times in the first two years of Obama's presidency.

Freddoso alleges that Stern was responsible for swaying the state government workers toward voting for Barack Obama. The statistics show that SEIU workers in the 2010 election were not only overtly Democratic but with 2.1 million members, the SEIU is the fastest growing American union. It is simply good politics to keep Stern happy. This may be the books one accurate conclusion.

The role of lawyers is another Freddoso target. He accuses the president of supporting virtually any special interest tied to liberal lawyers. Freddoso maintains that Vice President Joe Biden told a fund raising group of lawyers: "There are two groups that stand between us and the barbarians at the gate. It's you and organized labor." Rather than making fun of Biden's comment, as Freddoso does, one should consider its validity. The blue-collar, middle class worker and many professionals, who are represented by labor unions, earn wages and have benefits that wouldn't exist without a labor union. The role of lawyers is to prevent the big money right wing forces, like the Koch brothers and Grover Nordquist, from subverting traditional, and constitutionally guaranteed, civil liberties.

The right wing nut house would end the union movement and institute right to work laws that are blatantly measures to impose low wages, poor working conditions and end worker benefits.

Perhaps the most egregious misrepresentation of the Obama administration is Freddoso's contention that the Democrats in the White House are attacking civil liberties. He uses the term "Obama's Gang," to trumpet his cynical view of the decline of American civil liberties. This argument is a mystifying one.

Freddoso supports the policies of Grover Nordquist. A conservative right wing lobbyist with an ego the size of Mount Rushmore, Nordquist, has convinced a large number of Congressman and a small number of U. S. Senators to sign an agreement, which pledges them to oppose all tax hikes. The Nordquist Pledge is one of the most frightening aspects of recent America politics. He is a lobbyist who controls a portion of the House of Representatives on matters of tax hikes. This is extraordinary power. When he appeared on the television show, 60 Minutes, Nordquist giggled when he was asked if he could defeat a Congressman who raised taxes. After he was finished giggling he demonstrated his power. He would defeat any candidate who went back on the Nordquist Pledge. Those who have signed the pledge and changed their mind find that Nordquist pumps millions of dollars into an opponents campaign. Those who repudiate the pledge are sent into political retirement. This is a clear violation of civil rights or more appropriately the power of key conservatives.

Not surprisingly, health care comes in for major criticism. Freddoso argues: "President Obama has stretched the constitutional limits of federal powers beyond their breaking point." This is the same tired and out-of-date criticism leveled toward President Franklin D. Roosevelt. But Freddoso has complete confidence that President Obama will not survive the 2012 presidential election. If Obama is re-elected, Freddoso can still bank the money from his aggressive half-baked books with sloppy research but great writing. Another good thing he still looks good in a suit on television.

As an author, Freddoso has zero accountability. There are no rings of emotional truth in his writing. The discipline, perseverance and the capacity to meet challenges that define Barack Obama are missing in Freddoso's writing.

Chapter 8
IF I HAD BRAINS I WOULD BE IN THE BIG TIME: DAVID LIMBAUGH'S, CRIMES AGAINST LIBERTY AND THE INDICTMENT OF PRESIDENT BARACK OBAMA AND PAMELA GELLER'S OUTRAGEOUS CLAIMS AND A BATHING SUIT

"SHE'S A FRINGE CHARACTER...WHO EVERY DAY IS ON CNN, FOX, THE WASHINGTON POST AND THE NEW YORK TIMES," IBRAHIM HOOPER, COUNCIL ON AMERICAN-ISLAMIC RELATIONS SPEAKING OF PAMELA GELLER

The younger brother of Rush Limbaugh would not have surfaced as a writer without his famous sibling. David Limbaugh does have a marvelous education with a cum laude degree in political science and a law shingle from the University of Missouri. He is also a patriot who served six years in the National Guard. His columns and various publicity releases established his anti-liberal credentials. There is, however, the question of his famous brother, Rush. He is one of the most famous conservative talk show hosts; David is always in his shadow. This is the reason his writing is over the top. David Limbaugh also has five children to support, so his books must sell.

How did David become a well-known conservative critic? To quote David Brock, Limbaugh is part of the Republican Noise Machine that chronicles every misstep in President Obama's political path. Limbaugh has no answers just vexing criticism. He has no substance and little understanding of the political system.

The influence of Christian propagandists, Norman Geisler and Frank Turek, is all over Limbaugh's harsh, right wing message. For some reason, Geisler's sixty books intrigue Limbaugh. "I'm put here for the defense of the Gospel," are the first words on Dr. Geisler's website. He is the author of more than sixty books that advocate "moral absolutism." This is a theory that certain actions are absolutely right or wrong. From Limbaugh's point of view, what Geisler argued was that there are not two sides to an issue, there is no reason to accept compromise, and it is necessary to do everything to destroy the enemy. Translated into American politics, Limbaugh took Geisler's teachings as a mandate to defeat President Barack Obama for a second term. He convinced Limbaugh to overstate his message.

It is Limbaugh's use of language that makes his writing interesting. In a column on February 16, 2012 that appeared in Town Hall.com, Limbaugh compares Moses' parting of the Red Sea to President Obama's attempt to secure bipartisan legislation.

If David Limbaugh has a sister it is Pamela Geller. She is in her early fifties, and she is described as an author, blogger, political activist and social critic. Her argument is to suggest that America is on the verge of becoming a Muslim nation. She founded the American Freedom Defense Initiative Plan (AFDI) and Stop The Islamization of America and co-authored a book, **The Post-American Presidency; The Obama Administration's War On America**. She issued a warning that Islam was taking over America. Her Ayn Rand inspired blog **Atlas Shrugs** is so extreme that even some in the right wing nut house take issue with her.

Limbaugh and Geller have one thing in common; they are making a fortune from pillorying Barack Obama. Their arguments are arcane and innocuous. But Geller has had some success with her pressure groups.

THE AMERICAN FREEDOM DEFENSE INITIATIVE ACTION PLAN

Geller's AFDI is a well-meaning human rights organization dedicated to preserving constitutional rights. Along with Robert Spencer, Geller attacks the academics that are too kind to Islam. She also is critical of the Courts. She believes that they protect immigrant rights while preserving Muslim religious practices. Geller is determined to educate people on the dangers of Islam.

"AFDI acts against the treason being committed by national, state, and local government officials...." Geller writes. Her supporters meet and challenge any and all demonstrations that argue for Islamic rights. She is adamant that Sharia law is encroaching upon the American legal system.

AFDI believes that the U. S. government is being infiltrated with Islamic jihadists. She has a website Jihad Watch that daily warns of Islamic forces plotting to take down the U. S. Jihad Watch is as much the brainchild of conservative icons David Horowitz and Robert Spencer, as it is of Geller. The Anti-Defamation League and the Southern Poverty Law Center have identified Jihad Watch as a hate site. In London, Abdel Bari Atwan, the editor in chief of the London based Pan-Arab newspaper, **Al Quds Al Arabi**, editorialized that Jihad Watch did a better job of keeping track of Islamic extremists than the FBI and MI6. The Council of American-Islamic Relations (CAIR) charged that Jihad Watch was an "internet hate site." Robert Spencer argues that this is nonsense, he stated that Jihad Watch stands for equal rights and freedom of expression.

When Pamela Geller and David Limbaugh demonize President Barack Obama, they share a belief that the U. S. is headed for Islamization due to the Democratic Party. They appear like strange bedfellows, politically speaking, but they have a great deal in common.

LIMBAUGH AND KELLER: BAD BREATH, BAD CLOTHES AND BAD OPINIONS

Why are Pamela Geller and David Limbaugh together in a chapter on right wing nuts? There are many reasons: 1.) They are both very good appearing on the media, and they are sophisticated and intelligent bloggers. 2.) They both push the issue of Muslim radicalism and President Obama's lack of leadership. 3.) They both have a strong definition of what America is and isn't, and they claim to envision an apocalyptic future. 4.) Geller is Jewish and concerned about the growing Illumination, as she calls it, of America. She went too far when she suggested, with a mock up of her in a Nazi uniform, that Supreme Court Justice Elena Kagan, who is Jewish, supported Nazi ideology. She also has falsely clamed that Obama's mother "was involved in pornography." 5.) Geller also suggests that Muslims have sex with goats. When she has been called to task for her comments, Geller remarks: "You can't make jokes or make fun." She is the female Don Imus of the right wing nut house without Imus' intelligence, media savvy and warm personality. But she does look better in a bathing suit. She frequently posts pictures of herself on the Internet in skimpy garb.

Big Boy Roberts: "I think these people have bad breath, bad manners and bad opinions, but I love their books." Apparently Big Boy Roberts has been in Southern Arizona too long. It is Limbaugh's four books, published by Regnery, that have brought him into the forefront of the right wing nuthouse.

DAVID LIMBAUGH'S FOUR BOOKS ARE ALMOST FICTIONAL

For a decade, David Limbaugh's propaganda pieces have found a receptive conservative audience. His books have premises that are difficult to accept. In 2002, Limbaugh's **Absolute Power: The Legacy of Corruption In The Clinton-Reno Justice Department** came out with a thud. I was an inspector with the Bureau of Alcohol, Tobacco and Firearms for four years and two days, and then I regretfully resigned to return to a professor's position. I mention this because there is not one fact associated with ATF that is correct in Limbaugh's book. He writes that the federal government is attacking the tobacco industry. The truth is that much of what the tobacco industry does through ATF is self-regulation. They do a good job, and ATF's regulation powers are strong and non-partisan.

LIMBAUGH'S STYLE AND SCANDAL

The most egregious error in Limbaugh's book is the notion that the government makes more money from the tobacco industry than the cigarette manufacturers. But it is scandal that intrigues Limbaugh. His chapter, "The Mother Of All Scandals," is a look at campaign finance misdeeds in the Clinton administration. There is nothing new here and the facts are distorted. The British author Ambrose Evans-Pritchard's book, **The Secret Life of Bill Clinton** is a much better interpretation of the same material. Limbaugh's writing is also like carving on stone. That is, it is flat, uninspired and convoluted. That's the good news. You don't want the fact check sheet that I have compiled. David is an incredibly shoddy researcher whose books a sixth grader would criticize. It would take the sixth grader the entire school year to finish the criticism.

Things got worse in 2004, when Limbaugh's **Persecution: How Liberals Are Waging War Against Christianity** appeared to an adoring fundamentalist audience. This book is a joke, but it sold so well that Harper's put it out in a deluxe paperback edition. Right wing books sell. Even if the material is a comedy act.

It is the title of David Limbaugh's book, **Crimes Against Liberty: An Indictment of Barack Obama** that gives one the feeling that he is not fair and balanced. Like most critics, Limbaugh accuses President Obama of something close to treason. Thank God for Rush Limbaugh. If he didn't exist, we would not have to read the ranting of his brother. David Limbaugh is the minor league version of his brother. He has the same cigar. He has the same awful hair. He has he same bad clothes. He has the same nasally voice.

DAVID LIMBAUGH'S INFLUENCE ON SENATOR MCCONNELL

The rising number of fear inducing e-mails, the use of incendiary language, and the scurrilous attack on President Obama's character has created a new American politics. Obama's detractors include Kentucky Republican Senator Mitch McConnell who said it best when he stated that his goal is to keep Obama from a second term.

Senator McConnell uses his Kentucky seat and his role as Senator Minority Leader to lambast President Obama. There is not a semblance of fairness in his opinions, and it appears that he is David Limbaugh's disciple. He has accused the president of "arrogance." This is a strange charge, because McConnell is short on the facts and long on opinions.

In press conferences, Senator McConnell lacks personality. He is simply an obstructionist who will go to any extreme to oppose President Obama. McConnell looks like a constipated owl. He is a person who says he is strong on principles, and he views the president as an opportunist. The hard left agenda that he ascribes to President Obama prevents any form of compromise. "The single most important thing we want to achieve is for President Obama to be a one-term president," McConnell remarked to Joshua Green. McConnell allegedly remarked to his wife, Elaine Chao, "Goodness Elaine there is a Negro in the White House."

DAVID LIMBAUGH'S ISSUES

The issues that David Limbaugh and most other irresponsible right wing critics argue are: 1.) Liberals, Progressives, Marxists, Communists and Feminists are jumbled together into an anti-American stew; 2.) President Obama is not really an American but he is an Indonesian; 3.) Obama's mother and father were radicals with anti-American leanings; 4.) He applied to Harvard as a foreign student; 5.) Obama is a Muslim in faith and a black nationalist in politics; 6.) His inner White House circle has similar politics; 7.) Obama's birth certificate, social security number and education records are secret and sealed. He also charges that the documents have been manipulated. It is this same old tired theme of America heading into a socialist nation that dominates Limbaugh's thinking.

Limbaugh, like his brother Rush, describes himself as a conservative who is critical of the media. He is also a constant critic of environmentalists, and those who promote climate change. One wonders if the Koch brothers are funding David Limbaugh.

WHAT MOTIVATES DAVID LIMBAUGH'S CRITICISM?

Since David Limbaugh is a minor figure in the right wing nut house, what motivates him? The answer is failure. He served on the Cape Girardeau City Council for eight years, he was mayor pro-tem for six years, and he is on numerous city boards and committees. His inability to move beyond local politics inspires his hateful criticism. He is a regular contributor to the right wing website Worldnetdaily.com, and he writes for the **Washington Times**. What motivates Limbaugh is a belief that liberal media bias controls American politics.

"President Obama is calling for dramatic defense cuts that could threaten our national survival while obstructing structural reforms to our entitlement programs that are essential for our national financial survival," David Limbaugh wrote on January 5, 2012. From this convoluted prose, one can see that Limbaugh fails to understand the simple premise behind President Obama's foreign policy. The U. S. will have a strong presence in the world without military occupation.

THE DANGERS OF LIMBAUGH'S CRIMES AGAINST LIBERTY

David Limbaugh's **Crimes Against Liberty: An Indictment Against President Barack Obama** is a dangerous book. In fifteen well-written and erudite chapters, he uses his considerable intellect to indict the president. The book begins with the notion that the President is a narcissist, and he is unable to accept criticism. This is a ridiculous conclusion. It gets worse. The book charges that Obama is so ego driven that he has given up much of what past American presidents have earned as policymakers. He uses Fox TV News minion Charles Krauthammer, who is trained as a psychiatrist, to advance the idea that the president doesn't represent the U. S. He is strictly a self-motivated, ego driven person. A section on clinical narcissism has Limbaugh acting as a medical doctor. The idea of anyone with the name Limbaugh complaining about narcissism is laughable.

After attacking Obama's character, a chapter, "Fraud Against The Electorate," argues that the president has neither the personality nor the fortitude for leadership. A chapter "The Liar," needs no explanation. Limbaugh informs us that President Obama is not non-partisan. Does Limbaugh realize how inane this comment is or how it reflects his political naiveté? Limbaugh continues by informing the reader that the president is the same good old boy that has caused America its present unemployment, foreign policy and housing problems. Apparently, Limbaugh has never heard of George W. Bush. This chapter is long on opinion and short on key facts. Limbaugh concludes about Obama: "His outright, habitual lies are a fundamental aspect of governance." (p. 89)

In chapters four through eleven, Limbaugh continues to argue that it is American institutions that suffer from President Obama's lack of leadership. Once again the writing is crisp, clear and interesting, but the facts and key examples are missing to prove the charges. While ranting about healthcare reform, bowing down to Arab leaders and coddling Communists, Socialists and other radicals, Limbaugh accuses President Obama of violating the rule of law, terrorizing the private sector and generally disregarding American business interests.

The last section of Limbaugh's tome argues that the president is taxing America toward bankruptcy. This threatens the general welfare as well as national security. This section of the Limbaugh book has some merit. The problem is that he is blinded by his hatred for President Obama. Yet, many of his arguments hit the mark. He points to waste in government spending, and his list of thirty problematical government-spending areas is one that Republicans and Democrats alike could consult. (pp. 286-288) His examination of the government debt and spending practices is a sober and generally correct one. But he is overly concerned with blaming the Treasury Secretary, Tim Geithner, for economic failures rather than tracing these problems back to President George W. Bush.

On the foreclosure controversy, Limbaugh is angry that President Obama is working on various plans, including Harp 2.0, to help homeowners escape the burdens of a rapidly descending housing market. It is in this section that Limbaugh shows little knowledge of and interest in explaining the Obama administration's approach to the depressed housing market. Limbaugh describes the three to five month loan modifications with little knowledge and less accuracy. (p. 303)

Limbaugh cites statistics on the home bailout program: "In June, 2010, it was reported that more than a third of the 1.24 million borrowers who enrolled in the mortgage bailout program had already dropped out." (p. 303) What they failed to understand or appreciate is that the 400,000 people who dropped out of the mortgage bailout program did so because they sold their homes. The Democrats provided a bailout that prevented these homes from going into foreclosure.

The most egregious argument that Limbaugh brokers is that Barack Obama is anti-American. In the right wing nut house, this is a primary contention. Richard Hofstadter observed that when people can't prove government duplicity, they explain it with conspiracy theories. The idea of a Muslim majority in America is one of the right wing nut house pet theories. But there are smaller, less significant, charges brandished from the right. At the Random Hills Trailer Park in Mesa Arizona there is a right wing crazy that claims that the Obama administration will place a guard at banks to catalogue what you take out of your private banking box. The argument is clear, there is no longer a respect for privacy or traditional civil liberties.

Limbaugh concludes his book by suggesting that a Saul Alinsky America is on the horizon. (p. 389) His argument is that "America is in a dangerously rapid nosedive under Obama's navigation." (p. 390)

DAVID LIMBAUGHT ATTACK ON PRESIDENT OBAMA: THE GREAT DESTROYER

In June 2012, David Limbaugh's **The Great Destroyer: Barack Obama's War On The Republic** argued that the end of the free market economy and the principles of limited government threatened the nation. The attack on federal bureaucrats and left wing socialists who Limbaugh sees running the country was strident.

In order to prove his points, Limbaugh analyzes Obamacare, and he concludes that it will cost more than one thinks. The level of medical care also will decline. The key to the book is the notion that Obama is ignoring the Constitution by having appointed bureaucrats who erode American democracy on a daily basis.

The use of footnotes is one of the academic tricks of the right wing nut house. Not surprisingly, Limbaugh has 1184 footnotes. By examining the footnotes there is not one manuscript collection, there is not one academic dissertation, the **Washington Post**, the **New York Times**, the **Wall Street Journal** and most other mainstream newspaper are represented by only a few articles in the footnotes. The mainstream political press is not represented. Whether or not you like the **New Republic**, the **Economist**, **Time**, **Newsweek**, the **Atlantic Monthly** or the **New Yorker**, they do represent a responsible media segment of American politics. Limbaugh conveniently ignores these sources. What you have are such obscure and insignificant sources as **RealClearPolitics**, **Townhall.com**, the **Tea Party Tribune**, the **American Thinker**, and **TheStir.CafeMom.com**. Who needs the mainstream media when you have such reliable sources? This pitiful book ends with the comment: "I must thank my brother Rush for personally inspiring me, for opening up doors to me directly and indirectly, for leading the charge for American conservatives...." (p. 407) Yuck!

PAMELA GELLER'S CONNECTION TO THE RIGHT WING NUT HOUSE

Pamela Geller succinctly states her ideas in her blog and in her books. She left Hofstra before completing her degree. She is almost like the sister that David Limbaugh never had and she looks better in a bathing suit. Somehow she convinced Simon and Schuster to publish her book, **The Post American Presidency: The Obama Administration's War on America** which argues:: "In the first month as President, he showed himself ready to give up American sovereignty for the primacy of international law...." (p. 1). As ridiculous as her arguments sound, she sold a large number of books by frightening Americans about their future.

In **The Post American Presidency**, Geller brings out all the right wing nut house themes. She argues that Obama is not an American, his mother and father were Communists, his birth certificate is false, his social security card forged, his education records are suspect and she believes that he was a foreign student at Harvard. She also argues that he is a Muslim and a black nationalist. To Geller's way of arguing, he is a socialist-communist who employs a circle of like thinking bureaucrats.

Not only is the book full of errors, sloppy writing, convoluted thoughts and misinterpretation, it is slanderous and dishonest.

Geller is in league with the mustached former U. N. Ambassador John Bolton, who wrote the forward to her book. They are Bush neocon's that believe that President Obama is a threat to our liberties. Geller may be in the top five of writers in the right wing nut house for sheer audacity.

PAMELA WHO IS PAMELA GELLER AND WHY IS SHE IMPORTANT?

Beauty, photogenic good looks, a blog and a media presence are among the requirements for membership in the right wing nut house. Geller is also a brilliant business person who worked for a decade at the **New York Daily News**. Then she discovered blogging and the Internet. Fortunately, the tools to research and write dispassionately are not among the requirements for conservatism. Pamela Geller is the brains and editor behind Atlas Shrugs.com, and she is also the executive direction of the American Freedom Defense Initiative and the Stop Islamization of America organization. There is a picture of her with Robert Spencer on the Internet in a tight dress that is scant. She is obviously headed toward Ann Coulter territory.

As a columnist for the World Net Daily, she is an informed conservative. David Horowitz recognized her contribution in 2010, when she received the Annie Taylor Award For Courage

Geller is also a serious blogger. When the controversy over building a Mosque near New York's Ground Zero emerged, Geller was in the forefront of the opposition. Her blog stated that she was in "my Burka." So I looked. It was a two-piece bathing suit that revealed all you need to know. I couldn't read the article because she looked so good in her swimming pool in a skimpy bathing suit. Oh, the blog. Well, she opposes building the Mosque near Ground Zero. Sorry, I am still looking at her in the bathing suit. I wonder if Newt Gingrich has gone on her web sight. He did. Of course, it was for political purposes.

The liberal **Huffington Post** labeled Geller "The Queen of Muslim Bashers." In her campaign to prevent the construction of the Grand Zero Mosque, Geller placed anti-Muslim ads in several city newspapers. She quickly became a major television presence. She has also accused President Obama of anti-Semitism, as well as posting a blog that stated that Barack Obama was the love child of Malcolm X.

The issue that Geller loves is the Barack Obama birth certificate controversy. She claims that Obama's mother, Stanley Ann Dunham was in Washington State in August 1961 when Barack was born. Her evidence is that the University of Washington removed material on Stanley Ann Dunham from the registrar's office. At Mercer Island High School, it is alleged that Stanley Ann Dunham read the Koran. Sounds logical to me. She has a blog stating that the final report on Obama's birth certificate is in, and the fraud advisers for the Association of Fortified Fraud Examiners, the American College of Forensic Examiners and the International Information Systems Forensics Association all agree that the birth certificate has been altered. Homer Simpson also agreed that it was a fraud. Beavis and Butthead are still considering the question.

There are other ridiculous charges. But I think you get the point. The Media Matters For America labels Geller's blogs "extreme." She also has some interesting thoughts on Jews. "It galls me that the Jews I fight for are self-destructive, suicidal even," Geller wrote. The reason she thinks Jews are self-destructive is that most of them vote for the Democratic Party candidates.

One Internet site labels Geller "The Looniest Blogger Ever." That is debatable but she is in the running for the looniest blogger. Some of Geller's observations include: 1.) The allegation that the president has "strange sexual predilections" and "he should be investigated." That is a new charge. 2.) She claims there were only two reasons to travel to Pakistan in the early 1980s: drugs and jihad. 3.) "Obama deceitfully hid his Muslim background…." This observation is not new but the venom in Geller's prose is unmistakable. 4.) She accuses the president of "bald-faced lies to the Jews." Is this better than big hair lies? There is no need to continue her comments. They reflect ignorance, hostility and unhealthy political opinions. This is America, you can say what you want.

She has other views. Some of these opinions are in the mainstream. The Tea Party is one of her causes. Not surprisingly, she became a darling of the Tea Party for her anti-Islamic observations. Jeffrey Goldberg labeled her a "bigoted blogger." You have to decide for yourself.

Chapter 9
OVERSTATED LANGUAGE: MICHELLE MALKIN ON THE CULTURE OF CORRUPTION: OBAMA AND HIS TEAM OF TAX CHEATS, CROOKS AND CRONIES

"I'VE BEEN ASKED. 'WHAT DO YOU OLD FOLKS DO NOW THAT YOU'RE RETIRED?' I'M FORTUNATE TO HAVE A CHEMICAL ENGINEERING DEGREE...ONE OF THE THINGS I ENJOY MOST IS CONVERTING BEER, WINE AND VODKA INTO URINE. THEN I PISS ON A PHOTO OF OBAMA!" HAROLD SCHLUMBERG

The hostile feelings toward President Barack Obama are reflected in Harold Schlumberg's inane comment. His picture and words on the Internet, in a site that praises beer, is a new low in the right wing nut house. A beer praising website that talks about pissing on the president! Boy have we come a long way. This attitude is the product of Fox TV News and female political terriers like the irrepressible Michelle Malkin. She loves Schlumberg. His comments have made him an instant celebrity. Not for talking about beer but for crude remarks that make no sense about the president. The old fart is talking about urinating on the president. He is constantly on the Internet that is when he can tear himself away from Fox TV News. Then he goes out on the front porch to scream about the Obama administration. Good old Schlumberg. He sits in front of the Fox TV News network and genuflects for Michelle Malkin. She has the same over the top delivery and a nasty look on her face as he does when he is on his porch. She also has overstated language, and she is after all a minority. As a Filipina, she detests, despises and attacks liberals. That is as long as the paychecks keep coming into her sizeable bank account. Ironically, I was warned about Michelle Malkin almost two decades ago. When I spoke in the Philippines for the 1996 Century Centennial, I was told by half a dozen high ranking government officials to beware of Michelle Malkin. As former Philippine Vice President, Salvador Laurel remarked: "She is an attack dog in the conservative right wing nut house." She has not gone unnoticed in the Philippines, as she is a well-respected local celebrity. But she is closer in attitude to Schlumberg.

The quote from Harold Schlumberg suggests the depth of feeling toward the president. It is sad, tragic and ironic that the right wing nut house has so much media presence. The fact that these opinions are all over the Internet is even more tragic. The right wing nut house has some college degree folks screaming about President Obama. Malkin has a B.A. from an excellent liberal arts college. All those Communist professors trained her to think independently. This is further proof that those Communist college professors aren't doing their job. She can't tell a liberal from a conservative. They all look alike to her.

What has happened to liberalism? Fortunately, we have Michelle Malkin to tell us what is wrong with American democracy. Not to mention the perilous and ill-advised journey that liberalism has taken since she received her first paycheck.

In analyzing Michelle Malkin remember that she has a sharp tongue and a brassy attitude. Her story begins in 1992 when Salvadore Laurel, a Vice President in the Philippines, recognized her skilled writing and acerbic criticism.

PHILIPPINE VP SALVADOR LAUREL ON MICHELLE MALKIN

In 1996, I was a featured speaker at the 100 Year Centennial of Philippine Independence. I had written a book, **Jose Rizal: Philippine**

Nationalist As Political Scientist as well as three others books on Filipinos in California. They were all well received in the historical journals and popular press. A phone call from Salvador H. Laurel, who was Vice President of the Philippines from 1986 to 1992, under Corazon Aquino, led to a few drinks and dinner in Manila. He wanted to talk about Michele Malkin. I had never heard of her.

When I returned to California, I found that Malkin recently had been a fellow at the Competitive Enterprise Institute. As I journeyed home to teach my courses, I had no idea that the first Filipino journalist to attain national stature in America would be a staunch, conservative Filipina. She would turn out to be a famous and well-paid conservative right wing critic. Not only is she an attack dog, she is articulate and well educated.

Malkin qualifies to enter the right wing nut house by her frequent, incendiary statements on Fox TV News. She made untenable claims about President Obama, and she displayed perpetual envy over his leadership. There is no doubt that Malkin is upset over affirmative action. Whether or not she is an affirmative action baby is not clear. What is clear is that she believes any special preference program is a mistake. She has not just a dislike for President Obama, she also displays a persistent hatred. This mind set has led to some outrageous claims. While much of what Malkin writes is interesting, there is a dark side.

An excellent example of Malkin's dark side is a January 6, 2012 post in which she criticizes President Obama for issuing orders to his "constitution-subverting minions…." This comment came after the administration created a $1.5 billion dollar summer job program. She gets a paycheck and believes others should suffer. But this is only one of her outrageous statements. A list of Malkin's seven worst Obama statements for 2011 calls her credibility into question.

MICHELLE MALKIN'S SEVEN WORST 2011 OBAMA STATEMENTS
1. "THE SCANDALOUS BANKRUPTCY OF SOLYNDRA (A SHADY CALIFORNIA SOLAR POWER COMPANY) THAT RECEIVED $535 MILLION IN STIMULUS FUNDS AND IS NOW UNDER INVESTIGATION BY THE FBI…." SEPTEMBER 14, 2011
2. "IMMEDIATELY AFTER PRESIDENT OBAMA TOOK OFFICE, HIS HOLLYWOOD BENEFACTORS CLAMORED FOR THE CRE-

ATION OF A SECRETARY OF CULTURE." IS THERE A POINT HERE? JULY 20, 2011

3. "THE WASHINGTON POST AND NEWSWEEK BOTH INDULGED IN TRANSITION-MANIA, LAUNCHING WEBSITES FEATURING THE BY-THE-MINUTE BLOGGING OF BARACK OBAMA'S 'HISTORIC' AND 'UNPRECEDENTED' ASCENSION TO POWER." GEE MICHELLE THERE IS AN AFRICAN AMERICAN IN THE WHITE HOUSE. QUOTED IN MICHELLE MALKIN, CULTURE OF CORRUPTION, p. 3

4. "KA CHING, KA CHING. PRESIDENT OBAMA'S PERPETUAL CAMPAIGN CASH-O-MATIC MACHINE KICKS INTO HIGH GEAR....AS THE PRESIDENT HEADS TO HOLLYWOOD...." MICHELLE YOU SOUND ENVIOUS, APRIL 20, 2011

5. "BARACK OBAMA'S NEW ERA OF CIVILITY WAS OVER BEFORE IT BEGAN." MICHELLE YOU ARE A SORE LOSER, FEBRUARY 25, 2011

6. "PRESIDENT OBAMA'S GRABBY-HANDED ENVIRONMENTAL BUREAUCRATS HAVE EARNED YET ANOTHER SPANKING FROM THE FEDERAL JUDICIARY," MICHELLE YOU ARE AN ENVIRONMENTALIST LIKE OTHER RIGHT WINGERS, FEBRUARY 2011

7. "NO MATTER HOW YOU REARRANGE PRESIDENT OBAMA'S INNER CIRCLE, IT STILL LOOKS, SMELLS AND TASTES LIKE A ROTTEN CHICAGO DEEP-DISH PIZZA." BE CAREFUL MICHELLE, ANGELO AND BRUNO MAY GET UPSET, JANUARY 5, 2011

THE ROAD TO MEDIA STARDOM STARTS IN HIGH SCHOOL

When Malkin's father arrived in America, he was a doctor trained in the Philippines. A high level education began a successful medical career. Growing up in the small town of Absecon in southern New Jersey, Michelle had a normal, if somewhat boring, childhood. Her mother was a teacher and the family was upper middle class. Her parents were Reagan Republicans who had little interest or knowledge of politics.

By all accounts, Michelle Malkin is a talented musician and writer. In high school, she edited the school newspaper, as she trained to become a concert pianist. She had tremendous discipline, was well read and wrote incessantly. At Holy Spirit Roman Catholic High School, she was a shy but model student. This is a private Catholic school, and it maintains a rigorous academic reputation. Her obsessive-compulsive desire to achieve made Malkin an academic and extracurricular star. She not only edited the school newspaper. She displayed liberal political ideas. Her ideas often ran counter to her teachers. Then she went on to study at the liberal arts college, Oberlin, in 1988, and she found the liberal professors obnoxious. At least for a brief time, she was a typical college liberal. Somewhere along the line at Oberlin, she morphed into a raging conservative.

At Oberlin, she attacked the affirmative action program. She detested special admission requirements for minorities and women. While Malkin criticized the affirmative action program, she suddenly found herself verbally attacked by her left wing counterparts. Malkin balked at what she termed the liberal terror at Oberlin. This created a life long conservatism that matured over the years into brilliant, if erratic, blogs and an honorary membership in the right wing nut house. There is a great deal in her educational background that explains her blatant and unperceptive conservatism.

When she entered Oberlin, with the intention of majoring in music, Malkin quickly changed her concentration to English. At Oberlin, she was a blue-collar working class student with part time jobs as a tax preparation aide, a press inserter and a network news librarian. Along the way, she became angry about what she perceived as the elitist, selfish, trendy liberal, well-financed and dilettantish Oberlin students. Malkin wasn't one of them. She became hostile over her elitist education. A liberal education, she told close friends, was a waste of time. Malkin looked around the campus, and the affirmative action program continually disgusted her. It not only brought in minority students, but she allegedly wondered if they qualified for admission. She has never stated whether or not she was admitted due to affirmative action.

JESSE DYLAN MALKIN'S CONSERVATIVE INFLUENCE

She displayed a writing talent that made her the envy of her peers. Her intellect and writing skills soon led to a boy friend. She met Jesse Dylan Malkin, a Jewish student who grew up in the shadow of the University of California, Berkeley. As Jesse matured in this liberal Berkeley hotbed, he evolved into a staunch conservative. He was much like his future wife, a contrarian who could not stand liberalism. He was also a superb athlete. Jesse was captain of Oberlin's cross-country team, and he was a Rhodes Scholar. He studied for a year at England's Oxford University. While at Oberlin, Malkin had political aspirations, and he began writing for a right of center student publication. Soon Michelle Maglalang began working with Malkin, and she was on the road to becoming his wife. He also helped her define her conservative credentials. By the time she graduated, one of her friends remarked that, she was still more of a left of center student than a conservative right-winger. That would soon end with work in Los Angeles and Seattle for daily newspapers. It was Oberlin that helped Michelle frame her political philosophy.

Looking back on her Oberlin days, Malkin labeled her experience as one that was "radically left-wing." When she attacked Oberlin's affirmative action program, in a school publication, she unwittingly set her future writing career in motion.

What Malkin fails to mention is that her husband not only established a conservative journal at Oberlin, he received funding from the right wing nut house. His newspaper, founded in 1989, was a venue for a group of students who were recruited as conservative students to earn PhDs to teach in college. In other words, Malkin was furious with the political concepts of his professors, and he became a lead neo-conservative. He would find and help to train conservative college professors. This was a strange notion for an undergraduate at a major liberal arts university. To find people to spread the conservative message, Malkin needed a ready money source.

The Institute For Educational Affairs (IEA) funded Malkin's conservative message. William Simon and Irving Kristol sought out promising PhD candidates and then helped them through graduate school. Not surprisingly, this was Malkin's goal. The support of big business, notably Coca-Cola, Dow Chemical, Ford Motor Company, General Electric, K-Mart, Mobil Oil and the Nestle Corporation, is indicative of the level of big business interest in altering the campus message. If college professors couldn't contain their liberalism, IEA would train and support conservative scholars.

One of IEA's most important recipients, Dinesh D'Souza, followed the conservative line with **The End of Racism**. In that book, he outlined conservative principles for a multiracial society. In reality, D'Souza's book is a polemical attack on affirmative action. He argues that Christian whites study harder than minority students. There is no need to denigrate anyone by suggesting that his book should be read. Pass on it. If you agree with D'Souza, you may want to thank IEA for it.

MICHELLE MAGLALANG'S FORMATIVE YEARS: ON THE WAY TO BEING A MALKIN

When Michelle Maglalang began working for Malkin's newspaper, it was love at first sight. She quickly turned romance into domestic tranquility. Political tranquility was another matter. As H. Y. Nahm observed, Michelle became "the radical right's Asian pit-bull."

Her first assignment for Malkin's newspaper was to renounce Oberlin's affirmative action program. The sight of a Filipina screaming out about special preference made her an instant favorite in the right wing nut house. "It was seeing the violent paroxysms it caused on the Left that really put me on my way to a career in opinion journalism," Michelle remarked. One of the things she might do as an English major is to make better word choices. Paroxysms suggests there is too much emotion on the left, she should check the right and her own writings. But she was still in college, so we can give her a pass.

After she married Jesse Dylan Malkin in Los Angeles in 1993, she began working in the newspaper field. It was at the **Los Angeles Daily News** from 1992-1994 that many of her early political opinions crystallized. The liberal Democratic, ethnic stew that was Los Angeles politics caused her to look askance at left wing goals and accomplishments.

In the San Fernando Valley, the **Los Angeles Daily News** is a small step above the free shopping news that is tossed on every doorstep. It was here she learned to produce quick copy. This is one reason for her productivity. She also appealed to the less educated, blue-collar, suburban lower middle class individual. These folks were quick to accept her slanted conservative opinions. Her columns on illegal immigrants caught the attention of conservatives. She received positive mail on her columns and national recognition was in the offing.

Oberlin College and the **Los Angeles Daily News** had a dramatic impact upon Malkin. When she returned to Oberlin, fourteen years after graduation to deliver a speech, she remarked: "Liberals see racism where it doesn't exist, fabricate it when they can't find it, and ignore it within their own ranks." She evolved into one of America's more prominent conservative voices. How she got there is an interesting story.

When she left Southern California, she complained that the **Los Angeles Daily News** was a cesspool of journalistic incompetence. She already had a view of her greatness, and she would pursue it in the Pacific Northwest.

Her husband completed a PhD at the Rand Graduate School, which is attached to the conservative political think tank, the Rand Corporation, and he moved as a Rand consultant to Seattle.

As Malkin looked back upon Oberlin she described her alma mater as "radically left wing." There were many incidents at college that shaped her unyielding conservatism. "That's where I first really encountered the vicious response you can get when you stand up to a political orthodoxy," Malkin continued. "I was not a huge lightning rod until the end of my tenure at Oberlin." When she entered the journalistic arena, Malkin was determined to become a lightning rod. She succeeded beyond her wildest expectations.

THE LOS ANGELES AND SEATTLE COLUMNS: STARDOM BECKONS

When Michelle Malkin began her journalistic career, she was not exactly a household name. She realized it. So the language and intent in her newspaper articles, and, later in her books, sought out a conservative audience. It worked. In less than a decade, she became one of the darlings of the radical right. As a writer, who is Michelle Malkin? That is the million-dollar question.

In Los Angeles, when she began writing a weekly column for the **LA Daily News**, there was room for a liberal woman columnist. She quickly proved that this was not her forte. She had a conservative message, and she was incensed that the liberal media wouldn't listen.

Malkin wrote effectively complaining about illegal immigrants, liberal politicians and Democrats who used the minority vote. She was already a conservative pit bull, when she left to work for the **Seattle Times**. She clearly saw her future. It was as a vociferous right wing critic. One who would tilt at Don Quixote type windmills. She learned her craft in Los Angeles. It was now time to hone her arguments.

The tenure with the **L. A. Daily News** infuriated Malkin. She recalled: "When I was twenty-four and making less than twenty-five thousand dollars a year, I did it by eating Spaghetti-O's, Ramen noodles and Swanson pot pies for dinner." It never occurred to Malkin to have her husband get a job. But the economic difficulties at home definitely spurred her conservatism. It also intensified her negative feelings about liberals.

In 1995, Malkin was a Warren Brookes Journalism Fellow at the Competitive Enterprise Center in Washington D. C. This is an organization that states its goals as "free markets and limited government." It is a training ground for entry into the right wing nut house. The CEC advertises itself as a center to promote "freedom and fairness." The truth is that it is to end governmental policies at the state level. Influencing the media is one of CEC's stated goals. To that end the fellowships train conservative journalists.

The depth of Malkin's conservatism is traced to Seattle, Washington. She looked at the famous yachts, the upscale Mercer Island homes where millionaires like Bill Gates lived as well as the latte-cappuccino lifestyle of liberal Seattleites. She skewered the local culture in her opinion and editorial pieces.

In 1996, she wrote popular columns for the **Seattle Times**. In three years her writing was syndicated through Creators Syndicate. She now had a national audience. What Malkin observed in Seattle was that the Asian population was political, vocal and worked within the system. She argued that the liberal Democratic tone in and around Seattle held back the Asian-American population. This view radicalized her thought and writing.

In Seattle, Malkin began her rise to stardom. The real impetus to fame and fortune came when her husband accepted a RAND consulting job in Maryland. She began writing columns on national politics that were over the top. One column: "Sluts And Nuts-And Our Daughters," called Britney Spears "insipid and shameless…." Along the way Malkin argued that environmental factors had nothing to do with breast cancer. She also went after actress Julia Roberts in an April 14, 2004 column: "The Truth About Erin Brockovich." Other women were a target of her acid tongue. Senator Elizabeth Dole was attacked when Malkin called her "Sugar Lips." Malkin wrote that Dole "has been wading inside the Beltway for decades, like a giddy queen bee in a bottomless pot of taxpayer-subsidized honey." Nice writing but there isn't an ounce of truth to it. The use of facts or proofs is not a part of Malkin's writing. She is a writer with a florid style and little substance.

ON HER WAY TO BLOGS AND JOURNALISTIC RICHES

Malkin's conservative blog and a syndicated column are popular with a number of news shows. Fox TV News, MSNBC and C-Span have her appear as a frequent guest, and she tailors her message for the programs. She is a career blogger and conservatives are a perfect audience for her truncated message. The right wing publishing company, Regnery Books, releases her conservative book diatribes. By the time that she appeared on Fox TV News, Malkin was a well-received conservative. She was a regular on the O'Reilly Factor. Then abruptly in 2007, Malkin claimed that derogatory statements made about her by Geraldo Rivera prevented her from appearing with Bill O'Reilly. She had an agenda.

From 2007, she spent more time writing, blogging and securing well paid public speaking engagements. She appeared on Fox And Friends from time to time, and in 2009 she began writing for the **St. Louis Globe Democrat**. This was another major turning point. Her writing increasingly found a larger and more receptive audience.

Her political blog, MichelleMalkin.com helped to pave the way for increased popularity. It was one of the five most visited conservative websites. When she attacked the hip hop artist Akon for nasty comments about women, his label the Universal Music Group, took down some of his music from You Tube. She is a strong supporter of censorship. Malkin censors all responses on her website. Isn't this the conservative way?

THE MICHELLE MALKIN BLOG

Her blog is an interesting and informative one, and she is constantly criticizing the Democratic Party, liberals and President Obama. If you go to her website, http://michellemalkin.com/2012/05/15/obamainhistory/ you will find a treasure trove of conservative information.

She uses her blog to compose editorials, publish faux news stories and generally harass and intimidate the Democratic Party. Her blog comments read like a junior high school government class that is unhappy with the prospect of attending high school.

Malkin is not stupid. There is a note to Michelle Obama that Malkin doesn't approve of all the blogs. Then there are ten pages of blogs about the Obama's marriage. One suspects that Edward Klein's dreadful book, **The Amateur: Barack Obama In The White House** or the equally insipid 2010 Klein and John LeBoutillier tome **The Obama Identity: A Novel Or Is It?** appears to have benefitted from Malkin's blog. For a review of Klein's book that suggests the author believes that President Obama is a confirmed Muslim, see, Adam Peck, "Ed Klein, Author Of New Anti-Obama Book, Suggests Obama Is Secretly A Muslim," **ThinkProgress.org,** May 17, 2012 http://thinkprogress.org/election/2012/05/17/486380/ed-klein-obama-muslim/

By 2012 Malkin's blog, **Hot Air**, was influential and profitable. She is interesting if strange. One of the best pieces has to do with Mitt Romney's alleged first day as president, and it was written by conservative blogger Ed Morrissey. Who is Ed Morrissey? He is the ex-husband of the Rev. Mary Manin Morrissey. She is the founder of the Living Enrichment Center and a former pastor at the New Thought church. Her husband pleaded guilty to money laundering and using church funds for personal expenses. There is no one I would like to hear from more than

Ed Morrissey. He can really straighten me out politically. Just remind me to keep my hand on my wallet. Quality control is not one of Malkin's concerns on Hot Air. After all it is only Hot Air. But it is fun Hot Air. Who cares if there is any depth, accuracy or content. This is after all the right wing nut house.

MALKIN'S BOOKS ARE NOT RELIABLE

Uniformly, her books are among the least reliable in the conservative movement. They are provocative, sensational, well written and they sell well. They just don't stand up to any form of intellectual scrutiny.

Malkin's critics point out the abundance of free airtime that she receives to sell her material. She is adept at selecting interesting minor stories and expanding them into major arguments. A good example took place on the View when Malkin said: "We have a technology czar who is a convicted shoplifter." This was a reference to Vivek Kundra who stole $134 worth of shirts in 1997 while in college and received an eighty-hour community service sentence. Kundra, born in New Delhi, India, served as President Obama's first Chief Information Officer until 2011. He then went on to Harvard University and he has served in D. C. and Virginia government positions. A youthful indiscretion had little to do with his subsequent political success. This is typical Malkin, as she finds a small piece of the historical puzzle and proceeds to create a mammoth generalization.

In 2002, **Invasion: How America Still Welcomes Terrorists, Criminals And Other Foreign Menaces** was published with little fanfare but respectable sales. It hit upon themes that appealed to those fearful of Muslim terrorism. As Malkin told Dr. Laura Schlesinger: "Invasion shows how every component of immigration enforcement has failed…I tell the stories of dozens of Americans who died as a result of lax and incompetent immigration enforcement." Fortunately, this book wasn't reviewed in any major journal. A few conservative organizations praised it.

The earliest review in the October 7 issue of **The American Conservative** was fawning and overly complimentary. The critics in the right wing nut house pointed to Malkin's columns appearing in more than one hundred newspapers as proof of her wisdom. Her defenders praised her for ignoring political correctness. Serious critics, academic historians, political scientists and serious journalists writing on American government derided the book as shoddy reporting with spurious conclusions. Why was Malkin's book a failure?

The premise was too vague and Malkin's language too radical. It did reach number fourteen on the **New York Times** non-fiction bestseller list. If labeled as fiction, it would have crested at number one.

Malkin placed much of the blame for immigration and terrorist problems on the Democratic Party. (pp. 30-31) She also argues that terrorists have been allowed "to disappear in the United States." (p. 8) It took another two years to complete what she called "an academic book." Most professors were falling on the floor laughing at this pronouncement.

MALKIN ON JAPANESE AMERICAN INTERNMENT: SHE IS A DISGRACE

It is fashionable to write a book with a new twist. Michelle Malkin's **In Defense of Internment: The Case For Racial Profiling in World War II And The War On Terror**, published in 2004, is a national disgrace. This is the worst written tome on ethnic history. I have reviewed five books for the **Journal of American History**, the most prestigious American history review, and more than a hundred reviews for other magazines, I have concluded that Malkin's study of Japanese-American internment distorts the facts, uses the primary material in a cavalier fashion and denigrates Japanese Americans. I have also written five books on ethnic subjects and not once have I encountered such an intellectual travesty as **In Defense of Internment**. What would possess Malkin to chastise Japanese Americans for complaining that their civil rights were compromised during World War II and its aftermath?

Why? The answer is a simple one. She wants to sell books. As the resident minority who hates minorities, she has a built in audience.

When my book, **The Fragmented Dream: Multicultural California**, appeared in 1997, it contained material on how white zealots marginalized ethnic minorities and were generally judgmental and condescending. Nothing has changed. The historical record is perverted and Japanese-Americans are marginalized in Malkin's extraordinarily inaccurate book.

Malkin begins this ill written and poorly thought out piece of historical analysis by stating: "Japanese American internment…is historically and legally inaccurate." (p. xv) She paints a rosy picture of Japanese Americans happily trotting off to what sounds like a Hilton Hotel. "My wife Elaine Black had to take legal action to accompany me to Manzanar," Karl Yoneda remarked to me in 1975. "The camp was dirty, the facilities were poor and there was little food. We pitched in and made it livable. Then some of us joined what became the 442nd Regimental Combat team and we fought for our country. We were Americans and proud of it." Karl Yoneda, an ILWU dockworker, is typical of Japanese Americans who proved they were first and foremost Americans. Malkin should be ashamed of herself for denigrating Yoneda's memory.

Malkin is brilliant in some ways. She connects Japanese Americans with the present War on Terror. When she accuses someone of anti-American behavior, she will mention that person and his "fellow travelers." She does this by painting Fred Korematsu as a radical. He defied Executive Order 9066 requiring all Japanese-Americans to leave the West Coast or be placed in internment camps. He sued the government and the U. S. Supreme Court heard the case. Korematsu v. United States upheld Korematsu's conviction for demanding his civil rights. In 1944, when the U. S. Supreme Court upheld Japanese-American relocation, Korematsu became a forgotten figure. Then his case was overturned. When Korematsu, now quite elderly, lent his name in support of Yaser Esam Hamdi, an American arrested in Afghanistan in 2001 and taken to Camp X-Ray at Guantanamo Bay, Korematsu emphasized that the U. S. had to have proof of radical activity. To hold someone, Korematsu argued, for alleged sedition was in violation of the U. S. Constitution.

When Korematsu was convicted of not reporting and complying with Executive Order 9066, his trial had a serious error. Charles Fahy, the Solicitor General of the United States, complained that Japanese American were a security threat. As Fahy argued this in Federal Court, an FBI and other military intelligence reports concluded that Japanese Americans posed no threat to national security. On November 19, 1983 Judge Marilyn Hall Patel of the U. S. Ninth District Court in San Francisco vacated the conviction, and Judge Patel remarked: "I would like to see the government admit that they were wrong and do something so this will never happen again to any American citizen of any race, creed, or color." President Jimmy Carter presented Korematsu the Presidential Medal of Freedom and Carter praised Korematsu for his integrity.

The State of California recognized Korematsu's bravery as a civil rights activist when on January 30 2011, the State of California celebrated "Fred Korematsu Day." He had been dead for almost six years, so it was a bittersweet victory.

The case of Yaser Esman Hamdi is a classic example of the type of American government action that drew Fred Korematsu's ire. He not only supported Hamdi and criticized the government, but he linked U.

S. action against Muslim radicals with the same intensity that plagued American during its Japanese American interlude in World War II.

Hamdi's supporters claimed that his civil rights were violated, and he was arrested simply for being an American Muslim. The government disagreed and labeled Hamdi a terrorist. Then Korematsu got involved, and he stated he did so because he believed that this was the same grievous wrong that ruined his life. Korematsu remarked that to incarcerate anyone due to public hysteria and lack of evidence was unacceptable. Malkin didn't think so, she saw Korematsu as an unrequited radical. His support for Hamdi prompted her to attack Korematsu as one who lacked a feel for America. She believed that he was typical of the radical Japanese-Americans.

Professor Greg Robinson, author of "By Order of the President," has more to say about Michelle Malkin's book "In Defense of Internment":

"Michelle Malkin engages in overkill. Her stated purpose is to prove that the removal and confinement of Japanese American aliens, and particularly of citizens, was based on justifiable fears of espionage and sabotage, rather than racism (and thus to make the case for racial profiling by the Bush Administration)."

WHAT IS WRONG WITH MALKIN'S INTERNMENT BOOK?

Japanese Relocation and the impact of World War II upon ethnic California is well documented. What Malkin does is to turn the historical evidence around, and in the process she distorts the facts and misinterprets the data.

Malkin falsely describes General John L. DeWitt, the Western Defense Commander, as a man who simply wanted to carry out his job. "DeWitt, who is often mistakenly portrayed by modern ethnic historians as the primary instigator of the West Coast evacuation, at first opposed any measure that encompassed American citizens." (p. 74) This description ignores the historical record. DeWitt spoke at California service organizations demanding internment, and he placed President Franklin D. Roosevelt in an impossible situation. As General DeWitt fanned the flames for Japanese Relocation, the Roberts Commission was formed to study the question of Japanese American loyalty. After the Roberts Report was released there was a demand for the relocation of all Japanese Americans from the West Coast. Hence, the reason for Executive Order 9066, which established the sand and cactus relocation centers that Japanese Americans were herded into for their alleged safety. Many historians credit General DeWitt with single handedly creating a mood of public opinion demanding Executive Order 9066.

General DeWitt stated that it was a military necessity to relocate Japanese Americans. He stressed the dangers of espionage and sabotage. When General DeWitt was asked why there had been no acts of sabotage in California. He responded that this proved there would be subsequent acts of violence. DeWitt argued that the specter of mob violence made relocation a necessity. On April 13, 1943, General DeWitt testified before a U. S. House Naval Affairs Subcommittee remarking: "The Japanese Americans are a dangerous element, whether loyal or not. There is no way to determine their loyalty…it makes no difference whether he is an American; theoretically, he is still a Japanese and you can't change him….You can't change him by giving him a piece of paper."

The **San Francisco Chronicle**, the **San Francisco Examiner**, the **San Jose Mercury**, the **Oakland Tribune** and the **Los Angeles Times** carried frequent quotes from General DeWitt concerning the danger of Japanese-Americans. He saw them as the perfect conspirators. They were citizens but they all acted and sounded alike. DeWitt never met a stereotype he didn't enjoy. Throughout World War II, General DeWitt fanned the flames of racism and resentment.

When President Harry S. Truman recognized the 442nd Regimental Combat Team, after World War II concluded, Truman praised the most decorated military unit in American history. Truman mentioned that they were Americans first and Japanese second, and they deserved thanks for their contributions to the war effort.

On General DeWitt, Malkin writes: "Derided today as a paper-pushing bureaucrat, DeWitt was an able theater commander…." This is a nice statement but it is contrary to the facts. His superiors described him as an inept field commander. He was reprimanded for his actions in San Francisco and replaced for incompetence.

She also ignores the contribution that Japanese Americans made in the Far East as translators, scouts, interrogators and soldiers. The 442nd Regimental Combat Team, a Japanese American unit, distinguished itself in Italy. It remains the most decorated military unit in American history. The 442nd motto "Go For Broke" was an indication of their courage. Malkin fails to realize the contribution that Japanese Americans made to the World War II war effort.

The hysteria surrounding Japanese-American internment was devastating. They lost most of their land. Japanese American businesses were taken over in San Francisco and the Grubb and Ellis real estate firms were the primary recipient of Japanese American riches. To distort the historical record is in itself a crime.

There were some minor acts of Japanese sabotage. When a Japanese submarine surfaced off the coast of Santa Barbara, it fired a shell that landed on the beach. The shell didn't explode and the army spent the next three years freshly painting it to remind Americans of the Japanese menace. The tragedy is that there is no record of massive internal Japanese American sabotage. Malkin points to Kibei's, who were Japanese Americans with a brief period of education in Japan, as the enemy. She describes them as "agents of Japan." (p. 23) The reality is that Kibei's were businessmen who had some Japanese sympathy, but, according to the FBI, they had no record of subversion. While some of the Kibei's lived here and were loyal to Japan, there was virtually no level of sabotage from this group.

Malkin's arguments evolve around a project known as Magic. The Magic messages were ones intercepted from Japan and they were used to shape President Franklin D. Roosevelt's policies. (pp. 37-51) There is no evidence the Magic transcripts had any impact on World War II. They were plans for Japanese sabotage of the West Coast that never materialized.

MALKIN LOOKING BACK ON HER CAREER: THE IDEOLOGICAL SIDE

In 2006, Malkin returned to her alma mater to give a speech. The Ronald Reagan Political Lectureship Series sponsored her lecture, "Exposing Liberals Unhinged," and it drew a capacity audience. She charged "liberals see racism where it doesn't exist, fabricate it…and ignore it within their own ranks." She prepared her lecture using a chapter from her book, **Unhinged: Exposing Liberals Gone Wild**. A chapter entitled, "One Sick Gook," refers to hate mail that she received, and she emphasized the material. Malkin loves to talk about racial insults that she receives from the left. The crowd booed as she accused them of racism. She couldn't understand why anyone at her alma mater was hostile. She was famous. She was rich. She is also one-dimensional.

The college crowd hooted at her defense of Japanese Internment during World War II. There is not a shred of evidence in the documents and history books to support her contentions. Perhaps, this is why she showed up with a bodyguard. That seems kind of strange. College campuses usually don't require a bodyguard. One spectator wondered if the college tavern was closed. Or maybe the sororities were on strike. She is a joke. The students at Oberlin were reminding her that they were embarrassed. How could she graduate from a major left wing, Liberal Arts College and turn into the Asian pit bull of the right?

Malkin wrote about her Oberlin visit in 2009, and she accused the school of closet racism. She pointed out that U. S. Senator Hugh Scott was hissed at Oberlin in 1963. If she knew anything about the pipe-smoking weasel, Senator Hugh Scott, she would have agreed with the students from the early 1960s. She even charged that the **Oberlin Review** printed an unflattering photo of her.

Then she used her Asian heritage in a manner that exhibited her rejection of racism. She told her audience that Asian students always see racism where none exists. This was a complete contradiction of comments she made a few years earlier. When a student challenged her views, she pointed out that she was Filipino. Then she charged that liberals on campus were fabricating race crimes. A student stood in the audience and remarked: "For every faked hate crime there are dozens of real incidents." When students pressed her for statistics and evidence to support her outrageous conclusion, Malkin remarked: "I can't put a percentage on it…."

Her lack of knowledge about American history was evident when she mentioned that Senator Strom Thurmond was a great man. Maybe! Maybe not! On the question of race, he was not a civil rights supporter. At least not until late in his career when the needed the African American vote for re-election. The students left with smiles on their faces. One remarked that he thought Malkin's talk was a comedy show. Somewhere Stephen Colbert was lurking in the shadows.

MAKING MONEY OFF THE ITNERNET: HOT AIR AND MALKIN

In 2006, Malkin launched Hot Air, the first Internet conservative broadcast network. She immediately claimed that she was not making enough money. Despite 220,000 hits a day, Malkin appealed to her fans for funds. Pork adobe must be expensive, as she continued ranting about liberals. The early rush from advertisers quickly subsided, as the shows amateur nature and lack of formidable news made it a parody.

The Hot Air site was so embarrassing that Bill O'Reilly no longer invited her on his show. O'Reilly is a lot of things, but he is not stupid. He recognized that she was an airhead with little to say and less to contribute.

When her producer, Bryan Preston, left hotair.com, he announced that he was going to work for Laura Ingraham. Malkin considered dying her hair blonde to compete. It didn't work.

In 2012, hotair.com remains healthy and profitable. With pictures of John Bolton and Newt Gingrich on the website it is not exactly **Playboy**. The articles have little value but the site appears to be one of the mainstays of the right wing nut house. By January 2012, Michelle Obama was criticized by Sarah Palin and John Bolton and then Malkin let us know that Mitt Romney was conservative enough to be president. It appears that Saturday Night Live is in danger of having serious competition from the right wing. Hotair.com is now a better comedy show. Stay tuned. The best is yet to come.

In February 2012, Malkin endorsed Rick Santorum for the Republican presidential nomination. Malkin remarked: "Rick Santorum represents the most conservative candidate still standing who can articulate both fiscal and social conservative values." She has changed her tone.

WHAT'S WRONG WITH THE CULTURE OF CORRUPTION?

In August 2010, Malkin's **Culture of Corruption: Obama And His Team of Tax Cheats, Crooks And Cronies** hit bookstores. The first few sentences clearly stated her viewpoint. "Janitors in newsrooms across America worked overtime in the halcyon days after Barack Obama won the presidency. It wasn't easy cleaning the drool off laptops and floors in the offices of journalists…." (p. 1) It gets worse. Mrs. Obama was a target for the Filipina pit bull. Mrs. Obama's senior thesis at Princeton, Malkin claimed, was critical of the University's approach to African American students. That statement is hardly surprising, but it doesn't suggest the first lady doesn't like white people. This is Malkin's way of using innuendo to attack her subject.

The **Culture of Corruption** contains thirty-three specific references to corruption and President Obama. Malkin claims that he is corrupt in dealing with and protecting public unions. (p. 12) Obama's personal finances and public service have been intertwined in a corrupt manner, Malkin charges, and she suggests that Obama is "ethically corrupt." (p. 45) She says that the President has a history of "corruption and cronyism." (p. 112) She needs to go to her thesaurus and find another word for corruption. Perhaps right wing blogger. Conservative critic.

What is wrong with the **Culture of Corruption?** The answer is that it has little to do with the present state of American politics. It also has little to do with Barack Obama. It does, however, fit nicely into the right wing nut house perception that criminals in the White House are preventing economic recovery. Michelle Malkin is a strange political-economic figure. She is the right wing nut houses answer to the token ethnic. She is a wealthy and influential figure who is entertaining but politically naïve. Her fame rests on her attack dog persona. When she was shopping recently at the Lotte Korean Grocery Store, a customer told her nicely that she had "a confused identity." Malkin responded: "Fuck you." The professors at Oberlin are cringing in the English department. They can't believe her crude nature. Stay tuned. There is much more to come from the Filipina pit bull.

THE CULTURE OF CORRUPTION REVISED

The revised edition of **The Culture of Corruption** included three new chapters. The first one was in the forward and dealt with what Malkin labeled "The Anti-Corruption Referendum." The thesis is that everyone in and around the Obama administration is corrupt. She also suggests that the Democrats "strong armed Chrysler creditors...." (xiii) It gets worse. She charges the White House with bullying. Her source is Michele Bachmann. Then Malkin argues that Democratic malfeasance began with John K. Kennedy. She calls the Democratic administration "The Age of Da Boss Barack." (p. xxv) This is typical of her irresponsible reporting. But she continues: "The cajoler-in-chief and his political strategists may be in perpetual denial about the costly, rancorous side effects of their culture of corruption." (p. xxv) Again, this is beautiful writing. But it doesn't mean anything.

Another bonus chapter, "Obama's War On Whistleblowers" argues Obama terrified whistleblowers. The only problem is that there is little, if any, serious proof that President Obama is firing whistleblowers. The last new chapter "Married To The Mob" would make a good movie with Robert DeNiro. As a piece of analytical journalism it reads like Huey, Dewey and Louie wrote it. My apologies to Walt Disney and his people.

Michelle Malkin's writing is excellent, her thought is convoluted but her bank account remains healthy. So something is going right.

PART FOUR
I USED TO BE A DEMOCRAT OR A BEAUTY QUEEN: NOW I AM A PISSED OFF CRITIC

"EVER SINCE PRESIDENT BARACK OBAMA'S INAUGURATION, HIS RIGHT WING CRITICS HAVE DEVOTED COUNTLESS HOURS AND MILLIONS OF KEYSTROKES TO SPINNING THE PRESIDENT'S RECORD OF SUPPORT FOR ISRAEL SO FAR FROM REALITY THAT IT THREATENS THE HISTORICAL BIPARTISAN FOUNDATION OF AMERICAN SUPPORT FOR ISRAEL." MARC R. STANLEY, TEXAS JEWISH POST, JANUARY 9, 2012

The main danger of the right wing nut house is to confuse historical facts. There is no place where conservative critics have created more damage than in U. S. support for Israel. Among the worst offenders is a Jewish writer, consultant, lobbyist and self-promoter, Dick Morris. He has joined the right wing nut house to warn Americans of impending socialism.

Dick Morris is a political observer who bolted from President Bill Clinton's liberal political stable into the right wing nut house. He became a columnist for the **New York Post**, and he soon embarked on a career pillorying liberals. The **New York Times** described Morris as "a veteran of old fashioned, hardball politics." He introduced a web site asking voters to vote yes or no on political issues. Soon he was a media figure on Fox TV News and the book offers came in with large advances.

Why did Morris leave left wing politics? The answer is a simple one. He was broke. The Connecticut State Tax Board listed Morrison on their delinquency roles. Connecticut reported that Morris owed $452,367 in back taxes and the IRS filed a $1.5 million dollar lien in 2003. To pay his bills since 2003, Morris has authored six best selling books. The titles suggest his political direction: **Revolt: How To Defeat Obama And Repeal His Socialist Programs, A Patriot's Guide** and **Because He Could** an expose of Bill Clinton's personal and professional life. This book suggests the degree of antipathy that Morris has toward the Democratic Party and two of its more prominent leaders.

Morris takes on virtually every subject that makes money. His worst book in 2008, **Outrage: How Illegal Immigration, the United Nations, Congressional Ripoffs, Student Loan Overcharges, Tobacco Companies, Trade Protection, and Drug Companies Are Ripping Us Off... And What To Do About It** is a classic example of sensationalizing serious issues. One section of Morris' book has a box with the title: "The Amazing Democratic Gravy Train At Fannie Mae." He subtly blames those close to former President Clinton for Fannie Mae's fiscal problems. The Republicans and President George W. Bush, according to Morris, didn't have anything to do with the housing crisis.

There is no other reason for Morris' books and TV appearances other than making money. He lacks conviction and a commitment to honest criticism. But he does wear lifts in his shoes to make himself taller. He also knows Sherry Rowlands. That is enough to guarantee him legendary status.

In 2010, there were forty-six anti-Obama books published in the previous two years. These tomes had one thing to common, they demonize the president and present uneven, unfair and unsavory criticism. It is impossible to analyze all the books, there are some that stand out as some of the worst ever published. They are written for money, partisan politics and a sense of empowerment. It is a sad commentary on American politics that there are so few pro-Obama books.

Some reviewers are so incensed with the books in the right wing nut house that they have asked Regnery, the publisher of right wing propaganda, to remove their names from the reviewing list. **Time** magazine senior writer Jeffrey Kluger asked that his name be taken off all right wing books. Evelyn Leopold, a Huffington Post writer, called the conservative books "sensational rubbish." Ben Wyskida of **The Nation**, labeled

Aaron Klein's book "so offensive" and "so far afield" that it lacked credibility.

The attack dog Barbies in the right wing nut house are Ann Coulter and Laura Ingraham. One makes sense, Ann Coulter, and the other, Laura Ingraham, is a pale imitation of a Barbie TV host. Coulter and Ingraham have one thing in common, they are constant critics of liberals, Democrats, immigrants and government spending. Coulter is the number one Barbie, Ingraham trails badly. In November 2011, they argued over Newt Gingrich. Coulter appeared on Ingraham's radio show and the host praised Gingrich as "the only person who consistently gets crowds excited." Coulter vehemently disagreed. Coulter labeled Gingrich "a big government conservative." She also remarked that he was "a chubby boy who desperately wants to be liked." The two television personalities with their popular books have little to say that matters. But America listens.

The depths of the right wing nut house came to the fore when President Barack Obama and Vice President Joe Biden went to Ray's Hell Burger for lunch. A debate broke out over the President Obama's use of Dijon mustard. The scandal became known as dijongate and it is a joke. But it is an interesting insight into the right wing nut house. Whether or not the use of Dijon mustard by the president makes him an elitist is for you the reader to decide.

Chapter 10
I'M 5-4 BUT I AM TRYING TO BE 6-5: DICK MORRIS, THE POLITICAL CONSULTANT WITH A SEVEN-FOOT EGO

"HE IS THE CONSUMMATE MUTATION OF A POLITICAL CONSULTANT...IN HIS OWN WAY, HE REPRESENTS THE DARK SIDE OF POLITICS," LEON PANETTA FORMER CLINTON CHIEF OF STAFF

Ethics, integrity, political commitment, logic, personal honesty and straightforward talk are elements that have made politicians important. If you are a political consultant or a media guru, these traits are insignificant. The media can cover them up. Dick Morris is so taken with pontificating on radio and television and through his books that he forgets where the American political tradition began and where it is headed.

The problem is that Morris is five feet four inches with a little man's complex. He does wear lifts in his shoes, he has his office desk on a foot high platform and he meets people in places where he can stand two steps up and shake your hand. He definitely has a problem with his height. There are more serious issues.

He has strayed from his Jewish roots, and he embraces power as his religion. He stays in shape and lifts a few weights. He likes five star hotels and Michelin restaurants. For years, he was a Democrat. They don't like five star restaurants, so he wandered over to the Republican Party. It is the home of five star restaurant aficionados. He likes to get together with people and talk about his exploits. He seeks power and influential people as friends and colleagues. When he is not treated well, he is vindictive to the point of fanaticism. He likes to sit on a desk in front of an audience and talk about himself.

Morris is the author of six **New York Times** bestsellers. His fourteen books are interesting and well written. His wife, Eileen McGann, is the brains behind the operation. Dick wears a nice suit, he has a nice smile, he is articulate, but at times the lights are on but no one is home. McGann helps to direct his commentary. That is until Mr. Winkie takes over. But that is a subject for the Sherry Rowlands story. Stay tuned.

Since 2007, he has worked for TRN Entertainment offering "Dick Morris Reports" and "Moments With Morris." When he managed Bill Clinton's 1996 re-election campaign, he was angry that there was a double standard. Clinton could get away with anything. Morris was caught with a prostitute and crucified. He should have been; he allowed the call girl to listen in on one of President Clinton's confidential messages. But Morris didn't blame himself for this dismissal; he credited the media with exposing his malevolent deeds. He saw a conspiracy. He was ready for the right wing nut house.

RICHARD HOFSTADTER DEFINES DICK MORRIS

Richard Hofstadter warned us about fanatics. Perhaps Hofstadter's greatest error was to ignore the political consultants who warp, twist or reshape the political spectrum. No one has done this more intelligently or with more panache than Dick Morris. The blind ambition and the lack of perspective are key elements in his career. These traits also destroyed his left wing and liberal credentials. This allowed Morris to become a conservative convert. He promptly went over to the dark side. The Fox TV News Network welcomed his insights into the Democratic Party. He became the darling of conservatives. His writings about President Bill Clinton were applauded in conservative circles. He went where the money and power made him a media icon. The result is a loud-mouthed dwarf who has an opinion on everything. He is intelligent but not worth listening to on the key issues in American politics.

It is clear in Morris's quotations, and on his radio show, that he lacks a clear political direction, as well as a sensible view of the political process. But making money in the right wing nut house doesn't require any of these elements. He is the typical political consultant. The ends justify the means. Do what you have to do to have your candidate win. Unfortunately, Morris extended these noxious notions to his life. He is power mad, media savvy, and he will do what it takes to gain favor from the right wing.

What Richard Hofstadter called the traits of the paranoid style fit Morris beautifully. Hofstadter wrote that being "ruthless, angry, moralistic and dogmatic" were traits of the paranoid political mind. He didn't know Dick Morris, but he was writing about him. What dominates Morris' writing and radio-television commentaries is his paranoia over America's future.

THE ROAD TO POWER AS A POLITICAL CONSULTANT

Dick Morris began his political career as a friend and adviser to Bill Clinton while he was Arkansas' governor. Morris is credited with directing Clinton's 1978 gubernatorial campaign. Then Morris left the Clinton's. When Clinton was defeated seeking a second term as Arkansas governor, Morris returned as his principal political adviser. For the next decade, Morris directed the Clinton political machine. There was a raw, nasty side to Morris that the Clinton's were concerned about. They slowly shunted him into the political background. He was in the background as Bill Clinton won the 1992 presidential election.

It was during the 1992 presidential election, with James Carville and George Stephanopoulos leading the way, that Morris became disenchanted with Hillary Clinton. His later writings and media appearances would pillar Mrs. Clinton.

In 1993, Morris once again re-entered the White House as one of Clinton's advisers. When the Republican Party took control of both Houses during the 1994 elections, Morris was brought back into the inner circle. Morris' strategy of "triangulation" was a key to Clinton's 1996 re-election. Triangulation led to a campaign, which widened Clinton's appeal with independent voters. Morris also helped Clinton to appear as a "candidate of the people," as he distanced himself from professional politicians.

As a political strategist, Morris is brilliant. He adopted Republican and Democratic policies in a blend that promoted a neo non-partisan tone. After Morris directed Clinton's re-election campaign, he never felt appreciated by the Clinton's. This led to some hard line and unfair criticism. In later years, he penned several highly critical books on the

Clinton's. He is a venal weasel who joined the right wing nut house for fame and fortune.

The problem with Morris is that he needs constant gratification. He must be told that he is the most brilliant man in the room. His grandiose ego was his downfall.

THE BILL CLINTON FIGHT AND WHAT IT MEANT

There is doubt that Morris' strained relationship with Bill Clinton went back to an incident during Clinton's bid for the Arkansas governorship. The Clinton's were meeting with Morris and an argument ensued. Clinton took a swing at Morris and Hillary pulled her husband off his adviser. The right wing nut house blamed Clinton for the dust up. Those who criticize President Clinton cite his temper, and those who criticize Morris cite his excessive ego.

Morris explained his view of the fight: "Like Janus, the two faced Roman God, there are (sic) always been two distinct personalities in Bill Clinton," Morris concluded. During his Arkansas political career, Morris alleges he was tackled by the future President. "I was leaving, quitting the campaign," Morris remarked of his role in Clinton's run for the Arkansas Governorship, he continued, "I suddenly fell to the ground tackled by Bill Clinton. I saw his large fist coming at me. Hillary was trying to get between us, yelling, Bill, Bill stop it!"

When Morris repeated the story for his book **Behind The Oval Office**, he sent the page proofs to Clinton for approval. "He asked me to change the text and tone of the story. I did," Morris concluded. What does this story tell us? The answer is a simple one. Morris is cashing in on his connection to President Clinton.

There is another reason for the Clinton-Morris fight. Morris wanted to run the show. Morris always was the left wing Jewish intellectual in Clinton circles. As a campaign consultant, who helped Clinton poll voters and frame issues, Morris was important to Clinton. When Morris resigned in 1996 it was not due to policy differences. It was due to Morris' sex scandal.

MORRIS' SEX SCANDAL

During the Clinton years, Morris ascended to a position of preeminence that prompted him to convince the president to take a middle of the road political position. This allowed Clinton to escape the scandals that plagued his years in office. Just as Morris' power reached its nadir, he was involved in a sex scandal that prompted him to resign from the Clinton inner circle. A New York newspaper, the **Star**, alleged that he had sex with a prostitute on a balcony in a Washington D. C. hotel. There were also allegations of an illegitimate child. He allegedly compromised national security by allowing a prostitute to listen in to a private conversation with President Clinton. Ego and power destroyed his judgment. On August 29, 1996 Morris resigned as Clinton accepted the party nomination at the Democratic National Convention. There was trouble brewing.

Sherry Rowlands, according to the **Washington Post**, was the Virginia call girl that Morris showed the sighs (no this is not a misspelling) and sights of Washington D. C. She was interviewed by Hard Copy, and it was obvious that Miss Rowlands wasn't a Harvard graduate. On the television show, she remarked: "The only person I know in politics is Dick Morris." Apparently, the scholarship committee at Harvard called her with an offer for a four-year ride to America's most prestigious University. She told Dick Morris when she went to college she would study sociology, as she observed powerful people all the time. Those without their clothes on told only the truth. Viagra is trying to work up a commercial behind this story.

There was an excess of detail about this scandal as the **Washington Post** reported that allegedly Morris liked to suck Sherry Rowlands' toes. When he was asked for a comment, Morris replied: "No comment." Morris' wife, Attorney Eileen McGann, posing for a picture with her husband for **Time** magazine, remarked that she was "very upset." Really! She also had no comment. Sherry Rowlands continued to have comments. Most of Rowland's remarks came in paid interviews.

When Morris gave Rowlands the key to room 2005, it was to his regular suite, and he found himself without money. Consequently, he signed over a check for $824 from a speech at Memphis University to Rowlands, and she cashed it. The press discovered the check and the alleged Virginia call girl and the story was front page news. When he was interviewed by **Time**, Morris refused to talk about Rowlands. He was videotaped in a bathrobe with Rowlands and a tabloid, **The Star**, went public with the story. Her interview with Barry Nolan on the TV program, Hard Copy, had some hilarious moments. Rowlands commented: "Someone as intelligent as he is should have kept his lip buttoned when he unzipped his pants. I mean, how can you maneuver words, and he can't even control what he's doing in his own room with a paid lady." Maybe Sherry Rowlands should have been running Bill Clinton's campaigns.

Before his fall from power, Morris was on the cover of **Time** magazine as "The Man Who Has Clinton's Ear." Something happened to Morris after he left the Clinton inner circle. He was humiliated by the allegations of sexual misconduct, and he began to rethink his politics.

As he turned his venomous behavior on Hillary Clinton, he began earning enormous sums of money. It was a good career decision, financially speaking. When she made her bid for the presidency, he helped to produce a documentary, **Hillary: The Movie**. It was mean spirited and unfair. Morris was officially a turncoat.

Sherry Rowlands is the only person with fond memories of her time in Washington D. C. She let it be known it wasn't because she was paid a consulting fee. She got to listen into a conversation with Morris and President Clinton. Not even Monica Lewinsky can claim this feat. But Lewinsky has other firsts. Rowlands was a real rocket scientist on Hard Copy. She told the television program that Morris paid for sex because he loved his wife. "That makes him feel he is not cheating on his wife," Rowlands told Hard Copy. Cal Tech immediately offered Rowlands a scholarship to major in rocket science. Morris didn't have a comment. Neither do I.

WHEN MORRIS TURNED ON THE CLINTON'S

In 1999, the **Washington Post** reported that after two decades "one of President Clinton's closest friends and advisers, Dick Morris has turned on his former boss with a vengeance." The story wasn't surprising, what is strange are the personal stories that Morris began spinning in the media. As one of Morris's friends remarked: "Dick never let the truth get in the way of a good story." Another friend remarked: "The lifts in Morris' shows are affecting his mentality." Another friend recalled: "He was angry that Bill Clinton's sex scandal didn't derail his presidency." Dick Morris advised politicians for money, fame and fortune, but let's not forget Sherry Rowlands. Maybe she was an adviser of sorts.

When Morris testified before Kenneth Starr's grand jury in the Clinton impeachment proceedings, he went on Fox TV News to discuss his comments. He set himself up to become a right wing talk guru. Morris hoped that Congress would revoke Clinton's pension after the Monica Lewinsky scandal. He also talked about a White House secret police that dug up malicious material on Clinton's political opponents. Morris charged that House investigators feared for their lives because of the Clinton's special powers. This is of course patent nonsense. To the right wing conspiracy minded, it sounds like the ultimate truth.

The charges continued as Morris became even more ridiculous. As he showed up increasingly on right wing television, he talked of being fair and objective. In the next breath, he remarked of President Clinton: "He's a great president from the neck up." No doubt Dick Morris is fair and balanced. Just ask Sherry Rowlands. But don't ask her to comment from the neck up. The outrageous comments continued as Morris attempted to link **Hustler** magazine publisher, Larry Flynt, with the White House. There is no discernible reason for an Obama-Flynt link and there is also no evidence. Morris' ego prompted him to make this ridiculous charge.

THE EGO IS OUT OF CONTROL

There is no greater paean to Dick Morris' ego than his updating of Machiavelli's classic work on statecraft and government, **The Prince**. In a manifestation of an ego that no one could control, Morris' **The New Prince: Machiavelli Updated For The Twenty-First Century**, published in 2000, was an indication of his venal nature. In an unusually moralistic tone, we are told that the book is based on a single notion, Morris wrote: "If American politicians were truly pragmatic and did what was really in their own best interest, our political process would be a lot cleaner, more positive, non partisan and issue oriented." As Richard Hofstadter has pointed out, never let an excessive moralist get in the way of political analysis.

The main premise behind Morris' reinterpretation of **The Prince** is that voters have the right to take lawmaking into their own hands. The Tea Party loved the book. He also stresses that idealism is a key to electability. He uses clichés like issues over image and message over money to lecture his political followers. It sounds interesting, but it doesn't work. Even Machiavelli would be insulted.

The New Prince is a primer for politicians, according to Morris, and he drones on about its adaptability to the present day political environment. Hopefully, it will remain on sale for a penny at Amazon. This book offers a glimpse inside Dick Morris' ego.

The reviews for Morris' **The Prince** reflected the hostility to his personal life. One reviewer suggested that an amoral political adviser who worked for both Democrats and Republicans was acting with self-interest. Machiavelli would approve.

MORRIS BEGINS TO BELIEVE HIS CRYSTAL BALL

Dick Morris believes that he has a political crystal ball. He predicted that Hillary Clinton would run against the Republican candidate,

Condoleezza Rice, in the 2008 presidential election. Morris's tarnished crystal ball was largely the result of working for Latin American dictators, as he advised Fernando de la Rua when he ran for the Argentinean presidency, as well as advising Jorge Battle in Uruguay. He capped off his political advising working for Vicente Fox in the Mexican presidential election of 2000 and Raphael Troutman in Guyana in 2006. But Morrison was eager to return to American politics. Maybe he could find a dictator in training to support.

The notion that he believed his crystal ball was infallible was obvious to the casual observer. But there was a method to Morris' madness. He began ingratiating himself with conservative Republicans during George W. Bush's presidency. He craved the spotlight and media attention. Morris suggested that Hurricane Katrina would shape Bush's second term in the same manner that 9/11 influenced his first term. After this comment, Fox TV News made him a regular. He spewed venom about liberal Democrats. Morris was back, and he continued to publicize his crystal ball.

One wonders what level of integrity Morris possesses? He looks like a character that should be standing next to Marlon Brando in the Godfather. One intimate friend called him a "small sausage of a man." Another characterized him as being handsome with the looks of a movie star. Funny Morris described himself in the same manner. George Stephanopoulos says Morris is an "insincere prick." Stephanopoulos is the most media savvy and fair-minded person in the business. I think he got it right.

He does have his defenders. Sherry Rowlands, the alleged prostitute, that he showed the lights of Washington to and a few other things commented: "Dick Morris loves his wife." At an alleged price of $200 an hour I believe that Sherry Rowlands told the truth. I'm convinced that Morris is a great mind. He is also a fun guy. I wanted to know more about Sherry Rowlands. So I went on the Internet. They wanted to charge me five dollars to look her up. I guess that is better than $200 an hour.

But Morris has his defenders. Mike Huckabee called him the best political mind that left the synagogue in America. Then again Huckabee was having trouble getting elected to political office. It was rumored that Morris was advising him. He suggested that Huckabee lose weight and go into television. Morris also told Huckabee to quit playing the guitar. Christians don't like the guitar, and they hate rock and roll. It is the instrument of the devil. Good advice. Maybe that is why Huckabee is no longer in politics. The only person more ridiculous in this scenario is former U. N. diplomat John Bolton. In 2009, Bolton and Morris were on a cruise hosted by the **National Review**. They talked at length about President Obama and the danger he posed to America. That is after eating steak and lobster and swilling down fine champagne. "My God, John, there is a negro in the White House," Morris allegedly remarked. "Really!" Bolton answered as he slobbered on his mustache: "Obama is not doing his job." The cruise cost $3500. Most people wanted their money back.

There is no better example of using the media for personal gain than Dick Morris. Once he left the Clinton's in the mid-1990s, he became an apologist for the right wing nut house. He talked of being disillusioned with the Clinton's, he talked of the decline of American values, and he failed to discuss his limitations as a political consultant, as well as a husband. Along the way truth and objectivity were thrown to the wind.

There were more outrageous comments that suggested his credibility ranked zero to minus zero. He was able to trivialize the news. On 9-11 Morris remarked: "From the outset, the War On Terror was sharply different from other U. S. military actions in the strong support it received from American women." Morris continued: "Normally, men back military action by 10 to 20 points more than women do. But, after 9-11, women felt more endangered by terror...." Maybe this was Morris's way for making up for the Sherry Rowlands' interlude.

The bottom line is that Morris will do anything to further his career. This was demonstrated when he took his wisdom to Europe and Africa. No wonder we have so much trouble with our international image.

DICK MORRIS GOES ON TO ADVISE EUROPE AND AFRICA

After wearing out his welcome in American politics, Morris and his wife left for England. They advised the United Kingdom Independence Party in the 2004 European Parliament election. The couple moved on to advise the presidential campaign of Viktor Yushcehenko in the Ukraine. He won the election and took office in 2004, but he wasn't able to secure a position for the next Ukrainian Presidential election. Dick Morris was no longer around to create a media spin to keep him in office.

Then it was off to Africa where Morris offered his services to elect Kenya's Raila Odingo president in 2007. A brutal dictator who abused his people, Odingo was Morris' kind of guy. Morris worked pro bono. Was Sherry Rowlands in Kenya? Not surprisingly, Kenya's newspapers called into question the legality of Morris' work. When the votes were counted there were charges of voter fraud and manipulation of the electoral system. The foreign political consulting was important, as it made Morris not only more media savvy but American major publishers were lining up for his forthcoming anti-Obama books.

MORRIS GOES AFTER PRESIDENT OBAMA AND OTHERS IN HIS BOOKS

Once Barack Obama was sworn in as president, Dick Morris became a crusader to defeat him. When Obamacare was announced, Morris became a stringent critic of health care reform. As a frequent guest on the O'Reilly Factor and Sean Hannity's show, he warned of impending socialism. It is a message that the right wing nut house loves. It is his books that have made Morris so successful. Not to mention rich.

Much of Morris' writing comes from his vindictive, combative personality. He does have six **New York Times** best sellers and one that hit the top of the **Washington Post**. Drivel is the best way to describe Morris' books. He is angry and he wants to get even. In **Condi vs. Hillary: The Next Great Presidential Race**, he argues that only Condoleezza Rice could defeat Hillary Clinton in the 2008 presidential election.

Morris wasn't through with Hillary. When she published, **Living History**, Morris followed with **Rewriting History.** His wife, Eileen McGann, was the co-author. There were rumblings that Sherry Rowlands was in the neighborhood. While Morris was engaged in a pissing match with Mrs. Clinton, the right wing media anointed him. The coronation was held regularly on Fox TV News. This inspired him to write more of his insipid tomes.

It was Morris' nasty attitude toward Hillary Clinton that brought him fame and fortune. He portrayed her as "manipulative, cold and single minded." His connection to President Clinton allowed him to publish **Behind The Oval Office: Winning the Presidency In the Nineties**, which attacked his old friend Bill Clinton. His publisher put up a $2.5 million advance for an inside look into Clinton's White House. The book didn't sell well and the reviews were generally negative. But Morris did bank the money. The publisher is still waiting for a look inside the Clinton White House.

THE HATING BARACK OBAMA BOOKS: IT IS NO LONGER BILL AND HILLARY

Morris' **Fleeced: How Barack Obama, Media Mockery of Terrorist Threat, Liberals Who Want to Kill Talk Radio, The Do-Nothing**

Congress, Companies That Help Iran And Washington Lobbyists For Foreign Government Are Scamming Us…And What To Do About It was published in 2008 to convince voters to elect Arizona's John McCain. Fortunately, the electorate thought that Dennis Miller wrote Dick Morris' book, and it was a comedy tome. They also couldn't remember the title. The thesis that Morris and his wife, Eileen McGann, argue is that our government is fleecing the citizens.

In June 2009, Morris' **Catastrophe** was released. The sixteen chapters and 359 pages warn America in three sections that President Obama is working with Congress and special interests to cause a catastrophe. The tired argument that Obama is a socialist is buttressed with statistics and facts that bear little relationship to the current administration. The statistics are suspect, as are Morris' arguments.

It is the chapter titles in **Catastrophe** that appeal to the reader. "Obama's War On Prosperity," "The Bank Bailout That Bombed" and "Obama's Health Care Catastrophe" are samples from Morris' erudite pen. He posits no solutions, only criticism.

In March 2011, **Revolt! How To Defeat Obama And Repeal His Socialist Programs** continued the attack. The focus of Morris' prose is on how to defeat President Obama in the 2012 election. He sees the issues of budget, and debt limitation as a means of forcing the Obama administration to adopt Republican policies. Obamacare is another target and the requirement that everyone must buy national health insurance needs to be defeated. Morris worries that the government is taking over the Internet to silence conservative talk radio.

As a veteran of hardball politics, Morris is not concerned with what others think. He is a vain, petty little man with an ego the size of Texas, (P. S. Don't tell Rick Perry) and he is a self-serving megalomaniac. Beware of what he says and writes.

Where is Sherry Rowlands when you really need her?

Chapter 11
THE SIX BARACK OBAMA BOOKS FROM THE FRINGE

"POLITICS IS HIGH SCHOOL WITH GUNS AND MORE MONEY" FRANK ZAPPA

Aaron Klein and Brenda J. Elliott's, **The Manchurian President: Barack Obama's Ties to Communists, Socialists and other Anti-American Extremists;** *R. Lee Prescott's,* **Barack Obama's Plan to Socialize America and Destroy Capitalism;** *John Graham's,* **Obama's Change: Communism in America;** *Michael Savage's,* **Trickle Up Poverty: Stopping Obama's Attack on Our Borders, Economy and Security;** *Pamela Geller and Robert Spencer's,* **The Post-American Presidency: The Obama Administration's War on America,** *Mike Cullen's,* **Whiny Little Bitch: The Excuse Filled Presidency of Barack Obama**

The books listed above suggest the depth of hatred toward President Barack Obama. None show the antipathy or the feeling of depravity more than Aaron Klein's and Brenda J. Elliott's **The Manchurian President: Barack Obama's Ties To Communists, Socialists And Other Anti-Government Extremists**. When it was published in 2010, it was described as the work of a brilliant Jewish intellectual, who is a columnist for the **Jewish Press,** as well as a radio talk show host. His co-author, Brenda J. Elliott, is a persistent blogger and historian. This book is an over the top indictment of President Obama's life and electoral campaigns. Klein's argument is that Obama is the unwitting dupe of radicals, Socialists and Communists.

Why are Aaron Klein and Barbara J. Elliott important? They have hit a nerve with the conservative, book buying public. Why? The answer is obvious. They present arguments that appeal to the conspiratorial sense of the American voter. The notion that President Obama has been brainwashed by radical influences is a crazy one; yet, a small minority of Americans believe it. **The Manchurian President** is a title taken from the movie: "The Manchurian Candidate." This movie theorized that Communists were on the verge of controlling American government through brain washing techniques. A recent poll by a respected public opinion think tank revealed that just over twenty percent of Americans subscribe to the notion that President Obama is a socialist with radical political leanings. Therefore, he might be brainwashing the electorate.

THE ACORN SCANDAL AND PRESIDENT OBAMA: WAS HE INVOLVED OR NOT?

The theory behind this book is that massive research will expose government malfeasance. Klein picks issues that he claims proves President Obama's dereliction of duty. To that end, the publisher points out that there are 800 footnotes. Then the nonsense continues with the declaration that "Obama's deep ties to an anti-American fringe" defines his politics. It gets worse; Klein suggests that ACORN is affiliated with the president.

ACORN is the Association of Community Organizations For Reform Now. This organization is an unsavory one, as they administer federal funds to attempt to help foreclosure victims. Then California Attorney General Jerry Brown summed it up when he released a statement that said that ACORN engaged in "highly inappropriate behavior." This was a mild statement from Brown, after he announced that ACORN disposed of 500 pages of confidential records in a San Diego dumpster.

There was inadequate accounting, some allege outright fraud, and the scandals that erupted discredited ACORN. The House of Representatives voted overwhelmingly to cut ACORN's funding. The question remains: "Was President Obama involved in this?" His critics say yes. His supporters claim there is no truth to this malicious rumor.

The right wing nut house had a field day with ACORN. Stanley Kurtz, writing in the **National Review Online**, remarked: "What if Barack Obama's most important radical connection had been hiding in plain sight all along?" Then Kurtz charged that Obama and ACORN were conspiring to turn America into a socialist nation. Not to be outdone, the Filipina pit bull, Michelle Malkin, wrote of ACORN and President Obama: "He cut his ideological teeth working with ACORN as a community organizer…." The implication is clear to Malkin, ACORN is corrupt as is the president.

ACORN was a good idea that went awry. It was established to secure affordable housing and to provide social services for low-income families. The problem is that ACORN inappropriately designated its federal funds. There is no evidence that President Obama is in any way involved in or responsible for the ACORN misdeeds. The president signed into law the ACORN Funding Ban that included an end to spending for any affiliate or subsidiary. ACORN filed for bankruptcy and the scandal ended. To hear those in the right wing nut house, Obama is a co-conspirator. This is sheer nonsense. There is no evidence that President Obama contributed to ACORN's misdeeds.

The ACORN scandal guaranteed that community-organizing groups follow the rules for spending government funds. While ACORN attempted to prevent predatory lending practices from America's banks, its books were suspect.

In the aftermath of the ACORN scandal a great deal of interest was directed toward James O'Keefe and Hannah Giles who conducted an undercover video sting that exposed ACORN's misdeeds. The investigation revealed how ACORN spent its money. The conclusion from many was that they were engaged in alleged legal fraud. The housing programs failed to help foreclosure victims. None of ACRON'S programs, according to James O'Keefe and Hannah Giles, were successful.

Who were O'Keefe and Giles? They are an independent filmmaker, James O'Keefe and a columnist, Hannah Giles. O'Keefe posted as a pimp and Giles as a prostitute, and they asked ACORN for advice on how to run a house of prostitution. They wanted to use ACORN money to get started. There is a controversy over the veracity of the film, but in the subsequent investigation ACORN did not appear credible.

By all accounts ACORN was a travesty. President Obama is one of its staunchest critics. This didn't prevent Fox TV News from arguing that the media ignored the ACORN scandal. Dan Gainor, of the Media Research Center, complained that the major networks ignored the story. This was not close to the truth.

WHO ELSE IS A COMMUNIST?

One of the key arguments in Klein's book is that Communists influence President Obama. So is it surprising that he identifies those with a radical persuasion? He links Valerie Jarrett and President Obama's chief adviser, David Axelrod, to Communism. No wonder Communism failed. As a senior advisor to President Obama, Jarrett is responsible for Public Engagement and Intergovernmental Affairs. While this is an important job, it is not one that makes policy. As the Senior Adviser to the Chair of the White House Council on Women And Girls, she is in a position to implement positive social change. If anything she has too much to do, and she would probably flunk a basic test on the principles of Communism.

The problem with Jarrett, as Klein sees it, is that she is from Chicago and the product of the machine politics of Mayor Richard M. Daley. She is also a lawyer and that dams her. Klein's condescending attitude is because of her Stanford degree and law school credentials from the University of Michigan. She is too well educated for this critic.

But Jarrett has hidden problems, according to Klein, her father-in-law was once in the midst of the labor movement. He worked in the Citizen's Committee To Aid Packing House Workers. This organization, he alleges, is a friend to the Communist Party. The reality is that the CCTAPHW was largely a movement to gain wage and hiring equality.

Valerie Jarrett is criticized for seeking to promote her own goals. Klein charges that Jarrett, as a close friend and adviser to the president, has one thing in common with former Democratic presidential confidant, Dick Morris. They both want to promote their own agenda. She isn't always on the same page with President Obama. As a White House Senior Adviser, Jarrett is often the conduit for information to state and local officials. She is a strong and independent woman. President Obama loves this about her. Klein blanches at her superior intellect.

Jarrett's influence in Chicago politics helped her to push President Obama's programs while maintaining a close relationship with the business community. What Klein failed to recognize is that Jarrett is an important adviser who has helped the president formulate policy. She is uniquely qualified to represent President Obama and Klein's use of innuendo as well as his criticism of Jarrett does very little to establish his credibility.

KLEIN ON VALERIE JARRETT

Jarrett's father-in-law, Vernon Jarrett, was an associate of Frank Marshall Davis, the controversial labor movement activist who has been identified as an early influence on Obama. Vernon Jarrett worked with Davis in 1940 in the Communist Party-dominated organization, Citizen's Committee to Aid Packing House Workers. The groups own correspondence, previously uncovered by the *New Zeal* blog, describes its communist influence. Many of its leaders were tied to the Communist Party USA.

David Axelrod also comes in for a pummeling, as Klein links the president's advisor to a world wide Communist conspiracy. This is, of course, utter nonsense. Klein also sees the Nation of Islam and its outspoken leader, Louis Farrakhan, as another influence upon Axelrod. Klein argues "Axelrod...was himself mentored by a Communist." Klein was referring to Donald C. Rose who he described as "a member of a Communist Party front...." (p. 162)

Aaron Klein's job as head of the Jerusalem bureau for WorldNet Daily makes him uniquely qualified to judge radical political influences. Ironically, he is not a credible reporter. The reasons are many, but he uses facts loosely and his analysis is constantly flawed.

KLEIN SEES PRESIDENT OBAMA CONNECTED TO THE NATION OF ISLAM AND BILL AYERS

There is more craziness as Klein suggests that Obama has more than a tenuous connection with the Nation of Islam. When Obama's former Pastor Jeremiah Wright traveled to Libya with Nation of Islam leader, Louis Farrakhan, Klein proclaimed that Obama had ties to the Nation of Islam and Libya.

In **The Manchurian President**, there are twenty-two references to President Obama's ties to the Nation of Islam. None of these spurious facts connect Obama to the Nation of Islam. They are simply examples of spurious scholarship. Klein talks about meetings hosted by Farrakhan, but he fails to connect the president to this radical group.

The absolute fictional part of Klein's argument comes when he places Obama in close proximity with terrorist Bill Ayers. Who is Ayers? In his former life, he founded the Weather Underground in 1969, and this radical group conducted a campaign of bombing public buildings in the late 1960s and early 1970s.

During the 2008 presidential campaign, conservatives attempted to link Obama to Ayers. During the 1960s Ayers radicalism with the Weather Underground led to threats, deaths and jail sentences. Ayers is remembered for his role in the Days of Rage in Chicago in October 1969. Ayers went underground after a series of bombings connected to the Weather Underground and along with his wife, Bernadine Dohrn, evaded the FBI, but it wasn't until 1980 that Dohrn turned herself into the police. She was convicted on state charges in Illinois and fined $1500 and given three years probation. All weapon and bomb related charges against Ayers were dropped due to inappropriate FBI investigations.

While this activity was going on, Barack Obama had nothing to do with Ayers. In his 2001 memoir, **Fugitive Days: A Memoir**, Ayers pointed out that he did not have a significant relationship with Barack Obama. They met briefly, they talked of community organizing techniques. As Obama rose from local Chicago politics, he had no connection to Ayers.

In his second life, Ayers is an elementary school educational theorist. He is professor emeritus at the University of Illinois, Chicago. How does one connect President Obama to cloudy thinking college revolutionaries? There is no connection.

President Obama condemned Ayers past and many of Obama's critics suggested that the Ayers relationship should not be a campaign issue. Why the continued hostility of Ayers?

KLEIN'S INTRODUCTION

Finally, a word of reply to those who assert that in critiquing President Obama, we should all focus on his policies, and not on the man. Respectfully, we disagree. We do not believe in "guilt by association" nor in "the politics of personal destruction." In other words, a political figure should not be judged by his casual political relationships, nor by personal vulnerabilities—and certainly not by his race. We have instead labored to uncover the actual political history, beliefs, mentors, associates, appointments, and motivations of the 44th president of the United States.

The introduction to Klein's book employs one of the oldest literary tricks. He suggests that he is not being critical, he is just reporting the facts. Here is how he sees the facts related to Bill Ayers. 1.) He is a radical who educated Barack Obama. 2.) He is a socialist theorist who wants to transform American democracy. 3.) He is a professor who opposes the main contours of American history. 4.) He is a person whose beliefs make the U. S. prone to terrorist attacks. 5.) On Fox TV News, Klein made the ridiculous claim that Bill Ayers helped to draft President Obama's health care reform bill. There is no evidence the Ayers has had any influence upon the Obama administration.

Aaron Klein is in his mid-thirties, and he is an Orthodox Jew. Because of his religious persuasion, he views the future of the world as one of constant struggle between radical Jihadists and Jews. He also believes that President Barack Obama is dangerous, and he makes no apologies about pointing out the president's radicalism. His radio show, Aaron Klein Investigates, on WABC, is a popular conservative program that is responsible and well thought out. Klein was one of the first reporters to break the story on Van Jones, President Obama's former green jobs czar that led to Jones's resignation. Jones believed that President George W. Bush allegedly was responsible for 9-11. This comment from the left wing nut house, as well as Jones past political activism, led him to resign as the green jobs czar. The Obama administration pointed out that they had not vetted Jones properly. Klein believes that this type of lax security encouraged radicals and terrorists.

Van Jones is a committed environmental advocate, a civil rights activist and he continues to work for such issues as underwater homeowners. "They call it class warfare...if anything, it's warfare against people who have no class...they won't even return our phone calls when our houses are underwater," Jones remarked.

KLEIN ON BARACK OBAMA'S RADICALISM

Obama's exposure to Ayers' ideology, astonishingly enough, traces back to Obama's childhood and the Hawaiian church at which the future U.S. president attended Sunday school as a boy. While a firestorm ignited during the campaign over Obama's 20-year membership, as an adult, in the church of radical Reverend Jeremiah Wright, almost nothing has been reported about his Sunday school attendance at First Unitarian Church of Honolulu, a radical activist church that may have influenced the future president's early outlook.

The lack of evidence and concrete examples makes Klein's contentions laughable. But there is more nonsense. Klein sees Obama's college years as the foundation of his radicalism. While at Occidental College, President Obama was a quiet student who spent his time studying diligently. Few of Obama's professors remember him. So if he was a radical, he was a hidden one. Maybe he had some alternate thoughts. Klein appeals to the Fox News mentality and they love his conclusions.

When he attended Columbia University, Obama was an excellent student. His thesis, "Aristocracy Reborn," had an interesting comment. The future president wrote that the Founding Fathers "did not allow for economic freedom." The only problem with this quote is that no one has verified its accuracy. Did it exist? Who knows! The critics in the right wing nut house took this comment out of context to suggest that Obama is a socialist.

Like most other right-wingers, Klein sees a conspiracy in Obama's birth certificate. The notion that there were seven to nine alterations of his birth record suggests that he is somehow the Manchurian Candidate; programmed by the Communists to overthrow the nation.

Aaron Klein has written a book that is a fictional account of the 44th president. He has no real evidence for any of his conclusions and his mean spirited attack cannot be hidden by his declaration that he is a fair-minded citizen.

R. LEE PRESCOTT EMBARASSES CONSERVATIVES

R. Lee Prescott's, **Barack Obama's Plan to Socialize America And Destroy Capitalism**, published in 2009 by Pacific Publishing Studio, is a self-published book written for the lowest common denominator. When Prescott was through writing with his crayons, he left little to discuss. In ten chapters, Prescott misinterprets and misrepresents the Obama administration. He begins with a chapter "Bankrupting America," which not only has no relationship with the Democratic platform, but the author also fails to understand simple economics.

The ten chapters in Prescott's book are unusually trite, and he presents inane conservative arguments. He begins with the notion that Obama is bankrupting America. Along the way he accuses the administration of destroying capitalism, socializing medicine, destroying public education, ruining the energy industry by protecting the environment and creating a welfare state. This book is poorly written, inadequately argued and an embarrassment to liberals and conservatives alike.

JOHN GRAHAM: OBAMA'S CHANGE

John Graham's **Obama's Change: Communism In America from FDR to B & H Clinton To Obama** is an insulting book that fails to use the historical material properly. The thesis is that Franklin D. Roosevelt, then Bill Clinton, with the help of Hillary and now Barack Obama, are leading the U. S. to a Communist Utopia. This is an old and tired argument. The book is suspect when Graham writes: "I rely on Rush Limbaugh's radio show and Hannity and Beck on TV...." (p. 45) That tells it all. This is not a book that analyzes politics. It is one that relies on those in the right wing nut house for information and analysis.

There is an abundant literature on Communism in America. The author hasn't consulted one reliable history of Communism. Graham, an Assemblies of God Minister, has written one of the worst political books in history. There are a great many good books on Communism in the U. S. Some of the best books are by John Earl Haynes, a Modern Political Historian in the Manuscript Division of the Library of Congress. After receiving his PhD in 1978 from the University of Minnesota, he set out to write eight excellent books on the Cold War, spies and communism. He has a conservative point of view. It is an intelligent one combined with cogent research and skilled writing. Graham writes for an audience that lacks discrimination. Haynes offers serious histories of Communism.

Haynes 2002 book, **In Denial: Historians, Communism And Espionage** argues that the apologists for the Soviet Union run rampant in American universities. Haynes makes a reasoned case for academic excesses. If Graham had followed the same line of reasoning, he would have had an acceptable book. Good! No! Acceptable! Maybe!

While there is a great deal of material on radicalism and Communist-Socialist influences upon American politics, Graham failed to consult this material. Why? He probably can't read anything but the Bible. He is more concerned with selling his book at his church services.

Graham's book design is also insulting. The cover has a drawing of Bill Clinton with a nose and facial features similar to Barack Obama. Graham should show a little respect for the presidency. The publisher, Rose Dog Books, is a print on demand subsidiary of the Dorrance Publishing, and they are a reputable publisher. This is the only thing reputable about the book.

John Graham is an ordained minister in the Assemblies of God Church in Hot Spring, Arkansas. Of all the books discussed his is the least worth reading. He believes that President Obama is "corrupting our system," and his diatribe has little to do with the president. The church coffers allegedly are suffering from this book's sales. It is a shame that this book was published. Fortunately, there are no reviews.

While Graham's book lacks intellect and substance, there are those in the right wing nut house who are bright and well intended. Michael Savage is a good example of a brilliant right-winger. His radio shows are among the best in the conservative field.

MICHAEL SAVAGE'S LONG STRANGE TRIP

Michael Savage was born Michael Alan Weiner on March 31, 1942 in New York's the Bronx. At Jamaica High School in Queens, he talked incessantly and no one listened. When he graduated in 1959, Michael Weiner was remembered as a big talker with lofty goals and a penchant for overstatement. He also didn't like New York and New Yorkers. He is Jewish and his classmates remember that he was often critical of Jewish political issues. He was short, intense, and he wanted recognition. He graduated form Queens College with a degree in biology and earned an M.A. degree at the University of Hawaii in anthropology and botany. Then he traveled to Fiji to study the sedative kava and other Fijian plants. By the 1970s, he moved to California. Eventually, he earned a PhD from the University of California, Berkeley.

Eric Isralow, known as Doctor Rock on San Francisco radio, remarked that Savage's rise to prominence was "a long and strange trip." It was the San Francisco area with its hip subculture, large ethnic population, a penchant for supporting liberal causes and anti-war activity that shaped Savage's stringent conservatism. He is an attack dog from the right due to the liberal nature of the San Francisco Bay Area.

"I think that Michael Savage didn't care for his Jewish upbringing," Isralow continued. "He wanted to be famous as a writer, a comedian, a liberal, a professor, a dean but he had to settle for right wing radio. He told me he's a failure. Give me the money for that degree of failure."

NORTHERN CALIFORNIA FORMS SAVAGE'S CHARACTER

Savage has spent most of his adult life in Northern California. He was always into alternate modes of thought. In his spare time, he hung out in San Francisco's North Beach. He hoped to become a writer. That didn't work. He hoped to become an herbalist. That didn't work. Clearly, Savage was frustrated.

In 1974, after he settled with his wife in Fairfax, near where rock singer Van Morrison lives at times, he spent much of his time haunting the San Francisco literary scene. He had ambition to become a writer, and there he befriended North Beach Beat poets, Allen Ginsberg and Lawrence Ferlinghetti. He met Ginsberg briefly in Fiji. While drinking and eating in the Italian section of San Francisco's North Beach, Savage became a casual friend with Ginsberg, and they wrote ten letters and three postcards to each other. Savage sought acclaim, friendship and support from these beat icons, but he experienced indifference and rejection. The North Beach poet and biographer, Neeli Cherkovski, remembers Savage hoping to become a comedian in the style of Lenny Bruce. None of this materialized. Although he was born in the Bronx and swam naked with Allen Ginsberg, Savage was never a liberal or a beatnik. He was a kid looking to become famous. So he attended the University of California, Berkeley eventually earned a PhD.

MICHAEL SAVAGE: SHUNED BY UC, BERKELEY AND GETTING EVEN

Michael Savage is over the top like most broadcasters in the right wing nut house. The reason is that he was rejected by the academic life that he pursued without garnering a professor's position.

He is an academic, who not only earned a doctorate at UC, Berkeley in 1978, he also applied to become Dean of the Graduate School of the University of California, Berkeley School of Journalism. He never had a high level position in journalism, but he wanted to be the dean of a major journalism school. Grandiose thinking is his mantra. When he attempted to enter the mainstream of academic life, Savage was not only rebuffed, but he felt alienated by the liberal academics.

In 1980, Savage began his journey into the right wing nut house. He looked upon his North Beach artistic and literary cohorts with disdain, and he began talking to friends about conservative nationalism. He is hostile to illegal immigration, he supports the English only movement and he argues that liberalism is taking America down the road to ruin. His views are so extreme that the United Kingdom banned him from entering the country in 2009. The BBC censored his radio show. The alleged charge was that he "encouraged criminal acts and fostered hatred." The action of the British government made Savage an even more popular English figure. This is of course nonsense and it only created more popularity for Savage. When BBC News in May 2009 published a list of people barred from entering the U. K., Savage suddenly found himself on the list with Islamic extremists and white supremacists. He was neither of these folks.

By all accounts Michael Savage is a brilliant radio host and writer. His book, **Trickle Up Poverty: Stopping Obama's Attack On Our Borders, Economy And Security** is a serious, well thought out and well written book. As the host of Savage Nation, he has a syndicated radio show that is broadcast over more than 400 stations.

Much of Savage's message can be seen in his education. After receiving an M.A. degree form the University of Hawaii, Savage completed a degree in nutritional homeopathy PhD from the University of California, Berkeley. It is this education that led Savage to describe himself as emphasizing borders, language and culture. What does this mean? It means that Savage believes solving the illegal immigration problem, ending any restrictions on the English language or national holidays and controlling the excesses of liberalism are necessary goals. He also sees the infusion of other cultures as demeaning. He argues that multiculturalism is a weapon to destroy American history and culture.

The Savage Nation is a nationally syndicated radio show that brought Michael Savage to the forefront of American conservatism. However, unlike the nut job right-wingers, Savage is an educated, articulate and generally fair critic. Not surprisingly, he is the author a number of best selling books. How does Savage differ from the more popular right wing critic? Education, research, carefully articulated opinions and openness have led 8 to 10 million listeners a week on more than 400 radio stations to bring Savage a huge audience.

Michael Savage's life is one of attempting to become famous. Obnoxious, yes! Famous, yes! He has spent his life searching for fame and fortune. He has found it on talk radio and in the eighteen books he boasts about constantly. While he is Jewish, he makes lame jokes about Larry King and Barbra Streisand. He says nice things about fundamental Christians. In **The Savage Nation**, he complains of an anti-Christian bias in America. His ratings in the right wing nut house rose dramatically after that self-serving comment.

He is always a media publicity hound. In December 2011, he offered Newt Gingrich a million dollars to drop out of the Republican primary race. This publicity stunt was more about ratings in the right wing nut house than it was about politics. The main requirement for membership in the nut houses is monetary gain. Savage has the third highest rated political talk show in the nation.

As the 2012 presidential election approached, Savage's **Trickle Down Tyranny: Crushing Obama's Dream Of The Socialist States of America** continued the argument that a Stalin type dictatorship was imminent. Fortunately, most Americans didn't have a clue about Stalin. Had they known something about the Russian dictator, their knowledge would have discredited Savage's book. Savage's argument is a familiar one in the right wing nut house. He accuses President Obama of reducing the U. S. Navy to its lowest point since 1930, burdening the average citizen with increased taxes and printing money to cover his failures. The book contains 516 footnotes that include such respected journals and commentary sites as the **Canada Free Press, Sayanythingblog.com, sodahead.com** and **gunowners.org**. He has really done his research. He thanks his publisher for the willingness to "publish this, my most seminal work." Yuck. It gets worse. Savage writes; "What I've delivered in this book is the most important analysis you'll ever read of why we must stop the tyrant in the White House...." (. 267). At least Michael Savage is humble.

MIKE CULLEN IS A WHINEY LITTLE CRITIC

Mike Cullen, *Whiny Little Bitch: The Excuse Filled Presidency of Barack Obama* is a strange book. Mike Cullen begins by collecting incidents of President Obama whining. The book is a hoot. It is also a lesson to anyone who covets analysis, clear thought, fair criticism and good writing to search for another book.

Why would anyone purchase this book? Cullen argues that Obama has a "messianic complex." He calls the administration a "race baiting" one. The David Limbaugh school of truth seeking and journalism is the fountain for this brutal analysis.

The serious argument here, according to Cullen, is that liberals and Democrats destroyed the housing market. This is good to know. I can no longer blame the banks, the prevalent corporate greed or the appraisers and loan officers who brought on the housing debacle. Of course, speculator had nothing to do with it.

Cullen is a witty and a very good writer. Unfortunately, the truth, clear analysis and research are lost in the process. An example of Cullen's lack of fairness is: "Once he became president, Obama's first phone call was to Mahmoud Abbas, Chairman of the PLO...." (p. 22) Enough said. This is a dreadful book. Fortunately, Cullen makes nickels and dimes, but his colleagues are swimming in cash.

There are no clear records on the amount of money that the seven authors make from their place in the right wing nut house. Michael Savage is economically speaking the most successful as he has an estimated $18 million dollar net worth. John Graham's net worth isn't worth a paragraph. R. Lee Prescott is covered by a not for profit church. Mike Cullen has no public record as does Robert Spencer and Pamela Geller. Maybe books don't pay so well, that is unless you are Michael Savage with a popular radio show. That leaves us with Aaron Klein and he is worth less than Savage but more than the others. Klein is not as rich as George Soros. The message is clear. Write a book you can sell on a radio or television program.

Chapter 12
BARBIE ON STEROIDS: ANN COULTER'S DEMONIC: HOW THE LIBERAL MOB IS ENDANGERING AMERICA

WHEN A MAN CAN TAKE A POLL AND TELL WHAT EVERYBODY IS THINKING, THAT MEANS NOBODY IS REALLY THINKING ANYMORE," MARSHALL MCLUHAN, 1951

Marshall McLuhan would be appalled at the media. He would turn on his television set and see good-looking, photogenic airheads with a university education talking about politics. He would be looking at the Barbie's on steroids. The workout Queens who rule a small portion of the right wing news media. The Queen of the Barbie's on Steroids is Ann Coulter. She is the person who warns, "the liberal mob is endangering America."

Ann Coulter is a lawyer turned conservative political commentator. She is a well-known guest on Fox TV News, and her eight books appear regularly on the **New York Times** bestseller list. She has sold more than four million copies of books with suspect titles like **High Crimes and Misdemeanors: The Case Against Bill Clinton**. Her other books employ titles that emphasize slander, lies, treason and a Godless society to name just a few loaded words. Coulter is an articulate, beautiful, intelligent, media savvy woman who is in her early fifties. Like her idol,

Bill O'Reilly, she describes herself as "impartial, fair and a polemicist." If you criticize her, she will turn on you and call you a moron, tell you that you can't take a joke or that you are a liberal who is hopelessly out of the political swing of things. She is almost impossible to beat in an argument. She is bright and well educated.

FOX TV NEWS: CLEAN PORN AND THE NEWS

Not only is Coulter an example of the intelligent right, she is bringing home millions of dollars via her opinions. But she is not the Barbie on steroids that many suggest. Beneath the vitriolic rhetoric there beats the heart of an actress. Watching her you get the feeling that she is laughing at us, and that she doesn't believe her own incredulous opinions. The only thing that matters is her bank account. The road to media stardom was a long and twisted one for Ann Coulter.

It is her beauty, as well as her brains, that propelled Coulter to fame and fortune. That is if you think looking like a Park Avenue hooker is beauty. She is part of the Fox TV News Barbie showcase. They are all blonde, they are all beautiful, they all have designer clothes that don't fit over their midriff, they are all loud mouthed and they all have conservative opinions. Some feel that the Kardashian's took their model for their clothing line from the Fox TV News ladies. It is the Fox TV News version of "clean porn and the news." In June 2010, Jack Hitt, writing in **Harper's** magazine, asked: "Is Sarah Palin porn?" Why waste the voters' energy and people with issues. I like "Clean Porn and the News." This jab at Fox TV News was one of many. But it remains the most watched news channel in the U. S.

IF NOTHING ELSE ANN COULTER IS PROVOCATIVE

Ann Coulter is known for her provocative and intelligent quotes. She is not known for her insidious and sometimes ridiculous rants. By looking at Coulter's ten worst quotes, it is obvious that Barbie Coulter is in love with herself. She thinks her blonde hair is the next best thing next to heaven. Then again maybe it is the new trend at Fox TV News. Blonde hair, beauty and a lack of discretion are the key elements in the Ann Coulter package. She is my kind of woman.

ANN COULTER TOP TEN WORST QUOTES
1. "Clinton Masturbates in the sink." Geraldo Rivera Show Live, August 2, 1999
2. To a disabled Vietnam Vet: "It is people like you that caused us to lose the war." MSNBC quote

3. On Princess Diana's death: "Her children knew she's sleeping with all these men…it's the definition of 'not a good mother." MSNBC September 12, 1997
4. "I think women should be armed but should not…vote." Politically Incorrect, February 26, 2001
5. "Clinton is in love with the erect penis." This Evening with Judith Regan, Fox TV News, February 6, 2000
6. "The presumption of innocence only means that you don't go right to jail." Hannity and Colmes, August 24, 2001
7. "I think Whitewater's going to prevent the First Lady from running for the Senate," Geraldo Rivera, March 12, 1999
8. "The thing I like about Bush is I think he hates liberals," Washington Post August 1, 2000
9. "Originally I was the only female with long blond hair. Now, they all have long blond hair." Capitol Hillblue.com June 6, 2000
10. "Let' say I go out every night, I meet a guy have sex with him. Good for me. I'm not married." Geraldo Rivera Live, June 7, 2000

ANN COULTER'S TRAINING FOR TV BARBIEDOM

Unlike many right wing critics, Coulter is well educated with a degree in history from Cornell University. At Cornell, Coulter was not impressed with her liberal professors. She was a contrarian who challenged liberal views of U. S. history.

She went on to law school at the University of Michigan and her superior scholarship, as well as high grades, led to the editorship of the **Michigan Law Review**. Most of her classmates ignored her extreme conservative views.

After law school, Coulter worked in Kansas City for Pasco Bowman II on the United States Court of Appeals for the Eighth Circuit. It was here that she refined many of her conservative opinions. Judge Bowman, a former English major as an undergraduate, is one of the more literate justices to sit on a Federal District Court of Appeals. He spent hundreds of hours criticizing and rewriting Coulter's briefs. He is a Ronald Reagan appointee who is a specialist in criminal law. Many of Coulter's opinions on immigration were the result of working with Judge Bowman.

Coulter, a registered Republican, quickly caught the eye of party leaders. She went to work for the Senate Judiciary Committee when the Republican Party took control of Congress in 1994. Crime and immigration were the issues that she worked on for Senator Spencer Abraham of Michigan. She was instrumental in drafting legislation to deport aliens convicted of felonies. It was here that she found her anti-Muslim attitudes.

Her governmental successes prompted her to consider returning home to Connecticut in 2000 to run on the Libertarian Party ticket for Congress. It was this notion that brought her closer to conservative television. She realized that she had no chance for election. Coulter viewed her role as a thorn in the side of the majority. She believed that there was a "weak conservatism." She was determined to bring some fire to the right wing nut house.

Coulter wrote a column "I'd Burn My Neighbor's House Down," which appeared on September 15, 2000 in **Human Events**. What is **Human Events**? It is one of the leading conservative news sites on the Internet dealing with the sins of the left. While the Libertarians are not in this part of the right wing nut house, Coulter was determined to bring the party further to the right.

There was another reason for running on the Libertarian ticket. The Republican Congressman, Christopher Shays, who represented Connecticut's 4th District, had not voted for President Bill Clinton's impeachment. Coulter hated Shays. She vowed to ruin his career. Coulter knew that she had no chance to beat the Republican, Shays, in the general election. She hoped to draw votes away from him. Coulter vowed to elect the Democratic candidate. She caused so much trouble in Connecticut, that she was summoned for a meeting with Libertarian Party leaders. The Libertarians didn't want her, because she was too controversial and her politics were excessively right wing.

When the Libertarian Party met with her, they refused to endorse her candidacy. Harry Browne, the Libertarian Presidential candidate, sent a long letter to **Human Events** disavowing Coulter's opinions. He alleged that she was one dimensional and mean spirited.

Coulter dropped out of the race and went on radio and television with her complaints. Coulter was angry. This began her road to TV Barbiedom. She was already an established author with average sales. She was about to emerge as a best selling conservative commentator. Coulter's books have helped make her a media presence. In addition to being brilliant on camera and photogenic, she writes about controversial subjects from the point of view of the right wing nut house.

COULTER'S FIRST BOOK ON BILL CLINTON-PAULA JONES

Unlike most right wing critics, Coulter can write, think and present a coherent argument. In 1998, **High Crimes And Misdemeanors: The Case Against Bill Clinton**, resulted from her role as an unpaid legal advisor to Paula Jones in her sexual harassment suit against President Bill Clinton. As she wrote legal briefs for the case, Coulter formulated her book. She was also quietly critical of Jones' legal team. She realized that they were ready to settle the case. She wanted Clinton's hide. Coulter believed that Clinton should have apologized to Paula Jones, and she argued that the case was an airtight one.

It was Coulter who leaked to the press Clinton's distinguishing personal characteristic. Newsweek's Michael Isikoff's, **Uncovering Clinton: A Reporter's Story** claimed that Coulter informed the media of Clinton's bent penis. Coulter said that she views Jones as "a hero." When Jones fired her legal team, which included Coulter, she went to court and the case was dismissed.

Coulter was outraged at Paula Jones' decision. "Paula surely was given more than a million dollars in free legal assistance from an array of legal talent she will never again encounter…those lawyers never asked for or received a dime for hundreds of thousands of dollars in legal work performed at great professional, financial and personal cost to themselves," Coulter wrote.

Her **High Crimes And Misdemeanors: The Case Against Bill Clinton** was so mean spirited that most reviewers dismissed it. That is all except those at Fox TV News. They loved it. Her prose is highly emotional, but she failed to prove her case against Clinton. Like most people writing in the right wing nut house, she pulls out one historical anecdote after another to prove Clinton's guilt. But to quote Sir William Scrogg, in 1680, a Lord Chief Justice of the King's Bench, is a bit mysterious. Maybe Clinton was wandering around the English countryside having sex with the maids. This is the level of Coulter's venom, and her scholarship is second only to the Three Stooges. It was the Paula Jones case that drove her to be even more critical of the left.

When Paula Jones announced that she would pose nude for **Penthouse**, Coulter had no comment. James Carville said it best: "Drag a $100 bill through a trailer park, and you'll never know what you'll find." Carville continued suggesting that Paula Jones was a "fraud," at least to the extent of pretending to be "an honorable and moral person."

IT WAS 9/11 THAT BROUGHT COULTER FAME

While Coulter was well known for her conservative political opinions, it was the September 11 attack on New York's World Trade Center that brought her into the critical, conservative mainstream. The day after the September 11 attacks, Coulter wrote in a syndicated column: "We should invade their countries, kill their leaders and convert them to Christianity." As the media was attempting to maintain a reasoned and intelligent approach to the terrorist's attacks, Coulter fanned the flames of ignorance and filled her pocketbook.

Coulter has her media supporters. Richard Lowry, the editor of the conservative **National Review**, stated that Coulter lost a friend during 9-11, and she was writing out of grief. But Coulter wasn't listening. She wrote: "Congress should pass a law tomorrow requiring that all aliens from Arab countries leave…." When the **National Review** refused to publish some of her columns, because they were outrageous and libelous, Coulter's response was to call the editors "Girly boys." She was fired from the **National Review**.

Then things got really heated. Coulter was named the "Conservative Journalist of the Year" and she received the Clare Booth Luce Policy Institute award. What was ironic is that she was fighting with those in the right wing nut house in the same manner that she had gone after liberals. So it was about Ann Coulter not about politics.

In October 2001, there were those who predicted her downfall. Little did they know that all the controversy brought the book publishers running with lucrative contracts. Barbie on steroids was on her way to increased fame and fortune. Her quotes continued to intrigue and they helped to sell her books.

THE WISDOM OF ANN COULTER OR LACK OF IT

"The backbone of the Democratic Party is a typical fat, implacable welfare recipient." Coulter column, October 29, 1999

"Women like Pamela Harriman and Patricia Duff are basically Anna Nicole Smith from the waist down. Let's just call it for what it is. They're whores." Salon.com November 16, 2000

"Juan Gonzales is Cuba's answer to Joey Buttafuoco, a miscreant, sperm donor and a poor man's Hugh Hefner." Geraldo Rivera Live, May 1, 2000

"I think there should be a literacy test and a poll tax for people to vote." Hannity and Colmes, August 17, 1999

"If they have the one innocent person who has ever to be put to death this century out of over 7,000, you probably will get a good movie deal out of it." MSNBC, July 27, 1997

"I have to say I'm all for public flogging. One type of criminal that a public humiliation might work particularly well with are the juvenile delinquents...." MSNBC, March 22, 1997

"I am emboldened by my looks to say things Republican men wouldn't." TV Guide, August 1997

THE COULTER BOOKS CONTINUE

It was Coulter's second book that set the tone for her decade rise to conservative prominence. In 2002, **Slander: Liberal Lies About The American Right**, hit the number one slot on the **New York Times** nonfiction bestseller list. **Slander** argues that President George W. Bush's policies were stymied by unfair and biased liberal media coverage. What the second book established was that Coulter played loose with the facts. At this point her appearances on television increased, and she was a continual presence on the Fox News Network.

Her most ridiculous charge is that the book industry is liberal. This is utter nonsense. The bias in the book industry is toward making money. One of Coulter's literary tricks is a footnote. She included 780 in her book and they nothing to do with her thesis. After checking her footnotes to chapter 2, which she says is her favorite part of the book, it is apparent that the footnotes have little to do with the content.

Coulter's conclusions are more bizarre. She argues that liberals stoop to name calling, while conservatives seldom criticize. She must have ignored Newt Gingrich's career. Coulter complained that Barbara Ehrenreich praised the Communist Manifesto in **Time** magazine. There is no such article.

What Coulter objected to was Ehrenreich's status as a leading writer who is a feminist, democratic socialist and political activist with twenty-one award winning books. It was with a PhD. in cellular immunology, that Ehrenreich began her illustrious journalistic career. She is a serious writer who pursues important subjects. Ehrenreich didn't opt for a career in science. She authored award-winning books concerning women and health issues. Her book **Nickel And Dimed: On Not Getting By In America** is a brilliant study of the working poor. For Ann Coulter, Ehrenreich's greatest sins were supporting Ralph Nader in the 2004 presidential race and then switching to Barack Obama in 2008. She has the writing skill, the brains and the analytical ability that Coulter lacks.

The irony is that Barbara Ehrenreich is everything that Ann Coulter attempts to be in the media world. Ehrenreich is respected, an in-depth writer, an informative critic, if low key, a brilliant speaker and an author widely recognized for her sense of fair play and decency.

Coulter's third book, **Treason: Liberal Treachery From The Cold War To The War On Terrorism**, is purportedly a history of the Cold War. This is a breakthrough book with more than half a million sold in the first three weeks. The reason for the sales is that Coulter believed that the media maligned U. S. Senator Joseph McCarthy unfairly. The Wisconsin Republican is considered the most unreliable Senator in the early 1950s for his witch-hunt hearings to allegedly expose Communism.

Without a shred of evidence, Coulter maintains that McCarthy identified Communist sympathizers and spies in the U. S. government. Coulter then went on to argue that Senator McCarthy is the politician from the past that she most admires. He was a witless, low-grade demagogue intent on ruining the careers of low level government workers. What a role model for Ann Coulter.

In defense of McCarthy, Coulter wrote: "The portrayal of Senator Joe McCarthy as a wild-eyed demagogue destroying innocent lives is sheer liberal hobgoblins." If she bothered to check the facts she would see the college professors, high school teachers, government employees, Hollywood actors, union leaders and writers were fired, blackballed or forced to leave the country, because of McCarthyism. Most of these people never worked again. She ended her defense of McCarthyism by writing: "Liberals have a premature gift for striking a position on the side of treason."

Like Glenn Beck, she claims that liberal historians have gotten it wrong. After spending thirteen weeks on the **New York Times** bestseller list, Coulter was on her way. Historians criticized this book universally; as well as political scientists, popular columnists and liberals. The right loved it.

After Coulter rehabilitated Senator Joseph McCarthy, she re-examined the Whittaker Chambers-Alger Hiss controversy and bronzed President Ronald Reagan for his handling of problems with the Soviet Union.

PROFESSOR RON RADOSH EXPOSES COULTER

Ron Radosh, a history professor who has studied McCarthyism, observed: "I am furious and upset about her book. She uses my stuff, Harvey Klehr's, John Haynes', and Allen Weinstein's to distort what we actually say and to make ludicrous and historically incorrect arguments."

As a Professor Emeritus, which means he taught over thirty-five years and retired, Radosh has a keen eye for writing skullduggery. He exposed Coulter at her own game. She wrote a column on Robert F. Williams as a civil right hero. Most people had never heard of Williams.

Coulter wrote of Williams that he opposed Democratic Party supported gun control laws to keep guns out of the hands of African Americans. This is a reference to the post-Civil War period of Reconstruction. Then Coulter charges that without guns African Americans in the South remained in perpetual slavery after the Civil War. Then Coulter jumps up to the 1950s and 1960s, and she weaves the tale of a Black activist Robert F. Williams. He was the head of the Monroe North Carolina NAACP, and he demanded guns, so African American's in the South could defend themselves. Williams, a member of the National Rifle Association, argued for the doctrine of armed self-defense, and he defended his position by employing the segregated nature of Southern history.

What Coulter failed to mention is that Williams was a far left revolutionary with a Maoist determination. The state of North Carolina issued a warrant for his arrest after he allegedly kidnapped a white couple, and he went to Cuba where he operated a Havana radio station that beamed his left wing show, Radio Free Dixie, all over the South. While in Cuba, Williams wrote a book that supported the doctrines of Huey P. Newton and the Black Panther Party.

Things got worse when Williams left Cuba, because it wasn't radical enough. He moved his family to China where he became persona non grata. Williams then returned to the United States where he was arrested. The state of North Carolina dropped the charges. Williams was driven to extremes by racism and hatred. To have his legacy, his career and his impact compromised by Ann Coulter's shoddy reporting and unsupportable conclusions was the major crime to his illustrious career. That was worse than the racism and the insults.

Ann "Barbie" Coulter took a good story and turned it into fiction. She does a lot of that. To some observers, Robert F. Williams was a hero who fought racism and injustice. Then he veered too far to the left and became a self styled revolutionary. He is not a poster child for the National Rifle Association and gun control. Coulter attempted to put him into a place where he is a civil rights hero. The truth is that Williams' doctrine of "armed self defense" led to Huey P. Newton, Eldridge Cleaver and the revolutionary Black Panther Party. Whatever legacy Williams left behind he tarnished it with his later actions. Barbie Coulter didn't recognize this simple fact.

BARBIE DOESN'T HAVE ANYTHING TO SAY

After three best selling books, Coulter didn't have anything in the can. She was talking all over television, but there was no time to write. Thank goodness. So Crown Forum cobbled together her columns and released them as her fourth book, **How To Talk To A Liberal (If You Must): The World According To Ann Coulter** and this dreadful collection continued her fame. Her income rose to catastrophic levels and her writing plunged to egregious lows.

The fifth book, **Godless: The Church of Liberalism** charged liberals with ignoring God. She also suggested that people of faith were ridiculed and that liberalism was a religion in itself. By this point her sales brought another number one **New York Times** bestseller.

What is bizarre is that Coulter defines Christianity. "Christianity says that human progress proceeds from the part of divinity in the human soul; liberalism holds that human progress is achieved through sex…." She was on a roll and the next book, **If Democrats Had Any Brains, They'd Be Republicans** continued her assault on common sense. Sorry Thomas Paine! An essay, "Airport Security: Make Imams Take Buses" reflected her anti-Muslim tone. In "Christians Must Reproduce More," Coulter's opinions were put together in a piece that makes no sense. It gets worse. "Communism: A New Fragrance By Hillary Clinton" is a great title with a vacuous feel. The tragedy is that **If Democrats Had Any Brains, They'd Be Republicans** is not a book, it is a loose collection of quotes, television and radio commentary and as such it makes no sense. No problem. It still sold well.

GUILTY: LIBERAL 'VICTIMS' AND THEIR ASSAULT ON AMERICA

In 2009, Ann Coulter basked in the glow of her new book, **Guilty: Liberal Victims And Their Assault On America**. The book was dedicated to her parents, who immediately hid out from the media. Maybe it was because they were embarrassed.

Coulter commented: "Liberals always have to be the victims, particularly when they are oppressing others." (p. 1). The introductory chapter goes after Hillary Clinton when Coulter suggests that the former first lady championed the heroism of Officer Cesar Borja. Who was Officer Borja? He was an officer who responded to the 9/11 tragedy. The details differ. Coulter callously argues that the Borja's family claim that he was a hero, and the claim that he worked sixteen-hour days after 9/11 is questionable. She not only hurt his family, she disputed government records. Coulter believes that he was not the hero that Mrs. Clinton suggested. In a cruel and heartless manner, Coulter suggests that his pulmonary fibrosis had little to do with his heroism at 9/11. It had more to do with his pack a day cigarette habit. So not only is Coulter a lawyer, she is now a medical doctor. Whatever the cause of Borja's death, his family was heart broken by Coulter's callous, cruel and unjustified criticism. But it's liberals that receive the brunt of Coulter's vicious diatribes.

"Why do liberals keep coming up with hoaxes...." (p. 4) This sentence sets the tone for the rest of the chapter. She goes on to suggest that minority people use liberalism to make a case for themselves. She discusses "Margaret B. Jones," whose book on growing up half Native American in Watts was a hoax. Then Coulter goes on to show that any memoir about the holocaust is suspect due to liberals. Coulter concludes: "Liberals prey on this deep-seated American instinct to aid the afflicted...." (P. 32) Imagine wanting to help poor and displaced people.

BARBIE ON TV AND THE RADIO

Since 1996, Coulter has been a media darling. Her first spot was on MSNBC, as a legal correspondent. The network was too liberal for her. She was let go twice due to negative comments. In 1997, she insulted Pamela Harriman, the U. S. Ambassador to France, and then some eight months later she made fun of Robert Muller, co-founder of the International Campaign to Ban Landmines. In an egregious comment, she accused Muller of single handedly losing the Vietnam War. She claimed that she didn't know Muller was disabled when she made fun of him. Apparently her eyesight is not so good. She couldn't see his disability.

Coulter was too busy admiring herself in the mirror. Or at least this was her excuse. It didn't matter, she is articulate, beautiful and charming. Since she is photogenic and an intelligent speaker, the news networks couldn't get enough of her.

Soon Fox TV News began featuring her cute, but inane, comments. It was on Fox TV News that she revealed her lack of depth. She spoke of Canada as being one of our former but most loyal allies. She talked of Canada sending troops to Vietnam. They didn't. She continued to employ historical analogies that made Glenn Beck's use of history appear normal.

COULTER COURTS THE CHRISTIAN RIGHT

This is a smart woman. She courts the Christian right with comments like: "I don't care about anything else, Christ died for my sins and nothing else matters." Not surprisingly, the Christian right purchases her books in record numbers. She has been asked repeatedly about her religious views. Generally, Coulter cites privacy and fails to answer questions. There are, however, some indications of where she stands.

First, she is a fundamental Christian. At least this is what she suggests during interviews. "I am a Christian first and a mean spirited, bigoted conservative second, and don't you ever forget it," Coulter remarked.

American Jews are suspicious of Coulter's comments. Donny Deutsch accused Coulter of anti-Semitism in an October 8, 2007 interview on **The Big Idea**. What Deutsch complained about was Coulter's statement that the United States was a Christian nation that wants "Jews to be persecuted." This caused Deutsch to conclude that Coulter implied that she didn't understand Judaism. The Anti-Defamation League and the American Jewish Committee condemned Coulter. She immediately backed off from her comments. The Christian right rose to her defense. Even this gaffe worked to her advantage. Then the National Jewish Democratic Council asked the various networks not to invite her on their programs. Suddenly, she was quiet on issues regarding Jews and Israel. She did continue to prattle on about Christianity.

Despite her comments, Barbie on Steroids remains a favorite of the Christian right. She can talk about God, her country and her values in a dress that doesn't fit better than anyone in the universe. Who said arrogance and a Target dress doesn't sell books? The people at Wall Mart are making an offer for a Barbie on Steroids dress line.

BARBIE ON LIBERALS AND THE WOMEN WHO HATE THEM

Obama's Detractors

In 2007, Ann Coulter's **If Democrats Had Any Brains: They'd Be Republicans** was her sixth book. It was her worst. She introduced the book by writing: "Uttering lines that send liberals into paroxysms of rage, otherwise known as 'citing facts' is the spice of life." She ends by writing: "Fasten your seat belts! This time, I am going 'too far.'" (p. 31) She does without research, without the truth, without panache and without a dress that fits. (see the cover) By analyzing each chapter, don't worry in just a few words, it will become apparent that Coulter and a circus shill have a lot in common. A circus shill isn't as cute. Oh, sexist me.

Coulter's remarks on women would make Big Boy Roberts happy. She has a sense that there is something wrong with women who aren't political attack dogs.Big Boy Roberts: "Anyone who criticizes Ann Coulter has me as an enemy."

ANN COULTER IS A CONTRARIAN

Ann Coulter remains a dedicated contrarian. She once remarked that America would be better off if women couldn't vote. When she attacked Democratic presidential candidate, John Edwards, he called her a "she-devil." This didn't hurt her confidence; it was exactly what she wanted. Recognition. Power. Prestige. Media coverage. These are her elements.

She is also anti-gay. The Gay and Lesbian Alliance Against Defamation has complained that Coulter's sense of bigotry is one of the reasons that discrimination remains an issue. She denies the charges. In an irony that gays and lesbians appreciated, Arizona Republican Senator John McCain chided Coulter for her attitudes.

When Coulter appears on the Bill O'Reilly Show, she is so strong in her criticism of President Obama that O'Reilly seems to be defending the president. She is a contrarian for no other reason than to bring her pretty face into your living room. There is little content. If you like beauty and a Barbie tone, Coulter is for you.

When she is challenged, Coulter invariably invokes the Don Imus school of journalism. She states it is all a joke. She is the joke. The problem is that she complains constantly about "uptight white feminists," criticizing her. These women are hurting her career. She can't believe that a woman would criticize her. Whoopi Goldberg, on "The View," pointed out that Rush Limbaugh and Ann Coulter used the issue of Herman Cain's sexual harassment allegations to make it appear that they supported African Americans. No intelligent voter was caught up in this charade.

Then Coulter went after California Congresswoman Maxine Waters. What was Waters' sin? She spoke out against the bigotry of the Tea Party and the over the top quotes from Coulter.

Ann Coulter is neither a bigot nor a racist. She is a fame-seeking writer who will use any means to grease her publicity wheel. What is better than talking about race? You don't have to read any books or think, after all this is just your opinion.

BARBIE IS BLEEPED ON MORNING JOE

By looking cute and dressing provocatively, Coulter has fooled many television hosts. Not so with the Morning Joe program. The MSNBC early morning news program in late November 2011, bleeped her use of the phrase "douche bag" to describe John McCain. She complained that he consistently maligned conservatives, and this made her mad. She was bleeped out for thirteen seconds while she maintained that she preferred conservative principles to McCain's consistency.

When Coulter appeared on the MSNBC Morning Joe Program, the host, Joe Scarborough, tried to tone her down. Morning Joe was no match for Coulter's ranting and raving. On Morning Joe, as Barbie Coulter crossed her legs in a slinky black dress and tossed her bottle blonde hair in the air, she was campaigning for Mitt Romney. She defended Romney changing his political views constantly. She barely listened to the host Joe Scarborough. What sets Coulter apart from her friends in the right wing nut house is her complete lack of credibility. Barbie Coulter has gone so far as to call Ted Kennedy "a human pestilence." This is crass considering Morning Joe regular Mike Barnicle was a close friend of Senator Kennedy. When Scarborough suggested that Kennedy was a class act, Coulter made fun of him. Not only does Ann Coulter lack class, she needs to learn to dress and do her hair. She is increasingly looking like Pamela Anderson minus a couple of important items.

It is a form of street theater that Coulter practices on air. Morning Joe quit booking Barbie on Steroids. Now she can scream censorship.

THE TOP REASONS THAT COULTER'S DEMONIC IS WORTHLESS

When **Demonic** appeared it was not only a best selling book, but it contained material that is virtually worthless in a historical sense. Jamie Weinstein culled ten of her comments and they are worth analyzing. He points out that she calls Democrats anti-science. She quotes Gustav Le Bon who argues that the Democratic Party purposely downgrades science to control the populace. Who is Gustave Le Bon? He was a French social scientist who died in 1931 at the age of ninety. He was an amateur physicist, a sociologist, and an amateur psychologist, and he proposed theories of racial superiority that made Hitler look like a liberal. How Coulter equates the Democratic Party with LeBon is frightening. It gets worse. She dismisses liberals as not a part of American history. Maybe Richard Hofstadter is a figment of my imagination.

She sees no sign of racism in Southern history. Must be the collard greens that make you so smart Barbie. Coulter also argues that the left is responsible for all the political violence. Maybe John F. Kennedy killed himself. She equates Democrats with dictators. She calls President Obama a socialist.

Her strangest comment is that the Republican Party is the primary supporter of civil rights. She also supports the shooting of students at Kent State, and she blames the shootings on Martin Luther King's civil rights movement. Ann Coulter needs a remedial course in American history. Unfortunately, she is too busy in the right wing nut house to complete it.

RIGHT WING BARBIE ON THE 2012 ELECTION AND MICHELLE MALKIN HAS THE LAST WORD

In December 2011, right wing Barbie began beating up on Newt Gingrich. Why? Did she want to sleep with him? No! She questioned his character. The tired story of Newt's divorces and an affair with an intern, who is his present wife, made Coulter outraged. She also threw around the 2012 Freddie Mac money and chastised Newt for hanging out with Al Sharpton. She may have a point.

As Coulter supports Mitt Romney for President, the best is yet to come. Stay tuned. On the question of money made from the right wing nut house, there is only an estimate but it is a good one. Ann Coulter is worth conservatively $18 million dollars. The only good news is that the Filipina pit bull, Michelle Malkin, is attacking Coulter over her remarks about Sarah Palin. "This is a form of political fragging," Malkin wrote, and she went on to question Coulter's sincerity. It appears that Malkin wants to award Palin the Nobel Prize. Is there one for stupidity? There might have to be three awards.

Michelle Malkin has the last word. She blogs: "I am not the only one questioning her. I'm just one of the few to question her out loud." Be careful Michelle, if you lose the lawsuit your husband will have to get a day job.

Ann Coulter doesn't have to worry about a day job. She has too much money.

Chapter 13
SHE IS NOT QUITE BARBIE BUT TRYING: LAURA INGRAHAM'S BOOKS

"FOR THE GREATEST ENEMY OF TRUTH IS VERY OFTEN NOT THE LIE-DELIBERATE, CONTRIVED AND DISHONEST-BUT THE MYTH-PERSISTENT, PERSUASIVE, AND UNREALISTIC," PRESIDENT JOHN F. KENNEDY, YALE UNIVERSITY, JUNE 11, 1962

Laura Ingraham is an unlikely radio star. Her program **The Laura Ingraham Show** is the eighth most popular listened to radio talk show in America. She has more than five million weekly listeners. Like many other talk show hosts, she is angry as she looks back on her college education. At Dartmouth she earned a bachelors degree, and six years later graduated from the University of Virginia Law School.

What did Ingraham's college professors do to enrage her? They taught her a wide variety of viewpoints. They urged tolerance toward gays, immigrants, liberals and those who had a different view of American democracy. Her professors really had it wrong. She would convince them of their errant ways.

The dye was cast at Dartmouth, when she surfaced as the **Dartmouth Review** editor in chief. She was the schools first female editor. She attacked a Dartmouth music professor, Bill Cole, for what she considered unprofessional behavior. Cole later sued Ingraham for $2.4 million and Dartmouth paid his lawyer fees. He ended his lawsuit in 1985, and the matter was never resolved. It was settled out of court and allegedly Cole received an extra retirement income. As a child of privilege,

Ingraham lacked respect. The Bill Cole incident suggests her future direction.

THE BILL COLE INCIDENT: WHAT IT SUGGESTS

Bill Cole is a performing jazz musician who taught at Amherst College and then at Dartmouth. He is also the author of two well-regarded books on Miles Davis. Later, he wrote on John Coltrane's jazz. The Coltrane book grew out of his PhD dissertation, which he completed at Wesleyan University in 1974.

Laura Ingraham wrote a critical article for the **Dartmouth Review**, "Professor Cole's Song And Dance Routine," which appeared in the January 1983 issue. She complained about his unconventional teaching style. She also alleged that he was incompetent. He sued the paper for libel. She quoted Cole as saying: "A lot of you are racist or sexist or out to lunch. But that's your problem not mine." The war of words between Professor Cole and fledgling journalist Ingraham was a campus event that prompted Dartmouth to receive a great deal of unwanted publicity. She attacked his course for being second rate and insignificant to a college education. She also disparaged his teaching. Her lack of racial tolerance and her strident criticism went beyond good taste and sound judgment. Her stated goal was to rid the college of minority students.

As a result, Ingraham charged that Cole's class lacked the academic standards common to an Ivy League education. Ingraham quoted anonymous members of his class negatively talking about Cole's teaching. Ingraham said that he looked "like a used Brillo Pad." Then the article attacked Dartmouth's affirmative action program. Cole, who is African American, wasn't going to take this abuse. A large number of Cole's students were African American, and there was no common agreement that his class was insignificant. African American students applying to Dartmouth declined dramatically. Laura Ingraham won her first battle.

Professor Cole is a brilliant writer, an accomplished musician and a well-educated academic. A small coterie of students allegedly decided that he was not of the right lineage and he didn't possess the manners necessary for an Ivy League school. The personal insults toward Professor Cole were astonishing. The administration seemed afraid of the students. The incident did have serious repercussions. It triggered a demonstration by the Dartmouth Afro-American Society. They held a protest in support of Professor Cole. There was a tense racial atmosphere. The

African American students were outraged that a small group of **Dartmouth Review** students could treat a full professor with such disdain.

The conservative students argued that they were imposing standards. Ingraham accused Cole of disjointed ramblings rather than structured and tight lectures. Cole was quoted as calling reporters for the **Dartmouth Review** "racist dogs" and "scum of the earth."

How does Bill Cole fit into the Laura Ingraham story? Ingraham attacked Cole for what she termed "unprofessional" and "racist" behavior. Ingraham claimed that Professor Cole harassed and attempted to intimidate her roommate. Apparently, Cole swore in class and let Ingraham know that he was angry. When he sued Ingraham for $2.4 million dollars, the issue divided the campus. When Cole withdrew the lawsuit in 1985, he did not name the inaccuracies in Ingraham's article that prompted the initial lawsuit. She claimed this as a moral victory.

The swearing in class comment was the most ridiculous one. Since the majority of college professors are talking to theoretical adults, the swearing was not an issue. The issue was the ethnic studies department and its popularity among students. Professor Cole was also among the most popular instructors on campus. This did not sit well with those at the **Dartmouth Review**. Laura Ingraham disliked African American studies, and she did everything in her power to destroy academic offerings in that area.

What the lawsuit and the case was about was not Bill Cole. Ingraham used Cole as a means of attacking Black Studies and ethnic history. The paper attacked the faculty, the administration, some student groups and anyone with a liberal agenda. Even more incredible the white students, led by Ingraham's example, sued the school alleging racism because they were white. That case quickly disappeared.

The sad thing about the **Dartmouth Review** controversy is that some journalism students decided Professor Cole was incompetent. This is not their role, nor legally their job. But they harassed him into a lawsuit that was settled without explanation.

Dartmouth's attorneys did not want to air the college's dirty laundry. They did everything in their power to end the public battle. Dartmouth's perception as an elite Ivy League college was threatened.

The Bill Cole case was a featured story on 60 Minutes, and the ensuing publicity whetted Ingraham's appetite for fame and fortune. She also saw first hand the media's power. It was a lesson that she took to the bank.

The Professor Cole and **Dartmouth Review** case saw Ingraham, and her band of intellectual Nazis use the First Amendment to terrorize a full professor. But this was not the only controversy for Ingraham. The fun was just beginning for those who followed Ingraham's conservatism. This incident whetted her appetite for controversy and conflict, and she soon found other issues to condemn.

The sad thing is that Ingraham hurt many young students, who were from another culture, ethnicity or life style. She never apologized for her cruel behavior. Gays received her harshest criticism.

CHEERLEADERS FOR LATENT CAMPUS SODOMITES

Her behavior at Dartmouth was out of bounds. She labeled a Dartmouth gay rights group as "cheerleaders for latent campus Sodomittes." When the **Huffington Post** covered Ingraham's early years, they were shocked. Her defense was that she was simply using comedy. The Don Imus excuse for racism. While Ingraham often uses laughter as a weapon, she is innately cruel and demeaning. She is, according to one anonymous friend, angry that she is not Ann Coulter.

Perhaps the stupidest thing that Ingraham said came in October 2011 when she informed Bill O'Reilly that she wasn't sure that Barack Obama was African American. She did this by asking if Herman Cain "would be the first black president…." Insulting, yes! The truth no!

The Dartmouth Review characterized Ingraham as having the "most extreme anti-gay views imaginable…." One wonders how her gay brother, Curtis, felt about his sister. To her credit she did change her views and in a brief piece in the **Washington Post**, Ingraham recanted her previous statements. She blamed her action on the "callous rhetoric" of youth, and she announced her support for equal protection under the law for gays.

INGRAHAM, COULTER AND D'SOUZA COME FROM THE SAME PUMPKIN PATCH: IS CLARENCE THOMAS THE GODFATHER?

The **Dartmouth Review** was also the launching pad for Dinesh D'Souza's career and not surprisingly, like Ingraham, he outed gay students. Even stranger, D'Souza's wife looks like Laura Ingraham and Ann Coulter. Is this conservative cloning? Coulter hated her history professors. Ingraham didn't like the books she read in college and D'Souza complained that affirmative action babies were ill equipped for college. All three believed that Clarence Thomas had the right opinions on the U.S. Supreme Court, affirmative action and terrorism. One friend suggests that Thomas was the Godfather to conservative critics.

Not surprisingly, Ingraham clerked for Judge Ralph K. Winter, Jr. on the U.S. Court of Appeals for the Second District in New York and then went on to clerk for Clarence Thomas on the U.S. Supreme Court. The results were interesting ones. Justice Winter, a Ronald Reagan appointee, was concerned with foreign intelligence surveillance, and he was vocal about lax laws on terrorism. He also composed a number of decisions on the need to regulate Wall Street. From Winter, Ingraham developed a hostility to business malfeasance.

From Justice Clarence Thomas, Ingraham picked up the notion that President Obama appointed elitists to the U. S. Supreme Court. This was Ingraham's view of Elena Kagan, and it was influenced by interviews with Justice Thomas. He has great admiration for Ingraham. Not surprisingly, she shares many of his viewpoints.

Ingraham developed her political views with a dash of Ronald Reagan combined with a slice of Clarence Thomas. This means she supports a limited government and court decisions that harass, intimidate and restrict immigrants, the poor and the blue-collar worker.

FROM RONALD REAGAN TO CLARENCE THOMAS: FORMING INGRAHAM'S POLITICS

Her politics were formed in the 1980s, when she went to work as a speechwriter in the Ronald Reagan administration. She wrote speeches in the domestic policy sector, and this experience shaped her conservative views.

Before she landed permanently on radio, Ingraham had two stints on cable television in the later 1990s as a CBS commentator, and she hosted the MSNBC program Watch It. She was successful on both shows but Ingraham found it difficult to bring her increasingly conservative views to the fore. She realized that radio was the key to her future.

In April 2001, the Laura Ingraham Show debuted on XM Satellite Radio. With more than 300 stations carrying the show, she was an instant hit. She quickly became an official guest on the Bill O'Reilly Show. She is syndicated on AM radio and the Laura Ingraham Show remains a staple among conservatives. A new Barbie was about to enter the right wing nut house, it was Laura Ingraham.

By attacking the Democratic Party, Ingraham made her political reputation. In the Congressional elections of 2006, she urged her listeners to jam a toll-free Democratic Party phone line. Two years later, she had the number six show on talk radio. She learned a great deal from watching Fox TV News, the Don Imus Show and Ann Coulter's media appearances.

When it became apparent that she was a well-known radio-television personality, the book contracts came thundering into her office. The mainstream publishers looked at her as a minor league Ann Coulter. Even a minor league political figure could make a lot of money.

I'M NOT ANN COULTER BUT I'M TRYING

From 2000 to 2011, her five books have sold well but they tell us very little about politics. These books are filled with gossip, hurtful innuendo and speculation. They are also without fact. In 2000, **The Hillary Trap: Looking For Power In All The Wrong Places** indicted Clinton as a false feminist. She described Hillary as a victim, a dependent personality and a person dangerous to families. This ridiculous tome was followed by **Shut Up & Sing: How Elites From Hollywood, Politics and the UN Are Subverting America**. This 2003 book attacked liberal elites in politics, the media, the professors, the artists, the entertainment world, the business community and international organizations. Her goal was to provide middle class Americans with the respect that they were due in politics. The conservative publishing house, Regnery, spent an inordinate amount of money on publicity and the book sold well.

The publicity paid off as Ingraham's next book, **Power To The People**, released in 2007, shot to number one on the **New York Times** best seller list. She concentrates on the "Pornification" of America," and she stresses that family values are in decline. She argued that the election of Barack Obama threatened the family. This only whetted her appetite to continue to attack the Democrats and President Obama.

These early books couldn't compare to **The Obama Diaries**, which appeared in July 2010. This collection of fictional diary entries, supposedly made by Barack Obama, was a huge seller. She claimed it was satire, but the truth is that the essays were cruel, demeaning and mean spirited. She also didn't provide any insights into the president or the White House. When the book was criticized, she simply stated that the reviewer had no sense of humor.

The Obama Diaries, despite disastrous reviews, was a best seller and reached the number one slot on the **New York Times** bestseller list. It slipped to number two but stayed there for a month due to excessive and expensive media publicity. Who says that you can't buy a best seller! There was a controversy when the **New York Times** placed the so-called fictional **The Obama Diaries** on the non-fiction book list for best sellers. The **NYT**'s defended its action by pointing out that it was a "satirical fictional journal with commentary, by the conservative political commentator." In this convoluted explanation, the **New York Times** book editor, Sam Tanenhaus, took a stand. Ingraham and her publisher can call it fiction, but, as Tanenhaus suggested, this was a ploy to cover up their bad taste and libel suits.

Many of the entries in the book are racially insulting and Democratic Senator Harry Reid is attacked for giving a racist speech. Ingraham's book is a very weak and anti-intellectual satire that is uninteresting and never intelligent. The spin and distortion from Ingraham does little to provide credible information on the Obama administration. What **The Obama Diaries** accomplishes is to appeal to prejudices and stereotypes. But for Obama haters it is the quintessential book.

In **The Obama Diaries** there are a number of themes, and they all fit into the right wing nut house. She observes that President Obama is "disempowering the family." (p. 60) Ingraham continues by charging that Obama is frequently discussing abortion. (p. 44) A nice charge but there is no truth to it. She also argues that health care reform will pay for abortions. (p. 344) The truth is that the health care bill prevents use of federal funds for abortion. Ingraham characterizes Obama's foreign policy as apologetic. (p. 221) The truth is that President Obama has strengthened our position in world affairs. The most disingenuous attacks are on President Obama's family. They were so disgusting you would think that the writers for Beavis and Butthead and South Park got together. When Ingraham describes Obama's "twisted family tree," (p. 56) she goes beyond credible limits. Michelle Obama takes the brunt of Ingraham's criticism, when she describes the first lady as an angry woman who "derides patriots." (p. 8)

In 2011, **Of Thee I Zing** continued the use of humor with declining sales and little interest in her opinions. She disparaged Native Americans, and she talked about the decline of American culture. No one cared. Fortunately, this book didn't sell as well as her others. Hallelujah!

The subtitle to **Of Thee I Zing** is "America's Cultural Decline From Muffin Tops to Body Shots." The picture on the front of the book shows Laura Ingraham dressed as George Washington. Ego is a strange thing. It can change your persona. Maybe Ingraham is getting ready to save the country from Socialism, Communism, the Democrats, President Obama and Bono. My vote is for her to ban Bono.

Ingraham's books offer nothing significant about American politics. They are a cruel and callous attempt to cash in on the anti-Obama fever. It works for her. She is a millionaire. She is also clueless and witless.

WHY LAURA INGRAHAM IS A PROBLEM

Laura Ingraham sees Ben Affleck as the greatest danger to American democracy. You can see the danger in watching his movies. Insulting is the best word to describe Ingraham. When she called Meghan McCain fat, she went over the line. The good news is that McCain had never heard of Ingraham. She also told Ingraham to "kiss her fat ass." Maybe Meghan McCain should have run for president.

On the question of "her big fat ass," Ingraham's gym informed me that she wanted the figure of Ann Coulter and the voice of Rush Limbaugh. I applied for a permanent visa to write and teach history in Poland.

Laura dishes out the insults, but her ratings have protected her. After all it is all about the money. Certainly the truth bears little concern. When Ed Schultz called her a "right wing slut," MSNBC suspended him. His remarks were directed at Ingraham's critics who lambasted President Obama's Ireland trip. "President Obama is going to be visiting Joplin, Mo., on Sunday," Schultz remarked, "but you know that (Republicans are) talking about, like this right-wing slut, what's her name? Laura Ingraham?" Nasty! Nasty! He got suspended. If he had blonde hair, conservatism and high heels he wouldn't have been suspended.

Ingraham accepted Schultz's apology, because it continued her media presence. One wonders how she really felt. When Schultz called her a slut, not once but twice, the battle lines were drawn. MSNBC fined Schultz a week's pay. He did try to apologize. She did accept. End of controversy.

Shortly after President Obama came into office, Laura Ingraham's stock rose with the political right. She signed a new contract for twelve months of shows as her ratings continued to improve. She will be around for a long time. Who cares!

Chapter 14
RIGHT WING LUNATICS AND OBAMA'S DIJONGATE SCANDAL THAT INCLUDES CATSUP

"I'M GOING TO HAVE A BASIC CHEDDAR CHEESEBURGER, MEDIUM WELL, WITH MUSTARD….YOU GOT A SPICY MUSTARD OR SOMETHING LIKE THAT, OR A DIJON MUSTARD…." PRESIDENT BARACK OBAMA, MAY 5, 2009 AT RAY'S HELL BURGER.

"THE MCCAIN'S HAVE 7 HOUSES, 13 CARS AND A PRIVATE JET. OBAMA LIKES DIJON MUSTARD ON HIS HAMBURGER, WHICH ONE IS MORE AMERICAN," FOX TV ANCHOR

"THE REACTION PROVED ONE THING I ALREADY KNEW: THE CULT OF PERSONALITY SURROUNDING OBAMA IS REAL. AND MANY OF THE CULTISTS ARE DEMENTED, DANGEROUS OR BOTH." PROFESSOR WILLIAM JACOBSON, CORNELL LAW SCHOOL

The number of manufactured slights, insults and heavy-handed criticism from the Republican Party are legendary. Some are excellent. Others are stupid. Lets look at the stupid. Fox TV promotes this agenda for the ratings. Those who watch Fox put away their coloring books and turn on the one man who looks like a news anchor. The handsome, well-dressed and articulate Sean Hannity. He reported on President Obama ordering a burger at Ray's Hell Burger in Arlington, Virginia. Hannity remarked that the president had Dijon mustard on his burger. He then launched into a virulent and long-winded spiel on how much of an elitist Obama was due to the use of French mustard. But wait the issue is clouded. Dijon mustard is not always made in France.

The dijongate scandal tells us more about President Obama's critics than it does about Democratic Party politics. The amount of time Fox TV News and various bloggers have spent on the scandal is hilarious. On a more serious note, it suggests the degree of trivia that occupies right wing political pundits. The title of this book: **Obama's Detractors: In The Right Wing Nut House** was inspired by the argument over whether or not the use of Dijon mustard made President Obama an elitist.

What the dijongate scandal suggests is the depth to which the media transcends to find a story. As Javier, the busboy at Ray's Hell Burger, told me: "Man I can't wait to get back to Mexico. At least the Federales are fun guys that is if they don't shot you, those guys with the dark suits who came into Ray's Hell Burger. They were dangerous looking."

I asked Javier: "What you do think of the President?" I told him that I loved President Obama.

Javier looked at me like I was nuts. "I love the Mexican President, he can do no wrong. Your guy he's okay, I just don't get why he comes here for a hamburger." I wondered why it was such a big story. Javier is an oracle. He hit upon the main point. Why did President Obama and Joe Biden go out for a hamburger? It was for publicity. They were just two average guys having a burger. Those in the right wing nut house took exception. So did everyone else. The story took on mythical proportions.

If it hadn't been for Sean Hannity and Fox TV News, the escapade would have died in its infancy. It was Hannity who turned the incident into a sensational one. After Obama and Biden's visit to Ray's Hell Burger on May 5, Hannity brought in the big guns. Laura Ingraham and Rush Limbaugh, with his guest host Mark Steyn. They all weighed in on Obama's elitist desire for Dijon mustard.

A video on the Internet showed that the president wanted his burger well done with cheese and bacon. Then it was revealed on MSNBC that the president uses Grey Poupon. Even worse he used Grey Poupon on his meals in Chicago and in the White House.

A call to the owner of Ray's Hell Burger resulted in the revelation that it is an American variety of Dijon mustard that is served. Michael

Obama's Detractors

Landrum, the owner, wouldn't talk to me, but Javier the busboy did. My translation is as follows. I don't think the French are going to like any of this. So I called up Javier and asked him his opinion. As Ray's bus boy he knew all the secrets.

Howard: "Javier thanks for talking to me, did you meet the president?"

Javier: "The day before the president came for a burger guys in suits and earpieces came in. None had a burger. What president?"

Howard: "Javier, what did you think?"

Javier; "I think they nuts."`

Howard: "Did you see the president order Dijon mustard?"

Javier: "What is Dijon mustard?"

Howard: "Did you see the president?"

Javier: No, I went home, I'm not legal."

Well I guess my investigative skills didn't get to the bottom of the argument. So I researched Dijon mustard and found the president used an American brand. Boy was I relieved.

What could be more American than Dijongate? Laura Ingraham also remarked that American's were starving so President Obama could use Dijon mustard. Now I knew the cause of our financial crisis. It is Dijon mustard. I wrote Hannity thanking him for the insights. That was a year ago and I still don't have an answer.

This wasn't the end of the fiasco. Rush Limbaugh picked up the story when his guest, Mark Steyn, echoed the notion that Obama had a silver spoon, and the Dijon mustard was just another manifestation of his alliance with big business.

There were other elements to Obama's radicalism. He didn't always put catsup on his burger. What is more un-American that that? Limbaugh was so angry it looked like he was passing gas. Then Limbaugh-Steyn talked about a Grey Poupon commercial in which a wealthy English gentleman advertised the product. This was an even stronger indictment of our elitist president.

A bit of research clarified the issue. Grey Poupon is now owned and produced by the French Corporation. They make amongst the worst mustard in America. So Dijon is safe. Not only that but some of the Dijon mustard comes from Dubuque, Iowa. There is nothing more American than Dubuque Iowa. There is nothing less French than Dubuque.

There is also a line of other products from the Grey Poupon people. So all is not lost. There is more than mustard to Grey Poupon. The long list of products is due to Grey Poupon's ownership. It is manufactured by Kraft Foods. This is akin to salsa being made in New York City.

The catsup controversy is even more bizarre. Communists and Socialists don't use catsup. The French do. Maybe that is a reason to doubt President Obama. Maybe he is not American because he doesn't like catsup. It gets more interesting. Grey Poupon, manufactured by Kraft in upper New York State, has a rabbi supervising it to make sure that it is kosher. Maybe the analysts are right. This doesn't sound American.

Kraft Foods noticed the controversy, and they issued a press release asking the president to take action. Kraft wrote to President Obama: "We urge you to respond to 'Dijon-Gate' by issuing a 'pardon' to any American who has ever been criticized for putting a liberal spread of Dijon mustard on a burger or a conservative dollop on a ham and cheese sandwich."

But then again Fox News may have it right. According to Hannity, the Dijongate scandal proves that President Obama is a Communist. The proof is that President Obama took President Dmitry Medvedev to Ray's Hell Burger in June 2010. They shared an order of French fries then they ordered burgers. What could be more Communistic? Sharing isn't that a Socialist or Communist ploy? He also took Vice President Joe Biden there. Maybe they are all Communists. Thanks to Fox News for enlightening me.

When President Obama and Russian President Medvedev went to eat at Ray's Hell Burger, the Russian leader added jalapeños, mushrooms and onions to his cheeseburger. They sat at a small table and everyone looked around in amazement. There is nothing like a Ray's Hell Burger for Obama. But eating with a Communist leader. I think this proves Glenn Beck right. You can't trust the president. A guy who has jalapenos on his burger is also suspect, but the Russian press couldn't find a translation for jalapeño, so Medvedev is safe. At least until Bill O'Reilly exposes this indiscretion.

Right Wing talk show host Laura Ingraham cleared everything up for me when she asked: "What kind of man orders a cheeseburger without ketchup but Dijon mustard?" A good question. It certainly couldn't be an American.

Hannity stated it even better: "I hope you enjoyed that fancy burger Mr. President." Boy Hannity cleared things up for me. What a guy.

At the Horeb Mustard Museum, just outside of Madison, Wisconsin, founder Barry Levenson, was furious, and he pointed out that Dijon mustard is a rather common one. While its origins are in France, it is now more often made in the U. S. Levenson added with "too much salt." It is not like the French Dijon. I called Levenson and he told me to come up to the museum, and he would show me more than five hundred mustards. I bought a bottle of Tums and flew to Madison. A week later, I was home with an upset stomach Now I have to worry about the president's blood pressure, as well as my own, there is too much salt in all the mustards. But make no mistake, there is nothing better than 500 hundred mustards.

There is one thing I can't forgive President Obama for when he visited Ray's Hell Burger. He could have had an Old Dominion Brewing Company root beer or a Cherrywine soda or even a Bell's beer. My favorite Ray's Hell Burger beer is Lucifer from Belgium, which is a strong blonde ale. I think the Christian right is powerful, I called Brouwerij Riva S. A. and they told more that they no longer brewed Lucifer. It is a retired beer. It's a good thing they are no longer making it as the right wing could say that he was both a Communist and the Devil.

Maybe Ray's Hell Burger should raise their beer prices for what's left of Lucifer. Jerry Falwell would approve. What kind of person would drink a beer called Lucifer? Charles Manson!

There is one last serious problem with Dijongate. MSNBC didn't fully report the story. As conservative critics looked on the liberal MSNC hosts Andrea Mitchell and Kelly O'Donnell, live from Ray's, reported that two regular guys were out for a burger. Am I missing something? Two regular guys! Then Fox News charged that MSNBC had not accurately reported the story. They alleged that the MSNBC sound and lighting crew made so much noise no one could hear the president's order. They singlehandedly sabotaged the event. It was subversive on his part to hide the request for Dijon mustard.

Professor William A. Jacobson, who has the title Associate Clinical Professor at the Cornell Law School, has the most outrageous posting on Dijongate. He labels MSNBC President Obama's favorite network and Jacobson alleges: "the cover-up is getting deeper." What Professor Jacobson complains about is the edited version of the president ordering a burger. Then just in case Barack Obama is re-elected the professor remarks: "I happen to agree with the president, American mustard is crap." No doubt this is an important issue. Or maybe the professor should get a real day job. Remind me not to hire any of his students.

COMMENTS ON PRESIDENT OBAMA'S USE OF DIJON MUSTARD

Sean Hannity: "As you all know, President Obama is a real man of the people. And yesterday he dropped by a popular Virginia restaurant to grab a burger....Now take a look at him ordering his burger with a very special condiment...Dijon mustard?"

Laura Ingraham: "I don't even like the way the man orders a hamburger."

Mark Steyn: "What kind of man orders a cheeseburger without ketchup but Dijon mustard."

Huffington Post: "President Obama and Vice President Biden made a historic trip to an Arlington, Va. Hamburger joint, to celebrate the 'stress tests' or something...."

Fox TV News Staffer: "Andrea Mitchell and MSNBC covered up the Dijon mustard scandal."

Professor William Jacobson: He called the controversy "Dijongate" on his blog.

Professor William Jacobson: On his blog he accuses Kelly O'Donnell, of MSNBC, of helping Andrea Mitchell cover up Dijongate. Hope the professor has time to teach. Hope the students aren't listening too carefully.

Yuhay's Gun Shop, Union City, California: "Dijon mustard is a condiment that the French invented to feed their godless elitists. It was a vulgar attempt at overthrowing the all-American Ketchup from America's tables. The President doesn't know he was duped."

Sean Hannity: "I hope you enjoyed that fancy burger Mr. President."

Howard A. DeWitt: "I ate at Ray's Hell Burger. It was great. Ray is intelligent. Maybe he should be the president. Then again Javier makes even more sense."

Mark Steyn: "People are talking a lot about the Obama hamburger and this business about him ordering Dijon mustard...and ordering the Grey Poupon. And I have to say, speaking as a foreigner, that I deeply resent Barack Obama cashing in as the Grey Poupon spokesman."

Carolyn A. DeWitt: "My husband has written twenty one books, if he does another one like this I am moving to my home country." (editor's note; Mrs. DeWitt is a Croatian)

I am really glad that Sean Hannity is around to show me the real truth. Maybe Andrea Mitchell and Kelly O'Donnell are also Communists. I can't thank Fox News enough for informing me of the dangers to our democracy.

The last word on the Dijon mustard scandal came from Cornell Law School Professor William A. Jacobson, who concluded that the Obama administration went out of its way to create "a real guy kind of quality image." I wonder did the Professor pass English 101? What does his remark mean? Maybe he has watched too much Fox News. The culprit in this story may be the waitress. She asked President Obama if he wanted regular mustard. He said: "No." The search went on for the Dijon. America has no other problems, so this is a significant subject. Rumor is the French are inviting Obama to Paris and the numerous makers of French Dijon mustards are paying for the trip. It is in recognition of a sharp increase in their sales.

In 2011, the Dijongate scandal continued when Jacques Hazon, the president of the Federation of School Pupils and College Students Parents Council in France, pointed out that the school system banned ketchup. The French government reasoned that if President Barack Obama didn't use ketchup, none of the French students deserved this condiment. Who said Dijongate didn't have a far-reaching significance? Ketchup may be in trouble in America.

Cornell University Law Professor, William A. Jacobson, remarked that Obama had a long history of liking Dijon mustard. One hopes the professor is teaching his law students about more serious matters. Sean Hannity, on Fox, looked seriously into the camera and chided Obama for his "fancy burger." The search for a specialist took us to Canada where Baine Fritzler, of the Saskatchewan Mustard Development Commission, informed me that Dijon mustard is for the regular guy not the elitists.

Baine Fritzler told me that most of the Dijon mustard seed is grown in Canada. The French are going to be angry. Fritzler said that elitists prefer organic mustard. Barack Obama doesn't use organic mustard. " Dijon is pretty common mustard nowadays," Fritzler remarked. I am glad President Obama is an average guy after all. I was worried. Thank you Sean Hannity for bringing all this to my attention.

For the mustard industry, the Dijongate scandal benefitted everyone. The Mustard Museum in Wisconsin reported a thousand per cent increase in those going through the exhibit. When I sent this essay to the French Mustard Company, I received a case of Dijon mustard. I sent the same chapter to France and it was sent back with a note stating that they did not publish the writings of Americans. Then I sent the chapter to Canada and I received a nice letter from a farmer in Saskatchewan asking if I wanted a job. For me Dijongate had a few perks. I received a letter from my friend Claude. It was a one-sentence letter. "Are you nuts?" I don't think so. But who knows!

Arizona Governor Jan Brewer sent me a nice note stating that the chapter was interesting. She also hoped that I was a Democrat. The last copy of the chapter went to my neighbor, former NBA star and TV commentator Charles Barkley. He asked: "What does this have to do with my golf game?" That ended mailing my chapter to critics. I worried that maybe MSNBC had covered up the scandal and Charles Barkley or Governor Jan Brewer wouldn't comment. I showed Claude and Peter the letters. Claude had a one-sentence comment: "Are you nuts?" Peter had no answer. I am looking at MSNBC's cover-up.

IS THERE IS A DIJON MUSTARD COVER UP?

The question of whether MSNBC purposely covered up President Obama's use of Dijon mustard is a marvelous window into the American political mind. Professor William A. Jacobson wrote: "The cover-up is getting deeper. Here is an MSNBC website version of the video in which they cut off the audio just before the mention of Dijon mustard. The Hell Burger theme of the coverage doesn't sound so tough when it's topped off with Grey Poupon." This is from a major law professor teaching at a major university. As a taxpayer I want my money back. Then Jacobson wrote: "There may be addictive behavior involved. Here is one of Obama's **favorite** lunch recipes: **President Obama's Tuna Salad** Tuna, Grey Poupon mustard, mayonnaise, chopped gherkins." I want to thank my newfound friend Professor Jacobson, for explaining the key problem with the Democratic Party and President Obama. It is a plot. You see what has happened. When President Obama ordered a cheddar cheeseburger with Dijon mustard on his first flight on Air Force One, he ignored some problems in Iraq. The President compounded his dilettantish behavior by ordering a medium-well cheeseburger with fixings and fries on a flight from Chicago to Washington D.C. At least Professor Jacobson has convinced me President Obama can't run the country, he is too busy eating cheeseburgers.

Professor Jacobson is about to be inducted into the right wing nut house so he should have almost the last word. He is convinced that there is not only a conspiracy at MSNBC. Jacobson comments: "Andrea Mitchell (does she have nothing else to do) reported that Obama ordered a burger and mustard. Sounds like it had that real guy kind of quality." Let's see Professor Jackson who is more prone to wasting my time? It is you Professor Jacobson. Please don't refer to her as "Andrea." You don't know her. Perhaps this would upset a famous economist. Spend more time in the classroom.

It must be difficult for Professor Jacobson in the classroom. He is described as an Associate Clinical Professor. That means he has tenure but is a long way from being a full professor. You earned full Professor recognition with in-depth articles, serious books and professional papers. There is not a blogger in any university in America who has become a famous professor by online writing. This makes Jacobson angry. It is the fault of all those liberals. It might even be the work of all those Communists. Now he is getting his revenge as a spokesperson against Communist Mustard.

What is the final word on Dijongate? The final word is that those in the right wing nut house, particularly Sean Hannity, could have ignored the story and it would have gone away. Is it important? I don't think so. Then why have I written ten pages about it? Also, will my In And Out Burger taste the same? I don't think so. Because I now bring my own Dijon mustard to the red, white and blue hamburger place when I sit down and polish off a double cheeseburger. At least the restaurant is a patriotic color.

PART FIVE
THE RIGHT WING CRITICS WHO SOMETIMES MAKE SENSE BUT ARE STILL OVER THE TOP

> "COMPASSION IS DEFINED NOT BY HOW MANY PEOPLE ARE ON THE GOVERNMENT DOLE BUT BY HOW MANY PEOPLE NO LONGER NEED GOVERNMENT ASSISTANCE."—RUSH LIMBAUGH

The right wing critics who make sense are the ones who are wary of political correctness. They generally do not use excessive language. They have reasoned opinions that they declare to be fair and impartial. The problem with right wing critics is that they have defined their own level of political correctness. In 2003, when the Dixie Chicks criticized President George Bush, Bill O'Reilly of Fox TV labeled their actions "treasonous."

Despite the less than gracious comments by the Dixie Chicks, virtually no one defended their right to free speech. The so-called "fair and balanced" conservative media almost destroyed the Dixie Chick's career. Fortunately, they are talented and survived. The same cannot be said for many in the right wing nut house. A number of conservative pundits pointed out that Americans are looking for entertainment news. As a result, the Dixie Chicks story became a hailstorm of conservative criticism. The reason is that the three major networks present little in the way of interesting news.

The U. S. network news stations, CBS, ABC and NBC are a hopeless brand of mediocrity. With the exception of Brian Williams, the nightly network news is in flux or is redesigned. This is not true of the cable news shows, as they continually refine their message. On occasion there is hard news but it is always entertaining. The two cable news networks that have some political punch, CNN and MSNBC, are to the left but often tilted to boredom. Fox TV News shares none of these characteristics. Fox TV News, created under media mogul, Rupert Murdoch, represents a confrontational form of shouting at the major news events. Despite being rigidly conservative, Fox TV News uses the description "fair and balanced." This is a brilliant marketing statement that bears little resemblance to reality. People repeat it like a mantra from the Holy Land. It is anything but fair and balanced. The statement should read fear and attacking.

Fox TV News is personality driven. Such big names as Neil Cavuto, Mike Huckabee, Bill O'Reilly, Sean Hannity, Glenn Beck, Greta Van Susteren, Michelle Malkin and Shepard Smith make Fox TV News a viewer favorite. Then there are the whiny, midget guests. Dick Morris is the perfect example of the attack dog midget in a dark suit. His hair is dyed black in the front and remains gray on the sides. He looks like an advertisement for a new form of old age punk rock. As a former liberal under President Bill Clinton, Morris now has his revenge. He is a whiney little turd with nothing to say in the right wing nut house. At least writers like David Freddoso look good on television. He also has something to say. Morris is also so far to the right that Hitler is rolling over in his grave.

A good example of the kind of intellectual Nazis that run Fox TV News occurred when Al Franken used a term in his book **Real Journalism**, he subtitled "A Fair And Balanced Look At the Right." Fox TV News sued Franken as they had copyrighted "fair and balanced." But to their credit Bill O'Reilly, Dinesh D'Souza and Newt Gingrich are thoughtful, intelligent conservatives who attempt basic fairness. They don't always succeed but they try.

While Glenn Beck and Sean Hannity make outrageous, indefensible and essentially inane remarks about the president, Bill O'Reilly does give him a scintilla of credit. Obama sat down with O'Reilly prior to the Super Bowl, and there was a rapport between the two that was surprising.

Bill O'Reilly is the television anchor that excites the critics on both sides of the political aisle. One Internet site, O'Reilly-sucks.com, is a constant critic of the O'Reilly Factor. Steve Senti operates the site and it is a daily look at what is wrong with the O'Reilly show. He is also critical of O'Reilly's troll, Dennis Miller, and this results in some marvelous criticism.

Not only is O'Reilly the star of right wing critics, he sometimes make sense, but also he is the only one who occasionally admits to a mistake. His pompous and arrogant manner appeals to a certain person. These folks can sit around the television and feel informed. God help them if they ever read the Communist inspired **New York Times** or **Washington Post** or that liberal rag **The Economist**. Why read? Bill tells us everything that we need to know. The "no-spin zone" is a joke. But it sure is fun journalism.

Chapter 15
BILL O'REILLY: FAIR, BALANCED, INNFORMATIVE AND WELL INTENDED, AT LEAST IN HIS OPINION: IT'S REALLY PROPAGANDA

"AMERICANS WILL RESPECT YOUR BELIEFS IF YOU JUST KEEP THEM QUIET," BILL O'REILLY

The O'Reilly Factor is the number one cable news show. The reason is a simple one. Bill O'Reilly's forceful, often arrogant, personality appeals to Fox TV News listeners. He also is good at spinning the media. His program segment, The No Spin Zone, is a way of grabbing the viewer's attention. The O'Reilly Factor was the number one U. S. cable news show for 106 weeks from 2007 to 2009.

There are many reasons for O'Reilly's success, but the format is the key. He has two interesting segments, one is "Talking Points Memo" and the other is "Pinheads And Patriots." Both of these segments are entertaining and controversial.

As the author of ten books, O'Reilly's opinions are valued, and his show is one that purports to present a fair and balanced approach to the news. But make no mistake O'Reilly is a traditional conservative.

O'Reilly differs from his conservative commentators in that he is thoughtful and never predictable. He opposes the death penalty. He frequently hosts guests who seldom, if ever, appear on conservative television. Prior to Super Bowl XLV, O'Reilly interviewed President Barack Obama. The fourteen-minute interview established O'Reilly's superstar journalistic credentials as well as his humanity.

The strange thing about the Obama-O'Reilly interview is that they seemed to like each other. O'Reilly was respectful of the President. In turn, Obama was gracious and complimentary. It was more than just politics, they each recognized the others leadership. But O'Reilly did ask tough questions.

The road to fame and riches on cable news television took a long and circuitous road for Bill O'Reilly. Unlike many of his competitors, his education and training placed him in the forefront of conservative news television. A look at his background explains a great deal about his appeal.

THE EARLY YEARS, HIS EDUCATION AND ROAD TO MEDIA SAVVY

He has always been proud of his humble Irish-Catholic roots. Along the way, his education at prestigious Catholic schools helped to crystallize his political thinking.

It is his Irish heritage, which makes O'Reilly a curmudgeon and a contrarian. It was at Catholic high school and later Marist College, where in 1971 he received a B. A. in history that O'Reilly developed his ability to question authority. An athlete, as well as an honor student, he had a Walter Mitty existence. He pitched for the New York Monarchs in a semi-pro league and in college he was a kicker on a club football team. The years as a competitive athlete bred a toughness.

Throughout the 1970s, O'Reilly worked for a variety of television stations. In 1980, he anchored the local news-feature program, the 7:30 Magazine, at WCBS in New York. By 1982, he had won two Emmy's for breaking sensitive stories. He was hired as a CBS News Correspondent. He went on assignment to El Salvador and the Falkland Islands. It was this training as a foreign correspondent which created his solid reputation for reporting hard news. He also learned what did and what did not work in reporting international relations.

An early example of O'Reilly's credibility and integrity came when his crew shot footage of key segments of the Falkland Island war. When Bob Schieffer aired a piece that didn't give O'Reilly and his film crew credit, he quit CBS over this incident. ABC News hired him. It was while working at CBS and ABC that O'Reilly paid close attention to Mike Wallace and Peter Jennings. He watched their intimate style. He soon had his own television manner. That is a forceful, yet intelligent, means of cutting to the core of an issue. There was still need for training. O'Reilly found that tabloid television had its own direction and rewards.

INSIDE EDITION AND TRAINING FOR STARDOM

In 1991, he became a regular on Inside Edition, which is a tabloid news show specializing in gossip. One of the lessons that O'Reilly learned on Inside Edition was that ratings counted and they kept you on the air. The show competed with A Current Affair. It was O'Reilly who brought a credibility to Inside Edition that was previously lacking. He also brought excitement in reporting and a strong personality. In fact, his personal magnetism was so great that anchor, David Frost, was fired after just three weeks. As the anchor, O'Reilly took the show into a serious news direction.

While on Inside Edition, O'Reilly covered the fall of the Berlin Wall, and he obtained a number of exclusive interviews. What he demonstrated was the ability to take a mundane subject and make it interesting. He could also take a controversial subject and make sense of it. It was his news instincts that attracted other networks. At Inside Edition, O'Reilly looked back on his career, and he decided to make some personal changes.

O'Reilly wasn't sure that television was his calling, so he left Inside Edition in July 1994. Everyone questioned his decision. He decided to enroll at the John F. Kennedy School Of Government to receive a Master's of Public Administration. It was the financial world that attracted O'Reilly's attention. He was going to look toward a business career.

Fortunately, at Harvard, one of his major professors, Marvin Kalb, convinced him that the news could be controversial, intelligent, meaningful and profitable. Suddenly the thoughts of a business career went out the window. O'Reilly recognized that the news could be presented in a different format. The hostility over media bias was well known, and it was O'Reilly who pioneered the phrase "fair and balanced." The journey from Harvard to the O'Reilly Factor altered the direction of cable news television.

FROM HARVARD TO THE O'REILLY FACTOR

It was while he attended Harvard's John F. Kennedy School of Government that O'Reilly developed the concept for the O'Reilly Factor.

The road to this top rated television news show began when Roger Ailes, who was then the chairperson at Fox TV News, approached O'Reilly about a news show. Prior to coming to Fox, Ailes was a media consultant for Richard Nixon and others. He is also a staunch right wing conservative who believed that network television had an unwarranted liberal bias.

It was Ailes who moved O'Reilly into his present television slot. It was also Ailes who called the O'Reilly Factor a "blend of news and entertainment." If they get something wrong, they can say it's a joke, we are entertaining you.

Who is Roger Ailes? He is a conservative who advised Republican Presidents in the 1960s through the 1980s. In 1984, Ailes was a major figure in formulating policy issues and campaign directions that helped elect Ronald Reagan. He left political consulting in 1992, and he resurfaced on television. It was Ailes campaign advertisements in the 1988 camping that helped to elect George H. W. Bush. Ailes turned a double-digit deficit in the polls into a startling victory for the elder Bush. He did this with his savvy approach to television.

Ailes personality is a strong one. He called Clinton "the hippie president," and he employed the term "liberal bigots" to characterize those who attacked George H. W. Bush. The early hires at Fox TV News were raving conservatives, but they were intelligent and gifted. One of the most prestigious early hires, Catherine Crier, was a Republican Judge before entering journalism. Brit Hume was another conservative who was given a Special Report segment, which nightly featured a three-person panel who attacked the left. Fred Barnes, an evangelic Christian, was the most obviously biased guest. The viewers loved it, and the profits rolled into Rupert Murdoch's coffers.

Roger Ailes is a brilliant man. To deflect criticism from the left, he included some moderate to liberal guests. From time to time, Juan Williams a National Public Radio host appeared on the shows. Soon Williams became a regular contributor. William's who claims to be a liberal, has this position compromised by his continual defense of his friend, Supreme Court Justice Clarence Thomas. The concept of a left-right debate show brought Hannity and Colmes in a Crossfire type show that was more entertainment than hard news. Alan Colmes is a former stand up comic, who is embarrassing on a news show.

It is excessive television advertising that allows Ailes to dominate the news. He turned Fox TV News advertising revenue into a cash machine. He envisioned Fox TV as a news channel that rivals ABC, NBC and CBS. It was his belief that there was not a strong conservative voice at the national news level that led to Fox TV News. It was in the mid-1990s that Ailes' political attack dog mentality allowed him to employ television to go after his enemies. No one was more despicable to Ailes that Arkansas governor Bill Clinton. When Clinton decided to run for the presidency, Ailes made a decision. He not only had to oppose Clinton, but he needed to reformat the news to give conservatives an even stronger voice.

He worked against Bill Clinton in 1992, and he took over Fox TV News to prevent the liberal agenda from succeeding. Not only is Ailes typical of what Hofstadter labels "the paranoid style," but also he was now in a position to refute liberal political arguments. He needed a credible attack dog to foment hostility to liberals and other radicals. Bill O'Reilly had that elusive combination of intelligence and a media presence that made him appealing. He is on top of the issues and there is no doubt where his sympathies lie.

Much of the credit for the O'Reilly Factor goes to Roger Ailes. He convinced media baron Rupert Murdoch to take the Fox New Channel into a twenty-four hour direction with the emphasis on conservative thought. When Murdoch realized the advertising potential, he was on board with the idea. He also supported the O'Reilly Factor.

It was Republican comments that helped to put over the network. Mississippi Senator Trent Lott called Fox a great news source. George W. Bush labeled Fox News "an impressive transition to journalism." The idea was that Fox TV News challenged the liberal direction of the **New York Times** and the **Washington Post** worked. Fox TV News was a strong network from the beginning.

ROGER AILES HIDING THE BIAS

Ailes brilliance is in his ability to hide or obscure network bias. When Fox TV News aired as a twenty-four hour phenomenon in 1996, no one including its moneyman, Rupert Murdoch, envisioned its level of success and influence.

Fox TV News' legitimacy was enhanced in 2001 when Trent Lott commented to the **Washington Post** on February 5, 2001: "If it hadn't been for Fox, I don't know what I would have done for news." President George W. Bush echoed similar sentiments. When Fox TV News is accused of a conservative tilt they roll out the phrase "Fair and Balanced." The minions who watch Fox repeat the phrase. Then Glenn Beck comes on with his blackboard and lessons in American history. All of this is choreographed by Ailes.

Roger Ailes political background is impressive. He helped George H. W. Bush win the 1988 presidential race. While working as a political consultant for President's Nixon and Reagan, Ailes leaned to attack and destroy. This became Fox TV News' mantra. Ailes' hires extreme conservatives in management as well as anchors. The managing editor, Brit Hume is a well thought of conservative. The daytime anchor David Asman was too conservative for the right leaning **Wall Street Journal**, and he quickly joined Fox News. The list of hires from the Bush presidency include Tony Snow, who was the chief speechwriter in the first Bush administration, and Eric Breindel, who came over from the right leaning **New York Post**. Ailes has done a great job of setting of conservatives up positions of power and authority. The abundance of conservatives on Fox TV News is not accidental. There is an agenda, and it is to end America's liberal tradition. As Richard Hofstadter would point out, it is part of the American anti-intellectual tradition.

PARTISAN POLITICS AND THE FOX TV NEWS PERSONALITIES

The politics of the Fox TV news personalities is what sets them apart from other media personalities. Tony Snow, a Fox anchor, endorsed George W. Bush for the presidency. Snow covered the Republican Youth Caucus as a reporter and jumped up on stage to give a speech supporting conservative Republican thought. Bill O'Reilly gave the keynote speech at David Horowitz's Restoration Weekend. Sean Hannity frequently addresses conservative organizations. They all receive a nice stipend. But they are "fair and balanced."

There is no requirement that the media has to remain unbiased. So the Fox TV News personalities are introducing another element into American politics. They are using personality and ideological beliefs to influence the electorate. They are also cashing a nice paycheck.

THE MOST EMBARRASSING FOX TV NEWS STORIES

There are a number of Fox TV News stories that go beyond good taste. An embarrassing story on Jesse Jackson's sex life brought a new low to network television. Other shows like a panel discussion on Ronald Reagan, led by Tony Snow, was a one-sided love fest. A weird segment aired on how the United Nations was taking over private property.

It is Fox TV News employees who complain about embarrassing stories. When Don Dahler, a Fox executive, resigned it was because management changed a story that stated there was a lack of social progress among African Americans. When Fox TV News aired a daily hour special on the 1998 Clinton sex scandal they went beyond good taste, Dahler speculated.

The Political Grapevine is another segment on Fox TV News that is a bit nasty. It is a segment on news no one needs to know about, and when they analyzed why actor Ben Affleck failed to vote in 2000, the program segment reached a new low. There are often political reports that are meaningless. A good example is the report that a liberal Democratic member of the House of Representatives, California's Pete Stark, was reported to have used foul language at an airport. Despite these inane stories, the Grapevine is a hit. As they attacked liberals, Roger Ailes released a statement that Fox TV News "is not a conservative network!" No it's a comedy act.

Even worse Ailes suggested that the network had more religious programs because the news media beat up on Christians. Fox executive John Moody remarked: "It's always a story that beats up on Jesus." I feel better already as Jesus has his own television network.

THE O'REILLY FACTOR CHANGES THE NEWS

The O'Reilly factor from 1996 to 1998 set the tone for the Fox News Channel. It was a decade before it became the number one cable news show. When Bill O'Reilly appeared in 1996, Fox News was little more than a start up channel.

What made it so successful? The answer is a simple one. Controversial programs. Unique programming. As well as over the top explanations are the keys to success. Political attacks. Contrarian talk. All of these factors under the guise of "fair, unbiased, balanced and accurate." The liberal television watchdog, Media Matters, as well as another organization, Fairness And Accuracy In Reporting, frequently criticize O'Reilly's reporting. He is accused of distorting or misrepresenting the facts. O'Reilly is also prone to misleading or erroneous statistics.

He is heavy on sarcasm and criticism. Unlike most conservatives, he criticizes the Republican Party periodically. O'Reilly has been known to lash out at the right wing for insipid remarks. In March 2003, he appeared on Good Morning America and stated that he would not trust the Bush administration until they got rid of Saddam Hussein. The following year he apologized for his remarks and stated that he was wrong.

What sets O'Reilly apart from his contemporaries is his ability to intelligently attack issues. Unlike Glenn Beck, who is an attack dog devoid of brains, or Dick Morris who is an intellectual midget shouting at

Democrats, O'Reilly can take an issue and clarify it. But sometimes he does go too far.

On the issue of abortion, O'Reilly pointed out that George Tiller, a Kansas physician, was engaging in second and third trimester abortions. He called Tiller "a baby killer." In an acrimonious atmosphere of hatred, Tiller was murdered in late May 2009. O'Reilly simply stated: "every single word we said about Tiller is true."

Some of O'Reilly's comments hit the mark. A case in point is the controversy after the September 11 attacks, in which O'Reilly charged that the United Way of America and the American Red Cross did not properly account for donations, thereby preventing relief to those who needed it. No one proved O'Reilly wrong.

It is O'Reilly's use of statistics, which is suspect. He continually comes up with numbers he says are irrefutable. Then he changes them a short while later. He told one interviewer that 58% of all single mothers were on welfare and 54% of families receiving public assistance are from single parent households. Neither statistic holds up, but he delivers these opinions with such gusto and authority that he is seldom challenged.

When O'Reilly tirades that minority students were receiving too much financial aid, he pointed to Florida universities and stated that 37% of the student body was African American. It turned out at the highest percentage university it was 18% and lower at most other schools.

On international financial support, O'Reilly screams about the U. S. being the number one nation to dole out money to foreign countries. It is not even close. The U.S. gives less percentage wise to foreign nations than Italy. Even worse, when his guests use statistics to demonstrate that he is in error, O'Reilly dismisses them.

From 2005 to 2011, the O'Reilly Factor emerged as the top rated Fox TV News show. It attracts more than two million viewers each night. His daily radio program on 400 channels, and his books and newspaper columns add to the image that he is the King of right wing conservative politics. The O'Reilly Factor is broadcast in thirty countries and a recent political science survey claims that the O'Reilly Factor was responsible for three to eight percent of its viewers voting Republican.

In his approach to the news, O'Reilly has attempted to become the voice of the blue collar, working class American. There is a great deal of controversy over whether or not O'Reilly comes from a working class background.

Another aspect of O'Reilly persona is that he claims not to have a political party affiliation. If so, he walks, talks and analyzes like a Republican. Since 1994, he has been a registered Republican according to the **New York Daily News**. After this was made public, he reregistered as an Independent.

BILL O'REILLY ON RACE AND CLASS

Bill O'Reilly is not a racist. This is often the charge of left wing critics and it is a bogus one. He is also not one to disparage a guest because of class status. That said there is a danger to being a talk show host as from time to time there are incidents that arise which demonstrate strange attitudes on race and class.

In September 2007, O'Reilly went to dinner with Al Sharpton. He commented positively on the radio about Sylvia's restaurant. It didn't take long for these remarks to swell into a firestorm. Sylvia's is a well-known Harlem African American eatery, but to O'Reilly it was just like any other New York restaurant. When O'Reilly went on the air September 19, he talked at length about eating at Sylvia's. O'Reilly remarked: "I mean, it was exactly the same, even though it's run by blacks, primarily black patronship." O'Reilly continued: "I think black Americans are starting to think more and more for themselves...." O'Reilly must not have realized how condescending he sounded. What he tried to say is that he didn't approve of Al Sharpton or Jesse Jackson as political role models. In others words, O'Reilly was appealing to an independent, conservative African American. He found himself attacked by contentious liberals and condescending conservatives.

For some reason, O'Reilly's critics in the left wing nut house slammed his description of Sylvia's. It was punishment enough to eat there with Al Sharpton, but O'Reilly endured the inane barbs of the left with grace and intelligence.

On CNN, Roland S. Martin criticized O'Reilly for his demeaning comments. Martin was incensed with the notion that O'Reilly remarked that African Americans were beginning to think for themselves. What O'Reilly said is that they were for the first time valuing their education and participating in the political process. Martin remarked: "So maybe Bill ought to talk to some more African-Americans to get a better view than hanging out with Al Sharpton and Jesse Jackson." Juan Williams defended O'Reilly, and he labeled Martin's criticism disingenuous. Williams, an African American commentator on Fox TV News, is a brilliant analyst and he observed that O'Reilly's ideas "had nothing to do with racist ranting…."

In 2012, O'Reilly revisited the Sylvia's incident and others, when he complained that Media Matters made a issue out of a simple, harmless comment. "We are in a business to demonize with whom we disagree," O'Reilly remarked. This was an odd remark as O'Reilly is in the business of demonizing. When he is attacked he is upset. He can't afford to be thin skinned. O'Reilly defends his remarks. He claims they are taken out of context.

The intellectual pit bull of the right wing nut house, Michelle Malkin, came to O'Reilly's defense. So it was not about his remarks. It was about liberals and conservatives agreeing to disagree, as they ignored more important issues.

Where does O'Reilly stand on racial issues? He had trouble complimenting African Americans, as he told Professor Marc Lamont Hill. "Now we can't even say you're articulate. We can't even give you guys compliments because they may be taken as condescending,"

On Muslims, O'Reilly suggested that anyone who is a Muslim from age 16 to 45 should be detained at any U. S. airport. O'Reilly defended this as "criminal profiling." On immigration, he views the influx of illegal's as eroding white privilege. Maybe there aren't enough white dishwashers for O'Reilly. He intimated that only African Americans received jobs in the rebuilding effort after Hurricane Katrina.

O'Reilly has little, if any, racial bias in her persona or his program. He simply explains racial issues by an old standard with little knowledge of the present civil rights struggles. He has a sense of fair play, but it is difficult for him to understand the problems of African Americans. He is a born and bred New Yorker who understands diversity, but he went to schools that were predominantly white.

O'REILLY'S LINCOLN BOOK CONTROVERSY

One of the dangers of celebrity journalism is that a television or radio host is talked into writing a book that has little, if any, bearing on his or her expertise. Bill O'Reilly's **Killing Lincoln: The Shocking Assassination That Changed America Forever,** which is an account of Lincoln's assassination, has been banned from Ford's Theater due to factual inaccuracies. The story created a controversy that prompted O'Reilly to claim that the fact checkers didn't like him.

There are some errors. The references to the Oval House are strange as there was no Oval Office in Lincoln's time. The oval office was constructed in 1909. Ellen Fitzpatrick, a University of New Hampshire History Professor, reviewing O'Reilly's Lincoln book in the **Washington Post**, pointed out that O'Reilly resurrects a tale that Secretary of War Edwin Stanton was involved in a plot to assassinate Lincoln. There are at least a dozen books suggesting that this is not true.

Rae Emerson, the Deputy Superintendent of Ford's Theater National Historic Site, went through O'Reilly's Lincoln book, and she had some strong reservations about its accuracy. Most of the comments were minor points of error, and they didn't impact the story line. Howard Kurtz took O'Reilly's side in the argument. Kurtz, a former **Washington Post** reporter, pointed out that four minor errors were not enough to disregard the book. The minor errors did little to challenge the veracity of O'Reilly's book. O'Reilly's look at the Lincoln assassination is a compelling read. It is a rare history book that finds a broad readership. O'Reilly is to be congratulated for his sparkling prose, and he has the facts and events in the proper perspective. The criticism of O'Reilly's Lincoln book is often mean spirited. The reviewers are also prone to discussing other books often losing O'Reilly's in the fog of criticism.

Ed Steers' review of the Lincoln book for the **North & South Magazine** began by pointing out that there were more than 125 books on the assassination. Of these, only eight were researched and written by professional historians. With over 16,000 books and articles written about Abraham Lincoln, it is strange that only a little more than one hundred deal with the catastrophic events surrounding the assassination. There have been so many insignificant books about Lincoln, some examples are **Lincoln's Doctor's Dog** and **Lincoln Prayed**, so the question remains: Why so few books on Lincoln's assassination? With every aspect of his life from his finances to his sexual preferences covered, the absence of serious writing on the assassination is a void in Lincoln's life.

The reason that Lincoln's assassination has received so little attention is that tenured professors at the major universities are not interested. When Bill O'Reilly filled the void, the professor's were furious. He had done his homework and put the material together in a professional manner.

While the book is a good read, O'Reilly and his co-author have ignored some of the major evidence. There are 5,004 documents in the National Archives that were collected after Lincoln's assassination by Secretary of War Edwin Stanton and Judge Advocate General of the Army, Joseph Hold. These documents were given to Colonel Henry

L. Burnett and his assistant, John A. Bingham, for use at John Wilkes Booth's trial. These materials were published in 2009 by the University of Illinois press, William Edwards and Edward Steers, Jr., editors, **The Lincoln Assassination: The Evidence**. While O'Reilly didn't need to read these materials in-depth, it would have helped to have selective quotes.

The more serious charge is that **Killing Lincoln** had errors of people, places and events. O'Reilly refers to James J. Clifford, the John Ford Theater chief carpenter, his name is Gifford, and he was the architect who redesigned the theater. He later served as Ford's chief carpenter. The conspiracy to kill other members of the Lincoln administration is clear. The facts are sometimes jumbled. Lewis Powell, the man assigned to kill Secretary of State William Seward, did not speak with an "Alabama drawl," as O'Reilly suggests. He was from Florida.

There are numerous other errors, but they are minor and the story is told with excitement and accuracy. It is also extremely well written. O'Reilly clearly tells his audience why Lincoln was murdered. His book is also stronger in other key areas. The involvement of the Confederate Secret Service stationed in Canada is examined in depth, as is the close involvement of the Confederate rail line. The role of numerous key people in the plot clearly demonstrates a vast conspiracy. This is a good read and the errors, while serious to professional historians, are minor ones.

If historians can't write an interesting book, that is historically accurate, it is not Bill O'Reilly's fault. So much of the criticism is ill-conceived and it lacks substance. He has written a popular book that Lincoln readers will enjoy.

O'Reilly is not shy about answering his critics. He suggests that one million copies of his Lincoln book in print made it a number one on the **New York Times** bestseller list. It is hard to argue against this point. Read the book and decide for yourself. The only tragedy in this story is that John Wilkes Booth broke his leg and couldn't escape. If he had vanished, there would have been a much more plausible conspiracy.

The best book on the Lincoln assassination is by Ed Steers, Jr. who was a research scientist at the National Institute of Health in Bethesda, Maryland. When he retired in 1994, Steers began a second career as a historian and **Blood On The Moon: The Assassination Of Abraham Lincoln** won the 2001 Lincoln Group of New York's Award of Achievement. The O'Reilly book compares favorably to Steers, this is high praise.

There is no one on television that is more controversial or despised than Bill O'Reilly. Steve Senti leads the O'Reilly haters. His website O'Reilly-sucks.com http://www.oreilly-sucks.com/ is brilliant and intelligent. It is also at times unfair. Senti's hatred for O'Reilly often tilts his criticism. He has daily updates analyzing what is wrong with O'Reilly. Steve Watson is another critic. His article: "O'Reilly's America: Who Is The Real Hater?" is an excellent analysis of Fox TV News.

BILL O'REILLY'S POLITICAL PERCEPTION AND NET WORTH

The O'Reilly Factor has a credibility that allows him to spew out popular political opinions. He also has a strong political sense. That is the reason for his celebrity. He has a political perception that is unique and intelligent. While O'Reilly calls himself an independent thinker, as well as a devoted swing voter, he is strongly conservative. Yet, he is rational and to the point with most of his remarks.

When Fox came up with the slogan "fair and balanced," the network realized that it was the trademark of a brash, opinionated and highly patriotic news channel. Bill O'Reilly is the highest paid and highest rated news analyst on the Fox TV News. His books are best sellers and he speaks widely for handsome sums. The books about him are one sided and often unfair. Al Franken's **Lies (And The Liars Who Tell Them: A Fair And Balanced Look At the Right)**, published in 2003, was the first of many blasts at O'Reilly's career. There is also the substantial study by Peter Hart, **The Oh Really? Factor: Unspinning For Fox News Channel's Bill O'Reilly**, published in 2003. Both books took a dim view of O'Reilly's meteoric career and influence. Controversy pays. O'Reilly's net worth is over fifty million dollars and his annual salary is ten million. He can take the heat. O'Reilly's on air persona is that he is the son of a working class hero. That is true. What is also true is that O'Reilly now is as far as possible from the working class. When Michael Kinsley, the Slate.com editor, suggested that O'Reilly was an elitist, O'Reilly responded by defending his blue-collar roots.

Eric Foner, a noted historian, remarked: "I would not be surprised if there were historical errors as O'Reilly is better known as a TV polemicist than as a scholar." In the **Christian Science Monitor**, Jackie Hogan called O'Reilly out for ignoring the real history.

THE O'REILLY FACTOR: VICTIMS, VILLIANS AND THE VIRTUOUS

What is it that makes propaganda a part of the media? One aspect is that if O'Reilly influences popular public opinion, he does so with propaganda. One of the ways to be successful is to incite dread and a concern for safety. The fear of Muslims, the fear of immigrants, the fear of feminists, the fear of outsourcing jobs and the fear of a socialist president provide credibility for conservatives. O'Reilly employs the use of victims, villains and the virtuous to make his political points.

One of the best ways to induce propaganda is to identify an enemy. By demonizing the enemy, they are subject to hatred and ridicule. The person who identifies them, Bill O'Reilly, is viewed as a sage. It is in the "Talking Points Memo" portion of the O'Reilly Factor that he employs propaganda to make his salient points. On the first segment of the show, O'Reilly uses it to set a mood. Although this segment is only two minutes, it is important to incite listeners. This makes it easier to pass on opinions that may have only a slight grounding in fact.

Shrewdly, O'Reilly generally ignores name-calling. Rather he presents facts that destroy the person or issue that he is attacking. The facts are often glittering generalities, but they sound like important talking points. They aren't, and this gives O'Reilly the advantage of setting the agenda.

But there are exceptions to the name-calling. O'Reilly labeled University of Colorado professor Ward Churchill as following a Nazi philosophy, hating America, justifying murder and as a traitor to his people. These comments on the February 1, 2005 show are right on the money. Churchill is a radical academic who supported Native American rights. That is until 2007, when he was fired for shoddy research. Some allegedly called it plagiarized. O'Reilly was right in every way about Professor Churchill, but he should have toned down his language. Churchill is a person who gives professors a bad name.

The use of generalities is another O'Reilly device. He calls American troops aboard, "the good guys." He suggests that some government decisions are for "the greater good." These are clichés and O'Reilly never met a cliché that he didn't like.

The "No Spin Zone" is an iconoclastic approach to the news. In liaison with the claim, "Far and Balanced," it allows for political arguments that are volatile, lack objectivity and often result in shouting matches. Not only does O'Reilly blur the line between news reporting and entertainment. He blurs fact and opinion. The end result is a new type of news. It is the news of right wing propaganda. As O'Reilly injects fear into his commentary, his arguments appear lucid and convincing. It is all part of the strategy of the "No Spin Zone."

To make his point, O'Reilly often paints the media as the villain. Listeners love this tactic. The lack of media support for President George W. Bush is one of O'Reilly's favorite themes. It helped him win a massive audience.

The image of upholding American ideals is another O'Reilly media trick. He charges that the Obama administration victimizes the people, because Barack Obama is not a Christian or an American. He is a Muslim born in another country. O'Reilly never says this, because he is too smart. He suggests it through innuendo.

Democrats and left leaning organizations are cast as villains in O'Reilly's news reports. He also sees the American public as victims. The Muslims, the illegal immigrants, the welfare recipients and the liberals help to foment dissatisfaction. This in turn boosts his ratings.

SOME OF O'REILLY'S BOOKS THAT MAKE SENSE

Whether or not you like Bill O'Reilly, his books are wonderful. There are five required to understand the O'Reilly influence. **The O'Reilly Factor: The Good, The Bad And the Completely Ridiculous In American Life**, published in 2000, is a twenty-chapter masterpiece that analyzes everything from "the sex factor" to "the race factor." In his introduction, O'Reilly comments on getting a letter from his first grade teacher who disapproved of his comments. So he decided to divided the book into three parts. He analyzes what the average person is up to in America. Then he looks at personal relationships, and he ends the books with what is happening to the U. S. in the present day. Not surprisingly, **The O'Reilly Factor: The Good, the Bad, and the Completely Ridiculous in American Life**, quickly rose to number one on the **New York Times** non-fiction best seller list.

O'Reilly was stung by the barbs charging that he was racist. He began the book with a statement to the Rev. Jesse Jackson: "Jesse, you're wrong. Racism gets all the ink, but the heart of America's somewhat unfair social setup is class, not race. This fact might cut into your power...." (p. 4) Nasty, Bill. Maybe Jesse does or doesn't have class, but be nice he means well. Criticizing his clothes and haircut would have been more appropriate. What O'Reilly is doing is defending his right to criticize class differences. Richard Hofstadter was right. Loss of status, a concern for social standing and a feeling of losing your place in society is most important.

O'Reilly's is a thoughtful book in which class, not race, dominates his thinking. Then he goes on to talk about his life. It is charming. He paints himself as an average person. One of the best parts of the book is a note to a famous politician. This is a device to get your attention and it works.

On race and class, it is a note to Jesse Jackson, and on money it is a note to Hillary Clinton. At the end of the book, O'Reilly gives us a list of books to read, as well as brief sketches of key people. Only Bill O'Reilly could place Jonathan Winters and Mike Wallace in the same intellectual context. But not everybody escapes O'Reilly's caustic pen. On Donald Trump, he writes: "He is a playboy casino owner and luxury apartment builder who wrote in the Wall Street Journal that America needs him as president." (p. 148) It doesn't sound so crazy in 2012.

In 2001, O'Reilly's **The No Spin Zone: Confrontations With the Powerful And Famous in America** established his ability to handle controversial issues. It also was a number one **New York Time** best seller on the non-fiction list. In sixteen chapters, he deals with sex, violence, money, power, taxes, drugs, network television and capital punishment. A surprisingly thoughtful chapter, "The Bill Is Past Due," deals with President Bill Clinton's failures. This chapter features a debate with the bald headed genius who speaks terrible English, James Carville. O'Reilly claims not be a Clinton hater. Then he goes on the mention every time Clinton stubbed his toe or other parts of his body. In the love fest that followed O'Reilly and Carville agreed that the president would be better off without a publicity adviser.

O'Reilly has gone after the Reverend Jesse Jackson with a flair. In a chapter on Jackson's finances, he doesn't interview the good reverend. He has Sheldon Cohen, a former IRS Commissioner, as well as Jackson's attorney Lewis Myers debate O'Reilly, who did a marvelous job of pointing out the economic inconsistencies in Jackson's background.

It took a great deal of integrity to take on Jesse Jackson who is no stranger to the spin zone. What O'Reilly has done that most network talking heads wouldn't consider is to look into the complex and multi-layered Jackson finances.

In 2003, **Who's Looking Out For You** was dedicated to Roger Ailes. Not surprisingly, the media specialist who made O'Reilly's name a household word was impressed with the book. It was a number one **New York Times** best seller. This book deals, as O'Reilly wrote, with: "powerful entities (that) can crush you unless you understand them." (p. 5) He argues that the federal government is not good at helping real people. He goes on to suggest what the government is good at: 1.) letting Jesse

Jackson profit; 2.) keeping Camp David clean; 3.) incarcerating terrorists without charging them; 4.) sending Congress on lavish spending sprees; 5.) keeping investigations of corrupt politicians a secret and 6.) collecting taxes from individuals, not corporations. (pp. 36-37) Roger Ailes would be proud of this list. The contrarian nature of this book is refreshing. When a chapter "Minority Report" begins O'Reilly intimates that minorities have a more difficult time in the economy. It is the decline of the family, O'Reilly laments, which is part of the problem. O'Reilly's attitude on race in this chapter is liberal. He concludes: "It is still a much tougher road for minorities in America than for us whites." (p. 186)

In 2006, **Culture Warrior** came out with an argument that there is a battle between traditional values and those who hope to alter American into a "secular-progressive" nation. Once again this was a number one **New York Times** best seller. The book sold more than a million copies in its first three months.

The media receives a great deal of attention in this book. Peter Jennings is rated as a newscaster who favors traditional values, while Dan Rather and Tom Brokaw are described as rating mongers who have little regard for tradition. The lack of discipline in American society frightens O'Reilly. He sees the epidemic of drugs and crime as a major source of America's decline.

Critics of **Culture Warrior** rightly point out that there is seldom balance to O'Reilly's thought. For all the promises of "fair and balanced," his thoughts are directed toward the mainline conservative.

In 2008, **A Bold Fresh Piece of Humanity** came out with an introduction that stated: "Reading This Book Will Dramatically Improve Your Life!" The book begins when O'Reilly turned eight and was in Sister Mary Luarana's class. This is not a complete memoir but a charming and well-written look into his life. He made amends after the dreadful **Culture Warrior**. What this book does is to suggest that Rush Limbaugh and Sean Hannity are lightweights. They don't have the vision that O'Reilly possesses. O'Reilly, on the other hand, after visiting seventy countries, completing two tough degrees, dipping or stepping into every political movement possible and thoughtfully adjusting his ideology has turned into a sage. Limbaugh and Hannity are bellowing icons with little thought behind their comments. They give a bad name to conservatives.

The final O'Reilly book in this pantheon of his greatest hits, **Pinheads And Patriots: Where You Stand In The Age of Obama** is a take off on a segment of O'Reilly's show. In a unique marketing ploy, O'Reilly has a contract that requires his publisher, Harper-Collins, to send a copy of every book sold to a soldier serving in the Operation Enduring Freedom front.

Pinheads And Patriots examines President Obama's life and concludes: "the country is divided and exhausted by a brutal economy." (p. 54) He goes on to criticize healthcare, class warfare and there is a chapter "Loathing Obama," which tells one all you need to know about where O'Reilly stands in the political spectrum. He is not an independent. Rather, he is a conservative Republican with the same mentality as Fox TV News commentator Karl Rove. They are attack dogs with brains, skill and shaky facts. If you twist the facts the right way you have the complete spin zone. But his book is worth reading. It is fascinating as it ends with O'Reilly's reflection on interviewing President Obama. In what turned out to be a civilized interview, Obama and O'Reilly acted like they were old friends. It was a marvelous piece of journalism. The only criticism came from the far right who were convinced that O'Reilly had sold out. What they didn't recognized is that he is "fair and balanced." Something Roger Ailes and the rest of Fox TV News should consider.

Whatever you think about Bill O'Reilly and his books; they are well written, thoughtful, and full of insight. They are predominantly fair and reflect his concern for humanity. The bilious Karl Rove and the overfed Rush Limbaugh should take note. At times, O'Reilly is a liberal, most of the time he is a conservative, but he is always informed and civilized as a media icon. You can't ask for anything more.

Whether you like Bill O'Reilly or not, he is an excellent analytical television visionary. Stop and listen, he has something to say. It is not complete conservative nonsense; some of what O'Reilly says makes good sense. Even to a liberal.

Chapter 16
THE NINCOMPOOP NOMINEE: NEWT GINGRICH

"THERE WERE ENORMOUS DIFFERENCES BETWEEN THE ROLE OF THE PREVIOUS DEMOCRATIC SPEAKERS AND MY ROLE. THEY HAD BEEN ESSENTIALLY LEGISLATIVE LEADERS…I, ON THE OTHER HAND, WAS ESSENTIALLY A POLITICAL LEADER…SEEKING TO DO NOTHING LESS THAN RESHAPE THE FEDERAL GOVERNMENT ALONG WITH THE POLITICAL CULTURE OF THE NATION." NEWT GINGRICH, 1998

In late November 2011, **Newsweek** headlined: "The Nincompoop Nominee: Newt Gingrich." On the surface, this judgment appeared harsh. If one looks at his career, it is a roller coaster ride to success to failure back to success and who knows what is in the future? But Gingrich is hardly a nincompoop. Newt's characterization of himself runs from that of a political outsider who will reform the system to a politician with deep knowledge of history. Gingrich's intransigence hasn't always earned him plaudits. Yet, he is a brilliant man with an analytical mind.

On the personal side, he is an egomaniac with a flair for the ladies. He loves to answer questions from reporters by restating or reshaping the question. Then he provides his own spin on it. He has been accused of repeated adultery with younger women and his marriages, until the recent one with Callista, is the subject of intense media fodder. He has a charming personality and he has a way with words.

He has the unique tendency of comparing himself to historical figures. This is maddening, but it tells one a great deal about his personality. He has grandiose visions, and he sees himself as the historian who will take America into new and dramatic directions. These character traits demonstrate that he is a narcissist with a personality disorder. This is common to people who seek power. The continuing problems with his personal life plague his political future. The sex tales, the financial problems and the overstatement make him an interesting figure. He was fined $300,000 and reprimanded by the House for ethical wrong doing when he was the Speaker. It was the first time in the House of Representative's in its two hundred and eight year history that a Speaker was disciplined this harshly for ethical violations. Despite these flaws, Gingrich was until late April in the midst of the 2102 presidential race.

This book deals with those in the right wing nut house who make money from television, speaking engagements and books. Gingrich is an accomplished writer, a prolific speaker and a wealthy man. His opinions land him squarely within the right wing nut house. The problem is that his personal behavior negates his political brilliance. He is a walking contradiction. That is what makes him most interesting to the media.

IS NEWT GINGIRCH A BRILLIANT POLITICIAN?

Newt Gingrich is one of the most brilliant minds in American politics. He has claimed this title in numerous speeches and interviews. He is also a well-known author. His twenty-five plus books are an indication of his prolific nature. Because he has written so many books with co-authors, some critics question his productivity. He may not have written all of these books, but Gingrich is a remarkable intellect. It is his ideas that drive the books. A good example of his intellect came in mid-December 2011 when he delivered a speech on the subject of brain science, while campaigning during the Iowa Caucus.

This strange speech on brain science came after a group of students interrupted his presentation. It was typical Gingrich, as he then shifted to discuss his possible Republican presidential nomination. It was entertaining, informative and strange.

When he rose to Speaker of the House of Representatives, he exhibited unusual political ability. He has the power of persuasion, the gift of compromise, the depth of knowledge to make his point, and he has an uncanny ability to draw support from diverse political factions.

Then along the way, he became a serious presidential candidate. He has distinguished himself in state and national politics. While his personality is over the top, there is no question that he is well informed. Gingrich has a way of answering questions by cutting directly to the core. He is brusque, often insulting, and he is always intelligent and combative. This has resulted in a personality that is alternatively pleasing and protesting. Gingrich has strengths that he exploits in the political process. He also has some personal weaknesses. These traits are the result of an unfortunate childhood.

THE INNER QUEST OF GINGRICH: A PSYCHOLOGICAL LOOK AT POLITICAL MOTIVATION

When he was growing up, his paternal grandfather haunted Newt. It appears his grandfather passed on some genetic traits. Robert Kerstetter, born on August 30, 1888, had a number of non-marital liaisons, and he was a man about town. His conquest of the ladies was legendary. By the time that Robert died in 1953, he was known as the preeminent ladies man around Milroy, Pennsylvania. He had married at least three times and lived with a number of women while siring ten children. Robert never married Newt's grandmother, since she was fifteen and he was thirty-seven when they started living together. He worked in a steel machine plant as a laborer. He had a remarkable intellect and a blue-collar outlook. Kerstetter was a strong influence upon Gingrich.

It was Newt's parents who were a nightmare. His mother, Kathleen "Kit" Daugherty was sixteen when she and Newton Searless McPherson, who was nineteen married. By time that Newt's dad witnessed his son's birth on June 17 1943, his father already had a new girl friend. The birth was the major event in a marriage that lasted three days. Kit began raising her son alone. She also filed for divorce and received child support. His father joined the Navy. "My father grew up a very angry person," Gingrich told Gail Sheehy. "When he signed up for the Navy, the recruiting officer said, "Why did you fill out your application wrong?" Newt looked forlorn at Sheehy and he continued: "My father found out that he had been born out of wedlock." Newt went on to describe the emotional rages that followed.

Newt says his mother asked for the divorce while other sources suggest that Big Newt at six foot three and two hundred sixty pounds went off to marry another women while starting a new family. It was three years after their marriage ended that Newt's mother told her former husband, Big Newt, he could drop the child support payments, if she remarried. He agreed. Newt was traumatized by his manic depressive mother and his brutish father. One thing both parents possessed was a strong intellect. So Newt did get something along the genetic line.

When Kathleen married Bob Gingrich, he adopted Newt. Because of the family difficulties, Newt's mother, spoiled her son while encouraging him to read. By 1960, the seventeen-year-old Newt Gingrich was a psychological mess. He told Gail Sheehy: "I remember in the Scottish tradition...I would have been mythically called the McPherson." Newt was doing what he could to ignore his biological roots. He imagined that he was part Scottish and a comic book character. He may have been right. He is something of a fictional character.

There is psychological baggage from this experience that still haunts him. His stepfather shaped the family with lectures on government, religion and the future. In 1995, when Gingrich went on a twenty-five-city tour to promote his book, **To Renew America**, he talked at length about his rootless background. Using his publisher, Rupert Murdoch's money, there were insights gleamed into Newt's character that are frightening. While a Southerner in politics, Gingrich talked at length on this 1995 tour about his youth. Most of it was fictional, but he was a savvy politician, as he extolled his lower middle class, blue collar, working class roots. This was a clear distortion of his background, but it was important to his political evolution. He desperately wanted to be a man of the people. Even if he was a fictional one.

The first revelation from this 1995 tour came from Marianne Ginther Gingrich, the second Mrs. Gingrich. She told **Vanity Fair** that she couldn't envision herself as the first lady. If he wanted to run as president, Marianne would oppose it. She had a good reason. "Watching Hillary has just been a horrible experience," Marianne remarked. She went on to point out that she would discourage Newt from running for the presidency. He responded by divorcing her.

In the in-depth story for **Vanity Fair**, Gail Sheehy discovered that Newt takes his inspiration from John Wayne and action movies. Robert the Bruce, the main character from Braveheart, is another Newt favorite. Robert the Bruce is as much a lunatic as a historical figure. Gingrich remarked: "I'm a mythical person." Gingrich believes that he is a romantic political figure or for that matter a romantic individual.

While talking with Sheehy for the **Vanity Fair** piece, Newt told her that his relatives were "farmers, steelworkers or industrial laborers." He describes himself as a blue collar individual. This is a flight of fantasy unsupported by fact. Fiction dominates Gingrich's life. The inner New Gingrich is a fabrication. The personal side of Newt Gingrich reveals an egocentric, narcissistic personality with a penchant for overstatement. Yet, there are many strong points to the personal Newt Gingrich.

THE PERSONAL SIDE OF NEWT GINGRICH

As an accomplished writer, a refined speaker and a curmudgeon, he entertains liberals and conservatives. He is an interesting media personality. He has translated his television appearances into millions of dollars. On television, Gingrich has a deep understanding of American politics. It is this knowledge that he claims is his primary qualification for the presidency. He can answer a question better than anyone in American politics. His meteoric rise in the House of Representatives is a prime example of his political acumen. As the Speaker of the House, his power was unrivaled. Then he experienced a nasty personal and political fall. He is often said to be among the three historically most powerful House speakers

There are a number of serious character flaws in Gingrich's persona. He married his high school math teacher, who was nine years older. He divorced her. After he married his second wife, Jackie Battley, he began a long-term affair with his aide Callista Bisek, and after six years he divorced his wife and married Callista. The story that Gingrich presented his second wife with divorce papers while she was dying of cancer is not true. She is still alive and causing Gingrich grief. There were plenty of other Gingrich remarks about his ex-wife. When talking with President Jimmy Carter, Gingrich allegedly remarked of his first wife, Jacqueline, according to Robert Scheer in the **Los Angeles Times**: "She's not young enough to be the wife of the President." It is hard to believe that he admitted to this nefarious comment, but there was no retraction. It is in his youth that Gingrich was directed toward a political career. The early years explain a great deal about his later life. In numerous interviews, Gingrich is obsessed with his early years. He has never forgotten the period of his life, and he dwells on it.

THE EARLY YEARS EXPLAIN NEWT GINGRICH

While growing up in Columbus, Georgia, Gingrich traveled as a teenager to France. It was here that he stood at the memorial to the Battle of Verdun between the French and the Germans in 1916. This brief visit changed his life as he consumed history books. He was intrigued by this battle in World War I between the French and the German armies. It was this early lesson in history that caused him to major in history. At Emory University, he received a liberal-religious education, and he avoided the Vietnam War. He was a student and he received a deferment. "I should have gone over," Gingrich remarked of his ability to avoid military service.

At Emory, he was an aggressive, loud and highly opinionated student. He was thin with good looks and the ability to impress his professors. He entered graduate school at Tulane University and in four years he earned an M. A. and PhD in history. As a student Newt was intrigued with political leadership.

At Tulane, he spent years analyzing the political systems of various nations. After he earned a PhD in European history, he envisioned his political future. The irony is that he describes himself as an American historian. His doctoral dissertation was on a European topic: "Belgian Education Policy In The Congo, 1945-1960." It was not published and Gingrich went out on the job market without scholarly acclaim. He never recovered from the slights that the academic community perpetuated on his psyche.

While completing his degree at Tulane, he interviewed in the spring of 1971 at the annual meeting in New Orleans of the Organization of American Historians for a position in a university history department. He was appointed an assistant professor at West Georgia College. Along the way, he became interested in the Republican Party. It was while studying at Tulane that he attended the St. Charles Avenue Baptist Church in New Orleans. He did this to acquaint himself with the influence of religion on politics. It was this early combination of religion and politics that formed the basis of his political character. He was also interested in historical personalities and how they gained power.

From extensive reading, Gingrich was intrigued with the personalities and political machinations of Winston Churchill, Joseph Stalin, Benito Mussolini and Adolph Hitler. What interested him were their speeches, their use of language and their sense of history. He realized that these historical figures understood the importance of rhetoric. He also noted the importance of the big lie as well as image. He didn't consider character important. This was demonstrated in his early marital life. He could sweet-talk virtually any woman into doing his bidding.

While an assistant professor, he was known for his flamboyant speech and political statements. An example of how his early training directed his later political views came when he accused President Obama of running a political machine that was taking the country toward Socialism. He labeled Obama the most radical president in U. S. history. Newt made it clear that the nation was approaching permanent socialism. This rhetoric came from reading Friedrich von Hayek's **The Road To Serfdom**. It was this 1944 book stuck in the stacks of the Tulane Library that prompted Gingrich to talk at length about neoliberals. This is a philosophy emphasizing economic liberalism, which uses the principles of private enterprise to promote open markets. It is the role of the private sector that is most important to neoliberals. Government is limited and the private sector determines the political and economic priorities of the world. These views are the direct result of his doctorate. At West Georgia College, he found academic life stifling. Gingrich had a secret. He had a long buried history of liberalism. How does one earn a doctorate in European history without liberal credential? There were so many liberal ideas in his political soul that he had to hide these beliefs. He also had trouble with his academic colleagues.

While at West Georgia College, Gingrich did not get along with the other professors. He eventually switched to the geography department; he was an important force in establishing an interdisciplinary environmental studies program. He was a radical liberal and his colleagues had trouble with his over the top left wing views.

When he left West Georgia College after almost eight years he hadn't secured tenure in the history department. That is because he thought and did things differently than the other professors. He had a vision. He was so popular, as a lecturer, that he was forced out of the history department into the area of geography. It was all because Gingrich was too liberal.

GINGRICH'S LIBERALISM: WHAT IS MEANT

The irony of Gingrich's early years was that he was a doctrinaire liberal. Gingrich at one time was a Planned Parenthood advocate, he filmed a global warming commercial with Nancy Pelosi, and he lobbied for liberal causes. He had ideas on universal health care that are close to President Obama's. He toured the nation with Al Sharpton arguing for educational reform. He also sponsored 418 bills with Nancy Pelosi while in Congress. He supported amnesty for illegals. In 2008, Gingrich remarked that he would have voted for a TARP bail out if he were still in Congress. When he entered the political arena as an obscure professor in 1974, the media was attracted to his brains and eloquent speaking style. Liberalism was deeply in his soul.

In 1974, the **Atlanta Constitution** supported his bid for Congress as a liberal politico. As a politician, who has continually reinvented himself, Gingrich has as much baggage as Charlie Sheen. His early liberalism evolved from a campus professor model to one that was acceptable to conservative Republicans.

When he entered politics in the mid-1970s, Gingrich described himself as a Nelson Rockefeller liberal. An unusually talkative and eccentric thinker, Gingrich early on lectured anyone who would listen about the environment, the need for increased entitlements and facilities supported by big government. He advocated increased personnel and facilities for medical care. A strong supporter of the arts, Gingrich believed in federal grants to theater as well as poets and writers.

But Newt was a pragmatist. He wanted to get elected to public office. After four years as a liberal, he analyzed what he needed to do to win elections. It didn't take him long to ignore his earlier political pronouncements. In the beginning, he was a classic college professor liberal. He quickly evolved into a conservative to get elected to a public office. Pragmatism, not principles, ruled Gingrich's personality. Fuzzy thinking and lack of logic ruled Gingrich's political mind.

Few people realized that Gingrich was once a liberal. When he ran unsuccessfully twice against Jack Flynt for Congress, he emphasized environmental issues and reform themes.

Alvin Toffler, the futurist, was Gingrich's guru. What did Toffler offer Gingrich? It was Toffler's writings on technology and his influence on social change that attracted Newt. Gingrich learned some important lessons from his early liberal-academic years. The importance of attacking your enemies and overstating your position was his foremost lesson.

There is little consistency and even less ethics in Newt Gingrich's political career. He is a brilliant thinker, a spellbinding orator and he sounds as though he has thought out America's political direction. Don't be fooled. He has one interest-Newt Gingrich. But to become an electable politician, Newt realized that he had to evolve into a conservative.

NEWT GINGRICH'S ROAD TO RESPONSBILE CONSERVATISM

Newt Gingrich didn't became a conservative without training. In the 1970s, he analyzed what was politically significant and what was not politically acceptable. He developed a careful plan for electoral success. The initial campaigns for public office were disastrous. In 1974 and 1976 Gingrich made two failed attempts for a seat in the House of Representatives. It was while campaigning in Georgia's Sixth District that he learned some of the hard truths of politics. His opponent, Jack Flynt, an entrenched Democratic conservative with a segregationist background, understood Georgia voters. His contempt for Gingrich was legendary. Flynt remarked of Gingrich: "I'm going to beat the living hell out of this guy...he's an educated idiot." He had to toughen his rhetoric and his politics to succeed. On both accounts Gingrich evolved into a Republican attack dog.

In 1978, he became a full time politician. He left academic life. The truth is that Newt was a failed academic. He didn't write articles for scholarly journals, he didn't pursue writing critical book reviews or for that matter criticism in his field. He shied away from campus politics. In the academic environment, he demonstrated poor academic training, inadequate scholarship and a tendency toward blustery rhetoric. Gingrich had little substance.

One of the political lessons that Gingrich realized was that it was virtually impossible to defeat an entrenched incumbent. There was a great deal that Gingrich learned from challenging Flynt. His opponent had a strategy to remain in office. He continually evolved his political platform to remain in power. These ideas were always in line with voter thinking. Flynt was an anomaly. He was a segregationist who prided himself on treating everyone with respect. He was an old style Southerner with a mean personal streak. Gingrich did not forget this personality defect, and in some ways he came to embrace it.

GINGRICH'S RISE TO POWER

One of the political lessons that Gingrich learned early on was to dissect the demographics of the Sixth Congressional District. It was Georgia's wealthiest congressional enclave. By using the phrase, "the corrupt liberal welfare state," Gingrich endeared himself to those in the right wing nut house.

Gingrich was re-elected six times to the House of Representatives and along the way he established impeccable conservative credentials. In 1983, Gingrich founded the Conservative Opportunity Society. The COS met each week and the group held in-depth meetings to discuss key policy issues. It was due to this organization and these meetings that Gingrich became a well-known conservative. President Ronald Reagan adopted the "opportunity society" concept for his 1984 re-election campaign.

From 1981 to 1988, Gingrich established a power base in the House, as he continued to drift to the right. He opposed a ban on loans from the International Monetary Fund to Communist nations, but he did support a bill for a Martin Luther King, Jr. holiday. In many ways Gingrich was a contradiction.

He also had a social life that caused many to blink He screamed out about immorality in Congress, while he was cheating on his wife and openly having dinner with good-looking interns; one of whom became his present wife. But he was consolidating his power. He was also adept at ignoring his critics.

In May 1988, in league with 77 other House members and Common Cause, Newt brought ethics charges against Democratic Speaker Jim Wright. The allegation that Wright used a book deal to pocket money, thereby avoiding House ethics rules, led to his resignation. One irony of the battle was that Gingrich's book, **Window of Opportunity**, was criticized when his expenses were picked up by a limited partnership. Not surprisingly, Gingrich organized the limited partnership. He knew how to bend Congressional rules.

The ethics battle lead to Gingrich being selected in May 1989 as the House Minority Whip. He emerged as a major political figure. As House Whip, Gingrich concentrated upon publicizing his ethical politics. His power developed so rapidly that the Georgia Democratic party, who controlled the redistricting for the House of Representatives, attempted to redraw the lines in Gingrich's Congressional District. The Democrats did this to prevent his reelection. It didn't work. When the Democratic controlled Georgia General Assembly redrew Congressional districts, Gingrich's hometown, Carrollton, was placed into the Democratic dominated 3rd District. Five-term Democrat Richard Ray represented this Democratic power base. Georgia Democrats reasoned that Ray would defeat Gingrich. But Gingrich sold his home in Carrollton and moved to Marietta in the newly drawn 6th Congressional District. It was here that he once again won re-election. His antipathy toward the Democratic Party escalated.

MAKING HIS BONES IN THE HOUSE: GINGRICH'S POWER PLAYS: 1989

Much of Gingrich's power came from his isolationist foreign policy. In May 1989, there were talks about appointing a Panamanian administrator to supervise turning over the canal to the Panamanian government. Public opinion was outraged over returning the canal to the Panamanians. There were other domestic issues that Gingrich exploited. He organized the so-called Gang of Seven in the House. They went after what they termed "ethical lapses" in the Democratic Party. The Gang of Seven, led by Gingrich, included seven freshmen Republicans who made ripples in the 101st Congress in 1990. They condemned House banking and postal practices. One of the group's key members, John Boehner, helped Gingrich draft his "Contract With America." When he ascended to the position of House Speaker in 2011, Boehner had Gingrich to thank for his rise to power.

The Gang of Seven used the House banking and post office scandals to create a moralistic public impression of Republican politics. This led to the party taking control of the House in the 1994 elections.

ANOTHER LESSON IN POLITICS: BILL CLINTON AND OTHERS HUMILIATE GINGRICH

From 1994 to 1996, Newt Gingrich learned a number of major political lessons. He experienced the wrath and power of President Bill Clinton, and he was constantly at odds with members of the U. S. Senate. He found that presidential power was a formidable foe. As he rose to power in the House of Representatives, Gingrich was locked in a budget battle with Democratic President Bill Clinton.

In 1993, President Clinton's tax hike was designed to balance the budget. In 1995-1996, the U. S. federal government had a brief shutdown due to differences between Clinton and the Republican controlled Congress. The issue was funding for Medicare, education, the environment and public health. When President Clinton vetoed the spending bill that Congress sent him, the stage was set for a major political battle.

This struggle was essentially between Clinton and Gingrich. Because the president refused the budget cuts, there were two government shutdowns. As Clinton's approval rating fell dramatically, he blamed Gingrich. It was President Clinton who showed extraordinary leadership, as he demonstrated that Gingrich was a self-interested, plutocrat with a massive ego.

The media portrayed Gingrich as a new comer to leadership in American politics. He was increasingly described as power hungry. Clinton was looking for a way to humiliate Gingrich. He found it when the Israeli leader, Yitzhak Rabin, died.

When he attended Yitzhak Rabin's funeral in Israel with President Bill Clinton, Gingrich complained that he had to exit the plane from the rear door. Considering the depth of American political problems, his juvenile attitude drew harsh criticism. His comment made Gingrich appear to be a crybaby. The press crucified him. The so-called Clinton snub at Rabin's funeral escalated into open warfare. The **New York Daily News** had a cartoon of Gingrich on its front page with the headline: "Cry Baby: Newt's Tantrum."

For almost two decades, Jewish politicians have been wary of Gingrich. His comments on Israel and his disingenuous attitude toward

American Jews prompted Senator Carl Levin, Democrat-Michigan, to remark: "Gingrich's cynical efforts to attract attention to himself…will not help his presidential ambitions…." He accused Gingrich of attempting to appeal to the Jewish Channel by stating that Palestinians should not have their own state.

Levin was responding to an interview that the Jewish Channel did with Newt on December 9, 2011. In that session, Gingrich labeled the Palestinians an "invented people," and this caused a strong reaction among his Republican presidential challengers. It may have been one of the few times that Jews defended Palestinians.

Gingrich's approval rating plummeted, as the Republican leadership increasingly distanced itself from his politics. Things got worse. In 1996 Bob Dole, the Senate Majority Leader, was running for the Republican presidential nomination. On budget matters, Gingrich did everything in his power to derail Dole's nomination. There is no man with more integrity in American politics than Bob Dole. Gingrich failed to show him an ounce of respect. The press noted the arrogant attitude that Gingrich evoked.

GINGRICH IN THE HOUSE: HIS ROLE AND REPUTATION

On January 4, 1995 Gingrich became Speaker of the House and **Time** magazine named him "Man of the Year." His Contract With America led to changes in welfare reform, term limits, tougher crime laws and balanced budget legislation.

When he became the Republican House speaker, it was the first time in almost half a century that a member of his party presided over the House of Representatives. He was a key figure in four House sessions filled with in fighting. There was a great deal of productive legislation during his tenure. The Contract With America was a brilliant program. Gingrich drafted it with fellow minority Republicans, and it was unveiled six weeks prior to the 1994 election. This concept emphasized a comprehensive reform package that cut taxes, reformed social security and welfare, advocated legal reforms and emphasized the importance of term limits. The Contract With America is credited with the Republicans taking over the House and Gingrich becoming its Speaker.

As the 58th Speaker of the U. S. House of Representatives from 1995 to late 1998, Gingrich was one of the most powerful men in American politics. The Contract With America was a platform for the Republican Party. It was also a vehicle for Gingrich's power.

The balanced budget idea is perhaps the most important in Gingrich's plan. Welfare reforms and tax cuts were other significant cogs in his plan. Spending cuts were a key part of his program. He wielded extraordinary power. In many ways it was unprecedented power.

GINGRICH'S USE OF THE MEDIA AND THE RIGHT WING NUT HOUSE

Gingrich's inclusion in this book is due to his publishing deals tied directly and indirectly to the Fox TV News network. Rupert Murdoch, who created the Fox TV News network, is a Gingrich fan. He helped the former Speaker reach a massive audience.

Newt's first book deal had nothing to do with Fox TV News. In 1983, he persuaded a group of supporters to finance a corporation that would underwrite his publications. In this business arrangement Dolores Adamson charged that Gingrich wrote his books on office equipment paid for by U. S. taxpayers. In other words the federal government was subsidizing his work. In 1984, Gingrich's **Window Of Opportunity: A Blueprint For The Future** advocated an "Opportunity Society" predicated on space exploration and further advances in computer technology. The foreword written by science fiction guru, Jerry Pournelle, proclaimed: "It's raining soup, and Newt Gingrich has the blueprints for soup bowls." No one knew what that meant but Pournelle is a famous author and it sounded good. The book also had on the cover that Newt was the chairman of the "Congressional Space Caucus."

It was as if Gingrich copied his ideas from Alvin Toffler. This book, written with David Drake and Marianne Gingrich, continued to sell for five years at Gingrich's political conclaves. **Window Of Opportunity** intensified his efforts to continue publishing books for money. He was on his way to wealth via his books.

The **Washington Post** reported that for years Gingrich campaigned in what looks like a book selling tour that is "a for profit enterprise" disguised as a non-profit political event. In November 2011, he delivered a speech in Naples Florida, and then he walked over to a table to sell books. A few days later, in Charleston South Carolina, he delivered a speech seeking the 2012 presidential nomination. Then he walked out into the lobby and sat down at a table filled with books. The audience lined up with their dollars and checkbooks. He sold hundreds of copies of his latest product. But it just isn't books that he is selling. He has children's books, often written by his wife Callista, documentary movies, historical studies, novels and an assortment of other nonfiction books. On Amazon, Gingrich not only sells his books, but he has pink mugs, t-shirts, posters and his opponents even sell "Stop Gingrich" pins. There are over 1600 Gingrich related items for sale on Amazon. Not bad for a guy who couldn't secure a job at the major university after earning his PhD in European history. He has the publishing golden touch. He knows how to promote his product. It appears he writes very little of his product. He is too busy giving speeches, and he also delivers speeches for nice sums of money. Wisdom is after all a valuable commodity. An analysis of his publishing history suggests that he is not breaking the law, but he is carefully maneuvering around it.

His profits from publishing are in a tangled web. In his 2010 personal financial disclosure, required of candidates running for public office, Newt and his lovely young third wife, Callista, reported assets between half a million and a million dollars from Gingrich Productions. The issue was clouded when they also reported a promissory note worth between $5 million and $25 million owed to their production company. This promissory note appears to be profits from Newt's books. But who knows? The tax filing is cloudy and ambiguous.

It is while campaigning that Gingrich often answers questions with a nod to his books or movies. While speaking at a town hall meeting in South Carolina, Gingrich mentioned that he had produced a video of Ronald Regan and Margaret Thatcher. He made this remark after he was asked a question about Russia. He told the audience that they could learn a great deal about how to deal with the Russians from this DVD. The table containing the product sold out after Gingrich's speech. There is little distinction between campaigning and hawking books, DVDs, t-shirts, mugs and any form of peripheral product. Gingrich is a snake oil salesman of the best kind. Along the way he hopes to become president of the United States. Maybe a book-selling table will be set up in the White House. Then Gingrich could write a book on Lincoln. Sorry, Newt, Bill O'Reilly beat you to it.

NEW GINGRICH'S BOOKS DEALS AND CORPORATE ENTITIES

In 1984, Gingrich signed his first book deal with publishing tycoon Rupert Murdoch.

In 1995, Harper Collins, the publishing company owned by Rupert Murdoch, offered Gingrich $4.5 million for a book deal. After accepting the offer, Gingrich changed it to a more lucrative royalty based deal.

In 1999, the Gingrich group was organized as a for profit company. By 2011 when he sold the company the revenues were $55 million.

From 2001 to 2010, the companies that Newt and his wife owned had revenues of almost $100 million from books, movies, DVDs, etc.

NEWT GINGRICH: PROFESSOR OF PROFITS

It is not just the book deals that Gingrich finds profitable. In 2006, Freddie Mac, the government mortgage agency, paid Gingrich $300,000 for advice. There is nothing illegal here, but the deal smelled. What was Gingrich to supply? The answer is obvious. Political influence. But this was just the tip of the iceberg. The professor for profits was paid somewhere between $1.6 million and $1.8 million for additional advice. In 2010, Gingrich went after politicians with ties to Freddie Mac. He failed to note the irony and his hypocrisy. What is ironic about the Freddie Mac deal is that the government sanctioned lending institution went into receivership in 2008. Then in one of the strangest comments from a politician, Gingrich remarked of Freddie Mac: "My advice as a historian, when they walked in and said to me 'We are now making loans to people who have no credit history and have no record of paying anything back...that's what the government wants us to do, as I said to them at the time, this is a bubble." After this comment Gingrich continued to receive compensation from Freddie Mac.

The crown jewel in Gingrich's corporate mélange is the tax-exempt company American Solutions. This corporation allows him to promote his product while campaigning for the presidency. As Gingrich Productions turns out moneymaking DVDs, he criticizes those who use the economy to their advantage. He is so well connected to the moneyed establishment in Washington D. C., that it is frightening to even speculate on his wealth. Yet, Gingrich has the unmitigated gall to remark: "I do no lobbying of any kind." This is a sad comment on his lack of integrity.

The **Christian Science Monitor** revealed in December 2011, that Gingrich was the world's highest paid historian. The source was Gingrich's rival for the Republican presidential nomination, Mitt Romney. In a speech in Manchester New Hampshire, Romney called for Gingrich to return the fees that he was paid by Freddie Mac. Gingrich shot back with references to money that Romney earned from bankrupting companies and laying off employees at Bain.

THE CURSE OF POLITICIANS TURNED NOVELISTS

Not all of Gingrich's writing success is a blessing. History tells us that politicians turned novelists have a curse placed upon them. American publishers love to indulge politicians with literary ambition. They sell books. The question is: "What does it do for the politician?" The answer is they get rich. They also write some of the more convoluted and clumsy prose in fictional form. The novels of Gary Hart, Barbara Boxer, Scooter Libby and Ed Koch are among the most inadequate works in any genre. Their works are absolutely atrocious.

The worst offender is William Cohen, former Secretary of Defense and also a former U. S. Congressman and Senator, whose latest bomb, **Blink Of The Eye**, is a thriller that lacks anything remotely edgy. Forge Books brought out this travesty, which portrays a nuclear bomb destroying an American city. Of course, there are Muslims who want to bring down the world but Sean Falcone, the fictional hero, think William Cohen here, comes to the rescue. It is badly written and appeals to every stereotype known to man or woman. The only good news is that as the 20th U. S. Secretary of Defense, he did an excellent job for Democratic President Bill Clinton.

This brings us back to Newt Gingrich whose historical novels are painstakingly fully of drivel. With titles like **To Try Men's Souls: A Novel of George Washington** and **Never Call Retreat, Lee And Grant: The Final Victory**, Gingrich is mining a field full of fans who know little about history. They take his novelized approach as the word on a subject. What is the point? The point is the bastardization of the historical process. The Gingrich writing factory is not one full of research, diligent scholarship or well thought out opinions. Newt's historical piece, **Battle of the Crater** is a tome from St. Martin's Press that is convoluted fiction. The co-author William R. Forstchen is a Professor of History at Montreat College in Montreat, North Carolina. This is a religious college that is associated with Billy Graham and the two-person history department turns out propaganda rather than serious history. But Forstchen is trained as a historian. The sad thing is that he has used his considerable research and writing skill to become a conservative political polemic. It is a sad commentary on his education. He is a brilliant man, who has never met a religious feeling that he didn't embrace or for that matter a nice paycheck. Yet, his education is a traditional one.

Forstchen's PhD is in military history from Purdue University. He is considered an authority on the American Civil War. He has evolved from a serious historian into a historical fiction writer. He is an academic who has written forty books while attempting to teach. He is neither adept as a professor nor a writer. In 2002, he began the **Gettysburg** trilogy with Gingrich, and then he did two books on Peal Harbor with Newt. An American Revolution novel followed these in 2009 about George Washington. All of the co-authored books have reached the bestseller list. The only conclusion one can draw is that Forstchen is writing "fantasy fiction" disguised as "historical fiction."

What politicians who write fiction accomplish is to present a braver, more heroic version of themselves. They are in novel form smarter than the president, able to detect the nasty Muslims and they present solutions to world problems. If this were the real world it would be a revelation. Unfortunately, it is the fictional world.

In his novel, **1945**, Gingrich and his co-author William R. Forstchen concoct a plot where the United States partners with Japan to allow Germany to dominate Europe. Not surprisingly, the novel is set in the 1930s, and Hitler meets with the American President, Andrew Harrison, who is a fictional character of little presidential strength. There is a female spy who seduces the President's Chief of Staff, and the hero is Commander James Martel who realizes that the Nazis are dangerous. It is a fun book and a good read. It is also a book with a theme. That is the gun control nuts in America are taking away the right of Americans to defend themselves and their country. The book ends without solution and Gingrich promises a sequel, **Fortress Europe**, has yet to appear. Gingrich labels this book "an alternate history" with a message. Somewhere Philip K. Dick is rolling over in his grave.

What is alternative history? It has been the domain of some important writers. Philip K. Dick's **The Man In The High Castle**, published in 1962, theorized how America might have changed had Japan won World War II and occupied the U. S. Robert Harris's, **Fatherland**, published in 1992, suggests that the Axis triumph in World War II would have created a Cold War between the triumphant Nazi regime and the Americans. Harris employs the mystery novel genre, complete with a fictional detective, Xavier March, and the theme he explores is one that speculates on the post-World War II era. That the Nazis might have been preferable to the Russian Communists is one of Harris' themes. Harris's writing and plot are so compelling that he intelligently examines themes of anti-Semitism, technology, and scientific advances common to the 1960s. What Dick and Harris have in common is excellent writing, wonderful plotting and interesting conclusions. What Gingrich and his writing partner lack is believable material.

There are none of Dick and Harris's traits in Gingrich's books. In **Days of Infamy**, his novelization of Pearl Harbor, President Roosevelt is quoted: "Our civilization must not lose this war, or it would be, indeed, as Winston Churchill said: 'a thousand years of darkness." What is strange about this quote it is not from Churchill, but a remark that Ronald Reagan made in 1964. Then again, maybe Gingrich has FDR as a time traveler. It is, after all, fiction. When politicians attempt to rewrite history in novel form they do themselves a disservice and the nation pays with flawed information.

GINGRICH'S POLITICAL POSITIONS AND HIS NON-FICTION BOOKS

It is in his writing, as well as his books, that Newt Gingrich is able to articulate his political positions. Not only is he a best selling author, he is a wealthy man from the product of his pen. His books are ones that use historical illusion to make his points. In retrospect, he has developed a penchant for employing his PhD training in history to legitimize his viewpoint. But it is his non-fiction books that have the most dramatic impact upon his political positions.

As the nation geared up for the 2012 presidential election, Gingrich released a new book, **A Nation Like No Other: Why American Exceptionalism Matters**. This book, published in the summer of 2011 is well written and interesting. It has little to do with serious history. This is Gingrich's way of presenting his vision for America.

A Nation Like No Other presents some interesting points. Gingrich argues that American exceptionalism is the product of our history. Gingrich defines exceptionalism as faith, family, work, and the freedoms of civil society, the rule of law, safety and peace. With examples from American history, Gingrich makes a plea for his own leadership. Gingrich concludes that the Progressive Movement, 1900-1917, and the Franklin D. Roosevelt Presidency, 1932-1945 took America into dangerous directions. Then along came John F. Kennedy and Lyndon B. Johnson and the welfare state took over. It is Gingrich's view that government is now too big, too intrusive and too bureaucratic to govern effectively. The three parts of this book are interesting. In the first section, Gingrich examines who Americans are in a historical context. The second part defines and dissects American exceptionalism. This is an important segment as it uses American history to suggest why we are such a strong nation. The last part, "America Rising," analyzes how immigrants have shaped the American experience. The uplifting conclusion is that the U. S. will write its final chapter. Gingrich believes that he is the person to lead the nation in its ultimate path.

NEWT IN THE WILDERNESS

For a decade after he resigned as Speaker of the House of Representatives, Gingrich built his wealth to almost two hundred million dollars and in the process took hypocrisy to a new level. He is very clear about his political agenda. He wants to be President.

When he campaigned for the Republican nomination in Iowa in December 2011, he criticized Mitt Romney as the Golden Goose candidate. After the **New Hampshire Union Leader** endorsed him for president, Newt traveled to the state and informed reporters that Romney's wealth disqualified him for the presidency. It was a strange press conference as Gingrich voiced his criticism while eating at the exclusive Chez Vachon. He wasn't picking up the check.

What was strange about Gingrich's remarks concerning Romney is that they didn't make sense. He called Romney the man who bankrupted Bain Industries. The truth is that Romney saved the company from bankruptcy. It was Romney's business expertise that prevented Bain Capital from bankruptcy.

What Gingrich learned in the wilderness was to reinvent his candidacy as a positive one. For one of the most contentious politicians in modern history, this was a major task. But he achieved this goal. He was running for President, but he had little chance at the nomination. Newt is a narcissist egomaniac who found a brief moment in the spotlight. This moment quickly faded. He did hold the top spot in the run for the Republican presidential nomination for a nanosecond.

NEWT ON THE WAY TO THE 2012 PRESIDENTIAL NOMINATION: HE THINKS HE WILL HE GET IT?

In mid-December 2011, Newt Gingrich was the frontrunner for the Republican presidential nomination. The Iowa Caucus was on the horizon and his chief challenger, Mitt Romney, amped up the criticism. Michele Bachmann, who was dropping out of the presidential race due to her lack of expertise on domestic affairs, foreign affairs, and women's rights, hammered away at Gingrich's past. The old and tired accusation that Gingrich took $1.6 million from Freddie Mac for consulting was Bachmann's last gasp comment, as she left the national race. Bachmann remarked: "I was trying to see these two entities put in bankruptcy because they frankly need to go away, when the Speaker had his hand out and he was taking $1.6 million to influence senior Republicans." Despite her arcane and convoluted prose, Bachmann made a good point. The mortgage meltdown and Gingrich's politics had a lot in common.

Bachmann throughout the campaign discredited the conservative right with her ill thought out and poorly informed opinions. She degraded illegal immigrants, and she was applauded for it. She claimed that the mainstream media was hostile to her politics. She was right. Stupidity is not a requirement for the presidency. Or should one say she was so ill informed that she vanished as a candidate. Bachmann's comments made Gingrich look like Einstein.

Gingrich in his usual bombastic manner went too far in December when he promised to pull activist judges before Congress. He also allegedly remarked that the 9th Circuit Court of Appeals should be disbanded for ruling that "one nation under God" in the Pledge of Allegiance was unconstitutional. "Too many judges are grotesquely dictatorial," Gingrich continued. "As a historian I may understand this better than lawyers." This statement not only suggests the depth of his ego, but the ignorance of his statements. As a historian, Gingrich studied Africa and he has few insights into American history and politics. Then he pulls out the PhD card, and he mentions in an off-handed manner Saul Alinsky's radicalism, which had nothing to do with the U. S. Court system. Gingrich is articulate but he fails to make sense. But, as a professor, he didn't have to make sense. Maybe that is why he didn't get tenure.

The Republican right wing nut house had no winners by December 2011. At one debate Fox's Neil Cavuto suggested that Michele Bachmann and Rick Perry were the winners in a recent debate. This was the debate where Perry compared himself to Denver Bronco quarterback Tim Tebow. They are both Christians, and somehow Perry identifies with the late game heroics of football players. Delusional? Yes!

NEWT APPEARING ON FACE THE NATION: DECEMBER 2011

Gingrich's appearance on Face the Nation in December 2011 came at a time he was on top of the polls. He began his appearance with an attack on the court system. He compared federal judges to dictators. The U. S. Supreme Court, according to Gingrich, is supreme over the President and Congress. Rather than appoint conservative judges, Gingrich believes that the judiciary should be the weakest branch of government. In convoluted reasoning, that ignored the constitution and the scope of American history, Gingrich used historical analogy from the nineteenth century to argue that the nine judges are changing the law of the land. What Newt failed to realize is that judicial review exists to moderate the law of the land.

The law of the land is not up to the court system, Gingrich argued, and he believes that Congress and the President must take charge of the political system. He views the Court system as a dictatorship. Judges are not supreme in Gingrich's view. He sees the Court's as radicalizing America. "There is something profoundly wrong with the judicial system," Gingrich remarked to Face the Nation host Bob Schieffer. One wonders if Newt has ever read or understood the U. S. Constitution.

"I got into this race because of the steady growth of secularism," Gingrich continued. He won't stand for restrictions on holidays, and he has a strong feeling about political correctness. Gingrich wants Judge Biery to explain why he would put a superintendent of schools in jail if he used the word benediction. This was a reference to Judge Fred Biery, a Texan, who ruled that the Medina Valley Independent School District could not use the words "prayer" and "amen." Gingrich wants to know if judges are above the constitution? In this appearance, Gingrich suggested that Abraham Lincoln would not enforce the Dred Scott Case because it was wrong.

Gingrich's attack on the judicial system made his candidacy popular with the voters. Bob Schieffer countered that the judicial system needs to remain intact. Gingrich countered that elite politicians appoint judges. He sees America as becoming a secularist society.

As Face The Nation rolled into its second phase, Schieffer asked Gingrich about his ties to Freddie Mac. **The Wall Street Journal** attacked Gingrich for the money he received from the mortgage corporation. Gingrich defended himself saying that the Freddie Mac money went to a consulting firm. Gingrich defended his record of attempting to help the poor into affordable housing. Then Schieffer switched to immigration. On immigration, Gingrich remarked, that he believed that long-term immigrants needed to remain in America. He viewed them as a vibrant part of the economy. But if the border is controlled, Gingrich argued, the visa program is refined, a guest worker program is established, there are penalties for employers who hire illegal workers, and the result is that the immigration problem will decline. It will also make the deportation policy easier and allow a residency permit for long-term illegal immigrants.

There are eleven million illegal's and Gingrich suggested that seven to nine million should be allowed to remain in the U. S. The "humanity of the problem" and "the rule of American law" were phrases used by Gingrich to describe immigration.

As he pontificated on Face the Nation, the **Los Angeles Times** headlined: "Newt Gingrich Says He'd Defy Supreme Court Rulings He Opposed." Flush with his rise in the public opinion polls, Gingrich intensely courted right wing, conservative opinion. The only thing he failed to consult is the Constitution. When he said that he would ignore Supreme Court decisions as commander in chief. He failed to mention the War Powers Act of 1973, and its impact upon foreign policy. "I'm fed up with elitist judges," Gingrich continued, "who seek to impose their radically un-American views." The myth of "judicial supremacy" is what Gingrich said he was attempting to expose. "The courts have become grotesquely dictatorial and far too powerful," Gingrich told reporters on a conference call.

On same sex marriage, Gingrich remarked: "The Constitution of the United States has absolutely nothing to say about a constitutional right to same-sex marriage." Actually it does. The Constitution guarantees "full faith and credit" in Article IV, and this is the language that state courts employ to rule in favor of gay marriage. On November 19 2002, the Supreme Judicial Court of Massachusetts in a fifty-page ruling with four justices in the majority and three in the minority affirmed the right to marry in the state. The court noted that those states that passed a "defense of marriage act" could thwart gay marriage. Gingrich not only opposes gay marriage, but he also threatens to interfere with the federal courts if they upheld state statute.

When Gingrich advocated abolishing judgeships, Edward Whelan, a conservative legal analyst, remarked it was "constitutionally unsound and politically foolish." Whelan didn't realize that it is a smart move on Gingrich's part as the court system is under attack.

NEWT'S PROFITS FROM IN THE RIGHT WING NUT HOUSE

The profits from Gingrich's books are staggering. The best estimate is that his net worth from his books is almost $200 million dollars. The **Los Angeles Times** reported that Gingrich's 2010 earnings were $2.6 million. This is a jump from the $2.4 million that Callista Gingrich reported the couple was worth. The problem with Gingrich's net worth is that the Gingrich Group, LLC and Gingrich Productions shield some of his assets. If these companies are considered in his net worth it is in excess of $200 million dollars. Tax tricks, corporate organization, LLC's and donations made Newt Gingrich allegedly the top tax dodger in the right wing nut house.

The credit lines that Gingrich reports on his taxes are interesting. He has a million dollar line of credit with New York's Tiffany Jewelers. That line is now closed due to the political uproar. The Basilica of the National Shrine, a Catholic Church in Washington D. C, paid Callista Gingrich $5245 in 2006 for choir practice. That contract has been cancelled. Newt's stocks and an interest in a talent agency pay him about $200,000 a year. It is difficult to assess Gingrich's book royalties. One publisher told me that it is probably in the eight to twelve million-dollar range. Another suggested that it was in the five million dollar category. Whatever the figure, he is a for profit author. Nothing wrong with that, it's the American way. If that's what you in a president, vote Newt and purchase more books.

With Mitt Romney's net worth estimated at just above $250 million, Gingrich doesn't appear to be poor. But he sure makes a good case for his lack of money. Do you want that type of man in the White House?

THE RISE AND FALL OF NEWT

By February 2012, Newt Gingrich was out of favor with American voters. He had gone from a leading presidential nominee to the middle of the Republican pack. Since 1994, when he was the face of the new Republican Party, Gingrich developed a political career that has had highs and lows. The charges of poor character and a lack of fitness for office never bothered Newt. With only a 13 percent approval rate in the Iowa Caucus, he appeared dead in the water.

The reason is Mitt Romney and his lobbying group, Restore Our Future, spent $3.1 million dollars in ads targeting Gingrich's foibles. The anti-Gingrich ads didn't dissuade him from continuing what he called "a positive campaign." The reminder that an 89-count corruption investigation when he was the House Speaker made him unfit for office didn't phase Gingrich.

His colleagues also spoke about his misdeeds. Rep. Barney Frank, Democrat of Massachusetts, commented: "Gingrich invented the politics of venom." Representative Harry Waxman, a Democrat from California, commented: "He was erratic, undisciplined, said different things on different days...."

When he became the House Speaker in 1994, Gingrich abused his power. He attempted to make the Speakership a bully pulpit similar to that of the presidency. He failed miserably. When the government shutdown in 1995 and 1996 due to his conflicts with President Bill Clinton, the general public blamed the Republicans. It was Newt Gingrich who was responsible for the atmosphere that led to Bill Clinton's second presidential term. "His leadership was erratic," Senator Tom Coburn, a Republican from Oklahoma, continued. "His inability to discipline himself in his public comments was also a serious liability." Senator Lindsay Graham, a Republican from South Carolina, remarked: "He had a big ego, he was impulsive."

NEWT IN THE FRENCH RESTAURANT

At his select table at the L'Auberge Francois, an upscale restaurant in Great Falls, Virginia, Newt comfortably sits between lobbyists and beltway insiders to discuss politics. A typical Newt dinner at L'Auberge Francois features the six course $74 special. Newt loves to begin with La Salade d l'Auberge, followed by the lobster bisque. He tells the waiter that the French onion soup would disqualify him for the presidency. There is forced laughter. Then after finishing the first bottle of wine he orders the Jordan Merlot from California. This goes with the main course, La choucroute royale garnie à L'Alsacienne, cuite au crémant d'Alsace. This is a heart attack meal of sausage, duck and foie gras. The hot soufflé with Gran Mariner ends the meal. He doesn't order coffee. It is after all French roast. For a poor man with a blue-collar background this meal is a feast. He can order in French, he can eat food with names he doesn't understand and he doesn't use Dijon mustard. Gingrich is a real patriot. For reservations call Chef Jacques at 703-759-3800. Don't tell him you know what Newt likes to eat. After all Gingrich once discussed food stamps. I hope he didn't bring any to Chef Jacques.

He is concerned about the rise in food stamp usage, how the elites are destroying the middle class, and the need to defeat Obama liberalism. Then Gingrich cuts into his duck confit and drinks a one hundred dollar bottle of wine. It takes a great deal of strength to help the poor and downtrodden. Newt is a demagogue distilled in a fine French sauce and one of the meanest politicians running for president.

Since 1994,when Gingrich circulated his memo instructing Republicans to gain power through rhetoric, he has been one of the most divisive forces in American politics. In 2012, he is back at it. One critic remarked: "Newt thinks it is 1994. When he labeled Obama "the food stamp president."

In the Republican presidential debates, he snapped and snarled at the commentators. His constituency celebrates his half-truths, his criticism of the media and his bizarre attacks on President Obama.

NEWT IN APRIL MAY 2012: THE END IS HERE

The pathetic, but interesting, campaign that Newt carried on in April 2012 suggests that he is more interested in his place in history than the Republican Presidential nomination. His quest for the Republican nomination reached a new low in April when he finished below Ron Paul in four of the five Republican state primaries. There were rumors on April 25 that an announcement was coming from Gingrich.

By May 2012 Gingrich left the presidential race with massive debt, a bruised ego and a mammoth bill from his wife's hairdresser. The $3.8 million campaign debt didn't bother Newt, and he vowed to pay it off. He also vowed to lose fifty pounds, run a marathon and have dinner with Rodney King. He was gone. Good riddance. There was mourning in the right wing nut house. The cost of security is what placed Gingrich's campaign so far in debt. Callista needed a lot of security people so her wig boxes weren't stolen. You can never be too careful.

There are a number of Newt Gingrich's. He has opposed climate change, he has supported climate change and he has flip-flopped on issues. He has agreed with President Bush and President Obama and he has disagreed with them. This is the Newt we know and love. Stay tuned. There is another Newt coming to your local political arena.

Chapter 17
DINESH D'SOUZA AND THE ANTI-BUSINESS OBAMA

"CAPITALISM SATISFIED THE CHRISTIAN DEMAND FOR AN INSTITUTION THAT CHANNELS SELFISH HUMAN DESIRE TOWARD THE BETTERMENT OF SOCIETY." DINESH D'SOUZA

Dinesh D'Souza is a brilliant thinker, writer and speaker. The bad news is that he is a spokesperson for the radical right. His books are interesting. He loves God, he hates socialists, feminists and liberals. He allegedly believes that Communists should be shot on the spot. He is an academic type who writes like a professor. Witness his notion that President Obama is an "anti-colonial" ideologue. What does that mean? Nothing!

In September 2009, Dinesh D'Souza, writing in **Forbes**, labeled President Obama "the most anti-business president in a generation, perhaps in American history." This is, of course, ridiculous, but if you reside in the right wing nut house it sounds good.

D'Souza's arguments are clear and simplistic. They are well supported with factual data. This is uncommon among conservatives. To D'Souza's credit, he does at times make sense. What blinds him is his hatred for the Obama administration. He will do what he can to twist and distort the facts.

He sees the presidency as bringing back big government. Did it ever go away? He charges that Obama has a penchant to interfere with and arbitrarily regulate the economy. With taxpayer debt running into the trillions, the housing bubble bringing people near bankruptcy, health care reform causing concern, banking a controversial industry and the auto and energy industries in a state of flux, President Obama and the Democrats are in trouble. D'Souza has a lot to criticize. What looked like a sure two term president now appears to be a one-term occupant of the White House. At least this is Dinesh D'Souza's viewpoint.

WHO IS DINESH D'SOUZA?

Who is Dinesh D'Souza? He is formerly a fellow at Stanford University's conservative think tank, the Hoover Institution. The Hoover Institution is famous for educating right wing conservatives. It is also prestigious, and D'Souza's time there helped him secure a college presidency. He is president of King's College in New York. He is also a noted author of Christian and conservative books. He was raised as a Catholic, and he is now an Evangelical Christian. He was born in Mumbai, Maharashtra India and he arrived in the United States in 1978 to attend Patagonia Union High School in Patagonia, Arizona. It was here that his Christian and conservative political values were intensified.

Patagonia is a remote Arizona town in Santa Cruz County that began as a supply center for the mines and ranches. It is the type of settlement where individual initiative and conservative values dominate. The locals like to carry a gun. They don't like people from New York City. But here D'Souza was an honor student. He was admitted to Dartmouth, where he earned a B.A. in English. He was awarded the Phi Beta Kappa key for his superior scholarship.

He edited the **Dartmouth Review**, and he was a staunch conservative. He outed gay students in his writing, and he criticized Dartmouth's affirmative action program. He moved on to edit the conservative **Policy Review**, which is funded by the Heritage Foundation, and the Hoover Institution has since acquired it. As an ethnic minority, D'Souza was ready made for the right wing conservatives. They could point to him and suggest that there was no color line among conservatives.

DINESH D'SOUZA BECOMES THE DARLING OF THE AMERICAN RIGHT

D'Souza became the darling of the American right when he argued that liberals, like the Kennedy family, controlled or at least manipulated the Catholic Bishops. His writing attracted President Reagan, and in 1988 he joined the White House as an advisor.

Unlike most Evangelical Christians, D'Souza is a brilliant thinker and a reasoned writer. His main area of expertise is social forces in American democracy. When he wrote "Letters To A Young Conservative," he urged youthful activists to study classical liberalism. What is classical liberalism? It is a notion that limited-government, strict constitutional interpretation, a narrow rule of law, as well as complete due process and the liberty of the individual is preeminent. He suggests that liberal Democrats are destroying the free market and most American freedoms including religion, speech, press and assembly. When Barack Obama came to office, he openly stated that he feared for the nation's future.

Perhaps D'Souza's strongest argument came when the president supported drilling off the coast of Brazil. Many saw this as a sign of hostility to American oil interests. Like many conservative critics, D'Souza wondered why the Obama administration used tax money for foreign oil production.

What Dinesh D'Souza suggests is that Obama doesn't understand the basic premises behind the American oil industry. When the ban on offshore oil drilling was announced, the Obama administration informed the Brazilian government that it would provide the technology and financial support to develop its oil reserves. This help was not altogether altruistic. As President Obama remarked: "When you're ready to start selling…we want to be one of your best customers." The result was that the U.S. has a ready-made supply of oil to replace the BP leaks. It was smart politics to support Brazil, as they sell inexpensive oil.

The Obama administration did the right thing. Rather than grandstanding about the BP clean up, President Obama created an oil partner in South America. Petrobas, the government controlled corporation, allowed the Brazilians to keep and sell all the oil that was excavated with a two billion dollar loan from the U. S. Export-Import Bank. Not surprisingly, the U. S. benefits from its benevolence.

It is on the banking industry that D'Souza makes some strange conclusions. He alleges that the Obama administration attempted to prevent the banks from paying back their loans. He charges that Treasury Secretary Tim Geithner "might force the banks to keep the money." He is overly critical of the stimulus program. He has few, if any, facts to back his allegations. D'Souza cites the unemployment rate of 7.7% when Obama took office as compared to the 9.5% rate in late 2010. In what he considers another Obama faux pas, D'Souza points out that the so-called rich, or the one percent of the income earners pay 40% of federal taxes. He argues that this is more than equitable. Then the next 9% of taxpayers pay another 30% of the tax bill. D'Souza suggests this is 70% of the tax bill from the top ten percent wage earners. He clearly wants the rich to remain that way. D'Souza also has some statistical inaccuracies. The rich have grown proportionately wealthy while the middle class has declined. In California, those who earn $48,000 a year pay a top rate of 9.3% in taxes, whereas millionaires pay much less.

D'Souza argues that there is more bias and lack of thought in American foreign policy than in any other part of government. He unfairly charges that President Obama supports a Mosque being built near the 9/11 Memorial. When the president supported religious freedom in the Ground Zero Mosque controversy, the right harshly criticized him. What President Obama does not support is a 100 million dollar Mosque built for publicity purposes. Ground Zero remains for the president sacred. He is a strong supporter of religious tolerance, so he refused to enter the Muslim bashing controversy. He left that up to Pamela Geller.

Like many conservative critics, D'Souza sees a Muslim lurking in Obama's personality. He cites the compassionate release of the Lockerbie bomber, Zbdel Baset al-Megrahi, as an example of the Obama administration's support of Muslim radicals. The president reluctantly supported the release of the terrorist bomber because he was dying.

When D'Souza was completing **The Roots of Obama's Rage**, he noticed that NASA Chief Charles Bolden hoped to improve relations with the Muslim world. D'Souza charged that this pro-Muslim policy was unacceptable. He concluded that President Obama "wants to blunt NASA's space program, to divert if from being a symbol of American greatness to a more modest public relations operation that builds ties with Muslims...." (p. 201) Is there any need to comment on this insipid and inaccurate comment?

D'Souza ends his observations by stating that Obama doesn't understand the business world. The reason, according to D'Souza, is that Obama is a socialist. Then D'Souza suggests that this is the case with Franklin D. Roosevelt, John F. Kennedy and Bill Clinton. They all had radical, even socialist ideas. This ploy is a big part of the right wing nut house. If you make accusations and charge radicalism someone will listen. President Barack Obama is just a good Democrat and you know how they are about business.

When D'Souza began his writing career in 1984, he wrote a love letter to Jerry Falwell. His book, **Falwell: Before The Millennium, The Moral Majority Praised, A Critical Biography** is a piece of hagiography. What is intriguing is that liberal Christians come under the heaviest attack. The book is filled with sophomoric analysis. The notion that the U. N. hates children ignores the contribution of UNICEF. It is what D'Souza neglects to explain that makes this book suspect. Things get worse with his future books. No system is more open to criticism than the American University. D'Souza attacks it with a vengeance. He wisely goes after the most hated Universities. Harvard, Stanford, the University of Michigan, the University of California, Berkeley and Duke are among the elite educational institutions that D'Souza skewers. He doesn't skewer Dartmouth. They might take their degree back. They are easy targets because they are elitist and generally disliked.

D'SOUZA ATTACKS THE UNIVERSITY SYSTEM

D'Souza's rising star began in 1991 with the publication of **Illiberal Education**, which took issue with political correctness. The book landed on the **New York Times** best-seller list for fifteen weeks, and D'Souza was named one of America's five hundred leading authorities on international issues. **Newsweek** called him one of the most prominent Asian Americans in U. S. politics.

What made **Illiberal Education: The Politics of Race And Sex On Campus** a popular book was its message. D'Souza argued that the University of California, Berkeley discriminates against white students. Then he charges that multiculturalism eroded Stanford Universities academic reputation. He criticized the predominantly African American University, Howard, for its Afro centrism. The political correctness at the University of Michigan was skewered for its pioneering attempts to write a series of anti-harassment codes. Duke University was next on the list as they revised hiring and academic standards in accordance with affirmative action. Finally, Harvard University came under review for its innovative gender-ethnic studies programs.

D'Souza's goal is to find out how to include minority students in the university. He contends that the slotting of ethnic students is a form of discrimination. They feel that they have been admitted due to special circumstances, and this creates a sense of intellectual inferiority. He charges that the University of California, Berkley systematically attempts to keep the number of Asian American students low, so that African American students can take the slots. One can't call D'Souza a racist as he is from India and went to high school in one of the smallest areas in Arizona. One wonders did Dartmouth admit him as an affirmative action student?

He recklessly charges that minority students at major universities are among the earliest dropouts. This is due, D'Souza warns, to University policy that wants to count these students as statistically diverse. So the University of California is serving its own needs. He argues it has little concern with ethnic students. This is, of course, nonsense.

Stanford University is attacked for dropping the History of Western Civilization as a core requirement. Instead this course was replaced with a series of more diverse offerings. This so-called multicultural curriculum is a shift away from what D'Souza calls the "white, male, European, and heterosexual mentality," and he objects to the suggestion that the History of Western Civilization is a sexist, racist, ethnocentric and homophobic course. He labels "multiculturalism" both "phony and intolerant."

What D'Souza fails to recognize, and perhaps understand, is that the University is the center of unpopular, radical (both liberal and conservative), esoteric and divisive ideas. There is little consensus on a University campus and some colleges remain the center of ideas that can never be reconciled. To criticize the University for diverse thinking and innovative directions counters the very essence of a college education.

There is one point that D'Souza makes which is a strong one. That is the penchant of minority students to have their own graduation ceremony. I attended at San Jose State University and California East Bay University graduations for Hispanic and African American students in separate ceremonies. The students didn't seem to mind and the audience was a mixed one. Rather than intensify racial feelings on campus, these separate graduations were a morale boosting celebration of a University education.

D'Souza does education a disservice with his criticism. He misses the main point. That is the University system, particularly at Harvard and Stanford, have not been open to minorities for a century. U. S. Supreme Court Justice Clarence Thomas suggested, that when he was at Yale Law School, he felt that he didn't belong. Without this education, however, he would not be a member of the most prestigious court in the United States. D'Souza argues that discipline, respect and teaching as the essential ingredients of American life are in decline. He should be reminded teaching is not like a cookbook where you put in the ingredients and everything turns out fine. Sometimes the best professors are those who leave questions, colors of grey about controversial issues and most of all allow unpopular opinions. Of course, those professors are Communists.

There is no easy answer for the sins of a University education. Harvard frequently doesn't respond to admission forms or inquires. Stanford rejects many qualified applicants. The University is a competitive marketplace. There is no way to quantify fairness.

RONALD REAGAN IS MY HERO: BUT DON'T ASK ME TO DO RESEARCH

In 1997, D'Souza's, **Ronald Reagan: How An Ordinary Man Became An Extraordinary Leader** argued that Ronald Reagan's intellectual and political leadership was not appreciated and generally ignored by academics and popular writers.

This book is a tricky one. D'Souza suggests that President Bill Clinton's healthy economy was a result of the Reagan years. There is not an economist alive who subscribes to this theory. There is another problem with D'Souza in-depth look at Ronald Reagan. He failed to consult the most advanced sources. There are no manuscript collections, there are few in-depth popular and academic studies, and he compounds his faults by placing the California governor's years in eight pages. In case D'Souza missed it, Reagan was a two-term governor. The Reagan biographies that he consulted were ones by newspaper writers who dashed out quickie tomes, those who practiced hagiography and the non-critical, non-researched, non-footnoted varieties.

The California history years are filled with errors. He does Governor Reagan a disservice by suggesting that he came to work at nine and left at five, and he didn't seem to have a handle on the affairs of the Golden State. Quite the opposite is true. He instituted the no fault divorce, he cut back on welfare, he straightened out the California budget, he talked of less government as well as opposing undue federal taxation. Whether or not one agreed with Governor Reagan, his eight years in Sacramento were a training ground for the presidency. D'Souza trivializes this period.

Had D'Souza consulted my textbook, **The California Dream**, he would have had a list of Reagan's accomplishments. He also needed to examine how well Reagan worked with the Democrats and facilitated a bipartisan political atmosphere. This is something that is sorely missing from present day American politics.

D'Souza does get one thing right. Governor Reagan rallied Golden State conservatives against the counterculture. He opposed the Free Speech Movement at the University of California, Berkeley in 1964, and he was equally hostile to anti-war demonstrators.

The problem with D'Souza's treatment of Ronald Reagan is lack of in depth research and carefully thought out opinions.

DINESH D'SOUZA'S OTHER BOOKS

From 1984 to 2010, D'Souza's produced thirteen books. The majority of these tomes came from conservative publisher Regnery. They dealt with a wide array of themes. In 1991, his breakthrough book, **Illicit Education**, charged that political correctness restricted freedom of thought and speech at American universities. He was particularly critical of the University of California, Berkeley admissions program. D'Souza wrote: "Berkeley's abandonment of an effort to apply a neutral standard of academic excellence has cut the university off from the moorings of just principle…." Conservatives love any criticism of American education.

The issues of cultural change as well as entitlement programs are paramount in D'Souza's writing. In his view affirmative action and social welfare were destroying America. He also argues that intolerance toward conservative thought is rampant. His 2007 book, **The Enemy At Home: The Cultural Left And Its Responsibility For 9/11** suggested: "The cultural left in this country is responsible for causing 9/11, the cultural left and its allies in Congress, the media, Hollywood, the non-profit sector and the universities are the primary cause of the volcano of anger toward America that is erupting from the Islamic world." This is of course nonsense. In my two books, **A Blow To America's Heart: England Reacts To 9-11**, published in 2002, and **The Road To Baghdad**, published in 2003, I demonstrated that technology, a global economy, modernization, increased education in the Muslim world and the need for lasting political alliances with Western nations were some of the reasons for 9/11. The simplistic view that liberals caused it appeals to the right wing nut house. D'Souza's ideas aren't able to stand up to historical scrutiny.

What makes **The Enemy At Home** so annoying is its central point. This is that the U. S. has brought Islamic terrorism on itself by spreading its coarse culture around the world. If only Ronald Reagan was around to hop on a horse and shot the bad guys, that is the tone of D'Souza' polemical book. It will soon be made into a movie with Will Ferrell.

Even more ironic is the notion that D'Souza suggests that pious Muslims are more virtuous than impious Americans. The noxious notion that color television has promoted Islam unrest is something out of the crayon box. Bernard Lewis has made a good case for modernization, as the key to Muslim fundamental distrust of the West. "In this book I make the claim that will seem startling at the outset," D'Souza continues. "The cultural left in this country is responsible for causing

9/11...." It is much more complicated than D'Souza suggests, and, as I have shown in my book, **A Blow To America's Heart: England Reacts to 9-11**. D'Souza writes: "The holiday from history that began with President Ronald Reagan's inaugural...lasted through the Clinton Administration, blinded America to its world responsibility." One of the earliest critics of American decadence, the Egyptian writer Sayyid Qutb argued many of D'Souza's points. The Muslim Brotherhood embraced these ideas as founding principles.

Qutb, the founder of Islamic radicalism, is the theoretician who studied in America and after he watched students holding hands on campus, Qutb wrote of his disgust with American "decadence." His books became primers for Al Qaeda and Taliban violence.

What D'Souza fails to understand is the roots of Sayyid Qutb's radicalism. He was an Egyptian born in 1906 and after he studied in Cairo, he worked as a teacher. He became an official of the Egyptian Minister of Education, and he traveled for two years to America. He studied at the Colorado State College for Education in Greeley, when he was in his late forties. He was appalled by what he perceived to be loose sexual openness in American society. When he returned to Egypt he began writing and his twenty-four books were the foundation stones for the al Qaeda and the Taliban in their war on America and western decadence. D'Souza fails to analyze the complexity of Sayyid Qutb. Blaming the liberal left and cultural liberals for 9/11 is ridiculous. That is unless you are a career right wing pundit looking for fame and fortune.

WAVING THE FLAG FOR GOD AND COUNTRY

As an adopted American, D'Souza waves the flag and loves his new country. In his writing, he does make some important points. In a 2003 book, **What's So Great About America**, he challenges American's to take a global view of their country. He criticizes the Muslim world for its increased radicalism, he complains about multicultural advances, slavery reparations, and he is extremely critical of feminism. He opposes same sex marriage and told one interviewer that he believes "women civilize men."

He blames the Abu Ghraib tortures and the subsequent prisoner abuses on liberals, but he presents no evidence to support his claims. The most egregious thing that D'Souza suggests is in an article in **Forbes** in which he disparages the president's family. D'Souza claims that President Obama "is trapped in his father's time machine...." He argues that the U. S. is governed by the dreams of an African tribesman. By stating that Obama's father was a philandering alcoholic, he implicitly charges that perhaps the President has the same proclivities. Not only is this irresponsible, it is indefensible.

These views have made D'Souza the "house ethnic" on the Glenn Beck Show, Fox News shows and the Colbert Report. When he debated liberal activist Pete Singer at Princeton on May 15, 2009 the subject was "Can There Be Morality Without God." This debate further cemented D'Souza's conservative credentials, as Singer made him look like an ill informed college freshman.

His seminal conservative book, **The Roots of Obama's Rage**, published in September 2010, is one of the best written, most demeaning, and ill thought out tomes on the president. What is so strange about D'Souza is that when he heard about George Obama, Barack's half brother, living in a Nairobi slum, the conservative author set up a fund to help the brother study to be an auto mechanic. If you do that, do it anonymously. D'Souza charges that President Obama wouldn't help his poor half brother. But D'Souza aided brother George publicly.

The reality is quite different. George Obama was in the United States to sign a book deal with Simon and Schuster. The poor relative that the president was ignoring was in reality an opportunist. Politics are not always what they seem to be. D'Souza charges that the President launched a spending spree that did little to help the economy. This ignores the success of the bank rescue plan and the auto industry bailout.

The irony is that President George W. Bush signed the Economic Stabilization Act of 2009, known as the bank bailouts, into law on October 3, 2008. It was also Bush who announced the $13.4 billion bank bailout. President Obama agreed with both programs. D'Souza ignored the idea of President's Bush and Obama working together.

On President Obama's personal life, D'Souza alleges that he changed his first name back to Barack to assume an African identity. This is absurd. Barack was the name on his birth certificate. President Obama set the record straight on his use of Barack: "It was not some assertion of my African roots…not a racial assertion. It was much more of an assertion that I was coming of age. An assertion of being comfortable with the fact that I was different."

The worst offense is that D'Souza ignores the president's writing. Barack Obama faced up to his father's alcoholism and less than perfect behavior. D'Souza suggests that this was not the case. Anyone who has read Obama's books recalls his compassion and understanding. Not only for his father, but also for his ill-fated mother. Obama wrote in **Dreams From My Father**: "The old man began to drink heavily, and many of the people he knew stopped coming to visit because now it was dangerous to be seen with him." (p. 215)

D'Souza's books lack the foundation and sophistication for success. There is an unmitigated integrity to Obama's books. This is something that D'Souza and others in the right wing nut house fail to recognize. D'Souza is pandering to the conservatives who drank a martini, leave the golf course, and go home for a dinner in front of Fox TV News. Then it is off to the over 55 gated community for a card or pool game. They worry the poor might want to play cards or pool. It is in Obama's books that one can see what needs to be done to reform American politics.

In 2008, Obama's **Change We Can Believe In: Barack Obama's Plan To Renew American Promise** appeared as conservatives scoffed at his message. The President's message was a simple one. America needs change and new leadership. Obama called this era a "defining moment in our history." Whether or not you agree or disagree, he hit upon the key issue. The system needs changes and controls. The question is: how to alter the political arena and the manner in which to make the changes?

D'SOUZA'S MAIN MISTAKES CONTINUE

It is in the area of foreign relations that D'Souza is far off base. He suggests that Cuba and Venezuela were told by the president that they are "on an equal plane with the U. S." The reality was that President Obama quietly informed South American countries in 2009, at the Summit of the Americas that Latin American nations need to stop blaming America for their problems. He specifically informed Venezuela to change its attitude and behavior.

The list of D'Souza's falsehoods could go on forever, but he clearly cannot distinguish fact from fiction. I went to Dinesh D'Souza's website and it stated: "Dinesh D'Souza is one of the most original, insightful and penetrating minds in America today." Who am I to disagree? I also found the same statement on Warren Beatty's website.

Professor Alan Wolfe had the best answer to D'Souza's book, he called it "a national disgrace, a sorry example of a publishing culture more concerned with the sensational than the sensible." That comment in the January 21, 2007, **New York Times** perfectly sums up the book. The conservative critics wondered what made Professor Alan Wolfe such an authority. Had those in the right wing nut house done their homework they would have discovered that he is not only a Professor of Political Science, but also he is the Director of the Boisi Center For Religion And American Life at Boston College. In his latest book, **Political Evil: What It Is And How To Combat It**, he shows that theological thought from both the left and the right influences the course of democracy. One wonders if he wrote about how to combat political evil are reading Dinesh D'Souza. Just a thought!

An even stronger criticism of D'Souza's work came when the Colbert Report had D'Souza guest on his television show. The segment was hilarious. D'Souza said that Jimmy Carter began the road to 9-11, and then President Bill Clinton continued the drift to Islamic radicalism. "FDR gave away Eastern Europe through Yalta," D'Souza said, and he continued that this was the road to Osama bin Laden's triumphs.

The complete disregard for the facts indicate that D'Souza would have trouble passing the History of Western of Western Civilization.. The Colbert Report was excellent in the manner in which it demonstrated that Dinesh D'Souza is a ridiculously empty suit with a clear voice and little knowledge of American history or politics. He also pointed to American television for promoting a distorted view of the U. S. and its society. He had better watch out, Mark Harmon and the N. C. I. S. crew may be on the case.

D'Souza's **The Enemy At Home** is a joke. This book begins by echoing the statements of the Reverend Jerry Falwell who blames everything before and after 9/11 on homosexuals, feminists, lesbians and family planning. At least Falwell didn't blame the Kennedy's and the Democratic Party. They must have been sending his 700 Club TV show some donations. God loves money

What D'Souza fails to understand is the Muslim faith and the al Qaeda-Taliban mentality. On Osama Bin Laden, D'Souza writes: "What bin Laden objected to was America staying in the Middle East…." Apparently, Bin Laden didn't object to British or Russian influences.

DINESH D'SOUZA DID MAKE SOME POINTS

Here is the Top Ten List of Dinesh D'Souza's contribution to conservative thought.

1. He points out that Michigan, UC, Berkeley, Duke, Stanford and Harvard are universities that discriminate in admissions. Maybe that is why he had to go to Dartmouth. Not bad for a second choice. The serious side is the ability and openness of the University systems to take in students of all ethnic groups, as well as women and foreign students.

That argument is still a strong one as affirmative action and equal opportunity remains elusive.

2. The excessive influence of Christian values and religion is threatening to take over the political system. This is serious and frightening.

3. In his books D'Souza has set a new standard for nonfiction analysis. Warren Bass writing in **The Washington Post** said it best: "one has to wonder why his publisher, agent, editors and publicists went along for the ride." The answer Mr. Bass is for the money. It is not easy getting a paycheck in modern America. The unemployment rate is soaring.

4. D'Souza has little or no understanding of terrorism. His grounding in matters of foreign policy is minimal and it shows in the books.

5. When D'Souza announces that President Ronald Reagan made Libya's Momar Qaddafi retire from terrorism by his 1986 air strike on Libya, he ignored the bombing of Pam Am 103 two years later.

6. Osama bin Laden social-political ideas are ignored while D'Souza drones on with little historical knowledge about Muslim terrorists.

7. He claims that Christians, Jews and Muslims can live together. Then he suggests that the U. S. supports Jewish policy in the Middle East so as to divert attention from their occupation of Jerusalem and the killing of Muslims in that historic city.

8. He ignores the al-Qaeda goal of toppling America.

9. He fails to study Jahidist ideology or the books describing it. The work of Richard A. Posner, Jessica Stern, Peter L. Bergen, Steve Coll and Marc Sageman provides a great deal of useful in-depth information. Much of it is about the Jahidist mentality.

10. He does a wonderful job of demonstrating how to write for money.

HOW MUCH DOES DINESH D'SOUZA MAKE FROM THE RIGHT WING NUT HOUSE

There is no way to know how much money Dinesh D'Souza makes in a year. A call to the King's College in New York, where he is the president, brought a sharp "no comment." I persisted and told the president's secretary that I was a taxpayer and had the right to know his salary. She called me a name that was unkind. I have thought of myself as "a horse's ass." So I employed DeWitt science. I guessed from the facts.

There were some sources. When I called his speaker's bureau, they informed that his speaking engagement fee was revealed only to those with serious inquiries. Then I contacted his, book publishers and they returned my letters when I asked for a royalty figure.

So here goes. It is guesswork. A college president, particularly in New York, earns a half a million a year and a housing-travel-expense account.

In terms of net worth the best estimate is that D'Souza's books have earned just fewer than four million dollars. As a result his net worth is somewhere between four and six million dollars. He is definitely a low-end earner in the right wing nut house.

HOW DINESH D'SOUZA THINKS

Dinesh D'Souza is a political novice who doesn't understand Democrats or the party. He finds their views shocking and he can't explain Democratic Party ideas. The reason is a simple one. He has little, if any, understanding of American politics. What D'Souza does in his books is to defend elitism and nepotism. These notions are the heart of the Republican Party and the right wing nut house. In the 2000 book **The Virtues of Prosperity**, D'Souza writes: "For the state to enforce equal opportunity would be to contravene the true meaning of the Declaration of Independence and to subvert the principle of free society." This is D'Souza's view of American history. As D'Souza grew up as an elitist, he lost track of his origins and he does not appear to take pride in his American education. Those in the right wing nut house disagree, as they purchase his books in large numbers. This is a sad commentary upon the current book buying public, and it is a tragic reflection on American politics. D'Souza claims that President Obama is out of touch with Americans, he might look at his opinions and reflect on them.

Chapter 18
ANTI-OBAMA BOOKS SELL AND THE VANISHING CONSERVATIVES: A CONCLUSION

"ALL THAT IS NECESSARY FOR THE TRIUMPH OF EVIL IS THAT GOOD MEN DO NOTHING," EDMUND BURKE

In 2009, Amazon reported that three anti-Obama books were on the top of the best selling list. The three best selling authors Jerome Corsi, Dick Morris and David Freddoso inaugurated the literary right wing nut house. They are described simply as authors who write anti-Obama books. This is an oversimplification, as they all have an axe to grind. Corsi is a failed college professor, Morris is a Democratic political strategist let go by President Bill Clinton and Freddoso hopes to become Bill O'Reilly. As the previous chapters suggest, they had help from the Tea Party, Christian booksellers, grass roots activists and public relations firms. Nothing sells without hype. The hype is so great for the anti-Obama books that it has created a literary backlash.

The idea that Barack Obama is an ideologue tied to radical thought and political extremism is a constant argument on the right. Jerome Corsi labeled Obama the leader of "the cult of personality" and the right wing authors fell blindly in step.

Michael Moore's **Stupid White Men** is the best answer to these books. But Moore's sales don't equal those of the radical right. Dick Morris' **Fleeced: How Barack Obama, Media Mockery of Terrorist**

Threats, Liberals Who Want to Kill Talk Radio, The Do-Nothing Congress, Companies That Help Iran, And Washington Lobbyists For Foreign Governments Are Scamming Us…And What To Do About It* went through eight printings by 2008, and it sold more than a quarter of a million books. Morris is one of the more prolific and popular writers among conservatives.

There are so many anti-Barack Obama books it is tough to pick out the Top Ten. The list below is a personal look at the worst and most critical books.

THE TOP TEN ANTI-PRESIDENT OBAMA BOOKS

1. DAVID FREDDOSO, THE CASE AGAINST BARACK OBAMA: THE UNLIKELY RISE AND UNEXAMINED AGENDA OF THE MEDIA'S FAVORITE CANDIDATE

2. JEROME R. CORSI, THE OBAMA NATION: LEFTIST POLITICS AND THE CULT OF PERSONALITY

3. DICK MORRIS, FLEECED: HOW BARACK OBAMA, MEDIA MOCKERY OF TERRORIST THREATS, LIBERALS WHO WANT TO KILL TALK RADIO, THE DO-NOTHING CONGRESS, COMPANIES THAT HELP IRAN, AND WASHINGTON LOBBYISTS FOR FOREIGN GOVERNMENTS ARE SCAMMING US…AND WHAT TO DO ABOUT IT

4. MARK STEYN, AMERICA ALONE: THE WORLD AS WE KNOW IT

5. ANDY MARTIN, OBAMA: THE MAN BEHIND THE MASK

6. WEBSTER GRIFFIN TARPLEY, THE POSTMODERN COUP-THE MAKING OF A MANCHURIAN CANDIDATE

7. SHELDON FILGER, HILLARY CLINTON NUDE: NAKED AMBITION, HILLARY CLINTON AND THE AMERICAN DEMISE

8. GLENN BECK, ARGUING WITH IDIOTS; HOW TO STOP SMALL MINDS AND BIG GOVERNMENT

9. MARK R. LEVIN, LIBERTY AND TYRANNY: A CONSERVATIVE MANIFESTO

10. MICHELLE MALKIN, CULTURE OF CORRUPTION: OBAMA AND HIS TEAM OF TAX CHEATS, CROOKS, AND CRONIES

The list of anti-Obama books continues to grow. To understand the mania against the president, it is necessary to examine some of those not included in this book. There are four dreadful books by American conservatives and one excellent one by a British conservative.

Sally Pipes, **The Truth About Obamacare** is an attack upon health care reform. Pipes' argument is that the new health care plan will not only bankrupt America, but also it will lead to increasingly deficient health care. She argues that health care costs will increase so dramatically, as to make it less affordable and only a bare bones medical plan.

Equally ridiculous is Jason Mattera's **Obama Zombies: How The Liberal Machine Brainwashed My Generation**, released in March 2010. When Ann Coulter and Michelle Malkin reviewed it, the twenty-seven year old Mattera was accorded rave reviews. They must think he's cute, they couldn't like the writing or his dreadful analysis. They are both too busy to have read the book. His writing is tendentious and his thinking makes Attila the Hun look like a liberal. He is known as "D. C.'s Bad Boy Reporter," according to conservative websites. While attending Roger Williams University, he found his conservative calling. He reacted in a hostile manner to affirmative action. It wasn't his thing. Mattera is of Puerto Rican descent and an avowed Christian. Nothing wrong with that, but he is a calculating smug adolescent who has attacked militant gays, the Vice President and anyone with a liberal viewpoint.

Although a Puerto Rican, Mattera established a $50 white only scholarship to make his point about affirmative action. Mattera also attacked high tech people like Steve Jobs, Hollywood liberals and left wing media sources. The notion that they all followed President Obama like mindless zombies is insulting to the voter and to those with academic credentials. But, after all, Mattera is a born again Puerto Rican conservative hostile to the liberal establishment.

What makes Mattera's book ludicrous and even dangerous is his sensationalism. He writes of oral sex, reporters who were rewarded with administration positions, and he presents a six-point conclusion to stop the economic bleeding. But his ideas are so far out no one in his or her right mind would listen to them. "We've demonstrated that Obama is not the second coming of Jesus Christ," Mattera writes. (p. 195) Then he goes on to argue that young people need to be trained to be conservatives. Somewhere George Orwell is rolling over in his grave.

Mattera believes that his writing is cute. In fact, it is disrespectful. "John McCain was an atrocious presidential candidate. Gramps was uninspiring, inarticulate and uncharismatic and he looked like death." (p. 197). His prose gets worse. He wants American education reformed "before Michael Moore eats another young person for breakfast." (p. 207). The illusions of nonsense go on forever and why this book hit the market, let alone the bestseller list, is a mystery.

On the Mattera list of ridiculous books his 2012 opus **Hollywood Hypocrites: The Devastating Truth About Obama's Biggest Backers** begins: "Barack Hussein Obama has done more to destroy American freedom...than even his most committed Marxist zealots deemed possible." (p. 1) It is all downhill from that point on, as Mattera skewers the Obama administration with faulty analysis.

Mattera is particularly harsh on Hollywood. He points out that billionaire movie-record producer, David Geffen, movie moguls Steven Spielberg and Jeffrey Katzenberg not only put Bill Clinton in the White House but also conspired to get Barack Obama elected. Mattera writes: "The only group powerful enough publicly to resuscitate and resurrect Obama's 2008 mass popularity is the mob of Hollywood Leftists who got him elected the first time." (p. 221) Let's hope that Mel Gibson is not out campaigning for President Obama. That is the only thing that could defeat him.

The third worst book on President Obama is Jack Cashill's **Deconstructing Obama; The Life, Loves, and Letters of America's First Postmodern**, released in February 2011, by Simon and Schuster's Threshold Editions. If I was the publisher, Simon and Schuster, I would stay as far away from this book as possible. The thesis is that Barack Obama did not write either of his two best known books **Dreams From My Father** and **The Audacity of Hope**. Cashill describes himself as a literary detective. He is also a highly prolific author with books that not only elicit a right wing viewpoint, but he tends to rely on stereotypes. A good example of his defense of big business is **Popes And Bankers: A Cultural History of Credit And Debt, From Aristotle To AIG**. It is in reality a defense of Lehman Brothers and Bear Stearns. He blames the credit crunch on the borrowers. What Cashill is looking for is a contract from big business. He goes on to blame no-fault divorce for causing single mothers to purchase homes in California that they couldn't afford. There is more as he blames money from China for polluting our credit market. The tragedy is that Cashill is an excellent writer. As a thinker, researcher and critic he rates an F. As a writer he is an A plus. So this is a C book.

Robert "Buzz" Patterson's, **Conduct Unbecoming: How Barack Obama Is Destroying The Military And Endangering Our Security**, published in 2010 from Regnery, is a devastating critique of American

Foreign Policy. What is troubling about Patterson's book is its structure. His introduction "Barack Obama's Dereliction of Duty" and chapter 1 "Mr. Alinsky Goes To Washington" is a polemical critique devoid of fact. There is plenty of opinion but little in the way of substance. Patterson began his career working in the Bill Clinton White House. He was appalled by Clinton's foreign policy. "In Barack Obama we have elected a foreigner…he is half Kenyan and spent some time growing up in Indonesia." (p. 2). This is the tip of the iceberg as Patterson, who has a degree in political science, rants on about President Obama and his background.

Not only is Patterson's book devoid of fact, it has a fictional overtone. It is not fiction, it just reads like it. As a retired Air Force Lt. Col., Patterson told Fox TV News that then first lady Hillary Clinton "wanted to outlaw uniforms, military uniforms in the White House." Then Patterson went on over the years to suggest that Democratic foreign policy created a danger to American security. This is, of course, blatant nonsense. How does Patterson support his thesis? Here are a few examples. "It was in the home of Ayers and Dohrn that Barack Obama graduated from civil rights attorney, law professor, and community organizer to politician." (p. 19) What this quote intimates is that Bill Ayers and Bernadine Dohrn thrust Obama into the public eye. Like most right wing critics, Patterson links President Obama with Saul Alinsky. "This Chicago born radical is known for community organizing. He is a staunch leftist." Patterson writes: "Alinsky was street wise or educated in the streets like so many of Obama's associates…." Then he attacks Hillary Clinton and theorizes, she "is the original grassroots 'community organizer…." (p. 15) This type of writing makes the book less than credible.

The footnotes to Patterson's book read like a comic opera. In chapter 3, he uses Dennis Miller, the comedian, as his source to open a chapter he entitles "The Commander-In-Cool." Miller is a great comedian, as a TV news analyst he ranks up there with Pinky Lee. The remainder of the footnotes read like a who's who of right wing nonsense. Such sterling publications as **Christianity Today** and the **National Review Online** support his thesis that Osama Bin Laden's cohorts might soon be checking into the Holiday Inn. Where is Borat when you really need him?

The right wing nut house is not confined to America. In England, Daniel Hannan is a prominent British conservative who charges that President Obama is heading the U. S. down the road to European-style socialism. When Hannan upbraided English Prime Minister Gordon

Brown on the floor of the European Parliament, it earned him a place on Fox TV news. It also earned him a book contract with Harper/Collins. Someone smelled money. Hannan's **The New Road To Serfdom: A Letter of Warning To America** is actually a meaningful and intelligent look at Obama's president.

His argument is that the abandonment of history has hurt America. He sees the principles of the Founding Fathers ignored in the search for prosperity. He argues that the social programs since the New Deal are ones that have led to a form of socialism that threatens the nature of American democracy. Hannan, who has just turned forty, could use a hairpiece, but he has a marvelous mind.

Why does Hannan make sense and others in the right wing don't? The answer is a simple one. He is a politician first and a journalist second. So he does have some brains. Hair is another problem. But no one is perfect.

What sets Hannan apart from those in the right wing nut house is his political background. He is a member of the European Parliament representing South East England for the Conservative Party. He worked as a speech writer prior to his election to the European Parliament in 1999. He is a strong supporter of localism, which is much like states rights in the American model.

Edward Klein's **The Amateur: Barack Obama In The White House**, published in the late spring of 2012, is one of the more vicious and inaccurate books. Klein charges that Obama is not a centrist, that he has delusions of grandeur and that he is preoccupied with his place in history. These are Klein's conclusions by page three and it gets worse. Klein travels to Chicago, and he claims to interview those close to President Obama. The chapter title, "Hollow To The Core," paints the picture that no one knows anything about his family life. Dr. David Scheiner remarked: "I never heard anything about his family life." (p. 17)

When Barack Obama was an Illinois State Senator from 1997 to 2004, Klein alleges, "He hardly showed up at all." (p. 23) Then it is on to the influence of Reverend Jeremiah Wright. The chapter title, "The Man Who Prepared Obama For The Presidency," tells it all. Klein alleges that Obama wanted to meet with Wright secretly to discuss their relationship. His source is the eminent Rev. Wright. (p. 51) By describing President Obama as the "bungler in chief." (Chapter 7), he makes a case for inept leadership. Others who Klein skewers are Valerie Jarrett, Michelle Obama and Valerie V. Rahm, (chapters 9-11)

The coup de grace is Klein's description of the Jewish problem. "A sizeable number of American Jews...are having a serious case of buyer's remorse...." (p. 159) This statement is beyond ridiculous. Klein would have you believe that Jewish voters will join the Christian right in preventing Obama's second term. One of Klein's journalistic tricks is to find quotes from African Americans. He also has academic friends who employ the same trick. Michael Eric Dyson is the author of sixteen books and a Professor of Sociology at Georgetown University. Dyson wrote: "The president runs from race like a black man runs from a cop." It is a good thing that Professor Dyson is African American, or he might be accused of racial insensitivity. I wonder do white men run from cops?

In case you are wondering if Klein can top himself, he does in chapter twenty-one: "In Search of The Real Obama." He tells us why Obama has mishandled the economy, how he has bungled programs for African Americans and why he is a grand failure. Klein writes well and the book is interesting. Unfortunately, it bears little resemblance to reality. As I used to tell my students: "Never let the truth get in the way of a good story." Klein believes in this dictum.

Janet Maslin reviewing Klein's book in the **New York Times** remarked" "The Amateur" by Edward Klein is a book about an inept, arrogant ideologue who maintains an absurdly high opinion of his own talents even as he blatantly fails to achieve his goals. Oh, and President Obama is in the book too. Of course, Mr. Klein does not see himself as the amateur of his title." There is no better description of this book than Maslin's insightful critique of tome based on hot air and innuendo.

Race and class are important subjects. A book by a former Department of Justice employee, J. Christian Adams, **Injustice: Exposing The Racial Agenda Of The Obama Justice Department**, from Regnery in 2011, argued that there was a race bias in the White House. Adams, a former whistleblower, who resigned from the DOJ in 2010 to expose what he terms "the racialism" of Attorney General Eric Holder, is a good writer. He also has a wealth of useful information. Much of the book examines the Voting Rights Act of 1965, but the main thrust is the notion that the Obama administration is waging a war on white people. He bases this thesis on the Civil Rights Department of the Attorney General's office hiring more employees. Much of this book concentrates upon voter fraud by African American Democrats in the South. Adams, who lives in South Carolina, is upset that Obama is practicing "racialist policies." Jones makes some explosive claims. "In the view of the Holder

DOJ, whites aren't protected by Section 5 of the Voting Rights Act." (p. 69) This is not only a reckless charge, but it is indefensible and untrue. Then Jones quotes an African American DOJ employee: "I didn't come to work in the Civil Rights Division…to sue black people." (p. 53) Those who support Adams' book argue that white citizens are slowly losing their rights. This is a sad commentary on the present state of race and class in America.

Chapter 19
FROM THE COFFEE SHOP: A VIEW OF AMERICA: OCTOBER, 2011-JUNE, 2012

"AT THE ORINDA CALIFORNIA COUNTRY CLUB, I WATCH THE LADIES WHO HAVE PAID $195,000 TO JOIN WATCHING THE TELEVISION IN THE BAR. IT IS TURNED TO FOX TV NEWS. THEY ARE OFTEN NICE LITTLE LADIES WHO WATCH RUSH LIMBAUGH AND BILL O'REILLY. THEY TEND TO GET CONCERNED AND INSECURE ABOUT AMERICA'S FUTURE."
TOM MINKLER

Throughout America there are hundreds of coffee shops where the political process undergoes scrutiny. In October 2011, President Barack Obama took a three-day tour of the South. His bus journey through Virginia and North Carolina was a telling one. He won those states in 2008. As he shook hands with students, soldiers, average citizens and local businessman, he found that Virginia's Democratic politicians were often too busy to meet with him. The elections in three Southern States in November 2011 were ones that cast an ominous shadow over the 2012 Presidential election. The news was not on the surface good news for President Obama and the Democratic Party.

In Mississippi, the Republicans took the state house from the Democrats. The Republican candidate for governor, Phil Bryant, beat the Democrat, Johnny DuPree, soundly. But in Kentucky, Steve Beashear, the Democratic incumbent, won an easy victory. In Virginia there were only modest gains for Republicans. Yet, the 2011 elections did indicate one obvious point. President Obama has to win one of the following states: Florida, North Carolina or Virginia. Hence, the reason for his three-day bus tour.

The Republicans are the party to beat in the South. In Louisiana, the Republican Party annihilated the Democrats. In Virginia, the Republicans have taken over the Senate and the Republicans control every major Southern state except Arkansas, Kentucky and West Virginia. These are not key electoral states. It is economics, not foreign policy issues, that is the voters primary concern. "Obama's policies are too left of center," Milton Williams remarked. Williams, a contractor, is an independent with no hostility to Obama. Yet, he worries about the socialist direction of American politics.

The coffee shops in Virginia and North Carolina were the main source of information for the Obama campaign. What President Obama found out was that his policies needed clear explanation. He also learned that those who opposed him did so because they were primarily opposed to Obamacare.

In Boston, Sidney Glick sat in the Blue Moon Coffee Shop in Medfield Massachusetts. This is a famous local coffee and bagel bakery. Sidney sits drinking coffee, and he pointed out to me that it is located in the only city or town named Medfield in the U. S. Dan Freedman and his lovely wife Linda own the Blue Moon Coffee. Dan is a third generation baker, professionally trained and everything in this wonderful coffee emporium is baked fresh daily on the premises. It is the only place for political discussion in Medfield. Ed, Tony, Bruno and some of the other guys smiled as they cornered Sidney Glick and asked him for his political opinions. I listened. The owner, Dan, has no political opinions.

Sidney took a sip of coffee and told me to ask intelligent questions. I knew I couldn't go wrong on immigration. Sidney commented: "I think it's time to emigrate to Mexico." I pressed Sidney for his view of President Obama. "Nice guy but totally lacks and misunderstands leadership." Are you speaking about your cousin Ernie? "No," Sidney looked at me like I was nuts. "Let me be serious for moment." Sidney paused: "Congress needs to stop looking at today and start looking ten to twenty years in the future for what this country needs to become. We need to stop the partisan politics to go to a comfortable place. The government needs to look long term and they need to represent the people not themselves."

I came back to the coffee shop six months later and asked if President Obama would be reelected. "Yes," they all shouted in unison. But they all looked at me like I was a dumb shit. "There is not a candidate that they can put up against him that can be elected," Sidney Glick remarked. Suddenly a voice hollered: "Obama, Obama, Obama," it was the obscure guy who doesn't participate in the conversations. Then he talked for twenty minutes about the election. "The unfortunate thing about politicians is that they all say 'what's in it for me?'" Sidney Glick concluded. At that point everyone in the coffee shop smiled at me and asked: "Are you leaving?" Do I have a choice?

"Wait," Sidney screamed at me. "I want to read what you have written." He read it. Sydney had the last word. "You dumb shit, I am drinking tea." I got my revenge by not changing coffee to tea. You see, I am the writer.

THE BRIGHTEST PUNDITS IN THE RIGHT WING NUT HOUSE: THE OLD HOARY ARGUMENTS IN BRILLIANT BOOKS

The depth of feeling about the direction of American politics is formidable. It is in the coffee shops that one can see the future of American politics. Not surprisingly, President Obama is a big coffee shop guy. He realizes more deals are made at coffee shops than on the House or Senate floor. The Caribous Coffee shop across the street from the White House is a place where the Obama administration often conducts business. The K Street lobbyists who hang out there are able to talk politics and make deals.

Leonard Lee: "I eat breakfast every morning at Beth's Café on Aurora Avenue in Seattle. I hear people talk about Fox TV News. Those people are nuts, they talk about ending socialism. Then I see them go to their jobs at the post office, the Seattle Transit System and the local schools. They will all collect a pension. They tell me that they don't want socialism." Leonard was off to his job at the local bicycle shop. He has no pension; he has no 401K, and he has no health insurance. He also doesn't have all of his teeth. He leaves Beth's Café and hollers: "Let's reelect President Obama, I need health insurance."

The right wing nuthouse continued to explode in December 2011. Newt Gingrich called for Mitt Romney to pull out some television ads that were critical of the former speaker. In what was one of the strangest turns in recent election history, the bilious Gingrich demanded that an attack ad be cancelled because it was "dishonest." Everyone breathed a sigh of relief when Gingrich dropped out of the 2012 presidential race. Now he could concentrate on writing books critical of the president.

THE ANTI-OBAMA BOOKS PROLIFERATE

The number of anti-Obama books increases daily. A brief review of these works suggests the vast nature of the anti-Obama book industry. In 2010, Rand Paul, a Republican who ran for the U. S. Senate from Kentucky due to Jim Bunning's retirement, was elected with the help of the Tea Party. He is a Duke University School of Medicine graduate and he founded the Kentucky Taxpayers United. He is a staunch Tea Party advocate, and his book **The Tea Party Goes To Washington**, published in early 2011, declared that he was "elected to the US Senate campaigning on a traditional, constitutional platform, rooted in the founding of our nation and reflecting the values of individual freedom that have always made America great. With the Obama administration barreling in the opposite direction...that would have outraged Thomas Jefferson...." (p. 3) This presumptuous declaration is typical of those writing in the right wing nut house. The tone of the book is obvious. Paul opposes same sex marriage, and he cloaks his arguments in the states' rights mantle. He is also the son of the perennial Republican presidential candidate Ron Paul.

Stanley Kurtz' **Radical-In-Chief: Barack Obama And The Untold Story of American Socialism**, published in October 2010, is supposedly a two year investigation into the president's plan to socialize America. Who is Stanley Kurtz? The publicity surrounding his book describes him as "a veteran journalist." That is hardly an accurate description. Kurtz is an apologist for the right. He is a virulent critic of President Barack Obama. His credentials are impeccable. He earned a PhD in social anthropology form Harvard University. He has written on a wide variety of subjects including gay rights, affirmative action and the family, which he considers endangered. He also is critical of the policies of the Reverend Jeremiah Wright and former Weather Underground guru Bill Ayers. This reporting was the prelude to his attack on President Obama. He labels President Obama the **Radical-In-Chief**. Kurtz paints a sordid picture of the road to socialism.

There are other problems with Kurtz' book. It is not rooted in the literature of socialism. There are a great many excellent studies of American socialism. Kurtz apparently has not read or used any of this material. For a book on American socialism, it is surprising that there are only two references to the key American socialist Eugene V. Debs. In one reference Kurtz talks of a retreat in 1987 in which the Debs-Thomas Award was presented to Heather Booth. Kurtz writes that it was an event "which Obama could easily have attended...." (p. 188) So not only was President Obama not at the event, a check with the White House revealed that he was unaware of it and the award.

A check of Kurtz footnotes casts aspersions on his sources. When he discusses American socialists, his footnotes refer to a Glenn Beck book. An impeccable source! Kurtz book is a polemical tirade that is embarrassing.

In foreign policy, there is the compelling thesis that President Obama is somehow allowing the followers of Islam to overtake America. Ken Blackwell and Ken Klukowski's **The Blueprint: Obama's Plan To Subvert The Constitution And Build An Imperial Presidency**, released in April 2010, is not only an attack on Obama's foreign policy, it is a nasty, venal and highly personal criticism of his life. Not surprisingly, Blackwell is the former Mayor of Cincinnati, the co-chairperson of the Republican National Committee and a lifelong conservative pundit. He is an African American who not only hates President Obama, but also concocts a history of foreign policy that has little credibility. As the co-chairperson of the Committee To Re-Elect George W. Bush, Blackwell became a prominent Ohio political figure. In 2004, he headed the campaign to ban same sex marriage. He was defeated for the position of Ohio Governor in 2006. Blackwell's revenge is to go after President Obama. As an African American, Blackwell is embraced by the right wing nut house.

Blackwell's book, written with Ken Klukowski, who is a Washington D. C. attorney with a specialization in constitutional law, is a disaster. Like Blackwell, he is adamant that President Obama is taking the nation down the road to permanent socialism. **The Blueprint: Obama's Plan To Subvert The Constitution** is well written and well thought out, but it remains a polemical attack rather than a work of serious scholarship.

Bernie Goldberg's **A Slobbering Love Affair: the True (And Pathetic) Story of the Pathetic Romance Between Barack Obama And The Mainstream Media**, published in January 2009, brought a new low to the book industry. In addition to bad hair, inadequate writing plagues Bernie. He is an Emmy Award winning journalist who not surprisingly is on the Fox TV Network. But it is sports writing that is his real intellectual passion. He needs to return to that venue where he can share inane comments with Chris Berman. Or maybe he can be like Skip Bayliss and say nothing. Craig Sager could give Goldberg one of his suits.

In 2011, Phil Kerpen'a **Democracy Denied: How Obama Is Ignoring You and Bypassing Congress To Radically Transform America-And How To Stop Him** suggests that Kentucky politicians were about to save America. They would do so by passing the Reins Act limiting President Obama's power. This act would allow Congress to scrutinize and regulate legislation. The clear division of government power, established in the Constitution is ignored as the bill passed the House of Representative 241 to 184. Fortunately, for the nation it didn't pass the U. S. Senate.

This bill is the focus of Kerpen's book. He accuses the Obama administration of attempting to force workers into unions, control the Internet, regulate every aspect of a citizens' financial life, and grab as much land as possible. Not surprisingly, the Americans For Prosperity and the Koch brothers are behind this book.

Mark R. Levin's **Ameritopia: The Unmaking of America** is a sophisticated three-part analysis of what is wrong with America. The first section examines Utopian ideas and uses Plato's **Republic**, Thomas More's **Utopia**, Thomas Hobbes' **Leviathon** and Karl Marx's **The Communist Manifesto** to argue that Utopians, like President Barack Obama, "substitute glorious predictions and unachievable promises for knowledge, science and reason…." (p. 5)

The second section is on Ameritopia. Levin employs the writings of John Locke, Charles de Montesquieu and Alexis de Tocqueville to define the American character. "Locke opposed authoritarianism and sought to uncover the true nature of man…." (p. 123) What this has to do with Obama's presidency remains a mystery. When he discusses Tocqueville, Levin remarks about the sovereignty of the individual. Implicit in Levin's work is the thesis that we live in a society where: "Tyranny… is the use of power to dehumanize the individual and delegitimize his nature." (p. 241) The only problem with this archaic view from the right wing nut house is that America has strong institutions to prevent tyranny. The presence of mandatory elections, the role of public opinion, the use of the initiative, referendum and recall, as well as a host of other political devices at the state and federal level protect us from losing our liberties.

The right wing nut house is upset that Barack Obama became President. They believe he is not only too liberal but prone to socialist-communist tendencies. They also conclude that Obama's advisers have an agenda to socialize America.

The anti-Obama books argue that there is no hope for bipartisan politics. They also argue that President Obama is an ideologue who is pushing a radical agenda. There are other reasons for these books becoming successful and the main one is the support of Sean Hannity on Fox TV News. Steve Ross, of Harper Collins, pointed out that Hannity is an "enthusiast for books." This means he sells a lot of right wing tripe. What this comment fails to recognize is that he supports any book that bashes Barack Obama.

Newsweek is concerned about conservatism. This middle of the road, slightly Democratic Party leaning, news magazine created controversy when it published a cover photo of Michele Bachmann with the heading: QUEEN OF RAGE. Why the concern? The purpose of the **Newsweek** story was to demonstrate that the Tea Party was dangerous to American liberties.

In January 2012, **Newsweek** was once again in the midst of controversy. The magazine featured a story asking" Why Are Obama's Critics So Dumb?" This cover story produced a firestorm of criticism alleging that **Newsweek** was inherently biased. Andrew Sullivan's story took an interesting turn when he wrote: "Obama has delivered in a way that the unhinged right and purist left have yet to understand or absorb." While appearing on MSNBC's Hardball, Sullivan remarked that he believed that President Obama was a "sensible, pragmatic centrist."

WEBSITES FOR THE RIGHT WING NUT HOUSE

The websites for the right wing nut house provide interesting information. See the following list at http://obamalies.net/obama-lies-directory to understand the hostility to President Obama. These websites are devoted to exposing the president's alleged lies. There are more than seventy anti-Obama websites. The worst ones include Jewsagainstobama.com, Audacity of Hypocrisy, Stop-Obama.org, No-bama.blogspot.com and obamology.blogspot.com. All of these websites have a common theme. They argue that President Obama is not a citizen, and political radicals direct his policy. The insults continue, he doesn't know the truth from a lie, he is inexperienced politically and he is heading America in a socialist direction.

There are some nut cases on the web. The antiobama.net site quotes a Texan who argues that Texas can secede from the union. Incidentally, the nut is not Rick Perry. The secessionists argue that George W. Bush would become the President of the Republic of Texas. This whacko points out that under President Bush we haven't had another terrorist attack, and the Democrats ruined everything by lowering the qualifications for home loans. The whackos suggest that Texas controls 85% of the gas and this gives them power. Not to mention that over 65% of the defense industry comes from Texas. At least this is their argument. It appears that people with less than one percent of the brains in America follow this website. For these and other inane and factually incorrect assertions, check it out for yourself at http://www.antiobama.net/anti-obama-websites.html

The number of insulting websites continues. The worst is "Don't Vote For Obama, The Most complete Anti Obama Website at http://www.dontvoteobama.net/ What does this website has that no one can duplicate? It has a poster with President Obama asking you to join the Communist Party. The only problem is that there isn't a Communist

Party at least not in Russia. Our allies in China still have a Communist Party. Another egregious comment is that Obama is "the modern day incarnation of Adolph Hitler." It gets worse. The website owner suggests that President Obama is "the one who murders senior citizens (government healthcare), murders babies (abortion) and hates all whiter people (his own book)." Is there need for a comment?

THE REPUBLICAN PARTY 2012: WHAT HAPPENED?

The Republican Party has been transformed from a boring business minded entity with bald headed politicos who look like Dwight D. Eisenhower to radical, right wing zealots who want to bring the fervor of religion in politics and they look like Karl Rove.

The message is a clear one. Republicans are suspicious of big government. They are still reeling from Franklin D. Roosevelt's New Deal. The post Cold War liberalism that brought new entitlements to American society galls Republicans. Yet, the right wing nut house in 2012 is more moderate than Robert Welch's 1960 John Birch Society. While Glenn Beck is a loose cannon with a loud mouth and a pea brain, he is Einstein compared to those deep into the right wing nut house.

In Sidney Blumenthal's, **The Strange Death of Republican America**, which hit the book stores in April 2008, this well known journalist editorialized that the GOP was now "the minority party." This is the reason for the Tea Party. Some conservative Republicans no longer feel they have a voice. There is no repentance in the Tea Party, only zealous activism.

When the Tea Party helped to defeat Indiana Republican Senator Richard Lugar in 2012, it ended any speculation that the Tea Party was no longer an important influence. Lugar who came to office in 1977 was considered untouchable. His views on the major issues were contrary to the Tea Party and they defeated him. This caused people to reassess the Tea Party. In just two years they morphed in a sophisticated organization with political clout.

The Republican comeback in the Congressional elections of 2010 indicated that the Tea Party was much more than a group of right wing kooks. They understood the political process and they knew how to triumph in it. That is a frightening fact and on Fox TV News, the talking heads like Bill O'Reilly and Glenn Beck, the right wing pundits like Laura "Little Barbie" Ingraham and Ann "Big Barbie" Coulter as well as politicians like Newt Gingrich create what is now the right wing political nut house. The frightening thing is that they may elect a president.

The right wing nut house poses a fundamental threat to traditional civil liberties. Not only is their rhetoric offensive, but also the solutions from the conservative right to America's economic, political and social problems provide frightening insights into their mind.

TEN STRANGE OBSERVATIONS FROM THE RIGHT WING NUT HOUSE

1. "Barack Obama is the food stamp president," Newt Gingrich
2. "I never automatically trust anything the government does when they do an investigation…" Ron Paul on the 9-11 Investigation
3. "Like the average libertarian, Ron Paul is a dogmatic isolationist," Don Feder
4. "Bill Ayers is the one who ghost wrote Obama's "Dreams From My Father," Jack Cashill
5. My sons are all adults and they've made decisions about their careers and they've chosen not to serve in the military.…" Mitt Romney
6. "I don't want to make black people's lives better by giving them somebody else's money," Rick Santorum
7. "How do you say 'delicious' in Cuban," Herman Cain
8. "You're thinking of Europe as Germany and France. I don't…I think that's old Europe," Ron Paul
9. "I'm not a natural leader. I'm too intellectual; I'm too abstract; I think too much." Newt Gingrich
10. "I have enormous personal ambition. I want to shift the entire planet. And I'm doing it. I am now a famous person. I represent real power." Newt Gingrich

SOME THOUGHTS ON THE AMERICAN VOTER

Thomas L. Friedman observed in January 2012, that the presidential election was up for grabs. He made a number of excellent points writing in the **New York Times**. His initial observation was that forty-eight percent of the American voting public "would consider voting for a third party candidate." He went on to suggest that until we repair our infrastructure, the economy will suffer and significant reforms will be virtually impossible. President Barack Obama has programs for school, highway and unemployment reform. Partisan politics have delayed or diluted many of these programs.

The economy remains a problem as Christine Romer, former chairwoman of the Council of Economic Advisers, observed when she suggested that the government deficit and high unemployment hinder economic recovery. When the Bowles-Simpson Commission came up with a plan to cut four trillion dollars from the national debt, politicians paid lip service to the recommendation. As Friedman suggests, a politician who would reduce the debt while advancing the economy would be the next president. The only person capable of doing that is Barack Obama. The Tea Party and the right wing nut house will prevent substantial reform, and America will remain in crisis.

TV NEW POLITICAL BIAS: JANUARY 2012

There is a great deal of debate over whether or not the media has a liberal or conservative bias. While Fox TV News is generally conservative and MSNBC leans in the liberal direction, there is little agreement on the levels of bias. It is virtually impossible to quantify bias.

A recent survey from Mediate Metrics "TV News Political Bias Impact Ratings: January 16-20, 2012" turned up some surprising results. The three news outlets with the most Republican coverage were NBC, Fox and CNN while the Democrats had more stories on MSNBC, CBS and ABC. The surprise was that NBC was the network with the most Republican stories. While this doesn't necessarily prove slanted coverage, it is probably due to the Republican primaries and the drive for the party nomination.

There were some other surprises. The nightly network news on ABC, CBS and NBC have the highest viewer rating but the major networks have less impact because they are only thirty minute programs. In terms of quantifying the news the Democrats receive more airtime than the Republicans.

IS THE TEA PARTY BACK?

In late February 2012, the Tea Party reared its ugly head in Milford, Michigan as Mitt Romney addressed 500 of its finest members. As Romney spoke to the limited government advocates, he supported a litany of their demands. With eight separate Tea Party groups in attendance, Romney sharpened his small government message to hold off Rick Santorum. The tragedy is that the two Republican candidates spoke out against abusive federal power. The irony was that as Romney and Santorum called for tax cuts, the non-profit Committee For A Responsible Federal Budget released a report that pointed out Republican tax cuts would increase the deficit.

As President Obama's supporters watched the Republican presidential nomination circus unfold, they had a sense of victory. The right wing nut house increasingly took over the candidate's speeches, their actions and national television kept everyone informed. President Obama emerged as a quiet leader with integrity as the Republican candidates squabbled over abortion, immigration, budget and foreign policy.

President Obama's strengths were multiple ones. He ordered Osama bin Laden killed, thereby keeping American safe from the master terrorist. There was not another 9/11. The other concern among voters is the big Republican lies. The candidates say one thing about birth control and abortion, and the rank and file appears split on the issue. The Tea Party issues abortion and immigration statements that have hurt the Republican presidential candidates. The Tea Party advocates prompted former President Bill Clinton to bring out a book with his take on recent American politics.

BILL CLINTON'S BACK TO WORK

Bill Clinton's **Back To Work: Why We Need Smart Government** points out that a thirty-year antigovernment obsession has hurt the nation. Clinton views the 2010 Congressional elections as the high point of anti-government politics. Since that time, he alleges, President Obama has had difficulty governing due to a lack of bipartisan support.

The former president goes on to suggest why we need strong government. It is a simple answer. One most of us have forgotten. National Security is one reason. He also advocates assistance to people who cannot fully support or take care of themselves. The notion of equal opportunity is a corner stone of the former president's beliefs. Clinton suggests a level of economic development that encourages business to enter new markets. He believes this is important to economic recovery. These observations are contrary to everything that the Tea Party whacko's and the Fox TV apostles believe.

On the question of the national debt, the former president is optimistic. He argues that in the next ten to twenty years the debt must be reduced. He points out that reduced military spending is not the answer. He is also optimistic about social security. Clinton doesn't believe it is broken. He sees a cash flow problem. He sees the challenge as one of maintaining the long-term health of social security. Clinton also wants the Bush tax cuts on upper income taxpayers to expire in 2013, and he points to the arguments of the right wing nut house against letting the tax cuts expire.

Bill Clinton is a brilliant political thinker. Whatever you think of him as president, he has solid ideas on how to balance the budget while ensuring equality. The Tea Party can't say that. "We're in a mess now," Clinton writes, "we abandoned a proven path to shared prosperity in favor of….anti government ideology." As Clinton concluded, we are now paying the price for greed, capricious behavior and bullying the world. It is time for a new era.

PRESIDENT OBAMA'S SUPPORTERS WEIGH IN NEGATIVELY AND POSITIVELY

By the spring of 2012, there were two books by Democratic sympathizers and semi-Obama supporters that cast a pale over his economic policies. In September 2011 the headline line inducing David Susskind book, **Confidence Men: Wall Street, Washington And the Education of A President** argues that the economic collapse of 2008 is a political crisis that President Obama and his advisers handled poorly. Susskind's thesis is that President Obama needs to replace his economic advisers and look to Bill Clinton's economic policies. This sounds too political and it doesn't contain enough analysis. In 2012, Noam Scheiber's **The Escape Artists: How Obama's Team Fumbled The Recovery** continued Susskind's arguments in a more partisan manner. Scheiber, a senior editor at **The New Republic**, clones previous arguments that President Obama is naïve and too trusting.

Of these books, the Scheiber tome is one that carefully and judicially dissects President Obama's economic policies. The writing is dry, but the information is clear, concise and persuasive. That President Obama depends too heavily upon former Clinton advisors is one of Scheiber's main points. He also chides the president for emphasizing health care reform over jobs. Like Susskind, Scheiber argues that President Obama brought in "escape artists" from the Clinton presidency that failed to pull the economy from the doldrums. Scheiber doesn't believe that the Obama administration has a plan for economic recovery. "But even after winning the presidency, Obama was loath to accept that the economy was singularly important," Scheiber argues. This is Ron Susskind's argument. He supports it by suggesting that Obama's economic advisers were engaged in internal conflicts, petty ego maneuvers and faulty thinking that destroyed any chance of economic recovery.

While the right wing nut house garners most of the press coverage, there is a positive trend. A small number of books suggesting President Obama's miraculous journey from an obscure U. S. Senator to the presidency appear. Among the best is Gwen Ifill, **The Breakthrough: Politics And Race In The Age of Obama**, published in 2009 by Doubleday. Ifill is an African American who is the moderator and managing editor of Washington Week and she is also a senior correspondent for The PBS News Hour. Her book, released the day that Barack Obama was inaugurated, is a thoughtful look at changes in American politics. The theme is one that suggests Obama's election was a pivotal point in race relations.

On June 19, 2012, there was a media buzz as David Maraniss' **Barack Obama: The Story** was released amidst a huge publicity campaign. It was the first in-depth biography that was positive. It contained no surprise revelations, but Maraniss became the first biographer to analyze President Obama's career fairly, dispassionately and without rancor. There were few comments from the right wing nut house. While Obama has been portrayed as spiritual and intellectual, Maraniss points out that blind ambition and a strong work ethic brought him to the presidency.

What Maraniss has in his book that others missed is a ninety-minute interview with President Obama. During this session, Maraniss came to understand how Obama redefined his goals to move toward the presidency. He also shows that the president is very careful with his words, his actions and his public image. Not surprisingly, Maraniss demonstrates that marketing Barack Obama for the presidency promoted Hillary Clinton's campaign aides to complain that she wasn't running against Obama, but she faced his image. The book also reveals a deep intellect and a driving ambition. No one is surprised at this conclusion. As President Obama campaigned for a second term, the Maraniss biographer was a force in the voting process.

WHERE IS THE NATION IN APRIL 2012?

On Sunday April 1, 2012, Vice President Joe Biden weighed in on Face The Nation. He talked in detail about the future of American politics. It was Biden's fifty-fifth appearance on Face The Nation, and Biden suggested that Mitt Romney was the candidate to face the Democrats. "This is not your father's Republican party," Biden commented. Without mentioning the right wing nut house, Biden suggested that "there was a different language" in the Republican Party. He was gearing to go to battle with the Republicans.

Biden, with grace and good manners, suggested that Romney was out of touch with the electorate. "Everywhere I go in the country, there are millions of people benefitting," Biden remarked of Democratic health policies. "This is about the middle class and what affects them."

The Republican energy policy is non-existent, according to Biden. The Vice President made it clear that there is no viable Republican energy policy. On Obamacare, Biden suggested that there is no Republican alternative in the health care field. The notion that the Republican

Party is out of touch with the average voter is a theme that Biden evokes. It is ordinary middle class people that the Democrats believe need help.

Despite Biden's rhetoric, the Obama administration was in trouble. Unemployment figures inched up, the stock market was volatile, home sales lagged as foreclosures and short sales dominated the market. The continued difficulties in Iraq and Afghanistan, as well as problems with Iran's nuclear development program dominated foreign affairs.

On the housing market, Biden said that it was simple. Those people who have faithfully made their house payments need to refinance their loans to make ends meet. It is about their dignity. "The worst thing in the world for a parent is that they can't help their child," Biden concluded.

The Harp 2.0 refinancing program was the beginning of recovery for some homeowners. Republicans were critical of this government bailout and the Democrats pointed to its positive side.

THE MEDIA AND OBAMA'S DETRACTORS

The media is one of the prime sources for Obama's detractors. It is not just Fox TV news, but the media in general that features the attacks on the Democratic president. The mainstream media is not the main source of political news. When the Koch brothers were pictured as the financial arm of the Tea Party, it was Lee Fang, a blogger for the Center For American Progress, that broke the story. The Internet is increasingly the source of hard news. Much of that hard news is fed by an anti-Obama viewpoint.

CBS, ABC and NBC news no longer dominate. The rise of the entertainment news has led to Glenn Beck using a chalkboard to talk down to his listeners. One cannot imagine Walter Cronkite using such a tactic. There are only a few great newspapers left in America. The **New York Times**, the **Washington Post** and the **Los Angeles Times** still report the news accurately, but they are experiencing a dwindling audience.

There are also the sensational stories that bring people like Donald Trump into the midst of the political race. When Trump challenged President Obama's birth certificate, he was asked if he would run for the presidency. Trump's instant political credibility was due to this spurious story. Every network listened to Trump's birther argument, which had little, if any, merit.

By June 2012, the controversy over President Obama's birth certificate was replaced by the notion that his college transcripts were missing. Those in the right wing nut house concentrated on pointing out that they couldn't find records of his college work. The only thing missing was the brains from those who argued that there were no college records for the president.

The evening news with Brian Williams, Scott Pelley and Dianne Sawyer no longer attracts a large audience. The media is fragmented. MSNBC draws a liberal audience; Fox TV News a conservative listener and the MSNBC "Morning Joe" show mixes liberal and conservative views. In the middle, CNN finds it difficult to attract a lasting audience. When CNN fired Lou Dobbs for his political opinions, they lost listeners.

It is partisan journalism that dominates the news. The more sensational the story the more media coverage it is accorded. Arizona Senator John Kyl told one of the biggest lies in political history, and he received a huge amount of publicity. The Republican Senator from Arizona claimed that ninety per cent of all Planned Parenthood members support abortion. In fact, only three percent of the organizations activity is abortion related. Kyl was on the Senate floor when he remarked: "If you want an abortion, you go to Planned Parenthood, and that's well over ninety percent of what Planned Parenthood does." Whether or not Kyl realized his error is open to question. The point is that he received inordinate publicity for this ridiculous observation. The bigger the lie in the right wing nut house, the more publicity and acclaim is accorded.

The myth among those in the right wing nut house is that the media is liberal. The liberal media resides in MSNBC, the **New Yorker**, **Mother Jones**, the **Huffington Post** and **Talking Points**. The irony is that much of the liberal media comes from blogs. The sad state of affairs in the media is obvious when CNN hired the right wing attack dog, Erick Erickson, as a commentator. Erickson is the founder of a conservative blog **Red State**, and he is anything but fair and balanced. Erickson is extreme in comments, and he lacks good judgment.

During his first administration, President Obama received more positive, more negative and more trivial news coverage than any previous president. The point is that there needs to be more hard news. Conservatives have more success placing their message with the media. In its eagerness for news, CNBC presented more Tea Party coverage than was necessary. This was to fill dead air. The large number of television right wing talking heads attest to the increased interest in conservative issues.

From 2010 to 2012, President Obama faced a hostile Congress with entrenched Republican power mongers in the House of Representatives.

During his first two years, he accomplished a great deal. He banned the use of torture that the Bush-Cheney administrating endorsed. The "enhanced interrogation technique" was to President Obama inhuman. He stopped it. The American Recovery and Reinvestment Act, the so-called stimulus bill, brought $787 billion into the economy and health care reform took place that forced the insurance companies to spend 80 to 95 percent of their premiums on medical care.

PRESIDENT OBAMA: ACCOUNTABLE ON THE WAR ON TERROR

After 9-11 a number of al-Qaeda leaders were captured and put through interrogation. The CIA lawyers were asked to approve a battery of tests for tough interrogation techniques. A controversy broke out over whether or not the U. S. was violating international law by providing detainees with some rights. After all, they were terrorists, why did they need rights. Soon doctors, lawyers, psychologists, government officials and high-ranking White House staff were involved in defined terrorists rights. Only in America could the rights of those who want to destroy us be guaranteed.

When his term ended, the left roundly criticized President George W. Bush. His critics alleged abuses of power. The Bush administration's Office of Legal Counsel spent some time looking into detainee rights. Even the Republican appointees in the Office of Legal Counsel believed that power over persuasion hurt American intelligence. But the Office of Legal Counsel did document that the Bush administration did not run rampant over the detainee's legal rights.

President Barack Obama was among the strongest critics of the detainee policies. Obama believed that the U. S. position in world affairs was hurt by the detainee policy. He argued that there was a "moral responsibility" to comply with international law. What the president didn't notice is that things have changed. International law is murky regarding terrorists. When President Obama called the camps at Guantanamo Bay a "legal black hole," he framed the issue. He would have to shut down Guantanamo. It didn't work out. Even the president came to realize that this was a difficult issue, and the need for intelligence on terrorism was important to American security.

When the Democratic administration extended military commissions in 2009 they found it difficult to obtain intelligence. The military commissions were reinstated. While Obama stated that he is a peace president, there are three times more terrorists held in Afghanistan under the Democratic administration. Initially, President Obama was going to change the rules for handling enemy combatants. He didn't. Obama extended the surveillance measures in the Patriot Act and he targeted terrorists for killing. This led to the death of Osama bin Laden and a year later to his second in command.

The Congressional Intelligence Committees approve of President Obama's handling of the terror issue. The irony is that the Democratic policies differ very little from those of the Bush administration. This is a plus rather than a minus. It is an indication how well executive policy is working in the war on terrorism. The CIA's enhanced interrogation procedures still come under fire, but there is more leeway for terrorists to be vetted and interrogated.

The problem with American foreign policy and the war on terror is the difficulty of maintaining secrecy. In June 2102, the story broke that someone is leaking intelligence in the executive branch. It is virtually impossible to protect secrets and the leaks prompted Georgia Republican Representative Lynn Westmoreland to charge that the White House was responsible for the leaks. President Obama forthrightly disputed this charge.

The ensuing controversy over Justice Department leaks, the role of Attorney General Eric Holder in the leaks and the concern over the Bureau of A. T. F.'s "fast and furious" gun scandal prompted the Senate Judiciary Committee to hold hearings about the leaks. National security was the primary concern. Unfortunately, partisan politics reared its ugly head and the President and Congress were involved in a jurisdictional dispute. California Democratic Senator Dianne Feinstein was a lone voice of reason as she remarked: "To have a fight over how we do all this now will set back any leak investigation." Holder approached two Washington D. C. attorneys, Ronald C. Machen, Jr., the U.S. Attorney For the District of Columbia, and Rod J. Rosenstein, his counterpart in Maryland to investigate the leaks. Republican's on the Senate Judiciary Committee cried foul as they both supported Barack Obama in the 2008 election. In the midst of this partisan political mess the future of the American military was lost in the shuffle of partisan politics.

The final result is that Eric Holder became the first sitting Attorney General to be found in contempt of Congress for refusing to hand over additional documents beyond the more than 7,600 he had already given to Congress. In a press conference, Holder dismissed the contempt citation as simply the problems of "partisan politics."

There is no doubt that the American military is restricted by the legal and personal oversight toward its mission to protect the country. A lawyered army is a predictable army. This hampers the military actions and effectiveness. When American commanding general, David Petraeus, told his troops not to fire a round near the Shrine of Imam Ali in Najaf. "I don't want a single round, not even a ricochet, to hit the dome." This comment suggests the war on terror is endless and without a solution. The president does not have a free hand in the war on terror; it is such a highly politicized issue that a solution is difficult. The controversy over secret government leaks prevents an effective foreign policy.

RACE AND CLASS AND THE RIGHT WING NUT HOUSE

The place of race and class is one of the main arguments in recent American politics. In the White House the Obama's have gone out of their way to make race less of an issue rather than more of a concern. The Obama's are just an ordinary American family that is until they entered the White House. Then the question of race and class reared its ugly head.

Among the earliest indignities faced by President Obama and his family were the ones that came from Congress. Mitch McConnell, the Republican Senator from Kentucky, can't withhold his disdain for President Obama. Is it race? Is it class? No! McConnell sees "a Negro" in the White House. The rise of Ku Klux Klan type organizations and the revived national racism suggest that Americans shouldn't congratulate themselves for solving the racial problem.

Rachel L. Swarms' **American Tapestry: The Story Of The Black And White, and Multiracial Ancestors of Michelle Obama**, published in 2012, is a book that tells us more than we need to know about the first ladies family. There is one interesting theme and that is "uplift." The striving for a better position or the drive for a better class of life is part of the American dream. The critics in the right wing nut house should be required to read Swarms' book, as they would understand where the Obama's came from and why they are in the White House. Race and class is still important in American, President Obama demonstrates that education, hard work, intelligence and ignoring the nay sayers is the road to success.

WOMEN IN THE RIGHT WING NUT HOUSE

The facts are ugly concerning the Republican war on women. Senator Rick Santorum, who was a Republican front-runner for a time, argued that women must avoid "a license to do things in the sexual realm that is counter to how things are supposed to be." Santorum is not alone in attempting to abridge women's rights. Congress investigated Planned

Parenthood. The result was that a bill was introduced that would allow employers to fire a woman for sexual activity. That is illicit sexual activity as defined by the employer. This bill was narrowly defeated in Congress. Gay marriage, lesbian rights, and legal protection for gays are parts of the Republican political package. Right-wingers attacked the Indiana Girl Scouts because they supported lesbian membership. There has been no time in American history when women's rights have come under more intense scrutiny.

THE REPUBLICAN ATTACK ON WOMEN

1. THE REPUBLICAN'S IN CONGRESS WANT STO REDUCE FUNDING FOR ABORTION CARE.
2. A STATE LEGISLATOR IN GEORGIA WANTS TO CHANGE RAPE, STALKING AND OTHER DOMESTIC ABUSE LAWS BECAUSE THEY ARE TOO LIBERAL.
3. IN SOUTH DAKOTA REPUBLICANAS PROPOSED A BILL THAT WOULD MAKE IT LEGAL TO MURDER A DOCTOR WHO PROVIDES ABORTION CARE.
4. IN CONGRESS REPUBLICANS VOWED IN THE U. S. CONGRESS TO CUT A MILLION DOLLARS FOR FOOD STAMPS TO LOW INCOME WOMEN.
5. MARYLAND REPUBLICANS CURTAILED ALL COUNTY MONEY FOR LOW-INCOME CHILDRENS' PRE SCHOOL PROGRAMS.
6. AT THE FEDERAL LEVEL IT WAS RECOMMENDED THAT HEAD START PROGRAM BE CUT DRAMATICALLY.
7. TWO OF THE THREE ELDERLY POOR ARE WOMEN.
8. ALL FEDERAL FUNDING IS TO BE CUT FOR PLANNED PARENTHOOD
9. FAMILY PLANNING AND BASIC HEALTH CARE SERVICES WILL BE CONTINUALLY CUT IN FEDERAL BUDGETS. THIS IMPACTS MORE WOMEN THAN MEN.
10. VIRGINIA GOVERNOR BOB MCDONNELL SIGNED A BILL ALLOWING THE STATE GOVERNMENT TO FORCE WOMEN TO UNDERGO AN ULTRASOUND PRIOR TO THE ABORTION.
11. ROY BLUNT AND MARCO RUBIO ATTEMPTED TO PASS A BILL ALLOWING EMPLOYERS TO DENY WORKING WOMEN CONTRACEPTION CARE ON MORAL GROUNDS.
12. MITT ROMNEY WANTS TO REPEAL THE AFFORDABLE CARE ACT WHICH ENDS GENDER DISCRIMINATION BY INSURANCE COMPANIES.

Rick Santorum argues that contraception is dangerous. Rush Limbaugh, the radio voice of the right wing, called one feminist a prostitute, and he wanted her to post her alleged sex acts on you tube. The firestorm over Limbaugh's remarks prompted most Republicans to disassociate themselves with his remarks. Yet, many people believe that the Republican Party is not waging war on women. This is simply the opinion of important men who are attacking women.

President Barack Obama wants employers to cover contraception. Mitt Romney, Sanatorium and Limbaugh oppose this program. House Speaker John Boehner comments time and time again that the Republican agenda has done nothing to denigrate women. After saying this Boehner took a bill through the House reducing women's rights under the Violence Against Women Act. He countered his own argument by suggesting that women were being victimized. In the next breath, Boehner argued that women were too litigious. This is the stated reason that he supports amending the Violence Against Women Act.

In Virginia, Republicans are introducing legislation to require a series of medical tests, all of which are invasive, before an abortion. These tests would include sonograms and Christian counseling prior to the medical procedure. As a District of Columbia delegate, Eleanor Holmes Norton, asked for a chance to testify before the House on the need to continue abortions in the District of Columbia. Her request was denied. She was furious and pointed out that women's rights were lost in the battle over political viewpoints. She also walked out of a hearing on contraception to protest the insensitive Republican attitude toward women and the lack of respect that she received as a Congresswoman. Norton is a District of Columbia Congresswoman, but since D. C. is not a state, she is a non-voting member. So Republicans reasoned that they did not have to listen to her thoughts on contraception. She is also African-American and subtle racism permeated the House of Representatives.

In Arizona, Republican Governor Jan Brewer signed a bill making it more difficult to secure an abortion. The attack is on Roe v. Wade prompted politicians, like Governor Brewer, to reap their rewards at the polls. If Republicans had their way an abortion would be granted only if the woman was not expected to live. Governor Brewer is also in the forefront of a move to make access for women to health care more difficult. She signed a bill making it problematical that Planned Parenthood receive full state funding. The Arizona bill denies Planned Parenthood money for non-abortion services like cancer screening and family planning. Poor women need these services and without them their health is endangered.

Once the right wing nut house realized that they were in trouble with women voters, Speaker John Boehner denied the charge. The Republican Party and the right wing media launched on attack on the Democrats treatment of women. Rush Limbaugh accused Democrats of "launching a war on motherhood." Sharon Day, co-chair of the Republican National Committee, labeled the Democrats attack on Republicans over women's rights as "insulting and disingenuous." The right wing nut house produced statistics and comments that overall women favored the Republican programs.

It is on the equal pay debate that Republicans demonstrate the depth of their hostility to women's rights. Governor Scott Walker of Wisconsin is the poster boy for cutting women's wages. He signed a law making it difficult, if not impossible, for women to take legal action for equal wages. Walker defended his action as these law suits: "clogged up the legal system." President Obama spent three years attempting to put teeth into the Equal Pay Act of 1963. The right wing nut house has thwarted his efforts.

In Georgia, women were concerned about changes in the laws. State Representative Doug McKillip, a Republican from Athens, sponsored a bill signed by Governor Nathan Deal that alters the medical relationship between women and their doctors. The new law forces obstetricians to perform C-sections on women who go into labor early even when standard medical practice doesn't call for it. McKillip also supported a bill to enforce a twenty-week limit on abortions. Critics challenge McKillip's framing his arguments in a medically gray area.

The real reason for Doug McKillip's policy is that he is facing a challenge for re-election to the Georgia House. Regina Quick, who is challenged Rep. McKillip's, pointed out that he is playing to the crowd. Quick opposes abortion, but she is outraged that women are a pawn in the July 31, 2012 primary. She also believes that doctors, not politicians, should decide on abortion procedures. McKillip's answers with the slogan: "Conservative And Unashamed." This appeal to local voters is designed for re-election.

The critics of McKillip's bill point out that there is no provision for incest or rape in his abortion restrictions. McKillip's speaks out against what he terms "convenience abortions," and his opponents charge he has no concern for women's personal decisions. There was so much rancor over McKillip's abortion stand on a local television show prompted a woman to come on the TV set and present McKillip's with a Puppet Uterus. It gets worse, the Puppet Uterus is on You Tube.

The debate over women's rights rages on prior to the 2012 presidential election and beyond. There is no doubt that the Republican Party is supporting a subtle reduction in women's rights.

Whether or not there is a Republican war on women is a matter of opinion. There are some facts, attitudes and legislative bills suggesting that if there is not a war, there is modification of women's rights in Republican politics.

Republican arguments point out that women voted for the party in 2010 for the first time since President Ronald Reagan. The GOP argues that the war on women is a manufactured debate that insults and demeans the Republican establishment.

Senator Jeanne Shaheen, a New Hampshire Democrat, argues that the party should not hold back on the war on women. "I'm old enough to remember what it was like before Roe v. Wade, and I think access to reproductive health services for women is critical." She went on to point out that Mitt Romney stands with the Republican Party right wing. "We don't think government should tell us what to do on some of these issues," Senator Shaheen concluded. The question of contraceptive coverage for women should not be a government issue. At least not unless we are in the stone age in 2012 or perhaps the right wing nut house on the question of women's rights.

No one is stronger in his criticism of women than Georgia State Republican Representative, Bobby Franklin, who allegedly labeled women as "accusers" in select rape and stalking cases. It gets worse. Republicans in South Dakota are discussing a law that would allow justifiable homicide for people killing doctors who perform abortions. A number of Republican lawmakers complain that the words "uterus' and "vagina" should not be uttered in public. For those who believe that there is no Republican war on women, the facts don't lie. The war is on and John Boehner continues to support any House bill targeting a decline in women's rights.

THE WALL STREET JOURNAL WEIGHS IN ON PRESIDENT OBAMA'S ALLEGED ENEMIES LIST

By May 2102, with Mitt Romney assured of the Republican Presidential nomination, the forces of the right wing nut house took on a new urgency. On May 7, 2012, Tom O'Malley wrote a letter to the **Wall Street Journal** alleging that he was on President Obama's enemies list. Another letter followed from Richard Klitzberg of Boca Raton, Florida who alleged that he also made Obama's enemies list.

Klitzberg wrote: "Mr. Obama has chanted a message of 'fairness' in all matters from immigration to taxes to education, while declaring war on Wall Street." This reaction was due to a **Wall Street Journal** story that alleged President Obama was making war on natural gas and big business. But an enemies list. There is no proof of this allegation. The recent experiences of former President Richard M. Nixon suggest that this would not happen.

The Obama enemies list is an allegation from **Wall Street Journal** reporter Kimberley A. Strassel. She reports that President Obama was attempting to intimidate those who contributed to Mitt Romney's campaign. Not only is this a violation of the law, it would be an amateurish political move. President Obama is not noted for making such mistakes. Strassel wrote: "President Barack Obama, the most powerful man on the planet, singles you out by name. His campaign brands you a Romney donor, shames you for 'betting against America' and accuses you of having a less than enviable record." Strassel's statement is difficult to accept. She later goes on to allege that the SEC or the IRS can audit you for your campaign contribution.Strassel in a series of articles named people whom the Obama administration targeted. She charges that when Frank VanderSloot, the CEO of Melaleuca Inc. gave the Romney campaign a million dollars, the Democrats responded that VanderSloot was a less than reputable donor. The Obama administration had a point. It was that Strassel and the **Wall Street Journal** didn't get it. Not only is Strassel a strong critic of gay rights, he is a litigator who allegedly abuses the court system. His hometown, Idaho Falls, is a quiet and picturesque community. Rather than allow VanderSloot to harass, intimidate and bully gay Americans, someone hired an investigator to look into VanderSloot's past. Guess what they found? Friends describe him as a loveable, businessman who is politically conservative. They see none of the right wing arguments that Obama's supporters point out. He is simply a staunch conservative.

Frank VanderSloot was identified in the June 7 2012, issue of **Rolling Stone** as one of Mitt Romney's billionaire supporters. **Rolling Stone** estimated his revenues last year at over a billion dollars. He is the 86th largest landowner in the United States, and, in the past, he has donated more than half a million dollars to Republican candidates. VanderSloot wants less government regulation, and he is particularly hostile to the FDA for stating that Melaleuca Inc. made false and misleading claims. He disputes this charge. He also hates President Obama.

If there is one person who is the King of Obama Detractors, it is Frank VanderSloot. He also protested a PBS special on the gay lifestyle, and he donated large sums of money to pass California's ban on same sex marriage. He is described as divorced and lives in a seventeen-bed-room mansion. Everyone in Idaho Falls loves Frank and they are upset that he has been targeted by the left wing.

Why has the Obama campaign targeted VanderSloot? They claim that he has made repeated slurs and inappropriate remarks. The Democrats are simply calling attention to his callous behavior. All is fair in love and war. We are still waiting to hear from VanderSloot's ex-wife. It is only fair to let Frank VanderSloot have the last word, he told Kimberley A. Strassel: "I have many gay friends who I love and respect...." A great comment but just don't tell his present girl friend. Or maybe there is a wife.

THE SMALLER SCOPE OF PRESIDENT OBAMA'S 2012 POLITICS

What influence does the right wing nut house have upon President Obama's politics? The criticism from the right prompted the Obama administration to promise less and deliver more. Obama's advisers labeled this a minimalist election strategy. This is campaigning on one or two key issues. President Obama has ended war in Iraq; he has fulfilled campaign promises on health care and fiscal reform. The Obama administration worked on ending the recession, strengthening the economy in 2012 and creating jobs despite intransigent Republican opposition.

What the Obama administration desires is higher taxes on upper income Americans to insure an equal distribution of wealth and services. This policy guarantees strong opposition from conservatives. The popular issues that Obama embraced in 2012 include lower interest rates for student loans. He also supports the Buffett rule to increase on the wealthy.

Gay marriage is at the crux of Obama's political integrity. Rather than waffle and equivocate on the issue, the president came out in support of same sex marriage. President Obama made it clear, he supports it as a personal matter. He is not concerned with legal issues. The president was answering his right wing critics who accuse him of meddling with the court system. California's Proposition 8, and the 1996 Defense of Marriage Act are working their way through the courts. President Obama made it clear that he would respect court decisions on gay marriage. This is a smart political move.

The Democrats agenda is less ambitious than it was in Obama's first presidential run. But it is still an important message as the president attempts to spend more money on road and bridge repair, increase manufacturing, balance the budget and improve college funding.

The President has strengths and weaknesses. One of his glaring deficiencies is an inability to explain his successes. While Obama is a great speaker, he has trouble pointing out his achievements. Perhaps his greatest reform is in healthcare. Obamacare means that those people with pre-existing conditions will never be denied coverage. This notion drives the right wing nut house crazy. The idea of universal health coverage is anathema to conservatives.

On June 28 2012, the U. S. Supreme Court upheld President Obama's 2010 health care bill. Chief Justice John Roberts ruled that the Affordable Care Act is constitutional. By upholding the individual mandate, the requirement for all Americans to acquire health insurance, the Court upheld the heart of the law. This was a victory for the president, but there are still problems to be solved.

There are concerns over Obama's leadership. He needs to spend more time generating money to repair the nation's infrastructure. This would create jobs and enhance productivity. The Medicare and Social Security programs need a major overhaul. He must come up with an acceptable defense budget. The issue of the local economy is another important step to Obama's re-election. He has not addressed that question satisfactorily to many people.

In fairness to President Obama, he attempted to negotiate the "grand bargain" with House Speaker John Boehner. It failed. By the November 2012, election House Republicans thwarted any attempt at bipartisan compromise. The National Commission on Fiscal Responsibility And Reform, known as the Simpson Bowles Commission, was appointed by President Obama to research and propose solutions to America's fiscal difficulties. The eighteen-member commission didn't endorse its own findings. With six members of the House and six from the Senate on the Commission, along with six others, the committee failed to garner the fourteen votes needed to promote its recommendations.

THE FUTURE OF AMERICAN POLITICS

The present day political situation is a depressing one. The wit and wisdom of John F. Kennedy is long forgotten, the intellect of Adlai Stevenson resulted in his defeat in a presidential election, the easy going humor of Bill Clinton, the Zen wisdom of California's Jerry Brown and the straight ahead criticism of California's Nancy Pelosi are lost in the right wing nut house swirling around American politics. The specter of Michele Bachmann being taken seriously is a sad comment on the political scene. Bachmann's comments leave one wondering how she got elected to office. Among Bachmann's observations: 1.) "If we took away the minimum wage…we could potentially wipe out unemployment." This is a statement opting for an end to labor unions. 2.) Bachmann remarked: "When a judge will say to little children that you cannot say the pledge of allegiance, but you must learn that homosexuality is normal and you should try it." This statement indicates that she blames radical judges fir practicing judicial activism. That is, Bachmann claims, they are rewriting the laws not interpreting them. Bachmann calls these judicial decisions examples of "America's moral decline." 3.) "We also know that the very Founders that wrote those documents worked tirelessly until slavery was no more...." To do this Thomas Jefferson and George Washington would have lived well past the hundred-year mark. 4.) "I wish the American media would take a great look at the views of the people in Congress and find out: are they pro-America or anti-America?" She is suggesting that the House and Senate may contain some less than patriotic members. Bachmann is brilliant compared to Christine O'Donnell.

When Delaware Republican Senate candidate Christine O'Donnell suggested that masturbation was a sin, the press accorded her intense coverage. Soon signs showed up at O'Donnell rallies: "Atheists For Masturbation" and "Masturbate And Vote." Somewhere along the line the issues in political campaigns are lost in the midst of this nonsense. Masturbation! I can't remember that ever being a political issue. Thanks to the right wing nut house it is in the midst of American politics.

What is sad is that Obama's detractors have labeled him a left wing radical. Others call Obama a truculent Socialist. The truth is that he is a centrist who is almost too compromising. But that is another story. Stay tuned.

THE RIGHT WING NUT HOUSE AND LIBERALISM

Liberalism is almost a dirty word. The rise of right wing conservatism in the media, in the universities, in government institutions and in the corporate boardroom threatens free speech and individual rights. It is in carefully designed plans to thwart gay rights, and the attempts to end government funds for birth control, which highlights the successes of the right.

It is important to define why people embrace liberalism. To Sean Hannity, Ann Coulter, Glenn Beck and David Limbaugh, liberalism is a form of fascism. They view totalitarianism and Communism as a bastion of the Democratic Party. That is liberals have too much personal freedom and too little concern with government power.

Why does the right wing nut house hate liberalism? They fear big government, they fear liberal immigration policies and they believe restrictions on business are destroying the economy. The only way to prevent the federal government from accomplishing these goals is to create an intransigent form of government. Hence, House Speaker John Boehner and his criticism of the Obama administration.

What sets liberalism apart from conservatism is a lack of dogma. This is also one of the problems with liberalism. It is not a carefully defined idea or movement. That is the beauty of liberalism, as it is flexible and open to new ideas. This sets it apart from conservatism. The militant and optimistic spirit of Franklin Delano Roosevelt's liberalism is no longer existent. This is one of the present problems with American liberals. They fight fairly and they listen to both sides of an argument. Sadly, this is not true of the right wing.

Another problem with political liberalism is that since the 1980s, political, cultural, emotional and personal losers have represented it. Gary Hart, Michael Dukakis and Geraldine Ferraro are the prime examples. Others like President Jimmy Carter meant well in the political system, but he was devoured by it.

American conservatism is a totalitarian political religion and it needs to be combated. The right wing conservative nut house appeals to the white, over sixty, pensioned minions who go to the country club, play cards, pool. They go to concerts in the over age 55 clubhouses that house the right wing nut house and they recite the pledge of allegiance before each concert. They feel comfortable there with the other white reactionaries. In their spare time they turn on Fox TV News. They tell anyone who will listen that it is "fair and balanced." After all that is what Glenn Beck says, so it has to be true. He has a blackboard that teaches them history. They see liberalism as the bane of their existence.

There are many reasons for liberalism's decline. The role of political correctness, the influence of radical academics, the scandals involving state and local government pensions and the inability to explain federal or state spending are issues that create hostility to liberalism. These concerns have made liberalism a dirty word. There needs to be a reconfiguration of the tenets supporting liberalism, and a greater degree of political activism toward liberal causes.

THE POLITICAL FUTURE: MYTHS AND REALITIES

The economic downturn has humbled the American economy. Does the economic decline portend less political influence? There are some disturbing facts. In science and technology the U. S. is in trouble. With more than half of American patents granted to foreigners and Silicon Valley technology populated by a large number of well-qualified Indian and Chinese engineers, there is widespread concern for the future of American intellectual property. In science and technology, American students ranked twentieth. The American infrastructure is collapsing as Congress sits idly watching the roads deteriorate, the educational system crumble, key government buildings sag from lack of upkeep, and the construction industry is at an all time low. The right wing nut house demands less science and government research. This is a recipe for disaster. Federally funded research and development is at an all time low.

Jeff Flake, the Republican Representative from Arizona's Sixth Congressional District, in May 2012, introduced an amendment that passed the House of Representatives prohibiting the National Science Foundation from funding political science research. Flake called political science research "meritless." He also flexed his political muscle by pointing what was and what was not acceptable as scientific research. A chilling fear swept through the National Science Foundation as Congressional meddling in science reached epidemic proportions. Flake is also critical of political science journals. It is not surprising that political scientists are critical of Flake's meddling in scientific matters. This comes at a time when American science is in flux. Jeff Flake is looking over the National Science Foundation's shoulder and telling what is acceptable to receive federal money. Fortunately, the U. S. Senate defeated Flake's flakey proposal.

Flake studied political science at BYU. He harbors deep resentment, and he evokes constant complaints about the discipline. He view the journals as antiquated, the arguments as convoluted, and he argues that no one reads the political science journals. On a whim, he is putting a large number of people out of work and thwarting a discipline that is important to politicians, businessmen and the general public. Flake is getting even for all those political science classes that he hated. He is in the forefront of the anti-science agenda that is part of the Republican Party, and it is also a major force in the right wing nut house. By asserting politics in science, Flake has made a huge mistake.

During this controversy, Flake displayed his disdain for an Ivy League education and he suggested, using innuendo, that the entire field is useless. If Flake had only received higher grades this controversy wouldn't have emerged.

On June 28, 2012 the **Arizona Republic** reported that Flake testified before the Utah State Senate in support of South Africa's apartheid policy. As Flake began his campaign for the U. S. Senate seat vacated by Republican Senator Jon Kyl, Democrats attacked him for his pro-apartheid stand. Flake countered these charges with the statement: "Absolutely No," and he claimed to oppose apartheid. This issue is far from resolved.

But there those who see no American decline. Jeff Flake is among them. Asia and India are catching up with America in terms of its technology and the living standard. The idea that the U. S. is on the downside is contrary to research at **Yahoo Finance** and Daniel Gross's book **Better, Stronger, Faster: The Myth of American Decline…And The Rise of A New Economy** takes a different approach arguing that American exports are a key part of the economy. Gross argues that the federal government could do more to facilitate American trade abroad.

The conclusion is that the American economy is evolving in new directions, as is the political scene. The right wing nut house will have an influence on this journey.

SOME THOUGHTS ON PRESIDENT OBAMA

David Maraniss, a distinguished historian and biographer, was the first person to look deeply and fairly in Barack Obama's life. In June 2012 **Barack Obama: The Story** was released with a great deal of fanfare. It turned out to be a fair book with deep research and excellent writing. The analysis is superb, but, once again, there is a great deal of disagreement with his interpretations. That is for the brains in the political arena to debate. What is important about the Maraniss book is that there were signs of the depth of Obama's personality and character long before to became the president. In the third grade, living with his stepfather Lolo Montero, young Obama wrote an essay stating that he wanted to be the president of the United States. If there is one reason to elect Obama president it is his taste in music. He played Earth, Wind and Fire, the Rolling Stones, Billie Holiday and Jimi Hendrix among others while in college. Maraniss does a good job pointing out the kindness in Obama's personality. He was friendly with Kofi Manu because the young man was shy and had difficulty making friends. Maraniss writes: "Obama was especially friendly to people who seemed lonely or felt a sense of otherness….:" Perhaps Maraniss' most interesting conclusion is that Obama's college transcripts are the new battle for the birthers. The Maraniss book has a great deal of extraneous information, but the bottom line is that Barack Obama was a great young man.

One of the knocks on President Obama is that he has never had a real day job. Mitt Romney commented: "The president's a nice guy, but he's never had a job in the private sector." This is an interesting and also untrue comment. Obama worked at the Sidney Austin Law Firm in Chicago, and he also worked for a time at the Business International Corporation, where he edited a newsletter for an eighteen thousand dollar salary. He hated both jobs and went into politics. This is not exactly high-end employment. This information from the Maraniss biography indicates that President Obama is like no other person elected to the nation's highest office.

The exhaustively researched Maraniss biography suggests that no one with a convoluted family background, like that of Barack Obama's, has never ascended to the presidency. This not only makes him special, but it demonstrates his intellectual brilliance. He has had to overcome right wing criticism and unadulterated racism. He is still combating it in 2012. Much of what Maraniss writes paves the way for volume two, which moves from the early years toward the bastion of power that Obama occupies.

After almost four years in the White House, Barack Obama's transformation from a local Illinois politician into a world leader has been an often painful and frustrating one. He has persevered, despite the criticism and slights, and he is the first incumbent president since Woodrow Wilson to win the Nobel Prize. The public knows more about his early life than that of any American President. When the Maraniss biography appeared, one of his earliest girl friends, Genevieve Cook, allowed Maraniss to quote from a diary she kept while dating Obama. One of the key quotes from her diary was that he was too cool and distant for a serious relationship. Rather than being a negative, this comment was an early indication of his strength of character. This strength is essential to combating the right wing nut house.

The Maraniss volume is extraordinary in that it concludes with Obama driving an old, used yellow Datsun to Harvard Law School. It was here that the future president began his long and arduous journey to the White House.

When the Maraniss volume ends, Barack Obama is twenty-seven years old. His family history is a troubled one. From this he acquired strength and conviction. One inescapable conclusion from Maraniss' research is that somewhere along the line Barack Obama developed a personal charisma that took him from California's Occidental College to Columbia University, to Harvard, to Illinois politics, to the U. S. Senate and to the presidency. This is not the road Mitt Romney took from the silver spooned, billionaire childhood, to a silver spooned business career to a silver spooned political career. Is the next stop the silver spooned presidency? President Obama doesn't look like a bad choice.

BIBLIOGRAPHICAL SOURCES

PROLOGUE

For President Carter's remarks on race and his analysis, see "Carter Again Cites Racism As Factor in Obama's Treatment, **CNN Politics**, September 15, 2009 http://articles.cnn.com/2009-09-15/politics/carter.obama_1_president-jimmy-carter-president-obama-health-care-plan?_s=PM:POLITICS Also see, Ewen Mac Askill, "Jimmy Carter: Animosity Toward Barack Obama Is Due To Racism," **London Guardian**, September 16, 2009.

For Hank Williams, Jr's derogatory remarks about President Obama see Joe Queenan, "Revenge of the 60-Year-Old Has-Beens," **Wall Street Journal**, October 15-16, 2011, p. C 17. The thesis of the Queenan article is that American politics is filled with over sixty years of age politically crabby folks. On the 112th Congress see, Kathleen Hennessey, "Not Quite A Do-Nothing Congress, But It's Close," **Los Angeles Times**, July 4, 2011. The rhetoric of the right wing nut house is constant and complex and most of the books are dreadful. Harry Stein's, **How I Accidentally Joined The Vast Right Wing Conspiracy And Found Inner Peace** (New York, 2001) is a personal and interesting look at an intelligent person who found his political calling amongst conservatives. It is as much memoir as history, and it is a fascinating book. Stein is not part of the right wing nut house, he is an intelligent and thoughtful conservative, and the book is contrary is most written by right wing political thinkers. It is also well written and fascinating. Stein's columns for a decade in **Esquire** were brilliant and he discussed ethics in some depth.

Chris Mooney, **The Republican Brain: The Science of Why They Deny Science-and Reality** (New York, 2012) is a brilliant book that explains why Republicans deny that man-made climate change exists. Mooney also analyzes why and how the right wing Republican thinks. He demonstrates that there is a scientific factor behind the right wing nut house. He also suggests by studying the brain why Republicans are more likely to oppose new ideas, embrace modern science and depend upon the Bible. It is lack of a modern intellect that drives them. He shows that even college educated conservatives have a tendency to be skeptical of things intellectual.

PART I: THE PARANOID STYLE AND THE RIGHT WING

See Daniel Patrick Moynihan, "The Paranoid Style In American Politics Revisited," **Public Interest**, Issue 81, 1985 for a restating of Hofstadter's seminal theory and Scott Horton, "The Paranoid Style in American Politics," **Harper's**, August 16, 2007.

Also see, Floyd Brown and Lee Troxler, **Obama Unmasked: Did Slick Hollywood Handlers Create The Perfect President?** (Bellevue, 2008) for an interesting argument speculating that President Obama is a cult political figure.

A great deal of the material in this book depends upon Richard Hofstadter's writing. Also a number of books, notably, Chip Berlet and Matthew N. Lyon, **Right Wing Populism In America: Too Close For Comfort** (New York, 2000) and Seymour Martin Lipset and Earl Raab, **Politics of Unreason: Right Wing Extremism in America, 1790-1977** (Chicago, 1978) provide important historical background. The right wing nut house grew out of a long and complicated conservatism.

CHAPTER 1: RICHARD HOFSTADTER'S PARANOID STYLE IN AMERICAN POLITICS

See Richard Hofstadter, **The Paranoid Style In American Politics** (New York, 1964). On Richard Hofstadter's life see David S. Brown, **Richard Hofstadter: An Intellectual Biography** (Chicago, 2006) for the impact that this historian has had on American politics. Although Hofstadter died in 1970 his books, particularly, **The American Political Tradition**, championed liberal politics from the early days of the New Deal. In Hofstadter's view the radical right slowly took away our rights, attacked our values and controlled our media outlets. Now almost half a century later Hofstadter's words ring true. It is Hofstadter's brilliant writing, cogent analysis and vivid descriptions of the right that has made his work lasting.

The brilliant analysis provided by Richard Hofstadter has been criticized for lack of scientific materials. That is many of his critics point out that he is a glib writer with little proof for his assertions. Daniel Patrick Moynihan, "The Paranoid Style In American Politics Revisited,"

Public Interest, Issue 81, 1985, pp. 107-127 suggests the Hofstadter's ideas continue in the mid-1980s to have relevance. Other examples of the paranoid style in recent years include David Greenburg, "The Obama Haters: We Still Don't Understand How Fringe Conservatism Went Mainstream, **Slate**, September 23, 2009 and Laura Miller, "The Paranoid Style in American Punditry," **Salon**, September 15, 2010.

See Scott Horton, "The Paranoid Style in American Politics," **Harper's**, August 16, 2007 for the historical legacy of Hofstadter's argument. Horton is a New York lawyer educated at the University of Texas Law School, and he is also an adjunct professor at Columbia Law School. He is a left wing political activist and lawyer who has represented individuals charged with terrorism.

Many of the examples in this chapter are taken from Bill Press, **The Obama Hate Machine: The Lies, Distortions And Personal Attacks On The President-And Who Is Behind Them** (New York, 2012).

The radical right has a long and influential past. For the best books on this phenomena see, for example, David H. Bennett, **The Party of Fear: The American Far Right From Nativism To The Militia Movement** (Chapel Hill, 1988); David Brion Davis, editor, **The Fear Of Conspiracy: Images of Un-American Subversion From The Revolution To The Present** (Ithaca, 1971); Thomas Frank, **The Wrecking Crew: How Conservatives Ruined Government, Enriched Themselves And Beggared The Nation** (New York, 2009); Susan Jacoby, **The Age of American Unreason** (New York, 2008); Daniel Pipes, **Where The Paranoid Style Comes From And How It Flourishes** (New York, 1997) and Leonard Zeskind **Blood And Politics: The History of The White Nationalist Movement From The Margins To The Mainstream** (New York, 2009).

See Daniel Joseph Singal, "Beyond Consensus: Richard Hofstadter And American Historiography," **Journal of American History**, vol. 89, no 4 (October 1984), pp 976-1004. Also see Richard Hofstadter, **The American Political Tradition And the Men Who Made It** (New York, 1948) for the ideas on status. For reactions to Hofstadter's status theory and the paranoid style, see, for example, John Higham, "The Cult of the 'American Consensus': Homogenizing Our History," **Commentary** (27) 1959 and Charles Forcey, "Richard Hofstadter: Consensus In Conflict," Paper Presented to the 74th Annual Meeting of the Organization of American Historians, Detroit, April 1-4, 1981. Hofstadter work has been in print more than fifty years and it is as important today as it was when he published his first book. Hofstadter saw history as a part of literature, and he wrote so well that he was criticized for lack of empirical or scientific evidence. He has also been criticized as a consensus historian and this is unfortunate as Hofstadter's writing escapes categorizing. He is an original thinker and that is why his critics were hostile. Professor Richard F. W. Whittemore of Western Washington University beguiled me with Hofstadter tales when I was an undergraduate. Whittemore, like Hofstadter, was an original thinker. Nothing is more dangerous.

See David Greenberg, "Richard Hofstadter's Tradition," **The Atlantic Monthly**, November 1998, pp. 132-137. It is Hofstadter's elegant writing and cogent arguments that prompt Greenberg to conclude that the paranoid style is well and alive in American politics. Also see David Greenberg, "Richard Hofstadter: The Pundits Favorite Historian," **Slate**, June 7, 2006http://www.slate.com/articles/news_and_politics/history_lesson/2006/06/richard_hofstadter.html See Geoffrey Dunn, "Palin And America's Paranoid Style Politics," **San Francisco Chronicle**, September 6, 2009 for a brilliant look at how Palin continues to promote paranoid style politics.

Paul Krugman, "Paranoia Strikes Deeper," **New York Times**, March 22, 2012 is an excellent analysis of how Mitt Romney employed the "paranoid style" in his quest for the presidency.

On the Obama administration, see, for example Jonathan Alter, **The Promise: President Obama, Year One** (New York, 2010); David Remnick, **The Life And Rise of Barack Obama** (New York, 2010) and Richard Wolf, **The Struggle For Survival Inside The Obama Administration** (New York, 2010). John Wright, **The Obama Haters: Behind The Right Wing Campaign of Lies, Innuendo & Racism** (Washington, 2011) is an interesting look at some key negative attitudes.

CHAPTER 2: WHAT IS THIS GUY DOING IN A BOOK ABOUT RIGHT WING LUNATICS: WILL BUNCH, THE BACKLASH RIGHT-WING RADICALS, HIGH DEF HUCKSTERS AND PARANOID POLITICS IN THE AGE OF OBAMA

See Will Bunch, **The Backlash: Right Wing Radicals, High-Def Hucksters and Paranoid Politics In The Age of Obama** (New York, 2010) as well as Will Bunch, "The Tea Party, Right Wing Media And The Dog That Didn't Bark," **Huffington Post**, September 28, 2011, http://www.huffingtonpost.com/will-bunch/tea-party-right-wing-media_b_984395.html

See Michiko Kakutani, "The Engine of Right-Wing Rage, Fueled By More Than Just Anger," **New York Times**, September 13, 2010 for a review of the Will Bunch book. On the Tea Party see, "Tea Party Movement," **New York Times**, October 11, 2011. A thoughtful critique of Bunch is Scott Horton, "Tear Down This Myth: Six Questions For Will Bunch," **Harper's Magazine**, February 19, 2010. See Theda Skocpol and Vanessa Williamson, **The Tea Party And The Remaking of Republican Conservatism** (New York, 2012) for a brilliant look at how political elites and grass roots supporters have united against Barack Obama. Harvard University's Skocpol provides a reasoned account of why Tea Party supporters are hostile to Social Security, Medicare and military veteran subsistence.

See Jill Lepore, **The Whites Of Their Eyes: The Tea Party's Revolution And The Battle Over American History** (Princeton, 2010) is a thoughtful, detailed history of the Tea Party that places the movement in proper perspective.

For an indictment of the media see Sarah Palin, **Going Rouge** (New York, 2009), chapter 5. Also the Joel McGinnis, **The Rogue: Searching For The Real Sarah Palin** (New York, 2011). A much better researched and more critical study is Geoffrey Dunn, **The Lies of Sarah Palin: The Untold Story Behind Her Relentless Quest For Power** (New York, 2011).

On Republican foreign policy see the in-depth article by Ben Smith, "Mitt Romney Hawks New Hard Line On Foreign Policy," **Politico**, January 19, 2012 http://www.politico.com/news/stories/0112/71632.html; the critical article by Uri Friedman, "Foreign policy: What The World Makes of Mitt," **NPR**, January 18, 2012 http://www.npr.org/2012/01/18/145389531/foreign-policy-what-the-world-makes-of-mitt ; B. Stephens, "A Republican Foreign Policy: Credibility-Not Consensus-Should Be The GOP's Watchword," **Wall Street Journal**, June 21, 2011 and Max Fisher, "The Dangerously Unpredictable Foreign Policy of Newt Gingrich," **The Atlantic**, January 2012 http://www.theatlantic.com/international/archive/2012/01/the-dangerously-unpredictable-foreign-policy-of-newt-gingrich/251734/

The notion that Kris Kobach was one of the candidates supported by the Koch brothers in Kansas and what that meant to state politics is examined in Ari Berman, "The GOP War On Voting," **Rolling Stone**, August 30. 2011.

For Sarah Palin's death panels comment see Bill Press, **The Obama Hate Machine: The Lies, Distortions, and Personal Attacks On The**

President-And Who Is Behind Them (New York, 2012), pp. 266-268. Also see, Matthew Daly, "Palin Stands By Death Panel Claims," **Associated Press**, August 14, 2009 and Daniel Farber, "Palin Weighs In On Health Care Reform," **Political Hotsheet CBS News**, August 8, 2009 www.cbsnews.com/8301-503544_162-5226795-503544.html

CHAPTER 3: THE KOCH BROTHERS INVENTED THE TEA PARTY

The roots of the Koch families political conservatism is seen in Fred C. Koch, **A Businessman Looks At Communism** (Wichita, 1960) Neither of the Koch brothers appears to subscribe to all of the notions in this book.

For Herman Cain's support by the Koch brothers see article by a well respected political scientist, Will Durst, "Grope And Change," **Reader Supported News**, November 12, 2011 http://readersupportednews.org/opinion2/277-75/8368-focus-grope-and-change Also see, for example the notion that the Koch's have to much influence, Lee Fang, "Wall Street Titan Ken Langone, GOP Presidential Candidate Herman Cain At Koch brothers Meeting," **Think Progress**, January 30, 2011 http://thinkprogress.org/politics/2011/01/30/141486/langone-cain-koch/ and Guy Adams, "Why Liberals Are Rising Up Against The Koch brothers, **The London Independent**, February 1, 2011 http://www.independent.co.uk/news/world/americas/why-liberals-are-rising-up-against-the-koch-brothers-2200191.html Also see, Michael D. Shear, "Cain Stands By The Koch Brothers," **New York Times**, November 22, 2011.

The Koch brothers opposition to President Obama is described in Jane Mayer, "Covert Operations: The Billionaire Brothers Who Are Waging A War Against Obama," **The New Yorker**, August 30, 2010. Also see the incisive article, Hayley Peterson, "Internal Memo: Romney Courting Kochs, Tea Party," **Washington Examiner,** November 2, 2011 **http://campaign2012.washingtonexaminer.com/article/internal-memo-romney-courting-kochs-tea-party**

Tim Dickinson, "The Party of the Rich: How The Republican Party Abandoned The Poor And the Middle Class To Pursue Their Relentless Agenda of Tax Cuts for the Wealthiest One Percent," **Rolling Stone**, issue 1144, November 24, 2011, pp. 46-57 is an excellent analysis of how the radical right has taken over the Republican party.

On the Koch brother's political influence see the article by Democratic strategist, Peter Fenn, "Tea Party Funding Koch brothers Emerge From Anonymity, **US News**, February 2, 2011 http://www.usnews.com/opinion/blogs/Peter-Fenn/2011/02/02/tea-party-funding-koch-brothers-emerge-from-anonyMitty

"Koch brothers Fund Tea Party," **Media Freedom International**, February 2, 2011, http://www.usnews.com/opinion/blogs/Peter-Fenn/2011/02/02/tea-party-funding-koch-brothers-emerge-from-anonyMitty is a brief but important look at their political funding. Also see Ed Pilington, "Koch brothers: Secretive Billionaires To Launch Vast Database With 2012 In Mind," **London Guardian**, November 7 2011. For comments on politics by the Koch brothers see, "Exclusive Audio: Inside The Koch brothers' Secret Seminar," **Mother Jones**, September 6, 2011 http://motherjones.com/politics/2011/09/exclusive-audio-koch-brothers-seminar-tapes

On Koch Industries see, for example the strength of Koch Industries, "America's Largest Private Companies: Koch Industries," **Forbes Ranking of Private Companies http://www.forbes.com/lists/2010/21/private-companies-10_Koch-Industries_VMZQ.html**

Also see **Forbes**, October 28, 2010 and November 8, 2007. The following book is brilliant on management and market success, Charles C. Koch, **The Science of Success: How Market Based Management Built The World's Largest Private Company** (New York, 2007).

See Daniel Fisher, "Mr. Big," **Forbes**, March 13, 2006 for the Koch Brothers business activity.

Media reporting and speculation on the Koch brothers business and political activity is often one-sided and unfair. Some examples of fair and balanced reporting are Dan Voorhis, "Fertilizer Helps Koch Grow," **Wichita Eagle**, December 16, 2010; Josh Heck, "Red Cross Recognizes Three Fundraisers," **Wichita Business Journal**, May 18, 2011; Josh Heck, "Koch Responds to Bloomberg," **The Washington Post**, October 3, 2011.

On the paranoid style in American politics and the Koch brothers influence on American politics see, Matthew Continetti, "The Paranoid Style In Liberal Politics," **The Weekly Standard**, April 4, 2011, volume 16 no. 28 http://www.weeklystandard.com/articles/paranoid-style-liberal-politics_555525.html See Nancy Goldstein, "Koch Brothers Versus The Left In Palm Springs," **The Nation**, January 30, 2011 http://www.thenation.com/blog/158146/koch-brothers-v-left-palm-springs

The Koch brothers influence is analyzed in the decidedly liberal article by John Aloysius Farrell, "Koch Industries Is Spending Ten Of Millions To Influence Every Facet of Government That Could Affect Its Global Empire," **The Center For Pubic Integrity I Watch News**, April 6, 2011 http://www.iwatchnews.org/2011/04/06/3936/kochs-web-influence

See, Dick Dilsaver, "Fred Koch, Industrialist Dies In Utah," **The Wichita Beacon**, November 18, 1967 for an excellent description of the founding father figure.

For literature on Americans For Prosperity and the Koch brothers power brokerage see, for example, Tom Hamburger, Kathleen Hennessey and Neela Banerjee, "Koch Brothers At Heart of GOP Power," **Los Angeles Times**, February 6, 2011. See Charles G. Koch, "Why Koch Industries Is Speaking Out," **Wall Street Journal**, March 1, 2011 for the clearest expression of Koch's belief that crony capitalism and excessive government spending prevents entrepreneurs from success.

On the Solyndra scandal see, Suzanne Goldberg, "Billionaire Brothers Fund Solyndra Ad Against Obama," **London Guardian**, November 2, 2011. The media's concern and in-depth reporting with the Koch brothers is reflected in Paul Harris, "Koch Brothers Under Attack By Left Wing Film Maker," **London Guardian**, May 14, 2011 http://www.guardian.co.uk/world/2011/may/15/koch-brothers-leftwing-film-maker?INTCMP=ILCNETTXT3487 For the Koch attitude on labor see, for example, Rick Ungar, "Koch Brothers Behind Wisconsin Effort To Kill Public Unions," **Forbes**, February 18, 2011. Also see Andy Kroll, "Wisconsin Gov. Scott Walker: Funded By The Koch Bros., **Mother Jones**, February 18, 2011; Eric Lipton, "Billionaire Brothers' Money Plays Role In Wisconsin Dispute," **New York Times**, February 21, 2011 and Greg Sargent, "Americans For Prosperity To Run Ads in Wisconsin," **The Washington Post**, February 22, 2011. For a scathing critique of the Koch brothers, see Steven J. Guliti's excellent blog, "The Proof Of The Pudding Concerning The Koch Brothers," February 27, 2011 http://my.firedoglake.com/sjgulitti/2011/02/27/the-proof-of-the-pudding-concerning-the-koch-brothers/

See Mary Bottari, "Sarah Palin: The Koch Brother's Union Maid," **The Center For Media And Democracy's PR Watch**, April 18. 2011for her role in opposing Wisconsin's public sector unionization http://www.prwatch.org/news/2011/04/10609/sarah-palin-koch-brother's-union-maid On the use of the AFP to oppose health care see David Lazarus,

"Healthcare Debate Framed By Fear Mongering Ads," **Los Angeles Times**, August 9, 2009. Also see the in-depth analysis of Tea Party funding and its impact, Peter Overby, "Who's Raising Money For Tea Party Movement?" **NPR**, February 19, 2010 http://www.npr.org/templates/story/story.php?storyId=123859296

For the best description of the Koch brothers influence on American politics, Bill Press, **The Obama Hate Machine: The Lies, Distortions And Personal Attacks On The President-And Who Is Behind Them** (New York, 2012), pp. 176-236.

CHAPTER 4: THE PROFESSOR AS CRITIC: JEROME R. CORSI, THE OBAMA NATION: LEFTIST POLITICS AND THE CULT OF PERSONALITY

On Corsi's background see, Chip Berlet, "The Roots of Anti-Obama Rhetoric," in Donald Cunningen, et. al., editors, **Race In The Age of Obama, Research In Race And Ethnic Relations**, volume 16, (Emerald Group 2010), pp. 301-319. For reactions to Corsi's books, see, for example, Alex Brandon, "Democrats Say Corsi Book Full Of Lies," **Boston Globe**, April 16, 2008; Joe Miller, "Corsi's Dull Hatchet!" **FactCheck Annenburg Public Policy Center,** September 15, 2008; Eugene Robinson, "Obama Faces The Smear Machine," **Washington Post**, August 15, 2008; Sarah Weaton, "Anti-Obama Author On 9/11 Conspiracy," **New York Times**, August 14, 2009.

See John Fund, "Obama And Chicago Mores," **Wall Street Journal**, March 3, 2008 for the Tony Rezko connection. Also see, Binyamin Applebaum, "Obama Haunted By Friend's Help Securing Dream House," **Boston Globe**, March 16, 2008.

For the Tony Rezko housing incident see, David Jackson and Ray Gibson, "Rezko Sells Lot Next to Obama," **Chicago Tribune**, February 24, 2007; David Jackson, "I Trusted Rezko," **Chicago Tribune**, March 15, 2008: Chris Fusco and Tim Novak, "Obama Cuts Rezko Ties," **Chicago Sun-Times**, January 30, 2008. On the Four Seasons dinner where Obama met Nadhmi Shakir Auchi, see the sensationalist bog "Barack Hussein Obama, Antoin Rezko, Nadhmi Auci, Saddam Hussein=Strange Bedfellows," **Defend Out Freedoms**, October 3, 2010 http://defendourfreedoms.net/2008/10/03/barack-hussein-obama-antoin-rezko-nadhmi-auchi-saddam-hussein—strange-bedfellows.aspx Also see Andrew Walden,

"Lehman Brothers: Obama's Rezko-Auchi Conflict of Interest," **Hawaii 'I Free Press**, September 17, 2008 for another view of this controversy.

See, Saul Alinsky, **Reveille For Radicals** (New York, 1989) for community organizing.

The controversial side of Auchi's business career is analyzed in Paul Webster and Martin Bright, "Oil Scandal Billionaire Tells French Court Of Bribes," **London Guardian**, May 6, 2003; David Pallister and Rory McCarthy, "Corrupt Scandal Hits Senior Politicians," **London Guardian**, November 14, 2003 and David Connett, "Unwelcome Publicity For Oil Giant In Legal Battle With Billionaire," **London Independent**, May 4, 2008.

For a spirited and Marxist defense of Reverend Wright see, Malik Miah, "Reverend Wright And Black Liberation Theology," **Solidarity: A Socialist, Feminist, Anti-Racist Organization** http://www.solidarity-us.org/node/1469 See, Barack Obama, "On My Faith And My Church," **The Huffington Post**, March 14, 2008 for the best explanation of why the future President attended Wright's church. For other views of Reverend Wright, see, for example, Barack Obama, "My Faith And My Church," **the Huffington Post**, March 14, 2008; Rich Schapiro, "Reverend Jeremiah Wright Claims President Obama 'Threw Me Under the Bus In Letter To African Aid Group," **New York Daily News**, May 18, 2010; Michael Powell and Jodi Kantor, "A Strained Wright-Obama Bond Finally Snaps," **New York Times**, May 1, 2008; Jeff Zeleny and Adam Nagourney, "An Angry Obama Renounces Ties To His Ex-Pastor," **New York Times**, April 30, 2008 and Jeff Zeleny, "Obama Adds To Distance From Pastor And Opinions," **New York Times**, April 29, 2008. The strangest part of this controversy is when Reverend Wright alleged that Jews won't let him talk to Obama. For this controversy see, Gorman Gorman, "Reverend Wright Blames 'Them Jews' For Keeping President Obama From Talking To Him," **ABC News**, June 11, 2009 and "Reverend Wright Says 'Them Jews' Won't Let Obama Talk To Him," June 10, 2009. ABC News and Fox News seldom agree, they did on this story. On Wright's attempt to explain his anti Jewish remarks, see Brian Montopoli, "Reverend Wright: I Meant 'Zionists,' Not Jews," **CBS News**, June 12, 2009 http://www.cbsnews.com/8301-503544_162-5083816-503544.html For the anti-defamation league response see "ADL Expresses Outrage At Reverend Wright's Hateful And Inflammatory Comments," ADL Press Release http://www.adl.org/PresRele/ASUS_12/5548_12.htm

Obama's Detractors

For an interesting look at Reverend Wright see, Clarence Earl Walker and Gregory D. Smithers, **The Preacher And The Politician: Jeremiah Wright, Barack Obama, And Race In America** (Charlottesville, 2009). This is a book by an African American Professor of History at the University of California, Davis. It is an accurate and thoughtful academic treatise, well researched and written. One of Professor Walker's main points is that Afrocentrism is a dangerous concept. He doesn't view Africa of the cradle of civilization for African Americans.

On the cult of personality in Obama's politics and David Axelrod's role, see, Howard Wolinsky, "The Secret Side of David Axelrod," **Business Week**, March 14, 2008 and Christopher Hayes, "Obama's Media Maven," **Nation**, February 6, 2007.

Jim Rutenberg and Jule Bosman, "Book Attacking Obama Hopes To Repeat '04 Anti-Kerry Feat," **New York Times**, August 12, 2008 for the direction of Corsi's book.

See Janny Scott, **A Singular Woman: The Untold Story of Barack Obama's Mother** (New York, 2011) for Obama's early life.

The cult of personality that Corsi's describes is largely the vehicle used to link President Obama to Bill Ayers. There is more material on the Ayers-Obama friendship that one can digest. Some of the more interesting, although not factually support, and over the top right wing rants are "Cloward-Piven Strategy—The Left and Obama's Attempts To Destroy America," http://sadimtouch.wordpress.com/, "He Lied About Bill Ayers http://factcheck.org/2008/10/he-lied-about-bill-ayers/ and Hugh Hewitt, "Airing the Ayers-Obama Connection," **Townhall.com**. April 17, 2008 http://townhall.com/columnists/hughhewitt/2008/04/17/airing_the_ayers-obama_connection/page/full/

CHAPTER 5: WHY YALE, JOE LIEBERMAN AND THE COLLEGE PROFESSORS LED GLEN BECK TOWARD THOMAS PAINE

On Glenn Beck and the Hofstadter thesis see, David Greenberg, "The Obama Haters," **Time**, September 23, 2009. Also see the informative and in-depth article by, Alexander Zaitchik, "Glenn Beck Rises Again: Getting Clean, Getting Mormon, Getting Talk Radio And Going To Yale With the Help of Joe Lieberman, **Salon Magazine, Part 3,** September 23, 2009 http://www.salon.com/2009/09/23/glenn_beck_three/

See Matthew Continetti, "The Two Faces of the Tea Party," **The Weekly Standard**, volume 115, no. 39, June 28, 2010 for some of Beck's key political ideas. For Howard Kurtz' comments on Beck's TV style see Kurtz, "A Network Divided: The Glenn Beck Factor," **Washington Post**, March 15, 2010 also see "Glenn Beck Joins Fox News," **The Politico**, October 16, 2008, Rose Lacey, "Glenn Beck Inc." **Forbes**, April 26, 2010; Laurie Goodstein, "Christians urged to Boycott Glenn Beck," **New York Times**, March 11, 2010; Eric Deggans, "Glenn Beck Fans Say He Represents Their American Values," **St. Petersburg Times**, September 11, 2009; Brian Shelter and Bill Carter, "He's Mad, Apocalyptic, Tearful, And A Rising Star on Fox News," **New York Times**, March 30, 2009; Benjamin Wallace, "Is Glenn Beck The Most Annoying Man On TV? Or Does It only Seem That Way," **GQ**, September 2007; Brian Shelter, "A Folksy Guy In Recovery, About To Land Millions," **New York Times**, November 11, 2007; Rose Lacey, "Glenn Beck's $35 Million Empire Adds A News Site," **Forbes Blogs: Moneywood**, August 30, 2010; Brian Stelter, "Beck Leaving CNN For Fox News," **New York Times**, October 16, 2008; Matea Gold, "Fox News' Strikes Ratings Gold by Challenging Barack Obama," **Los Angeles Times**, March 6, 2009; Jack Mirkinson, "Glenn Beck To Transition Off Fox News Program," **The Huffington Post**, April 6, 2011; "Glenn Beck Talks About End of His Fox News Show," **The Huffington Post**, June 2, 2011; Steve Almond, "Glenn Beck Is the Future of Literary Fiction," **Salon Magazine**, September 12, 2009; Mark Schmitt, "Learning About The Left From Glenn Beck," **The American Prospect**, June 7, 2010 and Michael Boorstein, "Beck's Marriage of Politics And Religion Raising Questions," **Washington Post**, August 31, 2010.

See Glenn Beck and Joe Kerry, **Glenn Beck's Common Sense: The Case Against An Out-of-Control Government, Inspired By Thomas Paine** (New York, 2009) for his arguments.

For criticism of Beck see, Sean Wilentz, "Cofounding Fathers: The Tea Party's Cold War Roots," **The New Yorker**, October 18, 2010 and Bob Cesca, "Glenn Beck The Faith Healer Continues To Scam His Followers," **The Huffington Post**, September 1, 2010.

On Beck's misuse of history see, for example, the excellent article by Simon Maloy, "Glenn Beck's Revisionist History of Glenn Beck," **County Fair,** November 4, 2009 http://mediamatters.org/blog/200911040025 For a list of Beck's hostile racial remarks see, for example, Naima Remos Chapman, "Media Matters rounds Up Glenn Beck's Most Racist Moments," http://colorlines.com/archives/2010/08/glennys_greates_racist_hits.html

The argument against Al Gore's documentary on global warming is examined in "Beck On An Inconvenient Truth: It's Like Hitler," **Media Matters**, June 8, 2006 http://mediamatters.org/mmtv/200606080005

For Glenn Beck's mockery of 9-11 victims and his continual misuse of history see, for example, Danny Shea, "Stephen Colbert Rips Glenn Beck: Building His Career On 9/11," **Huffington Post**, April 1, 2009; "Glenn 'I Hate 9/11 Victims Families' Beck 9/12 Astroturfing," **Fox News Boycott.com** September 10, 2009; Katy Brutner, "Glenn Beck's Past Remarks About 9/11 And Hurricane Katrina Victims," **Athens Liberal Examiner**, September 7, 2009. See Simon Maloy, "Glenn Beck And The Paranoid Style," **Media Matters For America**, December 18, 2009 for the application of Hofstadter's ideas to Beck's politics.

See Daniel Hurtzman, "The 10 Craziest Glenn Beck Quotes of All Time," **About.com** http://politicalhumor.about.com/od/stupidquotes/a/glenn-beck-quotes.htm Also see the excellent, "Glenn Beck And The Radical Right," **Right Wing Nuthouse**, April 8, 2009 http://rightwingnuthouse.com/archives/2009/04/08/glenn-beck-and-the-radical-right/ See Bob Cesca, "Glenn Beck And The Consequences of Crazy Talk," **The Huffington Post**, October 31, 2011 http://www.huffingtonpost.com/bob-cesca/glenn-beck-and-the-conseq_b_184936.html

For the George Soros controversy see, James Besser, "Glenn Beck's 'Monstrous' Soros Accusations Rile Holocaust Survivors, Jewish Groups," **The Jewish Weekly**, October 31, 2011. For comments on Soros and the holocaust see, for example, Michael Calderone, "Glenn Beck Draws Criticism Over Latest Holocaust Comments," **The Upshot**, November 12, 2010 http://news.yahoo.com/blogs/upshot/glenn-beck-draws-criticism-over-latest-holocaust-comments.html Also see George Soros, **Financial Turmoil In Europe And The United States: Essays** (New York, 2012). Soros's comments on defeating President Bush are in an excellent article by Laura Blumenfeld, "Supremacist Ideology Fears Prompted Drive To Oust Bush," **Washington Post**, November 23, 2003 http://articles.orlandosentinel.com/2003-11-23/news/0311220187_1_george-soros-oust-bush-democratic-pa

There is an extensive literature surrounding George Soros. See, for example, Connie Bruck, "The World According To Soros," **The New Yorker**, January 23, 1995; Malcolm Gladwell, "Blowing Up" **The New Yorker**, April 22 and 29, 2002; Martin Pertetz, "Tyran-a-Soros: The Madness of King George," **The New Republic**, February 12, 2007 and Matt Welch "Open Season On Open Society: Why An Anti-Communist Holocaust Survivor Is Being Demonized As A Socialist, Self Hating Jew," **Reason**, December 8, 2003.

For articles written by Soros on a wide variety of subject, see, for example, George Soros, "Why I support legal marijuana", **The Wall Street Journal**, October 26, 2010; George Soros, "The Crisis and the Euro", **The New York Review of Books**, August 19, 2010; George Soros, "On Israel, America and AIPAC", **The New York Review of Books**, April 12, 2007; George Soros, "The Bubble of American Supremacy", **The Atlantic**, December 2003; George Soros, *The Bubble of American Supremacy*, audio recording of **The Atlantic** article via *Assistive Media*, read by Grover Gardner, 18 minutes; George Soros, "Soros on Brazil", **Financial Times**, August 13, 2002; George Soros, "Bitter Thoughts with Faith in Russia", **Moskovskiye Novosti (Moscow News),** translated from the Russian by Olga Kryazheva, February 27, 2000; George Soros, "The Capitalist Threat", **The Atlantic Monthly**, February 1997; George Soros, "Paulson Cannot be Allowed a Blank Cheque", **Financial Times**, September 24, 2008. On the billion dollar profit for Soros from business in the U. K. and Soros' business practices in general, see William Shawcross, Turning Dollars Into Change," **Time**, September 1, 1997 and Brendan Murphy, "Finance: The Unifying Theme," **The Atlantic Magazine**, July, 1993 http://www.theatlantic.com/magazine/archive/1993/07/finance-the-unifying-theme/5148/

On Glenn Beck's excessive criticism of President Obama's church attendance and the name change controversy, see, for example, "Glenn Beck: Obama's Church Attendance," http://www.glennbeck.com/content/articles/article/198/35933/

See "Glenn Beck: Newt Gingrich Supporters Who Oppose Obama Are Racist," **The Huffington Post**, December 20,2011 http://www.huffingtonpost.com/2011/12/10/glenn-beck-newt-gingrich-obama-race_n_1140920.html for an argument that Gingrich's supporters are racist. This argument lacks facts and most of all credibility.

For other critical articles on Glenn Beck's use of history, see, Joseph A. Palermo, "Glenn Beck: 'Historian' For A Troubled America," **The Huffington Post**, May 26,2010 http://www.huffingtonpost.com/joseph-a-palermo/glenn-beck-historian-for_b_591353.html and Alvin McEwen, "Glenn Beck's 'Historian' Uses Bad Information to Denigrate Gay Community," **The Huffington Post**, October 6, 2010 http://www.huffingtonpost.com/alvin-mcewen/glenn-becks-historian-use_b_753598.html

See Alexander Zaitchik, **Common Nonsense: Glenn Beck And The Triumph Of Ignorance** (New York, 2010) for an in-depth critique of Beck's politics on radio and television. This book presents an excellent cross section of Beck's opinions and he shows the malice and hatred that has propelled Beck to fame and fortune. Zaitchik is unusually cirtical, but he also shows conclusively that Beck has done a great deal to promote violence. Beck's books state do not use violence but the lawyers for the publisher obviously have a hand in that statement. They incite attitudes that foment critical comments that are on the brink of violence.

For Glenn Beck's Mormon influences and the religion's influence, see, for example, Alexander Zaltchik, "Fringe Mormon Group Makes Myths With Glenn Beck's Help," **Southern Poverty Law Center**, Spring 2011 http://www.splcenter.org/get-informed/intelligence-report/browse-all-issues/2011/spring/fringe-mormon-group-makes-myths-with-glenn-becks-help

On Cleon Skousen's influence see, Alexander Zaitchik, "Meet The Man Who Changed Glenn Beck's Life," **Salon**, September 16, 2009. A great story on his Beck helped his Mormon mentor is Lee Benson, "Glenn Beck Gives Skousen Book's Sales A Leap," **Desert News**, March 21, 2010 http://www.deseretnews.com/m/article/700018281

The Van Jones controversy is examined in "Van Jones Considers Legal Action Against Fox News, Demands Glenn Beck Retraction," **Huffington Post**, June 20, 2011 http://www.huffingtonpost.com/2011/06/20/van-jones-lawyer-sends-letters-to-fox-news_n_880907.html

On Beck's misuse of Thomas Paine's ideas see, for example, Hrafnkell Haraldsson, "How Glenn Beck Warped Extreme Liberal Thomas Paine Into A Teabagger," **Politicususa**, July 19, 2010 http://www.politicususa.com/beck-thomas-paine/; Chris Kelly, "Glenn Beck Is Thomas Paine, Except For Everything," **The Huffington Post**, April 15, 2009 http://www.huffingtonpost.com/chris-kelly/glenn-beck-is-thomas-pain_b_187102.html and John Halpin, "What Glenn Beck Doesn't Know About His Hero Thomas Paine," **Thinkporgress.org** October 16, 2009 http://thinkprogress.org/politics/2009/10/16/64807/beck-thomas-paine/?mobile=nc All quotes from Thomas Paine are taken from Michael Foot, editor, **The Thomas Paine Reader** (New York, 1987). See the **Tampa Bay Herald**, April 10, 2012 for Representative Allen West's comments on Communists in the House of Representatives. Also see, Jennifer Bendery, "I've Heard 80 House Democrats Are Communist Party Members," **the Huffington Post**, April 11, 2012 and Aaron Blake's blog in the **Washington Post**, April 11, 2012 http://www.washingtonpost.com/blogs/the-fix/post/republican-rep-allen-west-suggests-many-congressional-democrats-are-communists/2012/04/11/gIQApbZiAT_blog.html Also see Jonathan Mattise, "Allen West Hears Jeers, Cheers At Town Hall Meeting In Palm Beach, Jensen Beach," **The Palm Beach Post**, April 10, 2012.

For President Obama's link to past policies see, for example, Tom Cohen, "Obama Channels Roosevelt's New National, **CNN Politics**, December 6, 2011 http://articles.cnn.com/2011-12-06/politics/politics_obama-speech_1_obama-channels-obama-and-democrats-president-barack-obama?_s=PM:POLITICS

The importance of Theodore Roosevelt's New Nationalism and Woodrow Wilson's New Freedom is analyzed in Peri E. Arnold, **Remaking The Presidency: Roosevelt, Taft and Wilson, 1901-1916** (Lawrence, 2009), pp. 161, 189, 195-196.

CHAPTER 6: THE PROFESSOR IS AN ATTACK DOG: JEROME CORSI, WHERE IS THE BIRTH CERTIFICATE THE CASE THAT BARACK OBAMA IS NOT ELIGIBLE TO BE PRESIDENT

For the racial arguments motivating the birth certificate controversy, see, for example, Michael Tomasky, "Birthers And The Persistence of Racial Paranoia," **The London Guardian**, April 27, 2011; Dan Vergano, "Study: Racial Prejudice plays Role In Obama Citizenship Views," **USA Today**, May 1, 2011 and Amy Hollyfield, "For True Disbelievers, The Facts Are Just Not Enough," **St. Petersburg Times**, June 29, 2008.

On Donald Trump's remarks on President Obama and his 2012 potential presidential run see, for example, "Donald Trump Seriously Considers Running For President in 2012," **New York Post**, October 5, 2010; Kendra Marr, "Donald Trump, Birther," **Politico**, March 17, 2011' "Donald Trump, Whoopi Goldberg, Spar Over Obama On The View," **Wall Street Journal**, March 24, 2011 and "Trump Goes After Obama On U.S. Citizenship, Says Citizenship Questions Remain Unanswered," **The Washington Post**, April 7, 2011.

See Jerome R. Corsi, **Where's The Birth Certificate? The Case That Barack Obama Is Not Eligible To Be President** (Washington, 2011). The Corsi book is long on argument and short on factual examples that make sense.

Also useful are Andrew Sullivan, "Obama Still Isn't President In The South," **London Sunday Times**, August 9, 2009; Taegan Goddard, "Just 32% of Virginia Republicans Think Obama Is A Citizen," **Congressional Quarterly**, August 3, 2009; Eric Etheridge, "Birther Boom," **New York Times**, July 22, 2009; Leslie Savan, "The Birthers Of A Nation," **The Nation**, July 24, 2009; Rachel Maddow, "The Rachel Maddow Show, MSNBC**, March 13, 2009 and Sarah Abruzzese and Jon Ward, "Poll Finds Doubts On Obama's Birth," **Washington Times**, August 6, 2009.

On the racial side of the birth certificate controversy see, Tim Walker, "Let's Call The Birthers What They Really Are: Racist," **Minneapolis Star Tribune**, August 9, 2009. Also see John M. Woodman, **Is Barack Obama's Birth Certificate A Fraud?** (Springfield, 2011) for a conservatives analysis of the controversy who doubts the birthers. Woodman's book is well written and intelligent. It deserves to be considered more important than the Corsi volume.

The role of Orly Taitz in the birther controversy has a great deal of press coverage, see, for example, Dan Fletcher, "2 Minute Bio: Orly Taitz," **Time**, August 10, 2009; Martin Wisckol, "Orly Taitz: Natural Born Litigator," **The Orange County Register**, October 23, 2009

For Taitz' opinion on Obama's Israeli policies see, for example, Benjamin L. Hartman, "Orly Taitz: Obama's Policies Are 'Clear and Present Danger to Israel," **Haaretz.com**, April, 2011 http://www.haaretz.com/news/orly-taitz-obama-policies-are-clear-and-present-danger-to-israel-1.282161

Allison Hoffman, "In Doubt's Shadow: Soviet Jewish Émigré Orly Taitz Is The Queen Bee of the 'Birther' Movement," **Tablet Magazine**, July 28, 2009 and Martin Wisckol, "Queen of the Birthers: Attorney Gains Notoriety For Strange Challenges of Obama's Citizenship," **Orange County Register**, October 26, 2009 are important on the birther movement. On her court activity see, Michael Sheridan, "Birther Leader Orly Taitz Ordered By Supreme Court To Pay $20,000 Fine For Frivolous Lawsuit," **New York Daily News**, August 16, 2010 http://articles.nydailynews.com/2010-08-16/news/27072836_1_birther-nelson-mandela-orly-taitz

For the ruling by Arizona Secretary of State Bennett on Obama's birth certificate see, for example, Laurie Roberts, "Arizona Is The Nation's Laughing Stock," **Arizona Republic**, May 18, 2012 and Matthew Hendley, "Ken Bennett, Arizona Secretary of State, Plays To The Birthers," **Phoenix New Times**, My 17, 2012.

The English view of this controversy is Ed Pilkington, "Barack Obama Detractors, The Birthers, Face Challenge From Hawaii Governor," **London Guardian**, December 26, 2010 http://www.guardian.co.uk/world/2010/dec/26/barack-obama-birther-movement-hawaii

The background and reaction to President Obama's African roots is explored in Peter Firstbrook, **The Obamas: The Untold Story Of An African Family** (New York, 2010).

For the pulping of Corsi's birth certificate book see, Mark Warren, "Jerome Corsi's Birther Book Pulled From Shelves!" http://www.esquire.com/blogs/politics/jerome-corsi-birther-book-5765410 Despite the overwhelming evidence that President Obama's birth certificate is valid, Corsi continued his diatribe. He enlisted Phoenix Sheriff Joe Arpaio's volunteer posse to investigate the birth certificate. They concluded it was false. See the long-winded and highly insulting interview "Jerome Corsi Obama Birth Certificate, Marijuana In California," http://www.blogtalkradio.com/edtalkradio/2012/06/05/jerome-corsi-obama-birth-certificate

CHAPTER 7: SELLING BOOKS VIA A TITLE: DAVID FREDDOSO, GANGSTER GOVERNMENT: BARACK OBAMA AND THE NEW WASHINGTON THEOCRACY

For the most in-depth review of the Freddoso book see John K. Wilson, "David Freddoso's Hatchet Job," **The Huffington Post**, August 12, 2008 http://www.huffingtonpost.com/john-k-wilson/david-Freddosos-hatchet-j_b_118410.html For Michele Bachmann's use of the term "gangster government" see Melanie Starkey, "Bachmann Stands By 'Gangster Government Description," **Roll Call: the Newspaper of Capitol Hill Since 1955**, March 6, 2011 http://www.rollcall.com/news/-203887-1.html Also see, Glynnis MacNicol, "Michele Bachmann Still Thinks Obama Is Running A Gangster Government," **Business Insider**, March 7, 2011 http://articles.businessinsider.com/2011-03-07/entertainment/30031047_1_obama-administration-michele-bachmann-anti-american-views

The Nordquist Pledge and the legality of it is discussed in "Nordquist Pledge Violates Oath of Office, July 21, 2011 http://tiger.com/politics/nordquist-pledge-violates-oath-of-office/

For a positive review of Freddoso's second book, see Donald Lambro, "Gangster government Exposes The First Thug's Abuse of Power," **Human Events: Powerful Conservative Voices**, April 24, 2011 http://

www.humanevents.com/article.php?id=43114 A review of Freddoso's book that calls the Freddoso book a series negative biography is Ben Smith, "New Book: Obama A Lefty, Not A Reformer," **The Politico**, August 4, 2008.

On the Hugo Chavez incident see Philip Sherwell, "Barack Obama and Hugo Chavez Shake Hands," **London Telegraph**, April 19, 2009 and the nasty diatribe Jane Wells, "Why Is President Obama Kissing Hugo Chavez," **CNBC.com**, November 16, 2011 http://www.cnbc.com/id/45326469/Why_Is_President_Obama_Kissing_Hugo_Chavez

See Frank Marshall Davis, **Black Moods** (Urbana, 2002) and **Livin' The Blues** (Madison, 1992) for his political ideas.

CHAPTER 8: IF I HAD BRAINS I WOULD BE IN THE BIG TIME: DAVID LIMBAUGH, CRIMES AGAINST LIBERTY AND THE INDICTMENT OF PRESIDENT BARACK OBAMA AND PAMELA GELLER'S OUTRAGEOUS CLAIMS AND A BATHING SUIT

For David Limbaugh see David Brock, **The Republican Noise Machine** (New York, 2004) for a view of Limbaugh and others in the right wing nut house. Also see his blogs http://davidlimbaugh.com/

An intelligent look at Limbaugh is Peter Montgomery, "CPAC Leftovers-Peacemaking Pleas and Tea Party Coffee Books, **Right Wing Watch**, February 16, 2011.

On Pamela Geller see the conservative apology, Christian Toto, "Detailing Obama's Endless Radicalism," **Human Events; Leading Conservative Media Since 1944**, August 22, 2010 http://atlasshrugs2000.typepad.com/atlas_shrugs/2010/08/human-events-book-review-the-post-american-presidency.html For the Sutton story claiming that President Obama is tied to radical Muslims see, "Percy Sutton Reveals Association Between Khalid al-Mansur and Obama," **PA Pundits-International**, http://papundits.wordpress.com/2008/09/24/percy-sutton-reveals-association-between-khalid-al-mansour-and-obama/

Also see, Ben Smith, "Obama Camp Denies Sutton Story," **Politico**, September 4, 2008 http://www.politico.com/blogs/bensmith/0908/Obama_camp_denies_Sutton_story.html

See the articles on the in-depth conservative website **Stop Islamization of America** http://sioaonline.com/?page_id=153 also see "Memo To Media: Pamela Geller Does Not Belong On National Television," **Media Matters For America**, July 14, 2010 http://mediamatters.org/research/201007140035

On Geller's fears of the Islamization of America, see, for example, Chris McCrea, "The US Blogger On A Mission To Halt Islamic Takeover," **London Guardian**, August 20, 2010; Daniel Burke, "Pamela Geller, 'Queen of Muslim Bashers,' At Center of N. Y. Mosque Debate," **The Huffington Post**, August 20, 2010 http://www.huffingtonpost.com/2010/08/20/pamela-gellerqueen-of-mus_n_689709.html

On critical views of Geller see, for example, Doug Chandler, "The Passions (And Perils) of Pamela Geller," **The Jewish Week**, September 1, 2010; Chris McCrea, "The U. S. Blogger On A Mission To Halt Islamic Takeover," **London Guardian**, February 26, 2010; David Friedlander, "The Woman Behind the Anti-Ground Zero Mosque Bus Ads," **The New York Observer**, August 11, 2010 and Ahmed Rehab, "Untold Story Behind The So-Called Ground Zero Mosque," **Chicago Tribune**, August 20, 2010.

For Senator McConnell's attitudes on President Obama see, for example, "Sen. Mitch McConnell's Threat: Mean-Spirited And Undignified," **Baltimore Sun**, January 8, 2012 and Joshua Green, "Strict Obstructionist," **The Atlantic**, January/February, 2012.

The ability to write critically is the strength of Limbaugh's columns. They are thought provoking and the writing is generally excellent. For his best criticism, see, for example David Limbaugh, "President Margo Needs No Delphic Oracle," **TownHall.com**. February 14, 2012 http://townhall.com/columnists/davidlimbaugh/2012/02/14/president_magoo_needs_no_delphic_oraclea;

Another interesting article with strong language is David Limbaugh, "What Is It About 'No Free Lunch' That Obama Doesn't Understand?" **TownHall.com**, February 3, 2012 http://townhall.com/columnists/davidlimbaugh/2012/02/03/what_is_it_about_no_free_lunch_that_obama_doesnt_understand For the attempt to link President Obama with Moses, see David Limbaugh, "Obama Invites Backlash on Conscience Rule Betrayal," **TownHall.com**, http://townhall.com/columnists/davidlimbaugh/2012/02/10/obama_invites_backlash_on_conscience_rule_betrayal

For the idea that Pamela Geller is a "loony blogger, see Mooneye, "Pamela Geller Is the Looniest Blogger Ever," **Loonwatch.com**, August 31, 2009.

CHAPTER 9: OVERSTATED LANGUAGE: MICHELLE MALKIN, CULTURE OF CORRUPTION: OBAMA AND HIS TEAM OF TAX CHEATS, CROOKS AND CRONIES

For Malkin's return to Oberlin see, Jon Burckhardt, "Michelle Malkin, Alumna Pundit, Lambastes The Left," **The Oberlin Review**, February 17, 2006. A comment some years later on Michelle Malkin with sweeping generalizations, but intelligent ones, is Steve Volk, "Hitting The Nail On The Head," http://blogs.oberlin.edu/about/history_mission/hitting_the_nai.shtml Professor Volk wrote: "the discordant clip form Fox News' Michelle Malkin which insinuated 'But you have to question the timing of his speech," is a comment that shows how she twists her viewpoint. But Professor Volk's greatest comment is: "Malkin you have a choice. You went to Oberlin." She doesn't seem to get it. For an Oberlin alumnus who is embarrassed by Malkin see, for example, Cal Skinner, "Oberlin College Grads Cringe When Its Most Famous Graduate-Michelle Malkin-Speaks," **McHenry County Blog**, September 27, 2009, http://mchenrycountyblog.com/2009/09/27/oberlin-college-grads-cringe-when-its-most-famous-graduate-michelle-malkin-speaks/ On her early life see Jonathan Pitts, "Right At Home," **Baltimore Sun**, March 9, 2008, p. E 1 and Howard Kurtz, "A Hard Right Punch: Michele Malkin's Conservative Fight," **The Washington Post**, February 16, 2007, p. C 1.

See the inflammatory article, "Harold Schlumberg-Beer Chaser of the Month For August, August 29, 2011 http://thebeerchaser.wordpress.com/2011/08/29/beer-chaser-of-the-month/

See the comments on the summer job bill on Malkin's "Obama's Super-Czar Is On The Loose," http://michellemalkin.com/2012/01/06/obamas-super-czar-is-on-the-loose/

The best article on her formative years and the influence of her high school and college education is H. Y. Nahm, "Michelle Malkin: The Radical Right's Asian Pit-bull," **Goldsea.Com**, http://www.goldsea.com/Personalities/Malkin/malkin.html Also see Howard Kurtz, "A Hard Right Punch: Michelle Malkin's Conservative Fight Has Others Coming Out Swinging," **The Washington Post**, February 16, 2007. The Kurtz article highlights her distaste for Muslims.

On the Korematsu case see Roger Daniels, **Prisoners Without Trial: Japanese Americans In World War II** (New York, 2004_ and Steven Chin, "When Justice Failed: The Fred Korematsu Story (Austin, 1992. For the Korematsu case, also see Howard A. DeWitt, **The Fragmented**

Dream: Multicultural California (Dubuque, 1997), passim and Peter Irons, **The Courage of Their Convictions: Sixteen Americans Who Fought Their Way To The Supreme Court** (New York, 1988).

CHAPTER 10: I'M 5-4 BUT I AM TRYING TO BE 6-5: DICK MORRIS, THE POLITICAL CONSULTANT WITH A SEVEN FOOT EGO

On Morris' early political influence see, Eric Poole, "Convention '96" Who Is Dick Morris?" **Time**, September 2, 1996. Also see the in depth public television interview with George Stephanopoulos on, "Frontline: The Clinton Years Interviews," **PBS** 1995 http://www.pbs.org/wgbh/pages/frontline/shows/clinton/interviews/stephanopoulos4.html and Alison Mitchell, "President's Guru Goes Public, Back Home, Dick Morris Tells Tales Form the Clubhouse," **New York Times**, October 20, 1995.

See "Huckabee Advisor Dick Morris-Nominee, GOP Adulterers Hall of Fame," **Pension Review**, November 8, 2011 http://www.pensitoreview.com/dick-morris/ for his problems with a call girl. Howard Kurtz, "The Hooker, Line And Sinker," **The Washington Post**, September 4, 1996 for a hilarious story on Sherry Rowlands. Other excellent reporting is Richard L. Burke, "Call-Girl Story Costs President A Key Strategist," **New York Times**, August 30, 1996 and Steven A. Holmes, "Dick Morris's Behavior And Why It's tolerated," **New York Times**, September 8, 1996. Also see well written and researched article by, Richard Lacey, Jeffrey H. Barnaul, J. F.O. McAllister and Eric Poole, "Convention '96" Skunk At the Family Picnic," **Time**, http://www.time.com/time/magazine/article/0,9171,985081,00.html

For Morris' conversion to right wing conservatism see Howard Kurtz, "Dick Morris, High On The Critical List, **The Washington Post**, February 3, 10999, p. C1. See Richard Hofstadter, **The Paranoid Style in American Politics** (Cambridge, 1996 reprint), pp. 1, 15, 25. Also see, Dick Morris and Ellen McGann, **Rewriting History** (New York, 2004) for the use of Hofstadter's material to criticize Hillary Clinton. On Bill Clinton's fight with Morris see Dick Morris, "Bill Clinton's Temper Negatively Affects Hillary Clinton's Campaign," **Fox TV News.com**, January 25, 2008 http://www.foxnews.com/story/0,2933,325670,00.html

The best in-depth and critical review of **The New Prince** is Andrew Sullivan, "As The Focus Group Goes, So Goes The Nation," **New York Times**, June 13, 1999 http://www.nytimes.com/books/99/06/13/reviews/990613.13sullivt.html

Obama's Detractors

The notion that President Obama is stated in Dick Morris and Eileen McGann, **Screwed: How Foreign Countries are Ripping America Off And Plundering Our Economy-And How Our Leaders Help Them Do It** (New York, 2012). This book is a disaster with most of the footnotes reading Ibid. This means Morris had taken a book and simply rewritten one section after another. There are more serious errors. None of the key books in American Foreign Policy are consulted and the sources add little credibility to an idea book that has little to do with American Foreign Policy.

CHAPTER 11: THE NONSENSE BARACK OBAMA BOOKS: THE TOP SIX IN THE LUNATIC FRINGE

See Aaron Klein and Brenda J. Elliott, **The Manchurian President: Barack Obama's Ties To Communists, Socialists, And Other Anti-American Extremists** (New York, 2010). For a view that ACORN was not a major scandal and deserves little attention, see, John Tomas, "The ACORN Scandal: Then And Now," **The Colorado Independent**, March 5, 2010 http://coloradoindependent.com/48555/the-ACORN-scandal-then-and-now Also see Stanley Kurtz, "Inside Obama's ACORN," **National Review Online**, May 29, 2008 http://www.nationalreview.com/articles/224610/inside-obamas-ACORN/stanley-kurtz

For a contrary opinion suggesting Obama's duplicity in the ACORN scandal and the evidence against him, see, Matthew Vaduz, "Obama Uses Taxpayer Cash to Back ACORN Name Changes Used To Dodge The Law," **The Washington Times**, November 28, 2011 http://www.washingtontimes.com/news/2011/nov/28/obama-uses-taxpayer-cash-to-back-ACORN-name-change/

Also see Michelle Malkin, "The ACORN Obama Knows, **Michellemalkin.com**, June 25, 20008 http://www.nationalreview.com/articles/224610/inside-obamas-ACORN/stanley-kurtz

On Valerie Jarrett and the Obama administration, see, for example, Jodi Kantor, "An Old Hometown Mentor, Still At Obama's Side, **New York Times**, November 24, 2008, Jodi Kantor, "Longstanding Obama Adviser Gets Senior Role At The White House," **New York Times**, November 15, 2008 and Jodi Kantor, **The Osama's** (New York, 2012) a book highly critical of Jarrett. See Carol Feisenthal, "Valerie Jarrett 'Dedicated Her Life' To the Obamas' Plus More Details From Jodi Kantor's New Book," **Chicago Magazine**, January 12, 2012 http://www.chicagomag.com/Chicago-Magazine/Felsenthal-Files/January-2012/Valerie-Jarrett-

Dedicated-Her-Life-to-the-Obamas-Plus-More-Details-from-Jodi-Kantors-New-Book/

For Michael Savage's publicity stunt on the 2012 presidential primaries see, "Michael Savage Offers New Gingrich One Million Dollars to Drop Out of Race," **The Huffington Post**, December 12, 2011 http://www.huffingtonpost.com/2011/12/12/michael-savage-newt-gingrich-one-million-dollars-drop-out-race_n_1144323.html?ncid=webmail3

A San Francisco view of Savage is Ron Russell, "Inside the Savage Nation," **SF Weekly**, July 19, 2006. Also see Carla Marinucci, "Politics Blog: SF Radio Host Michael Savage Banned From Britain: Will They Ban My Listeners Too?" **SF Gate**, May 5, 2009 and Mark De la Vina, "The Man Behind The 'Savage Nation': Neo-Conservative Once Embraced The Counter Culture," **San Jose Mercury**, July 20, 2003. For a British view of Savage see, Guy Adams, "Michael Savage: Mr. Angry, **London Independent**, May 9, 2009. For the BBC list of people banned from entering the U. K. see **BBC News**, May 5, 2009 http://news.bbc.co.uk/2/hi/uk_news/8033060.stm Savage threatened to sue over his ban to enter the U. K. see "US 'Hate List' DJ To Sue Britain," **BBC News**, May 6, 2009.

For the ACORN scandal see John Atlas and Peter Drier, "ACORN Scandal Offers Key to All Charities, **The Huffington Post**, December 9, 2009 http://www.huffingtonpost.com/john-atlas/ACORN-scandal-offers-key_b_386064.html On the media ignoring the ACORN scandal see, Kathryn Jean Lopez "ACORN Scandal Has Deep Roots," **National Review Online**, September 21, 2009 and "News Outlets Largley Ignoring ACORN Scandal, Critic Says," September 15, 2009 http://www.foxnews.com/story/0,2933,550602,00.html and Glynnis MacNicol, "Rachel Maddow Compares 'Bogus' Scandal to Made Up 'Climategate," **Mediaite.com** April 4, 2010, http://www.mediaite.com/online/rachel-maddow-compares-bogus-ACORN-scandal-to-made-up-climategate

For the British view of Michael Savage, see, for example, Jennifer Harper, "Michael Savage Still Banned From UK," **The Washington Times**, July 12, 2010, Catherine Bennett, "Yes Jacqui, Let's Keep Out Those Dangerous Homeopaths," **The London Observer**, May 9, 2009 http://www.guardian.co.uk/commentisfree/2009/may/10/michael-savage-radio-homeopathy-jacqui-smith and "New U. K. Government Bans Michael Savage, **WorldNetDaily**, July 12, 2010 http://www.wnd.com/2010/07/177961/

The Bill Ayers-Barack Obama relationship is the subject of too much comment. The best sources are Bob Drogin and Dan Morain,

"Obama And The Former Radicals," **Los Angeles Times**, April 18, 2008; Scott Shane, "Obama And '60s Bomber: A Look Into Crossed Paths," **The New York Times**, October 3, 2008; Peter Slevin, "Former '60s Radical Is Now Considered Mainstream In Chicago," **The Washington Post**, April 18, 2008 and for some corrections see Bill Ayers, "Clarifying the Facts-A Letter To The New York Times, 9-15-2001 http://billayers.wordpress.com/2008/04/21/clarifying-the-facts-a-letter-to-the-new-york-times-9-15-2001/ Also see Ayers memoir, **Fugitive Days: A Memoir** (New York, 2003). For the influence of race in Chicago politics see, for example, Roger Biles, **Politics, Race And The Governing of Chicago** (DeKalb, 1995), William J. Grimshaw, **Bitter Fruit: Black Politics And The Chicago Machine** (Chicago, 1995) and David K. Fremon, **Chicago Politics Ward By Ward** (Bloomington, 1988)

Aaron Klein's books are at the heart of conservatism, see, for example, Aaron Klein, **Red Army: The Radical Network That Must Be Defeated To Save America** (New York, 2011) and **Schmoozing With Terrorists: From Hollywood To The Holy Land, Jihadists Reveal Their Global Plans-to A Jew** (Los Angeles, 2007) for conspiratorial views of American politics. Klein is an Orthodox Jew who argues that Islamic extremists are attempting a world revolution. He is singularly the best writer among conservatives.

For an update on Van Jones see Carla Marinucci, "Democrats Star Speaker Van Jones Fires Up Crowd-And Emerges Party Leader of the Future," **San Francisco Chronicle, February 11, 2012** and John M. Broder, "White House Official Resigns After G. O. P. Criticism," **The New York Times**, September 6, 2009.

CHAPTER 12: BARBIE ON STEROIDS: ANN COULTER, DEMONIC: HOW THE LIBERAL MOB IS ENDANGERING AMERICA

Coulter's early background is examined in David Horowitz, "Ann Coulter At Cornell," **FrontPageMag.com**, May 21, 2001, "Ann Coulter: Best Selling Author And Political Commentator," **Premierspeakers.com**

For Coulter's comments on Paula Jones see, Ann Coulter, "Clinton Can Sure Pick 'Em," **Jewish World Review**, October 30, 2000. Also see, Ann Coulter, "Trailer Park Trash' Strike Back" **Human Events**, January 30, 1998. Coulter answered her critics in Ann Coulter, "Answering My Critics," **Jewish World Review**, October 9, 2003. Also see Al Franken, **Lies And the Lying Liars Who Tell Them** (New York, 2003) for vitriolic criticism of Coulter. Another interesting article is Ian Austen, "Ann Coulter," **New York Times**, March 10, 2009.

For Coulter's religious views, see, for example, "Coulter: Press Either Incompetent or Full of Left-Wing Bias," **Editor and Publisher**, July 21, 2006; Jackson Thoreau, "U. S. Founders And Christ Were Liberals: We Cannot Let Right Wingers Like Coulter Define Liberalism" **OPEDNews**, June 9, 2006 and Tony Norman, "If Ann Coulter's A Christian< I'll Be Damned," **Common Dreams NewsCenter**, June 10, 2006.

For Coulter and gays see, for example, "Coulter Under Fire For Anti-Gay Slur, **CNN**, March 4, 2008 also see Rick Klein, "Edwards Calls Coulter 'She-Devil'," **ABC News**, August 17, 2007. Also see Jack Hitt, "Is Sarah Palin Porn," **Harper's**, June 30, 2010 for the notion that Fox TV News uses only beautiful blondes.

For Maxine Waters on Coulter see Frances Martel, "Eric Bolling To Ann Coulter: Is Maxine Waters' Tea Party 'Go To Hell' Comment Racist? **Mediaite**, August 23, 2011 http://www.mediaite.com/tv/eric-bolling-to-ann-coulter-is-maxine-waters-tea-party-go-to-hell-comment-racist/ Ann Coulter's comments on Newt Gingrich are many, see, for example,

For comments on the Senator Joe McCarthy controversy see **The London Sunday Times**, July 5, 2003; **Salon**, July 4, 2003; David Horowitz, "The Trouble With Treason," **Frontpagemag.com**. July 8, 2003; Brendan Nyham, "Screed: With Treason, Ann Coulter Once Again Defines A New Low In America's Political Debate," **Spinsanity**, June 30, 2003. Nyham writes: "As we documented back in July 2001, Coulter's writing is not just inflammatory but blatantly irrational." Also see, Bryan Keefer, "Throwing The Book At Her: The Bias Ann Coulter Documents Best May Be Her Own," **Salon**, July 13, 2003.

The book to consult on McCarthy is Thomas C. Reeves, **The Life And Times of Joe McCarthy: A Biography** (New York, 1982). The depths in Coulter's research errors are obvious after reading the Reeves volume. The problems with Coulter's writing are analyzed in Jamie Weinstein, "Top Ten Shocking Things In Coulter's Book 'Demonic' That Will Drive Liberals Crazy," **The Daily Caller**, June 6, 2011 http://dailycaller.com/2011/06/06/top-10-shocking-things-in-ann-coulter's-book-demonic-that-will-drive-liberals-crazy/3/

The Joe McCarthy influence is a negative one examined in detail in David Caute, **The Anti Communist Purge Under Truman and Eisenhower** (New York, 1979); Richard Fried, **Nightmare In Red: The McCarthy Era In Perspective** (New York, 1990) and Athan Theoharis,

Obama's Detractors

Seeds of Repression: Harry S. Truman And The Origins of McCarthyism (New York, 1971). Also see Athan Theoharis, **Abuse of Power: How Cold War Surveillance And Secrecy Policy Shaped The Response To 9-11** (Philadelphia, 2011) for a brilliant analysis of why it has been so difficult to contain terrorism and still maintain traditional civil liberties.

CHAPTER 13: SHE IS NOT QUITE BARBIE BUT I'M TRYING: LAURA INGRAHAM'S BOOKS

See "Laura Ingraham Isn't Sure If Obama Is Black," **Media Matters For America**, October 5, 2011 http://mediamatters.org/blog/201110050020

Also, see, Howard Kurtz, "Laura Ingraham, Reporting for W2004," **The Washington Post**, August 30, 2004, p. C 1. For her alleged anti-homosexual remarks and her defense, see, for example, "Laura Ingraham," Wikipedia http://en.wikipedia.org/wiki/Laura_Ingraham and Rory O'Connor, "Laura Ingraham: Right-Wing Radio's High Priestess of Hate," **Huffington Post Media**, June 9, 2008 http://www.huffingtonpost.com/rory-oconnor/laura-ingraham-right-wing_b_106034.html

"Ed Schultz Suspended From MSNBC After Calling Laura Ingraham A 'Right Wing Slut," **The Washington Post**, May 26, 2011 and Bill Carter "MSNBC Suspends Schultz over Ingraham Remark," **New York Times**, October 29, 2011. On the popularity of conservative radio see, Brian Stelter, "For Conservative Radio, It's A New Dawn, Too," **New York Times**, December 21, 2008. For Ingraham's remarks on the Irish trip see Aliyah Shahid, "Laura Ingraham Slams Obama For Drinking Guinness In Ireland While Tornado-Ravaged Missourians Suffer," **New York Daily News**, May 24, 2011.

On the Bill Cole law suit and the **Dartmouth Review**, see, for example Christopher McMahon, Preserving The Bastion: The Case of The **Dartmouth Review**," in Milton Heumann, Thomas Church and David P. Redalwsk, editors, **Hate Speech On Campus** (Evanston, 1997), pp. 192-212. See the **Dartmouth Review**, January 17, 1983 for Ingraham's article, "Prof. Cole's Song And Dance Routine." The reaction from alumni by Chris Witman, "Lies, Lies, And More Lies," **Dartmouth Review**, number 9, March 1988 is interesting regarding the First Amendment. Also see, Roland Reynolds, "Professor Cole Drops Lawsuit," **Dartmouth Review**, June 1985 and Alice K. Mandel, "Bill Cole vs. The Dartmouth Review," **Dartmouth Review**, number 5, June 1985.

For Laura Ingraham's anti-Muslim views on the Mosque to be built near Ground Zero see, Justin Elliott, "How the Ground Zero Mosque Fear Mongering Began," **Salon**, August 16, 2010 http://www.salon.com/2010/08/16/ground_zero_mosque_origins/

CHAPTER 14: RIGHT WING LUNATICS AND OBAMA'S DIJON-GATE SCANDAL

John Amato, "Crooks And Liars: Latest Right Wing Lunatic Smear About Obama: Dijongate," **John Amato's blog,** May 7, 2009. Although he has not commented on Dijongate, Mark Steyn's books, **After America: Get Ready For Armageddon** (Washington 2011) and **America Alone: The End of the World As We Know It** (Washington, 2006) both have the apocalyptic feel that characterize the righty wing. Steyn, a Canadian, lives in New Hampshire and appears on Fox with Hannity and he is also a frequent Rush Limbaugh guest. He has come up with a term Eurabie to describe the coming domination of Europe by Muslims. He seems to blame this on President Obama. If only the president had used mustard and ketchup.

See Jason Linkins, "Hannity Attacks Obama For Putting Mustard On His Burger," **Huffington Post**, May7, 2009 http://www.huffingtonpost.com/2009/05/07/hannity-attacks-obama-for_n_198851.html

Kevin Pang, "Barack Obama's Mustard: President Puts Spicy Mustard On Burgers And Lands In New Elitist Pickle With Right," **Chicago Tribune**, May 11, 2009. Also see the insipid article by William A. Jacobson, "Thou Shall Not Mock Obama's Mustard Scandal" http://legalinsurrection.com/2009/05/thou-shall-not-mock-obamas-mustard/ for a hilarious interpretation of the Dijongate debate. Also see William A. Jacobson, "MSNBC Hide Obama's Dijon Mustard, (aka Dijongate)" http://legalinsurrection.com/2009/05/msnbc-hides-obamas-Dijon-mustard-aka-Dijongate/

Also see, "Obama Mustard Attack Becomes Full-Blown Right-Wing Talking Point," **Huffington Post**, May 8, 2009 http://www.huffingtonpost.com/2009/05/08/obama-mustard-attack-beco_n_199953.html and "Dijon Derangement Syndrome: Conservative Media Attack Obama For Burger Order," **Media Matters For America**, May 7, 2009 http://mediamatters.org/research/200905070031

The number of blogs on the Dijongate scandal produced some of the most intelligent criticism of the radical right found on the Internet. Also see the Washington press for some hilarious coverage.

Obama's Detractors

See the story by the law professor and persistent right wing critic, William A. Jacobson, "MSNBC Hides Obama's Dijon Mustard (aka Dijongate) **Legal Insurrection**, May 5, 2009 http://legalinsurrection.com/2009/05/msnbc-hides-obamas-Dijon-mustard-aka-Dijongate/

for the President and Vice President's visit to Ray's Hell Burger. Also see Michael D. Shear, "Obama, Medvedev Chow Down At Ray's Hell Burger," **The Washington Post**, http://voices.washingtonpost.com/44/2010/06/obama-medvedev-chow-down-at-ra.html

The Dijongate scandal attests to the depths that the media will stoop for a non-news story. For a man obsessed with Dijongate see, William A. Jacobson's various posts and comments. He graduated from Harvard Law School and is now getting his revenge, for Jacobson's sterling credentials and brilliant career see, "About William A. Jacobson," **Legal Insurrection**, http://legalinsurrection.com/author/bill/

Among the more detailed and intelligent examinations with a sense of humor of Ray's Hell Burger is Patrick Pho, "President Obama Makes A Return To Ray's Hell Burger," http://www.welovedc.com/2010/06/24/president-obama-makes-a-return-stop-to-rays-hell-burger/

The Internet is filled with material on Dijongate, for a video, see "For Burger Fans: Obama And Medvedev and Rosslyn," **Rosslyn Blog**, June 24, 2010 for a video of the lunch http://rosslynblog.org/2010/06/24/presidential-burger-fans-obama-and-medvedev-in-rosslyn/

CHAPTER 15: BILL O'REILLY: FAIR, BALANCED, INNFORMATIVE AND WELL INTENDED

For O'Reilly's controversial side, see, for example, Howard Kurtz, "Bill O'Reilly And NBC, Shouting to Make Themselves Seen," **The Washington Post**, January 15, 2007; Peter Hart, "Fairness & Accuracy In Reporting, 'The 'Oh Really?' Factor: O'Reilly Spins Facts and Statistics," **Fairness And Accuracy In Reporting**, May-June, 2002mFair.org http://www.fair.org/index.php?page=1108 and

A good book on O'Reilly is Marvin Kitman, **The Man Who Would Not Shut Up: The Rise of Bill O'Reilly** (New York, 2008).

For those who despite O'Reilly see Steve Senti's blog O'Reilly-Sucks.com http://www.oreilly-sucks.com/linkpage.htm Also see, Steve Watson, "O'Reilly's America: Who Is the Real Hater?" http://infowars.net/articles/april2007/030407OReilly.htm

Perhaps the most egregious charge against O'Reilly came in the aftermath of the death of an abortion doctor, see, Gabriel Winant, "O'Reilly's Campaign Against Murdered Doctor," **Salon**, May 31, 2009 http://www.salon.com/2009/05/31/tiller_2/ Also see a defense of O'Reilly over the murdered doctor, Jay Bookman, "Don't Smear O'Reilly With Tiller Assassination," http://blogs.ajc.com/jay-bookman-blog/2009/06/01/dont-smear-oreilly-with-tiller-assassination/

One of the few studies to dispassionately analyze O'Reilly's influence and to do so in an academic manner is Mike Conway, Maria Elizabeth Grabe and Kevin Grieves, "Villains, Victims And The Virtuous In Bill O'Reilly's ""No Spin Zone"," Indian University School of Journalism http://newsinfo.iu.edu/news/page/normal/5535.html and the **Los Angeles Times**, may 16, 2007.

A good defense of O'Reilly is Ron Mitchell, "Stop Calling O'Reilly Names," **Los Angeles Times**, May 10, 2007. For =O'Reilly's power see Scott Horton, "How O'Reilly Got A Critic Fired," **Harper's**, August 23, 2010 http://www.harpers.org/archive/2010/08/hbc-90007521

For the controversy on race involving O'Reilly, see, for example, "O'Reilly Surprised There Was No Difference Between Harlem Restaurant and Other New York Restaurants, **Media Matters**, September 21, 2007 http://mediamatters.org/research/200709210007 This website is excellent as it analyzes the racial question from O'Reilly's visit to the Harlem restaurant Sylvia's.

For comments on O'Reilly's alleged racial statements see, Peter Hart, "O'Reilly's Racist Slurs-In Context," **Fair: Fairness and Accuracy In Reporting**, June 2003 http://www.fair.org/index.php?page=1147 Also see the interesting article if a bit biased, "CNN's Roland Martin On O'Reilly Comment 'List I Checked, I Didn't Hand Over My Brain To Reverend Sharpton," **Media Matters For America**, September 26, 2007 http://mediamatters.org/research/200709270001?f=h_latest

For the propaganda side of Fox TV News and O'Reilly see, for example, James Combs and Dan Nimmo, **The New Propaganda: The Dictatorship of Palaver In Contemporary Politics** (New York, 1993) and Mike France, "Is There A Marketplace For Nonpartisan News?" **Business Week**, November 29, 2004.

See the excellent and deeply research book by Peter Hart, **The Oh Really? Factor: Unspinning Fox News Channel's Bill O'Reilly** (New York, 2003). For the media see Werner Severin and James Tankard, **Communication Theories: Origins, Methods And Uses In Mass Media** (White Plains, 1997, 4th edition). Teun A. Van Duk, **Racism And The Press** (London, 1991). For the review of the Lincoln book see "Ford's Theater

Obama's Detractors

Historical Review of Bill O'Reilly's Lincoln Book," **Washington Post**, November 12, 2011 http://www.washingtonpost.com/politics/fords-theatre-historical-review-of-bill-oreillys-lincoln-book/2011/11/12/gIQA-C604FN_story.html Also see, Noel Sheppard, "Howard Kurtz Takes Bill O'Reilly's Side In Lincoln Book Battle With Washington Post," **News Busters: Exposing & Combating Liberal Media Bias**, November 20, 2011 http://newsbusters.org/blogs/noel-sheppard/2011/11/20/howard-kurtz-takes-bill-oreillys-side-lincoln-book-battle-washington-post

Ed Steers, Jr., **Blood On the Moon: The Assassination Of Abraham Lincoln** (Lexington, 2001) is the best book on the subject. Also see, the Abraham Lincoln's Assassination website

For the bias inherent in Roger Ailes' approach to the news see, for example, Keith Ackerman, "The Most Biased name In News: Fox News Channel's Extraordinary Right-Wing Tilt," **Fair: Fairness And Accuracy In Reporting**, July/August 2001 http://www.fair.org/index.php?page=1067

CHAPTER 16: WHETHER YOU LIKE OR NOT NEWT GINGRICH MAKES SENSE OR DOES HE?

For Newt Gingrich's background see, for example, "Biography of Newt Gingrich," **Biographical Directory of the United States Congress** (Washington 2007). On Gingrich in Congress see, Richard F. Fenno, Jr., **Congress At The Grassroots: Representational Change in the South, 1970-1998** (Chapel Hill, 2000) and Randall Strahan, **Leading Representatives: The Agenda of Leaders In The Politics of the U. S. House** (Baltimore, 2007), Chapter 5, pp. 127-180. Straham's chapter entitled "Newt Gingrich: The Transformative Leader As Speaker" credits much of the recent rights power to his activity as House Speaker. Also see, for example, Karen Foerstel, "Gingrich Flexes His Power In Picking Panel Chiefs," **CQ Weekly**, November 19, 1994; Major Garrett, **The Enduring Revolution: How The Contract With America Continues To Shape The Nation** (New York, 2005). On Gingrich's eventual resignation as House Speaker see, Guy Gugliotta and Juliet Eilperin, "Gingrich Steps Down In Face of Rebellion," **Washington Post**, November 7, 1998 http://www.washingtonpost.com/wp-srv/politics/govt/leadership/stories/gingrich110798.htm

On Newt's use of alternative history see, Hendrix Hertzberg, "Alt-Newt," The **New Yorker**, December19, 2011 and Gregory Beyer, "Newt Gingrich Publishes Eight New Alternative Histories of Himself," **The**

Huffington Post, January 3, 2012 http://www.huffingtonpost.com/gregory-beyer/newt-gingrich-satire_b_1180796.html

For Jack Flynt see, for example, Richard Fenno, **Congress At The Grassroots: Representational Change In The South, 1970-1998** (Chapel Hill, 2000), chapters 2 and 3. Fenno, one of America's most renowned political scientists, has two chapters on Flynt, the first deals with his strategy from 1970 to 1972 and the other details how he handled the changing electoral climate from 1972 to 1976 to remain in office. He provided Gingrich with lessons on how to win in partisan politics.

On Gingrich's early life and his political flip flops from liberal to conservative views, see, for example, Michael Barone, "Who Is Newt Gingrich?," **The Washington Post**, August 26, 1984; Peter Ostlind, "A Capitol Chameleon: What Will Newt Gingrich Do Next? **Los Angeles Times**, August 25, 1991; Dale Russakoff, "The Search For Newt Gingrich," **Washington Post Weekly**, January 2-8, 1995; Katharine Seelye, "Gingrich's Life," **New York Times**, November 24, 1994.

The number of articles detailing Gingrich's failings are many, but, see for, example, Timothy Burger and Owen Moritz, "Newt Plays House With New Squeeze," **New York Daily News**, August 12, 1999 and Andy Soltis, "Newt's Fooling Around With His Girl On The Hill," **New York Post**, August 12, 1999. Also see Paul Begala, "The Nincompoop Nominee," **Newsweek**, November 28, 2011, p. 6 for Gingrich's shortcomings.

On Gingrich's hidden liberalism, see, for example, Ed Kilgore, "Chameleon: The Long-Buried Liberal History of Newt Gingrich," **The New Republic**, March 3, 2011 http://www.tnr.com/article/politics/84568/kilgore-gingrich-liberal-policies

On the Gingrich-Clinton budget battle see, for example, Alan Fram, "Clinton Vetoes Borrowing Bill—Government Shutdown Nears As Rhetoric Continues To Roll," **The Seattle Times**, Mach 3, 2011; Deroy Murdock, "Newt Gingrich Implosion," **National Review**, August 28, 2008 and New Gingrich, **Lessons Learned The Hard Way** (New York, 1998), pp. 42-46. Also see, Steven M. Gillon, **The Pact: Bill Clinton, Newt Gingrich, And the Rivalry That Defined A Generation** (New York, 2008), chapter 10.

See P. F. Bentley and William F. Buckley, **Newt: Inside The Revolution** (Nashville, 1995) for a photo personality book that is abominable. Also see, Judith Warner and Max Berley, **Newt Gingrich: Speaker To America** (New York, 1995) and Dan T. Carter, **From George Wallace To**

Newt Gingrich: Race In The Conservative Counterrevolution, 1963-1994 (Baton Rouge, 1999).

On his early life see Gail Sheehy, "The Inner Quest of Newt Gingrich," **Vanity Fair**, September 1995 http://www.pbs.org/wgbh/pages/frontline/newt/vanityfair1.html

For Gingrich's comments on his first wife, see, for example, Robert Scheer, "Gingrich Puts A Price On Family Values: He Sheltered His $4-Million Book Bonanza From His Struggling, Non-Trophy Wife," **Los Angeles Times**, December 25, 1994.

On Gingrich's book deals see, Amy Gardner, "Gingrich's Book Selling Efforts Test Law," **Washington Post**, December 8, 2011, "As He Campaigns Gingrich Also Work For Profit," **CBS News Politics**, December 9, 2011 http://www.cbsnews.com/8301-501708_162-57339992/as-he-campaigns-gingrich-also-works-for-profit/, Joe Coscarelli, "Newt Gingrich, 'Cultural Teacher,' Is Also Campaigning To Sell Books," **New York Magazine.com** http://nymag.com/daily/intel/2011/12/newt-gingrich-is-campaigning-to-sell-books-too.html

On his 1989 ascent to political power, see, for example Maggie Haberman, "Newt Gingrich in 1989, the Pro-Rockefeller GOPer," **Politico**, November 289, 2011 http://www.politico.com/news/stories/1111/69204.html Also see, Steven Komarow, "House Republicans Elect Gingrich To No. 2 Spot, Chart Battle With Democrats," **Associated Press Report**, March 22, 1989.

The Professor For Profits heading is dependent upon Timothy Egan, "Professor of Profits," **Campaign Stops: Strong Opinions On the 2012 Election**, November 16, 2011 http://campaignstops.blogs.nytimes.com/2011/11/16/professor-of-profits/ See Kasie Hunt, "At $1.6 Million, Newt Gingrich Is World's Highest Paid Historian Says, Romney," **The Christian Science Monitor**, December 12, 2011 for a detailed description of the Romney's charge that Gingrich is taking financial advantage of his relationship with Freddy Mac. Also see Robin Abcarian, "Newt Gingrich Phones In Defense Over Freddie Mac Income," **Los Angeles Times**, December 17, 2011.

On the financing of the 2012 campaign see, Robin Abcarian, "Romney And Gingrich Caught Up In Money Talk," **Los Angeles Times**, December 17, 2011.

See Paul West, "Gingrich Scrambling Before Iowa Caucuses," **Los Angeles Times**, December 16, 2011. On Gingrich and the Supreme

Court, see David G. Savage, "Newt Gingrich Says He's Defy Supreme Court Rulings He Opposed," **Los Angeles Times**, December 17, 2011.

For Newt's comments on Israel and the Jewish reaction see the statement by Senator Carl Levin, December 10, 2011 http://levin.senate.gov/newsroom/press/release/statement-of-senator-carl-levin-regarding-newt-gingrichs-comments-about-the-palestinians Also see, Ali Abunimah, "Gingrich Comments On Palestinians For 'Jewish' Money, Former Strategist Says, **The Electronic Intifada**, December 10, 2011 http://electronicintifada.net/blog/ali-abunimah/gingrich-comments-palestinians-play-jewish-money-former-strategist-says

On events leading up to the 2012 Republican nomination see, for example, Shira Schoenberg, "Newt Gingrich Takes Aim At Mitt Romney And Massachusetts," **Boston Globe**, December 21, 2011. For the remark on gays in Iowa see Jason Glayworth, "Newt Gingrich To Gay Iowan: Vote For Obama," **Des Moines Register**, December 20, 2011. On Gingrich's net worth see Kim Geiger, "Newt Gingrich's Net Worth: $6.7 Million," **Los Angeles Times**, July 25, 2011. The Iowa Caucuses speech where he talked about brain science is covered in Sarah Hulsenga, "Gingrich Brushes Off Attacks, Discusses Brain Science," **CBS News Political Hotsheet**, December 14, 2011 http://www.cbsnews.com/8301-503544_162-57343313-503544/gingrich-brushes-off-attacks-discusses-brain-science/

On his rise and fall see, Gail Russell Chaddock, "Newt Gingrich's Rise-And Fall-Tied to His Reign As House Speaker," **Christian Science Monitor**, December 31, 2011. On Gingrich's three wives and their view of his presidential ambitions see Bonnie Goldstein, "What New Gingrich's Three Wives Tell Us About The President He'd Be," **The Washington Post**, January 2, 2012.

On Newt Gingrich's expert use of social media, see Jeremy Page, "Will Social Media Dictate A Tight Republican Race?" **ReadWriteWEb**, December 19, 2011 http://www.readwriteweb.com/archives/will_social_media_dictate_a_tight_republican_race.php

and Don Power, "3 Politicians With Expertly Run Social Media Campaigns, **Sprudinssights**, November 25, 2011 http://sproutsocial.com/insights/2011/11/social-media-politics/

For the Judge Biery decision limiting school rights, see, Todd Starnes, "Judge Prohibits Prayer At Texas Graduation Ceremony," **Fox News.com**, June 2, 2011 http://www.foxnews.com/us/2011/06/02/prayer-prohibited-at-graduation-ceremony/

Obama's Detractors

On Gingrich's punishment by the House of Representatives see John E. Yang, "House Reprimands, Penalizes Speaker," **The Washington Post**, January 22, 1997 and Curt Anderson, "Ethics Committee Drops Last of 84 Charges Against Gingrich," **The Washington Post**, October 11, 1998, p. A13.

On Gingrich leaving the 2012 presidential race, see, for example, "Newt Gingrich Out: Candidate Ending 2012 Presidential Campaign," (Video), **The Huffington Post**, May 6, 2012; Michael D. Shear, "Yielding To The Real World: Gingrich Tells Romney He Will Quit The Race," **New York Times**, April 25, 2012 and Amy Gardner and Karen Tumulty, "More Republicans Calling For New Gingrich To Leave GOP Race," **The Washington Post**, March 14, 2012 http://www.washingtonpost.com/politics/more-republicans-calling-for-newt-gingrich-to-leave-gop-race/2012/03/14/gIQAY01qCS_story.html

CHAPTER 17: DINESH D'SOUZA AND THE ANTI-BUSINESS OBAMA

See Dinesh D'Souza, "How Obama Thinks," **Forbes**, September 27, 2010 for the genesis of this chapter. Also see, "Obama Underwrites Offshore Drilling," **Wall Street Journal**, August 18, 2009 for drilling off Brazil. For D'Souza's remarks on the University of California, Berkeley and its admissions policies see D'Souza, **Illiberal Education: The Politics of Race And Sex On Campus** (New York, 1991). For a detailed study of California multiculturalism see, Howard A. DeWitt, **The Fragmented Dream: Multicultural California** (Dubuque, 1997). Also see Howard A. DeWitt, **Anti-Filipino Movements in California: A History, Bibliography and Study Guide** (Palo Alto, 1976); Howard A. DeWitt, **Images of Ethnic and Radical Violence in California Politics, 1917-1930: A Survey** (Palo Alto, 1975) and Howard A. DeWitt, **Violence In The Fields: California Filipino Farm Labor Unionization During The Great Depression** (Saratoga, 1980). What the DeWitt volumes demonstrate is that ethnicity is a complicated field with no easy answers. The problem with D'Souza's writing is that everything is black and white there are no grey areas.

For D'Souza's insensitive comments on 9/11 see Alex Koppelman, "How The Left Caused 9/11," **Salon**, January 20, 2007 http://www.salon.com/2007/01/20/d_souza_2/ This is an interview with D'Souza to promote his book **The Enemy At Home** and it panders to the most conservative fears. The problem with much of D'Souza's book is neither its tone nor its excellent writing, he simply over states his arguments, and he is loose with the facts. When he accuses Hillary Clinton and other liberals of causing 9/11, he does so with faulty logic and altered facts. For criticism of this book, see, for example, the argument by Carl F. Horowitz, "The Islamic Threat To America," **The Social Contract Journal**, Spring 2007 http://www.thesocialcontract.com/artman2/publish/tsc1703/tsc_17_3_horowitz_review.shtml

CHAPTER 18: ANTI-OBAMA BOOKS SELL: A CONCLUSION

On the Amazon list of anti-Obama books in 2009 and the birth of the phenomenon on the various bestseller lists, see, for example, "Anti Obama Books Are Best Sellers," **CBS NEWS** http://www.cbsnews.com/stories/2008/08/05/politics/main4323254.shtml

Hillel Italie, "Anti-Obama Books Are Best Sellers," **USA Today**, August 5, 2008. Also see John Avlon, "The Obama Haters Book Club," **The Daily Beast**, October 26, 2010 http://www.thedailybeast.com/articles/2010/10/26/anti-obama-books-the-secret-hate-driving-the-midterm-elections.html Avlon is an unusually perceptive critic. He founded No Labels, a 501© citizens movement of Republicans, Democrats and Independents to solve political problems. He also writes for **Newsweek**.

Also see a story on three books that hit the best seller lists without publicity, "Anti-Obama Books Are Best Sellers," **CBS News Politics**, June 18, 2009 http://www.cbsnews.com/stories/2008/08/05/politics/main4323254.shtml Also see, Fred J. Eckert, **That's A Crock, Barack: President Obama's Record of Saying Things That Are Untrue, Duplicitous, Arrogant and Delusional** (Beestone Books, 2012) for the name calling mongering of a former U. S. Ambassador and a one term U. S. Congressman.

A more mainstream attack on President Obama is Edward Klein, **The Amateur: Barack Obama In the White House** (Washington, 2012) and this book is a disaster. It has very little to do with President Obama and the general media dismissed it. Klein's tome comes out from Regnery, and he calls Obama "callow, thin skinned, arrogant and the leader of a messianic cult. The extraordinary thing about this book is that Klein sees Obama as anti-Semitic or at least anti-Israel. The forward by Dinesh D'Souza add little to the book.

For the carefully strategy beginning of the plan to attack President Obama see, Sam Stein, "Robert Draper Book: GOP's Anti-Obama Campaign Started Night of Inauguration," **The Huffington Post**, April

25, 2012 http://www.huffingtonpost.com/2012/04/25/robert-draper-anti-obama-campaign_n_1452899.html For more on the plan to defeat Obama see, **Do No Ask What Good We Do: Inside The House of Representatives** (New York, 2012). In this book Draper describes a dinner held at the time of Obama's inauguration that brought fifteen members of the House together and they made a pact to challenge every Democratic bill. Jon Kyl, of Arizona, showed his mettle when he went after Treasury Secretary Tim Geithner during his confirmation hearing. Draper demonstrates that intransigent opposition to Obama's economic policies have hurt the national recovery and provided the foundation for the lack of a bipartisan political coalition. The four-hour dinner was one where the Republicans planned attack ads, which aired two months after Obama's inauguration, they decided to use the media to attack the president, and they systematically had the goal of wining both the House and Senate for the Republican Party. What the Draper book highlighted was the intransigent opposition to President Obama. A sub-theme is that race had as much to do with Republican hostility as anything else.

CHAPTER 19: FROM THE COFFEE SHOP

For President Obama's favorite Washington coffee shop see, Eric Lachtblau, "Across From White House, Coffee With Lobbyists, **New York Times**, June 24, 2010. On Gingrich's demand that Romney pull attack ads see, Jonathan Weisman, "Gingrich Wants Ads Pulled," **The Wall Street Journal**, December 21, 2011, p. A 4.

To understand recent changes in the Republican Party, see, for example, Thomas Frank, **Pity The Billionaire: The Hard Times Swindle And The Unlikely Comeback Of The Right** (New York, 2012) and Geoffrey Kabaservice, **Rule And Ruin: The Downfall Of Moderation And The Destruction Of The Republican Party** (New York, 2012). On the Republican candidates in Arizona and Michigan in February 2012 see, Joseph B. White and Colleen McCain Nelson, "Romney Hits The Tea Party Notes," **Wall Street Journal**, February 25-26, 2012, p. A5.

Thomas L. Friedman, "American Voters: Still Up For Grabs," **New York Times**, January 22, 2012, p. 13 is a brilliant analysis of what is wrong with American politics. See Bill Clinton, **Back To Work: Why We Need Smart Government For A Strong Economy** (New York, 2012) for a look at the former president's take on the right wing nut house and what needs to be done to bring America back to its former preeminent position.

Gwen Ifill, **The Breakthrough: Politics And Race In The Age of Obama** (New York 2009) is the best book on race and politics. Also see, David Corn, **Showdown: The Inside Story of How Obama Fought Back Against Boehner, Cantor And The Tea Party** (New York, 2012).

See "Newsweek Obama Cover: Why Are Obama's Critics So Dumb?," **The Huffington Post**, January 17, 2012 http://www.huffingtonpost.com/2012/01/17/newsweek-obama-dumb-cover_n_1210182.html Also see, "Newsweek's Michele Bachmann Cover Raises Eyebrows," **The Huffington Post**, August 8, 2011 http://www.huffingtonpost.com/2011/08/08/newsweeks-michele-bachman_n_920860.html

For President Obama's alleged hit list of people and organizations against him, see Kimberley A. Strassel, "The Crucify Them Presidency," **The Wall Street Journal**, May 3, 2012. For the letters supporting the list see "Letters To The Editor," **The Wall Street Journal**, May 7, 2012m, p. A16. For allegations of the enemies list in depth, see, Kimberley A. Strassel, "Strassel: The President Has A List," **The Wall Street Journal**, April 26, 2012, http://online.wsj.com/article/SB10001424052702304723304577368280604524916.html Also see, Kimberley A. Strassel, "Trolling For Dirt On The President's List," **The Wall Street Journal**, May 11, 2012, p. A11.

The Republican attitude toward women is long and varied, see, for example, Sharon Day, "Democrats War On Women' Rhetoric Is Insulting and Disingenuous," **U. S. News And World Report**, April 10, 2012 http://www.usnews.com/debate-club/is-there-a-republican-war-on-women/democrats-war-on-women-rhetoric-is-insulting-and-disingenuous Also see, Norah Rothman, "Rush Limbaugh: The Democratic Party Launched A War On Motherhood," April 1,2 2012 http://www.mediaite.com/online/rush-limbaugh-the-democratic-party-launched-a-war-on-motherhood/ For the Republican attack on women, see the editorial, "The Attack Is Real: The Republican Assault On Women's Rights and Health Is Undeniable, Severe And Continuing," **The New York Times**, May 20, 2012, Sunday Review, p. 10. Also see, Jennifer Granholm, "Why Eleanor Holmes Norton Walked Out Of Congressional Hearings About Contraception," **The War Room**, February 16, 2012 http://current.com/shows/the-war-room/videos/why-eleanor-holmes-norton-walked-out-of-congressional-hearing-about-contraception For the notion that there is a fictional war on women from the Republican Party, see, for example, David Catron, "Republicans And Women's Rights: A Brief Reality Check," **American Spectator**, April 30, 2012 http://spectator.org/archives/2012/04/30/republicans-and-womens-rights

See Brian Doherty, **Ron Paul's Revolution: The Man And The Movement He Inspired** (New York, 2012) is well written, carefully researched and cogently argued study of Paul's influence upon the 2012 election. See Robert Merry, **Where They Stand: American Presidents In The Eyes of Voters And Historians** (New York, 2012) for an interesting analysis on executive leadership. Also see Nancy Gibb and Michael Duffy, **The President's Club: Inside The World's Most Exclusive Fraternity** (New York, 2012) is a brilliant look into the Executive Office.

For coffee shops frequented by President Obama see Manny's Coffee Shop and Deli in Chicago, the Coffee Mill, Cannon Falls Deli and the Zumbroata Coffee Shop are other coffee shops that the president has frequented and they provided some interesting comments.

The future of the U. S. economy and its relationship to the political scene is analyzed in Edward Luce, **Time To Start Thinking: America In The Age of Descent** (Boston, 2012) and Daniel Gross, **Better, Stronger, Faster: The Myth of American Decline…and The Rise Of A New Economy** (New York, 2012).

The proliferation of right wing attacks on President Obama is a two fold process. There are those by the newscasters, the media personalities and the writers and the other type of book is by a serious or quasi-academic or a popular historian. Some recent book authored by media personalities include Sean Hannity, **Conservative Victory: Defeating Obama's Radical Agenda** (New York, 2010); Sean Hannity, **Let Freedom Ring: Winning the War Of Liberty Over Liberalism** (New York, 2002) and Bernard Goldberg, **A Slobbering Love Affair: The True (And Pathetic) Story Of The Torrid Romance Between Barack Obama And The Mainstream Media** (Washington, 2009). For an example of a book hostile to President Obama by a former political figure, see, Andrew C. McCarthy, **The Grand Jihad: How Islam And The Left Sabotage America** (New York, 2010). Charles Goyette, **Red And Blue And Broke All Over: Restoring America's Economic Freedom** (New York, 2012) is a reasoned libertarian view of our current economic crisis. It qualifies for the right wing nut house by blaming virtually every American problem on President Obama. An example of Goyette's right wing paranoia is: "The Obama administration has taken a position… that can be used to prevent judicial scrutiny of blatantly illegal government activities and war crimes." (p. 37). For a reasoned and professional look at the Presidency by an eminent political scientist see, Samuel L. Popkin, **The Candidate: What It Takes To Win-And Hold-The White House** (New York, 2012).

See Jack Goldsmith, **Power And Constraint: The Accountable Presidency After 9-11** (New York, 2012). Goldsmith was a member of President George W. Bush's Office of Legal Counsel and he is a professor of law at Harvard University. In clear writing, filled with in-depth research, Goldsmith makes a case that the war on terror has not differed very much since Bush left office. He documents the difficulty that President Obama has had in redrawing procedures to interrogate terrorists. This is an intelligent and reasoned book that demonstrates that we are in a period of a new war. The old rules do not apply because of the war on terror. Also see, Daniel Klaidman, **Kill Or Capture: The War On Terror And The Soul Of Obama** (New York, 2012) who reports for **Newsweek** and **The Daily Beast**. The debate over President Obama's kill list is the central focus of Klaidman's book.

For the changes in Georgia law regarding women and the role of State Republican Representative Doug McKillip leading to many Republicans distancing themselves from his candidacy, see, Blake Aued, "Mayor Denson Backs Rep. McKillip's Opponent in GOP Primary," **Athens Banner Herald**, April 9, 2012. For the Puppet Uterus presented to McKillip and its You Tube video, which indicates the level of hostility in the campaign, see http://www.hipforums.com/newforums/showthread.php?t=450129&f=40 One of the show moderator's, when the Puppet Uterus was presented, remarked: "Since he loves controlling uterus,' she thought he may like one of his own." I have no comment.

For the future of the Republican Party see, Margaret Claire Hoover, **American Individualism: How A New Generation of Conservatives Can Save The Republican Party** (New York, 2011). Hoover is a life long conservative who worked in the George W. Bush White House. She is a conservative with a plan to bring the Republican Party back into the mainstream of American life. Hoover sees the Republican's as out of step with young voters and she has a plan to correct that flaw.

The Jeff Flake National Science Foundation controversy is covered in Ezra Klein, "Jeff Flake's Plan To Politicize The National Science Foundation," **The Washington Post**, May 12, 2012; Taegan Goddard, "House Votes To Slash Political Science Funding," **Political Wire**, May 11, 2012.]

Davis Maraniss, **Barack Obama: The Story** (New York, 2012) is a biography that ends in his twenty-seventh year and it is the single best book on the president's early years. Also see, James Mann, **The Obamians: The Struggle Inside The White House To Redefine American Power** (New York, 2012) for an interesting analysis of how President Obama's not only controls the direction of American Foreign Policy but how he has systematically redefined the role of the U. S. in world affairs.

See Douglas E. Schoen, **Hopelessly Divided: The New Crisis In American Politics And What It Means For 2012 And Beyond** (Lanham, 2012) for a thoughtful critique and Thomas Byrne Edsall, **The Age of Austerity: How Scarcity Will Remake American Politics** (New York, 2012) for the importance of the financial crisis to politics.

For the Dianne Feinstein remark on Eric Holder appointed two people to investigate the security leaks, see, Sari Horwitz and David Nakamura, "Attorney General Eric Holder Names Attorneys to Investigate Leaks," **The Washington Post**, June 8, 2012.

Senator Jeanne Shaheen's comments on the Republican war on women are in Patricia Zengerie, "Will The 'War On Women' Have Legs In November?" June 26, 2012 http://blogs.reuters.com/talesfromthetrail/2012/06/26/will-the-war-on-women-have-legs-in-november/

ABOUT THE AUTHOR AND ACKNOWLEDGEMENTS

Howard A. DeWitt is Professor Emeritus of History at Ohlone College, Fremont, California. He received his B. A. from Western Washington State University, the M. A. from the University of Oregon and a PhD from the University of Arizona. He also studied at the University of Paris, Sorbonne and the City University in Rome. Professor DeWitt is the author of twenty books and has published over 200 articles and more than 200 reviews in a wide variety of popular and scholarly magazines.

DeWitt is also active in a number of organizations to promote the study of history.

For more than thirty-five years he has taught two college level courses in the History of Rock n Roll music. He continues to teach the History of Rock and Roll music on the Internet. In a distinguished academic career, he has also taught at the University of California, Davis, the University of Arizona, Cochise College and Chabot College. In addition to these teaching assignments, Professor DeWitt is a regular speaker at the Popular Culture Association annual convention and at the National Social Science Association meetings. He has delivered a number of addresses to the Organization of American Historians.

He wrote the first book on Chuck Berry, which was published by Pierian Press under the title **Chuck Berry: Rock N Roll Music** in 1985. DeWitt's earlier brief biography, **Van Morrison: The Mystic's Music**, published in 1983, received universally excellent reviews. On the English side of the music business DeWitt's, **The Beatles: Untold Tales**, originally published in 1985, was picked up by the Kendall Hunt Publishing Company in the 1990s and is used regularly in a wide variety of college courses on the history of rock music. Kendall Hunt also published **Stranger in Town: The Musical Life of Del Shannon** with co-author

Dennis M. DeWitt in 2001. In 1993's **Paul McCartney: From Liverpool To Let It Be** concentrated on the Beatle years. He also co-authored **Jailhouse Rock: The Bootleg Records of Elvis Presley** with Lee Cotten in 1983.

Professor DeWitt's many awards in the field of history include founding the Cochise County Historical Society and his scholarship has been recognized by a number of state and local government organizations. DeWitt's book, **Sun Elvis: Presley In The 1950s**, published by Popular Culture Ink. was a finalist for the Deems-ASCAP Award for the best academic rock and roll book.

Professor DeWitt is a renaissance scholar who publishes in a wide variety of outlets that are both academic and popular. He is one of the few college professors who bridge the gap between scholarly and popular publications. His articles and reviews have appeared in **Blue Suede News**, **DISCoveries**, **Rock 'N' Blues News**, the **Journal of Popular Culture**, the **Journal of American History, California History**, the **Southern California Quarterly**, the **Pacific Historian, Amerasia**, the **Western Pennsylvania Historical Magazine**, the **Annals of Iowa**, the **Journal of the West, Arizona and the West**, the **North Beach Review, Ohio History**, the **Oregon Historical Quarterly**, the **Community College Social Science Quarterly, Montana: The Magazine of the West, Record Profile Magazine, Audio Trader**, the **Seattle Post-Intelligencer** and **Juke Box Digest** among others.

For forty plus years DeWitt has combined popular and academic writing. He has been nominated for numerous writing awards. His reviews are combined with articles to form a body of scholarship and popular writing that is frequently footnoted in major work. As a political scientist, Professor DeWitt authored three books that questioned American foreign policy and its direction. In the Philippines, DeWitt is recognized as one of the foremost biographers of their political leader Jose Rizal. His three books on Filipino farm workers remain the standard in the field. He has frequently been mentioned as the pioneer research force in this field.

During his high school and college years, DeWitt promoted dances in and around Seattle, Washington. Such groups as Little Bill and the Bluenotes, Ron Holden and the Playboys, the Frantics, the Wailers and George Palmerton and the Night People among others played at such Seattle venues as the Eagle's Auditorium and Dick Parker's Ballroom.

My thanks to my wonderful and supportive brother and sister in law, Ken and Barb Marich, for their sane and intelligent political views, as well as the wine and food; none of their opinions are in the book. My brothers Dennis and Duane DeWitt listened to me, and one of them, known as Nostradamus Junior, provided opinions on real estate, music and life. Fortunately, for the reader, none of his views are in this book. Nor are there any of his comments about real estate wedgies. He is a great guy. Marc and Gaby Magg Bristol are good friends and they publish my ranting on rock and roll music in **Blue Suede News**. Thank you Marc and Gaby for not only being critical editors but good friends. Neil Skok provides music and opinions on matters of culture as well as his friendship. Joe Gilliland's political views are all over the book thank you Joe. Homer Koliba's political views are not in the book but thanks Homer for the intelligent conservative conservation. Don't worry I won't tell anyone that you think President Obama is a Socialist. Yvonne Sanford edited some parts of the book and thanks go to her excellent and critical pen. Peter Serena provided critical comment on the last chapter. Thank you Peter for your forbearance. Arnie Weiner added a great deal of liberal information and support. None of my errors are due to my friend's criticism. James Hutton provided the coffee at Paradise Bakery and he wants all the readers to know that he had nothing to do with the book. Coffee that's all James provided. My good friends Claude Amerson and Ron Brock listened to my ideas as did Joe Hladik and they are still my friends despite my opinions.

Howard has two grown children. They both live in Los Angeles. His wife of forty plus years, Carolyn, is an educator, an artist and she continues to raise Howard. She is presently retired and vacationing around the world. The DeWitt's divide their time between Scottsdale, Arizona and the Silver Lake area of Los Angeles. That is when they are not in Paris looking for pieces of art, books and music.

Professor DeWitt has a private detective series that will be published shortly featuring a San Francisco P.I. and much of the story line will evolve around DeWitt's four years as an agent with the Bureau of Alcohol, Tobacco and Firearms. He was a street agent for the BATF and his tales of those years are in manuscript waiting for publication. He was also a key figure in the BATF Union.

He is currently working on a series of rock and roll mystery novels featuring Trevor Blake III, a private eye in San Francisco. The first novel

Stone Dead is in the stores and it can be ordered through Amazon. He also writes fiction under another name.

Any corrections or additions to this or the subsequent volumes that will follow this study can be sent to Horizon Books, P. O. Box 4342, Scottsdale, Arizona 85258. DeWitt can be reached via e-mail at Howard217@aol.com

www.ingramcontent.com/pod-product-compliance
Lightning Source LLC
Chambersburg PA
CBHW060232290526
45789CB00001B/20